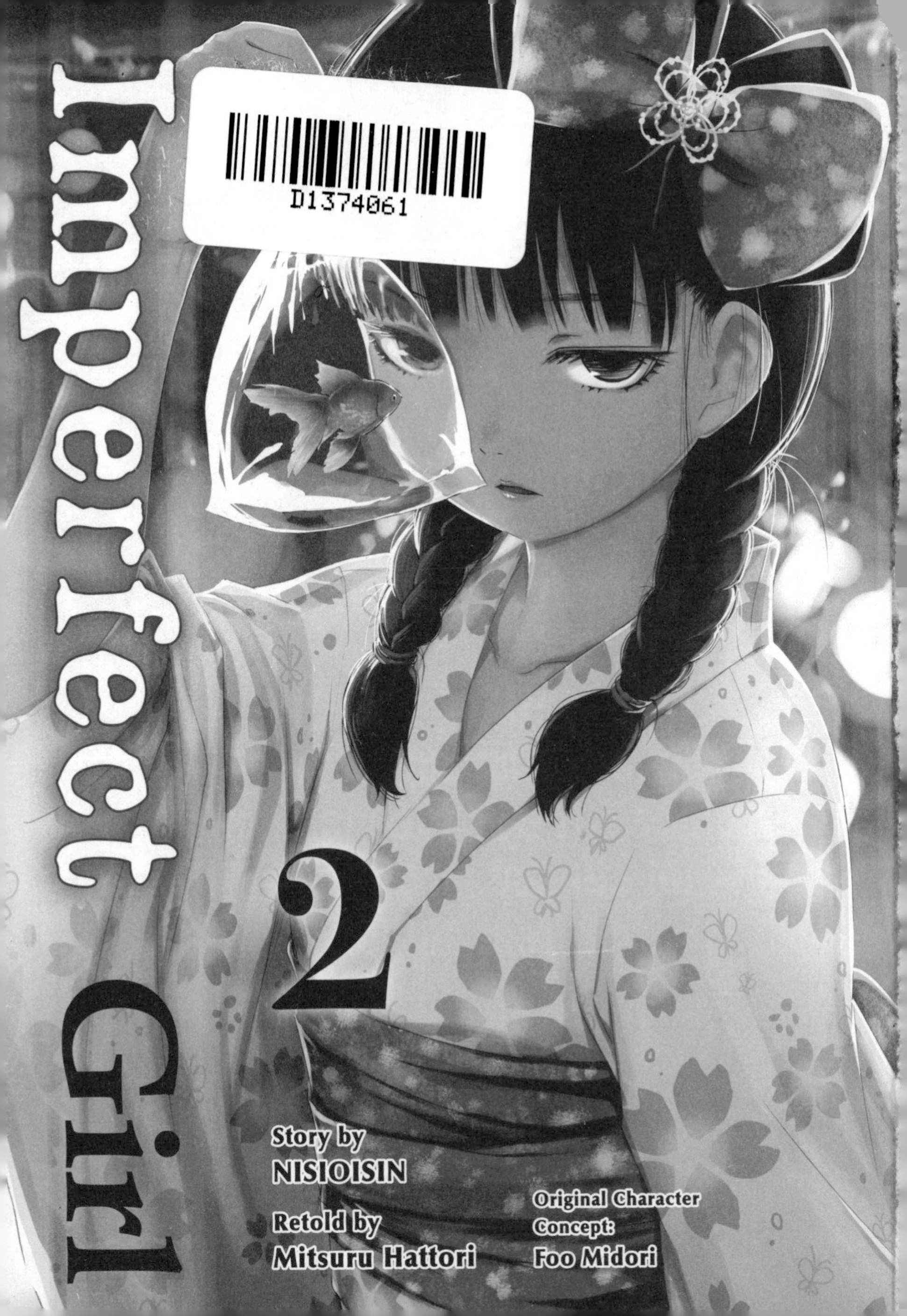
Imperfect Girl
2
Story by
NISIOISIN
Retold by
Mitsuru Hattori
Original Character
Concept:
Foo Midori

This was ten years ago.
I was a college student
at the time, and I had been
kidnapped and imprisoned by U,
an elementary school student.

I was nothing more than
an aspiring author then,
but this was the incident
that caused me to become
a real author.

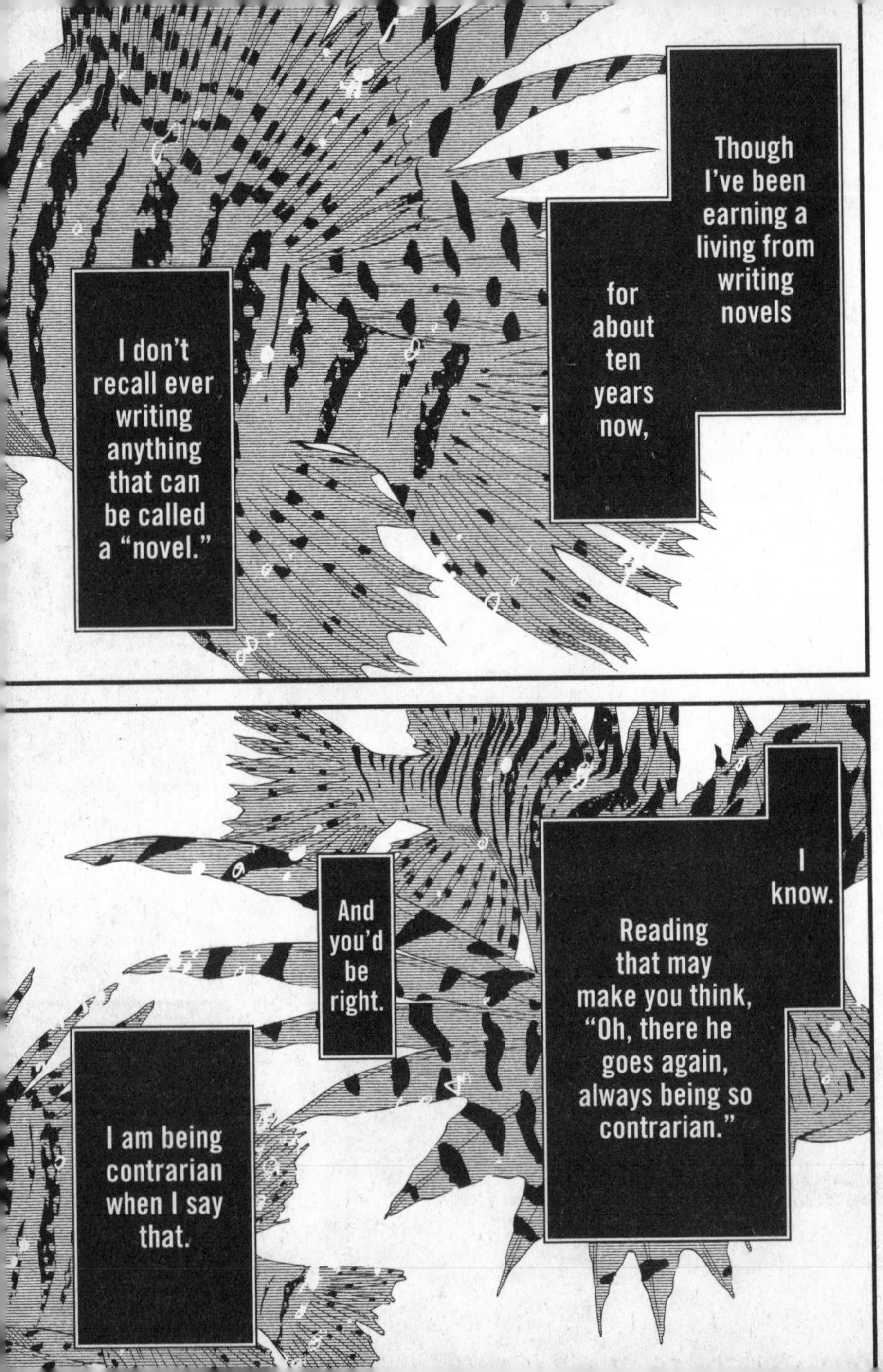
Though I've been earning a living from writing novels
for about ten years now,
I don't recall ever writing anything that can be called a "novel."
I know.
Reading that may make you think, "Oh, there he goes again, always being so contrarian."
And you'd be right.
I am being contrarian when I say that.

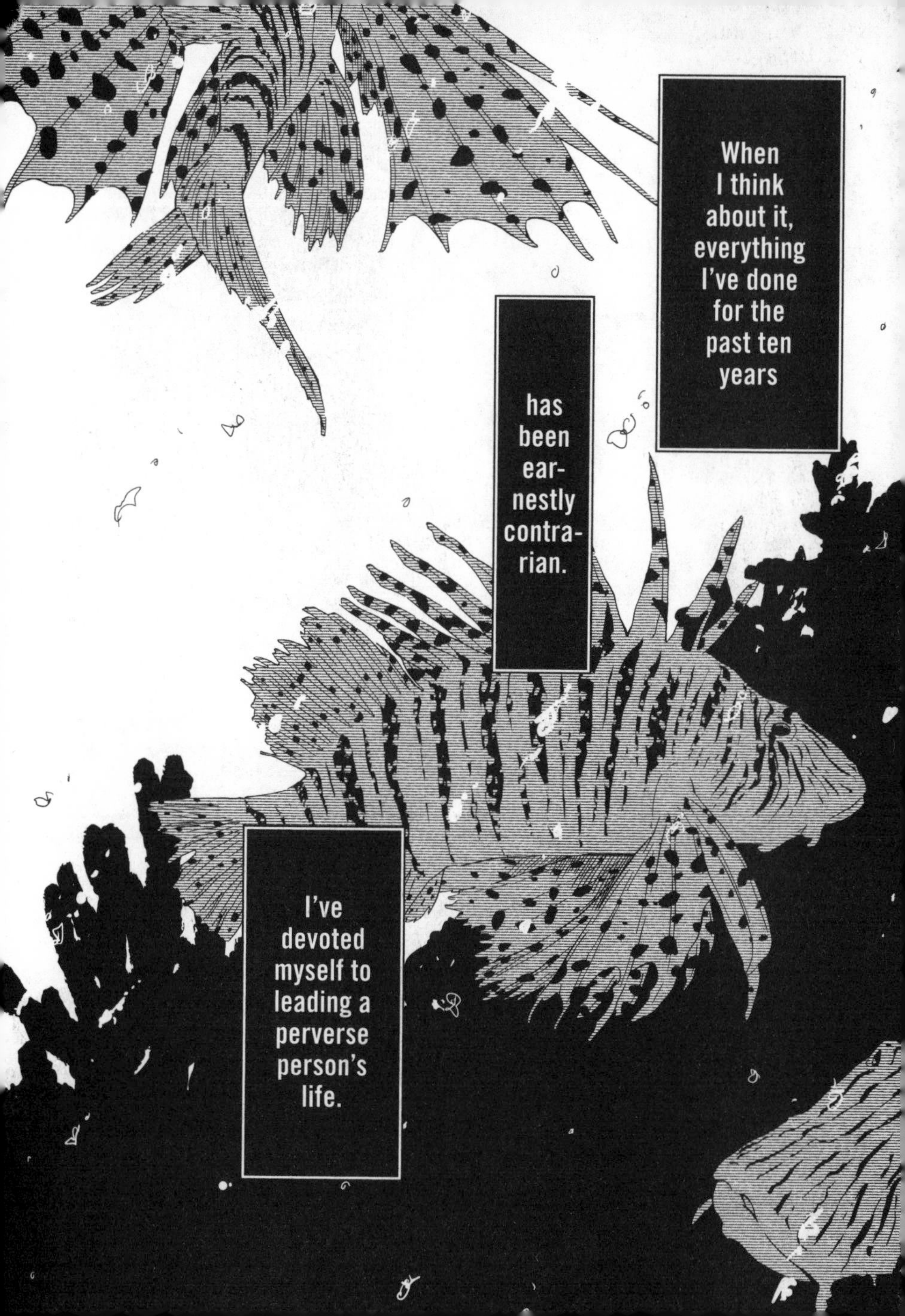
When I think about it, everything I've done for the past ten years
has been ear-nestly contra-rian.
I've devoted myself to leading a perverse person's life.

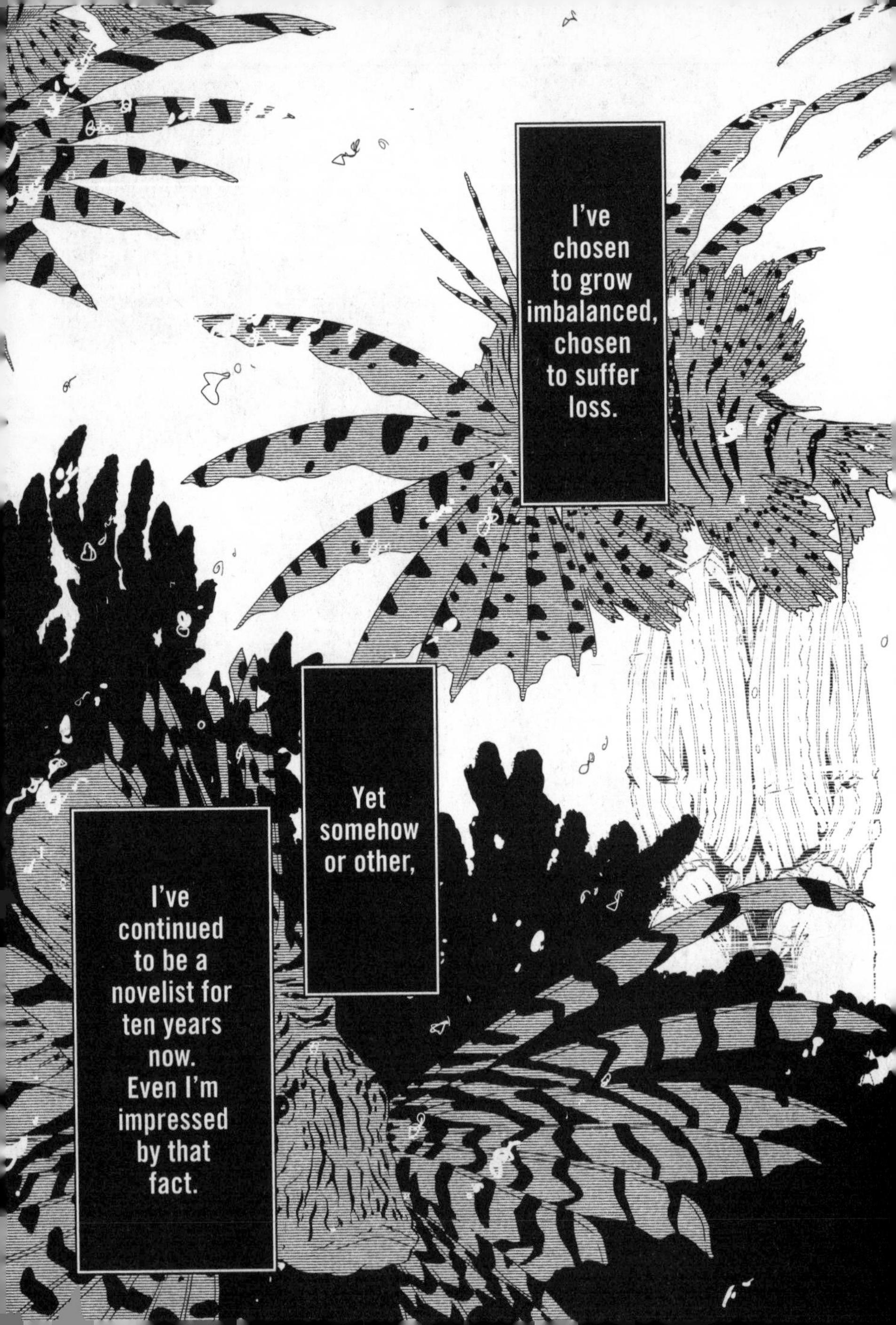
I've chosen to grow imbalanced, chosen to suffer loss.
Yet somehow or other,
I've continued to be a novelist for ten years now. Even I'm impressed by that fact.

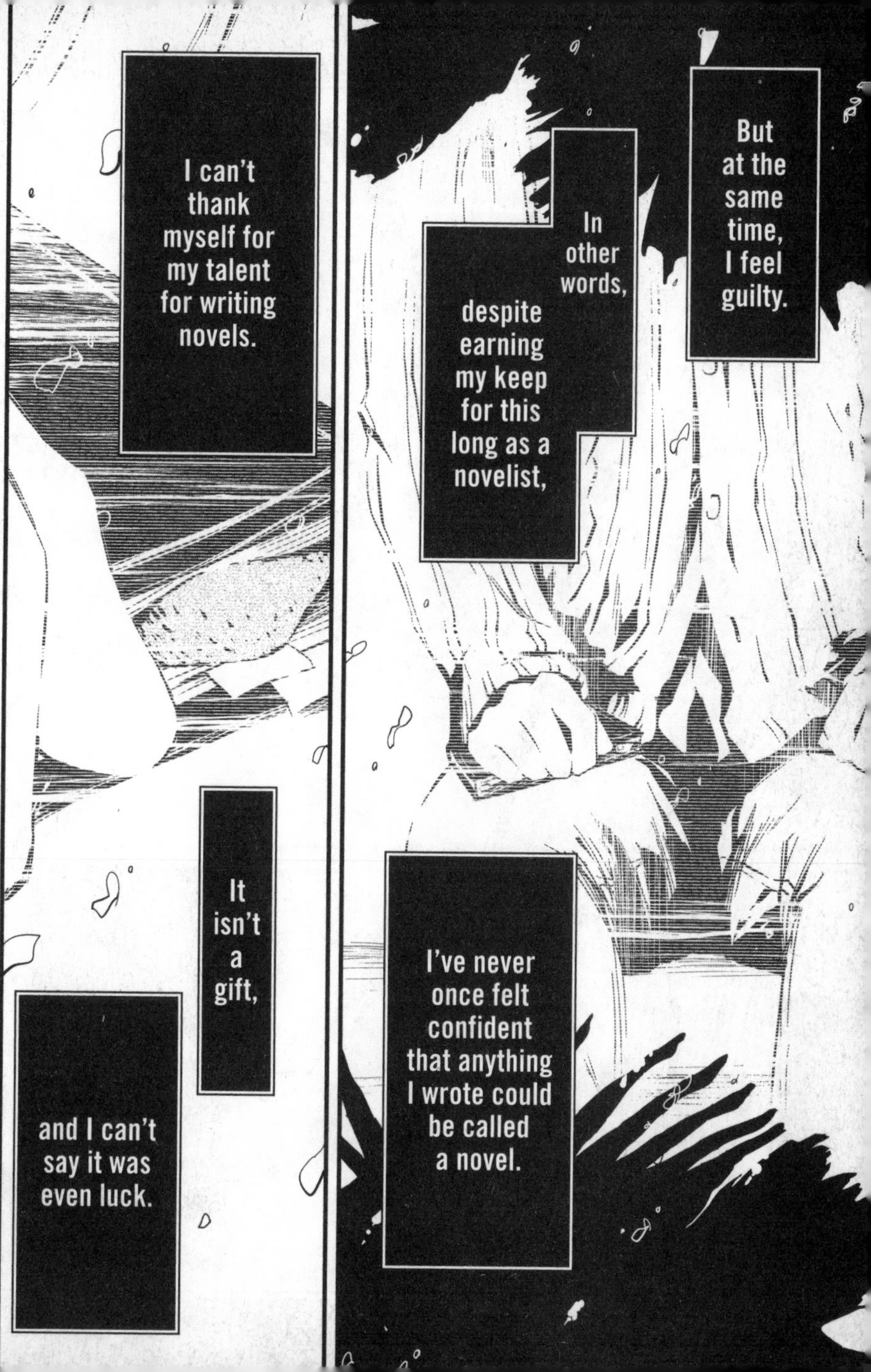
But at the same time, I feel guilty.
In other words, despite earning my keep for this long as a novelist,
I've never once felt confident that anything I wrote could be called a novel.
I can't thank myself for my talent for writing novels.
It isn't a gift,
and I can't say it was even luck.

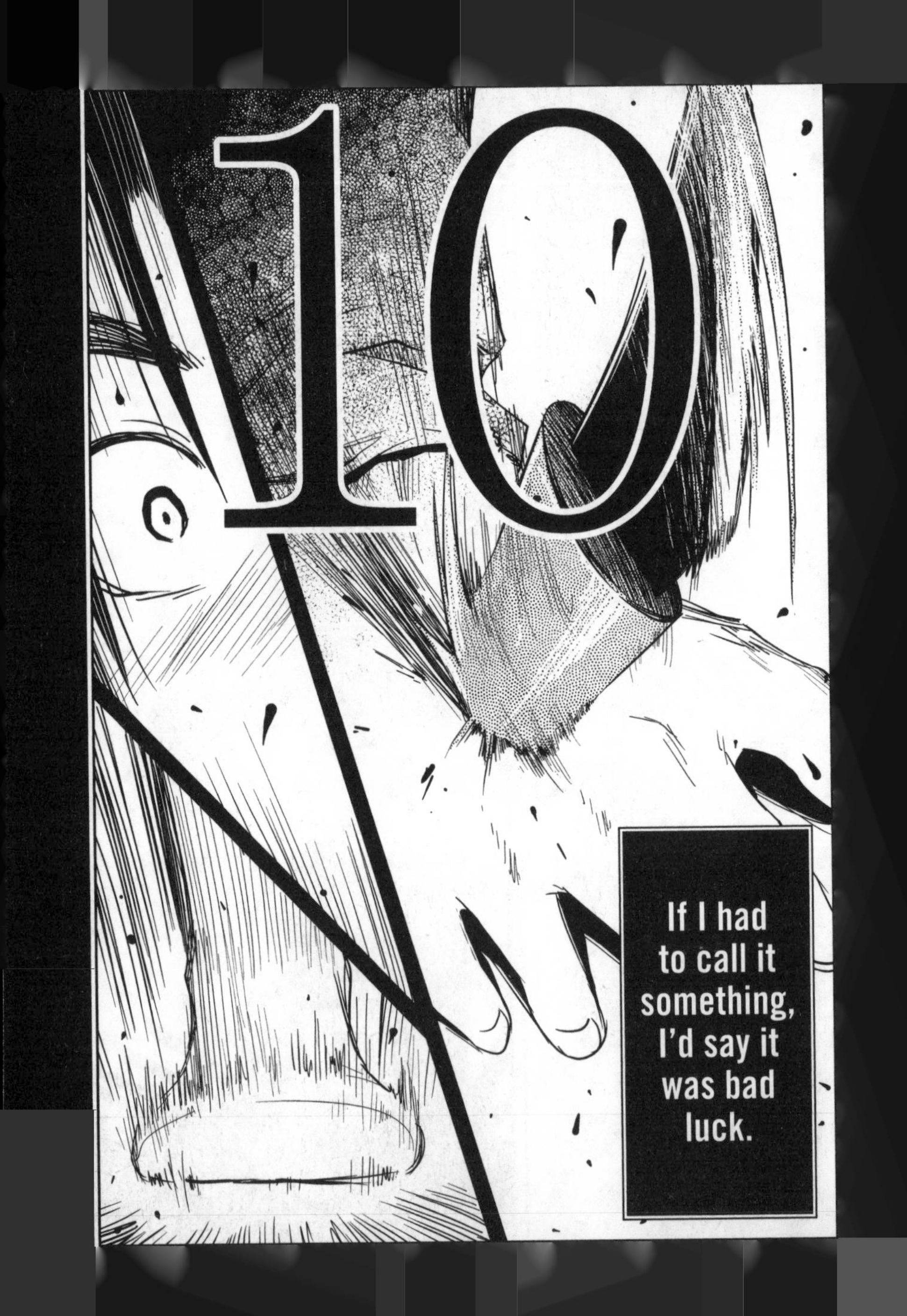
10
If I had to call it something, I'd say it was bad luck.

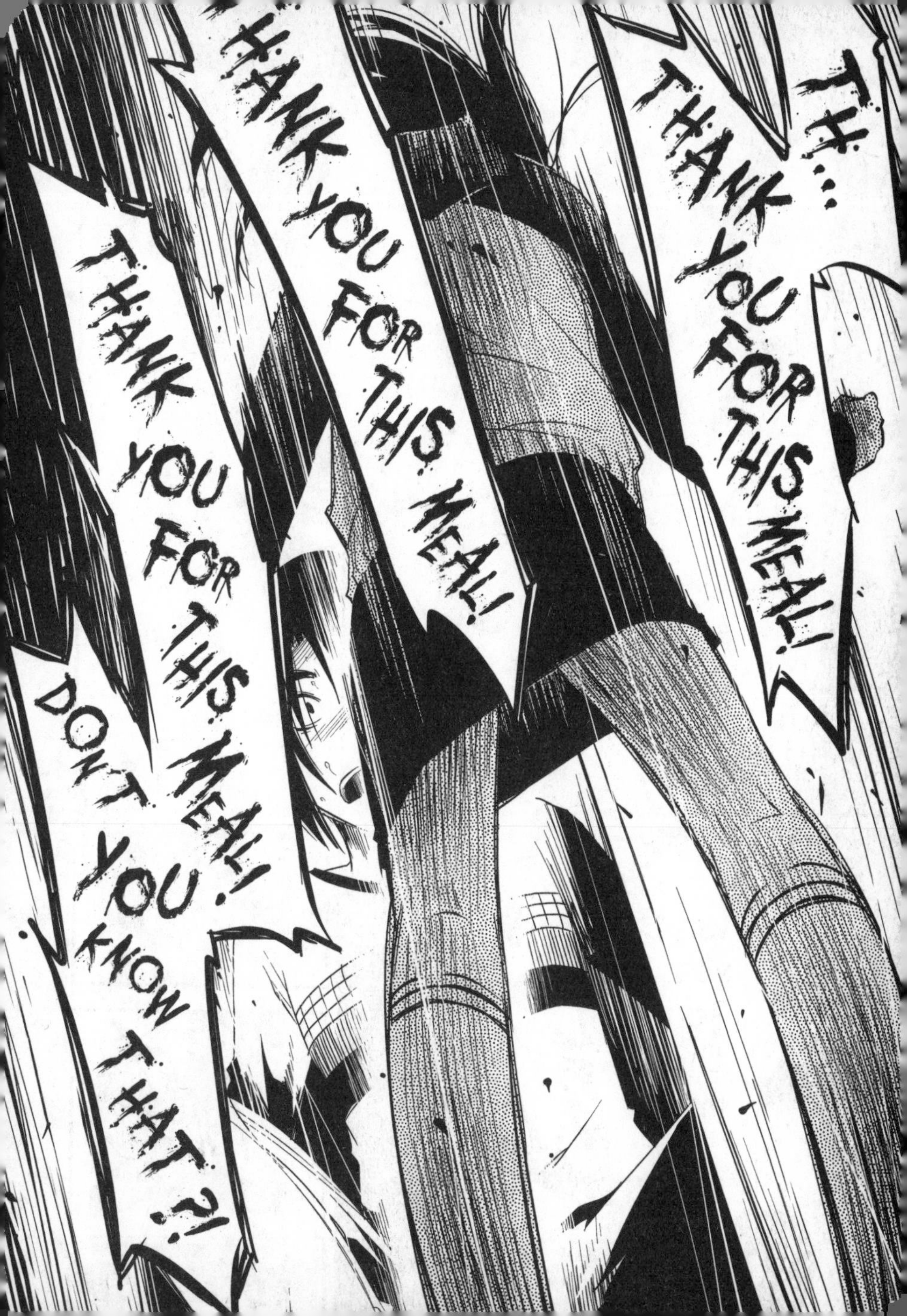
TH... THANK YOU FOR THIS MEAL!
HANK YOU FOR THIS MEAL!
THANK YOU FOR THIS MEAL! DON'T YOU KNOW THAT?!

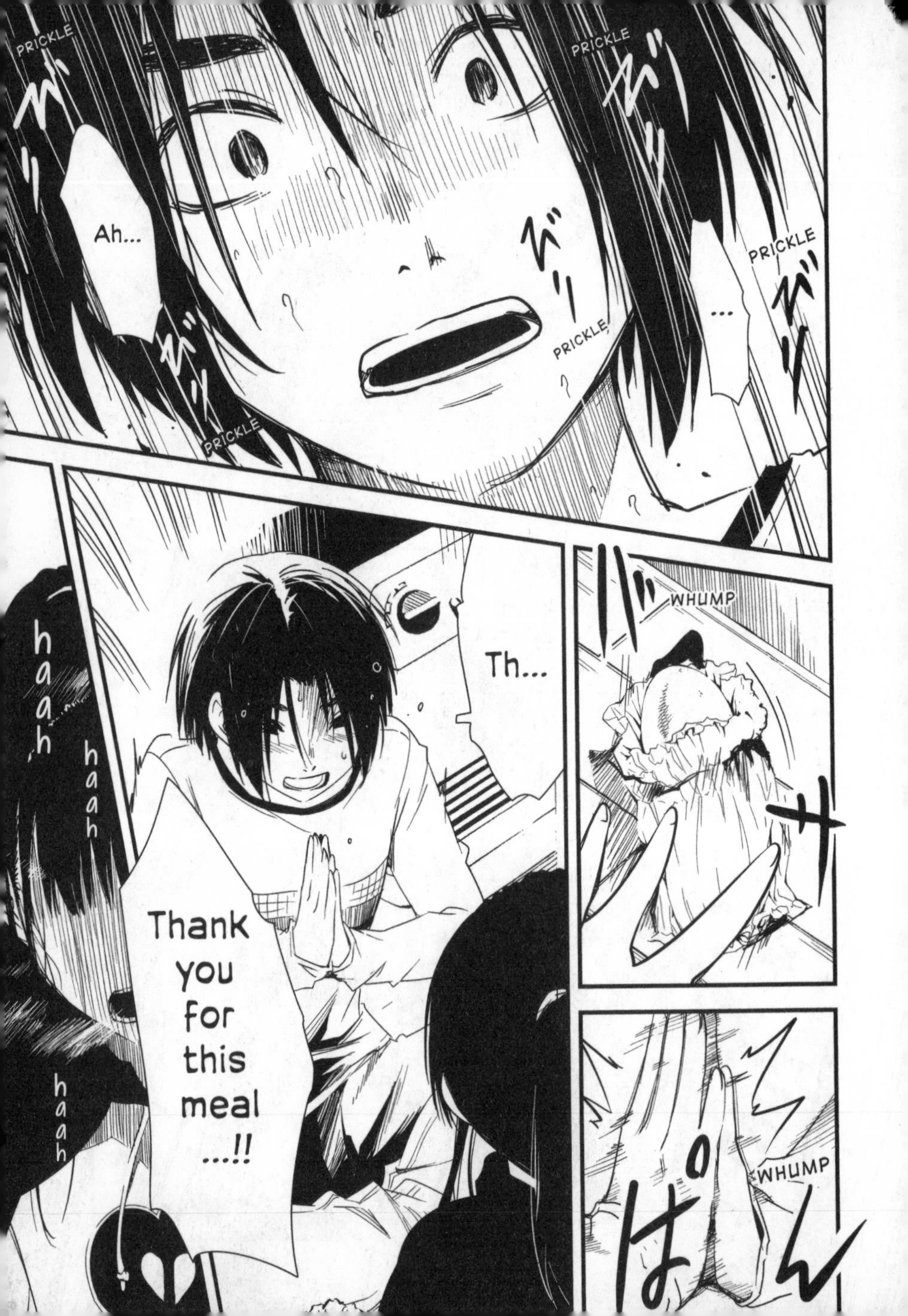
PRICKLE
PRICKLE
...
PRICKLE
Ah...
PRICKLE
PRICKLE
WHUMP
WHUMP
Th...
Thank you for this meal ...!!
haaah
haaah
haaah

haah...

haah...

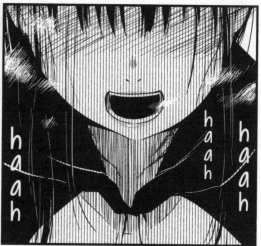

haah

haah

haah

haah

RATTLE

Hm.

Hey...
Wait—

GACHIK

haah...

ssk...

....

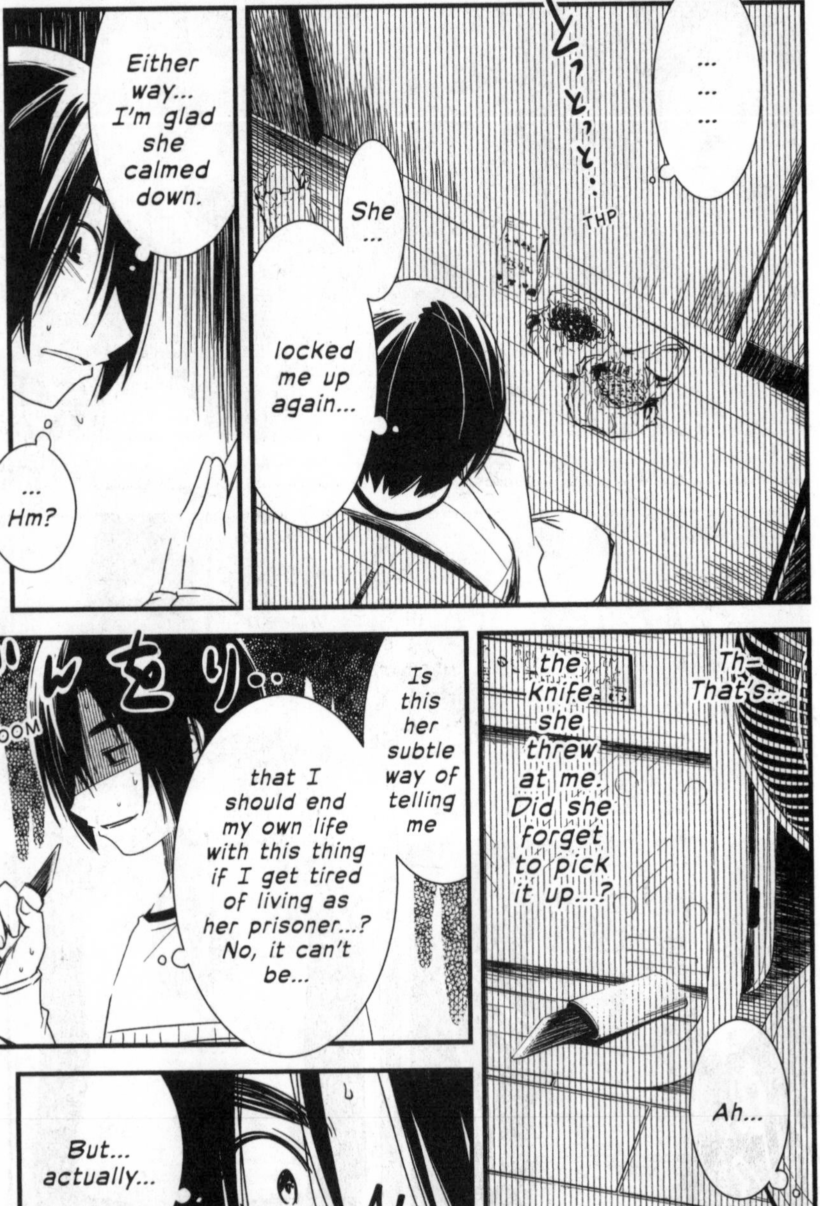

...
...
...
THP
She
...
locked me up again...
Either way... I'm glad she calmed down.
...
Hm?
Th- That's...
the knife she threw at me. Did she forget to pick it up...?
Ah...
Is this her subtle way of telling me
that I should end my own life with this thing if I get tired of living as her prisoner...? No, it can't be...
GLOOM
Ah
But... actually...

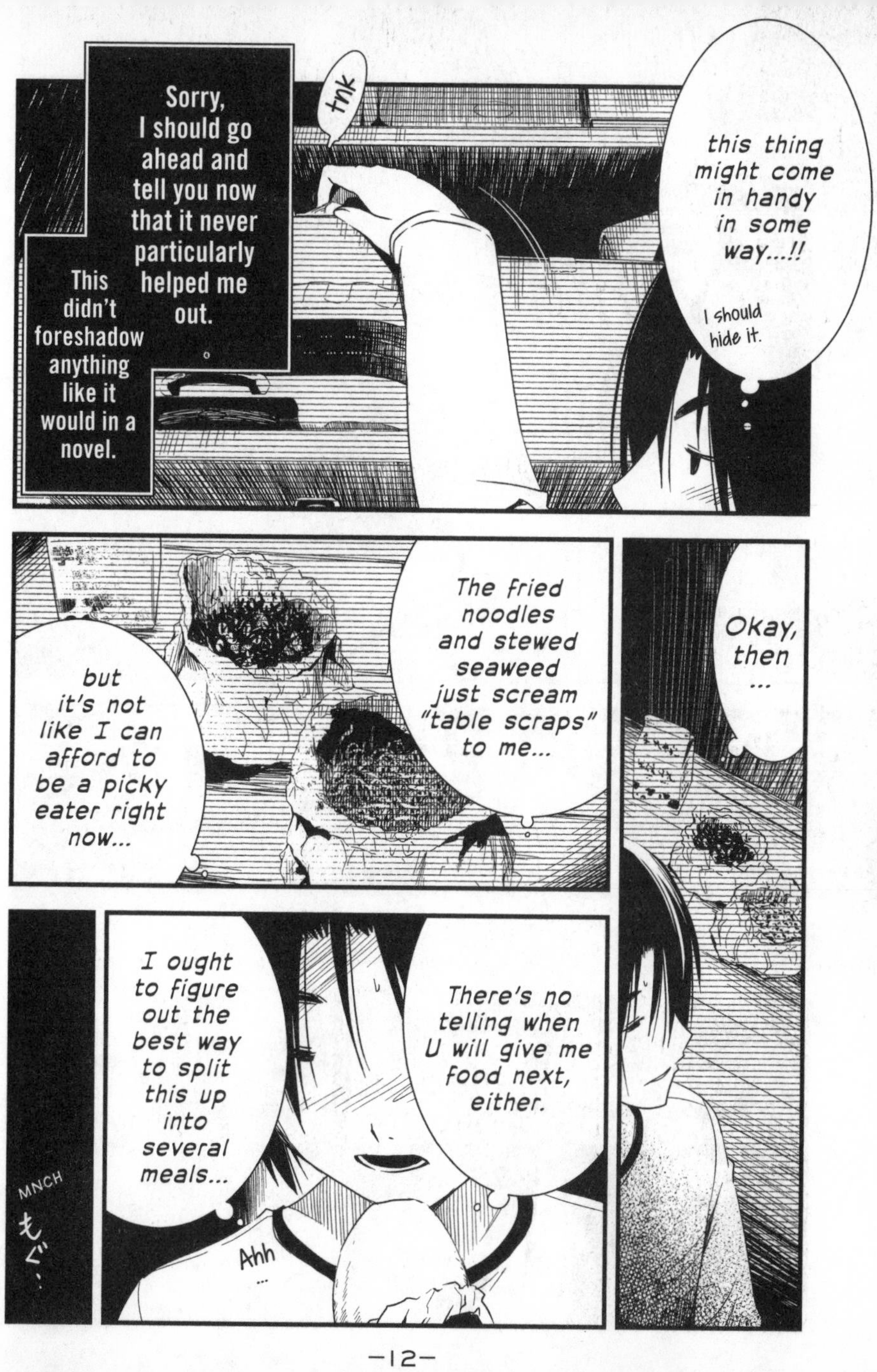
this thing might come in handy in some way...!!
I should hide it.
tnk
Sorry, I should go ahead and tell you now that it never particularly helped me out.
This didn't foreshadow anything like it would in a novel.
Okay, then ...
The fried noodles and stewed seaweed just scream "table scraps" to me...
but it's not like I can afford to be a picky eater right now...
There's no telling when U will give me food next, either.
I ought to figure out the best way to split this up into several meals...
Ahh ...
MNCH
もぐ..

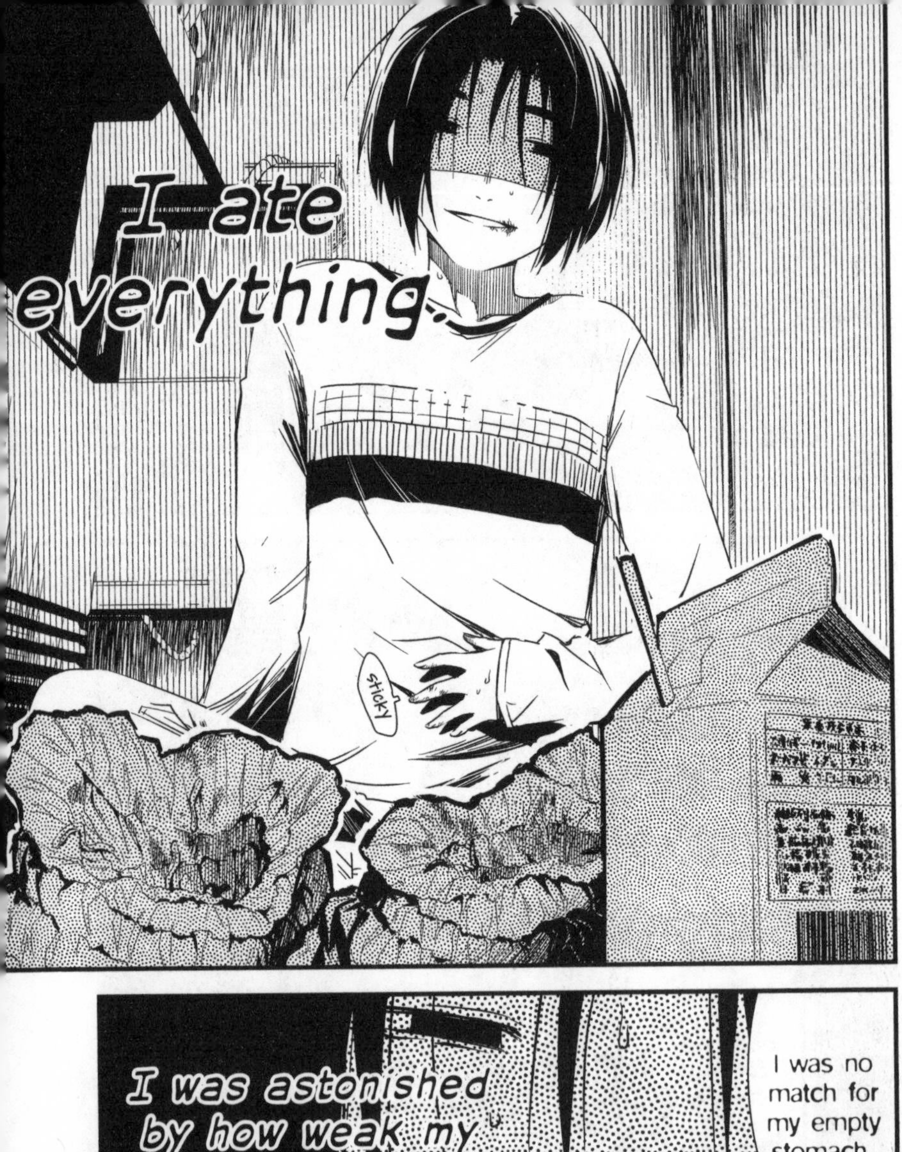
I ate everything..
sticky
I was no match for my empty stomach...
I was astonished by how weak my willpower was.
In fact, it wasn't enough for a single meal...

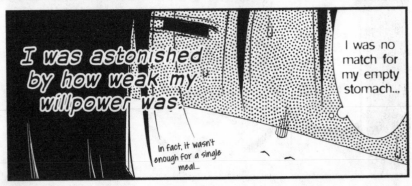

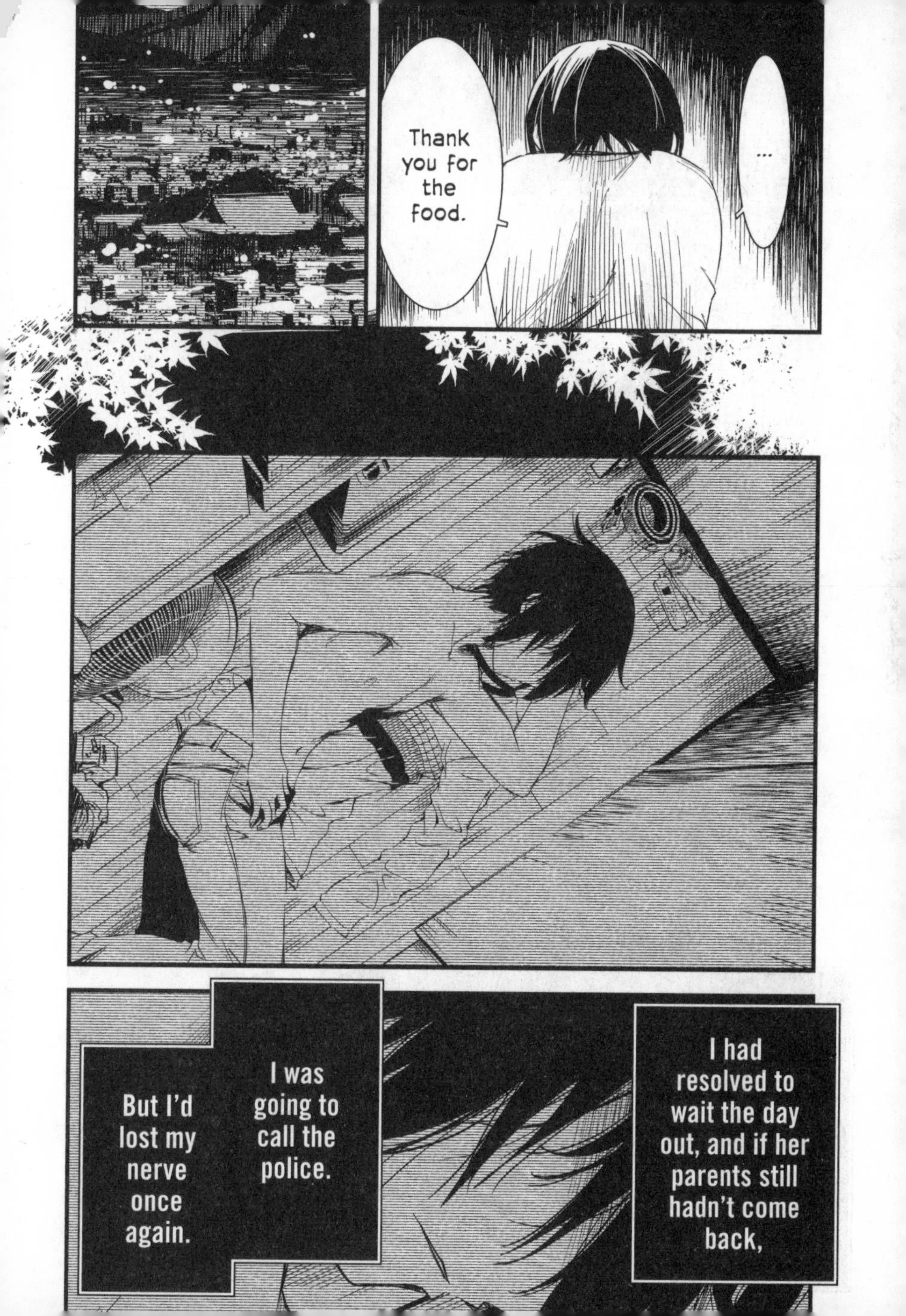
...
Thank you for the food.
I had resolved to wait the day out, and if her parents still hadn't come back,
I was going to call the police.
But I'd lost my nerve once again.

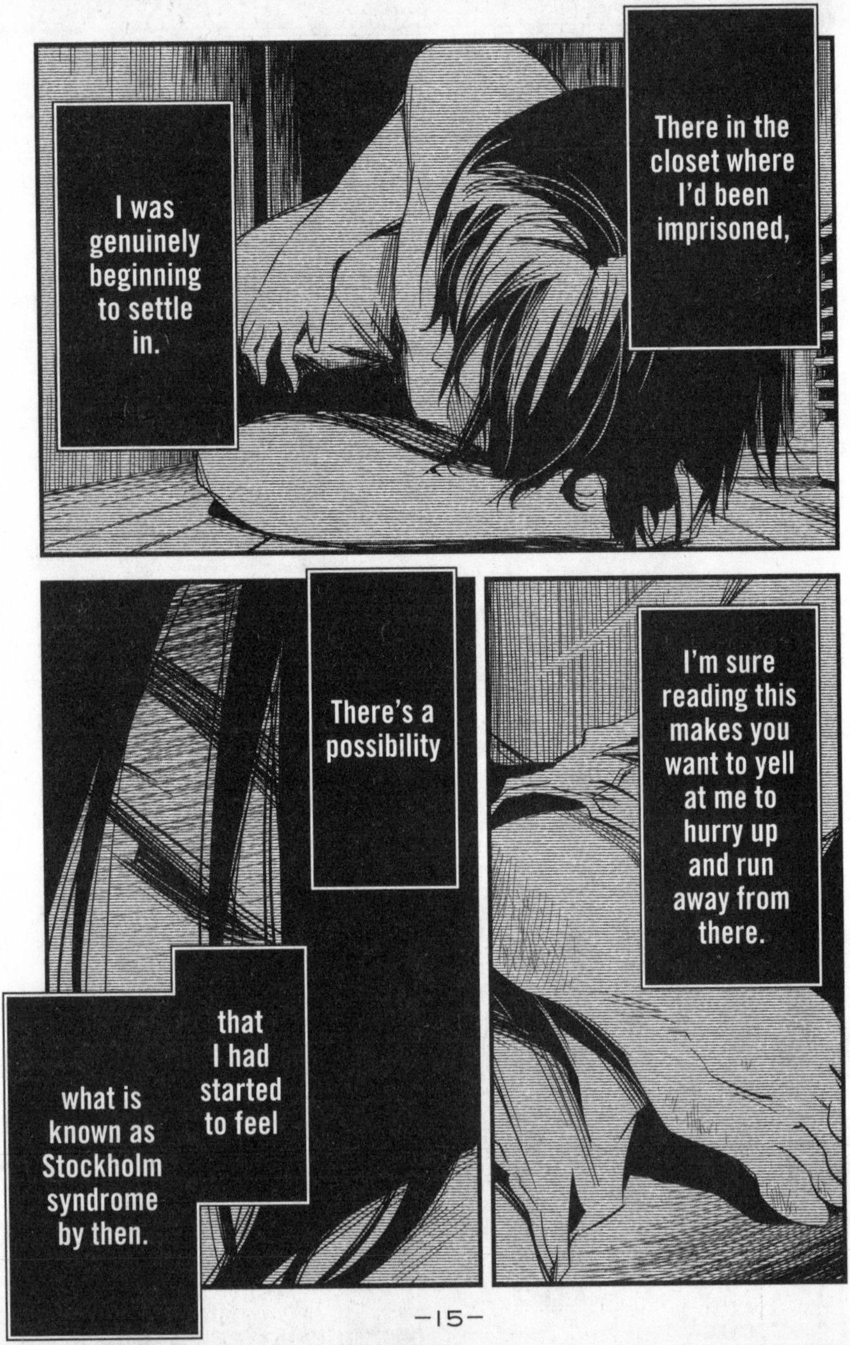
There in the closet where I'd been imprisoned,
I was genuinely beginning to settle in.
I'm sure reading this makes you want to yell at me to hurry up and run away from there.
There's a possibility
that I had started to feel
what is known as Stockholm syndrome by then.

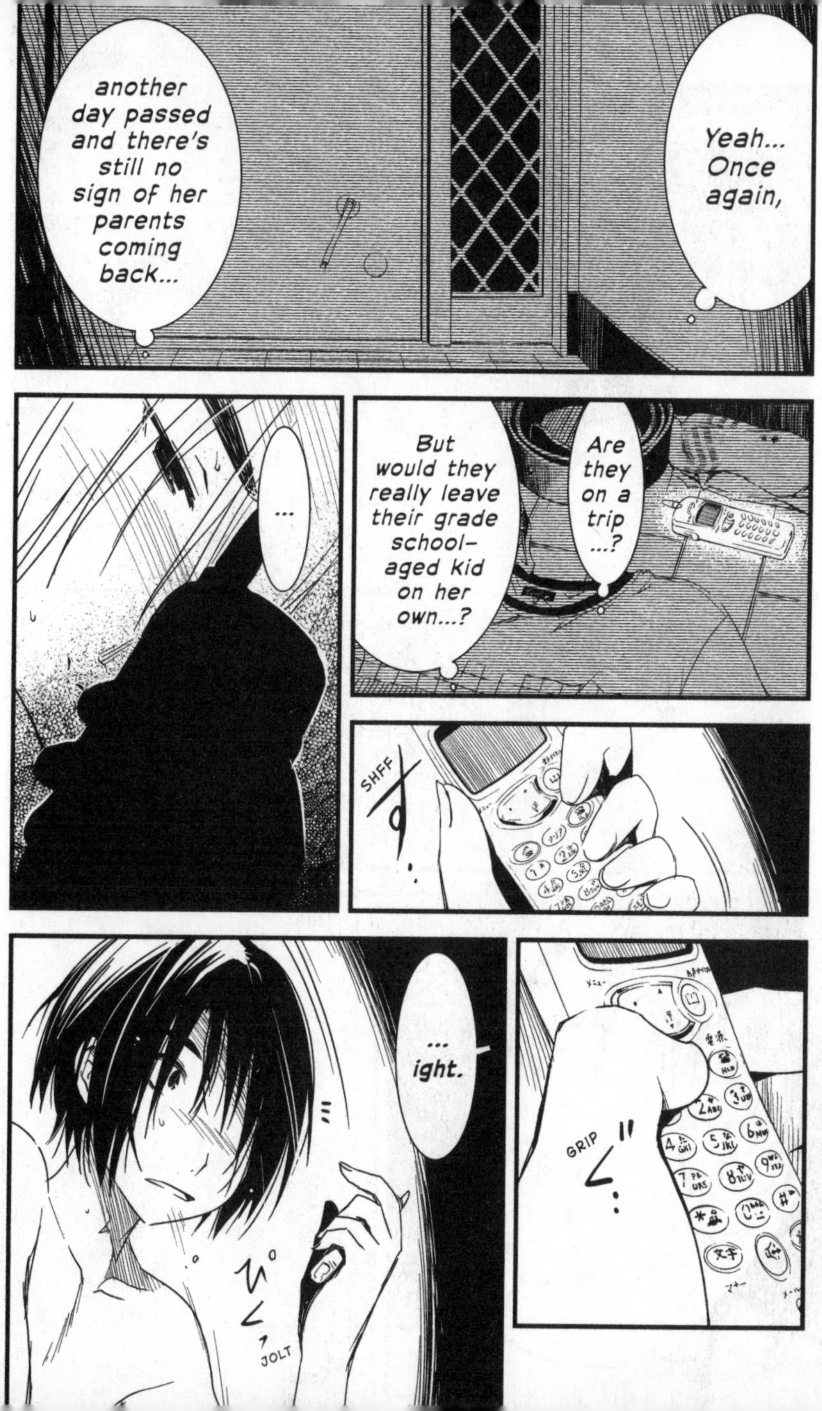
Yeah... Once again,
another day passed and there's still no sign of her parents coming back...
Are they on a trip ...?
But would they really leave their grade school-aged kid on her own...?
SHFF
...
GRIP
... ight.
JOLT

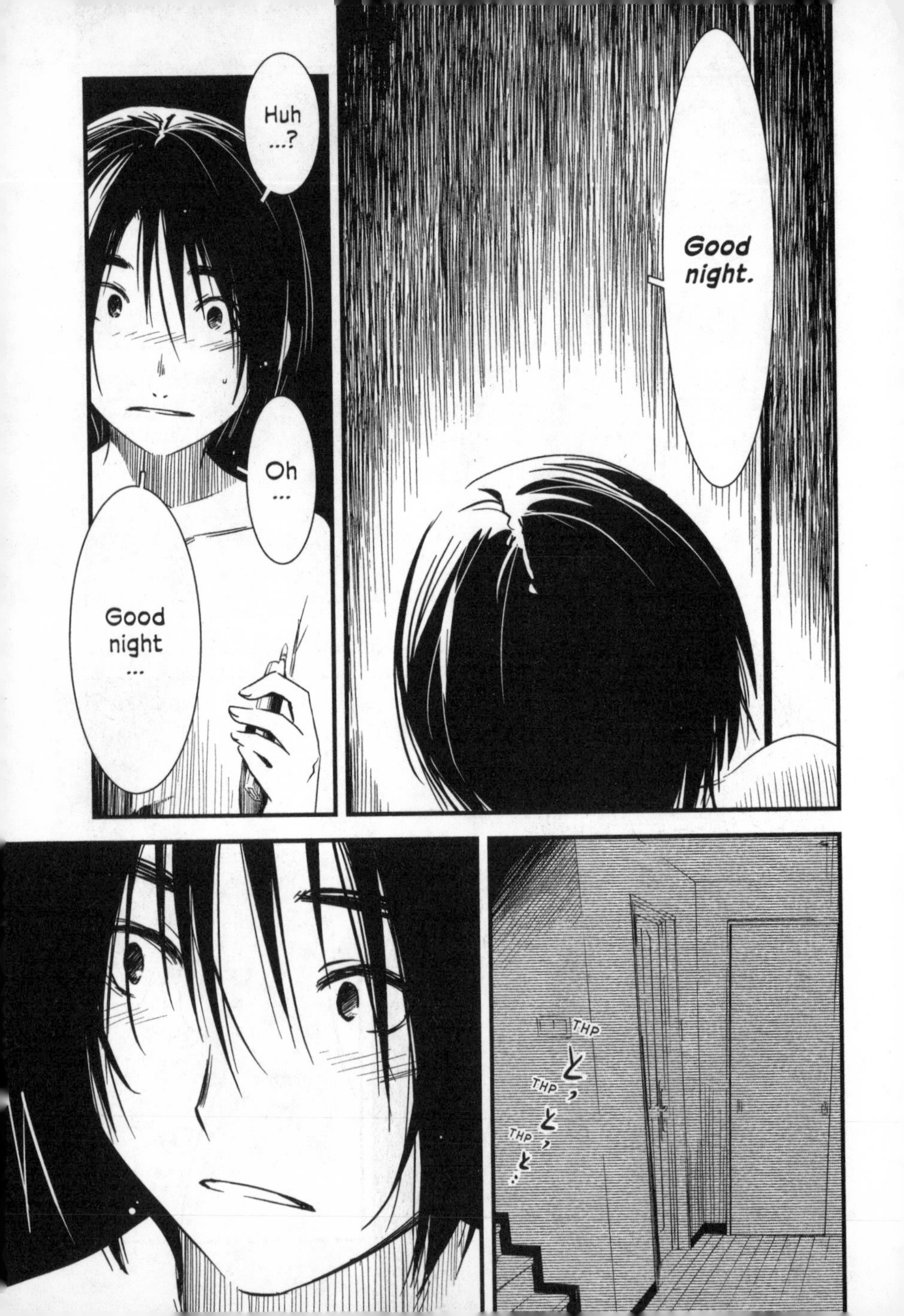
Good night.
Huh ...?
Oh ...
Good night ...
THP と,
THP と,
THP と...

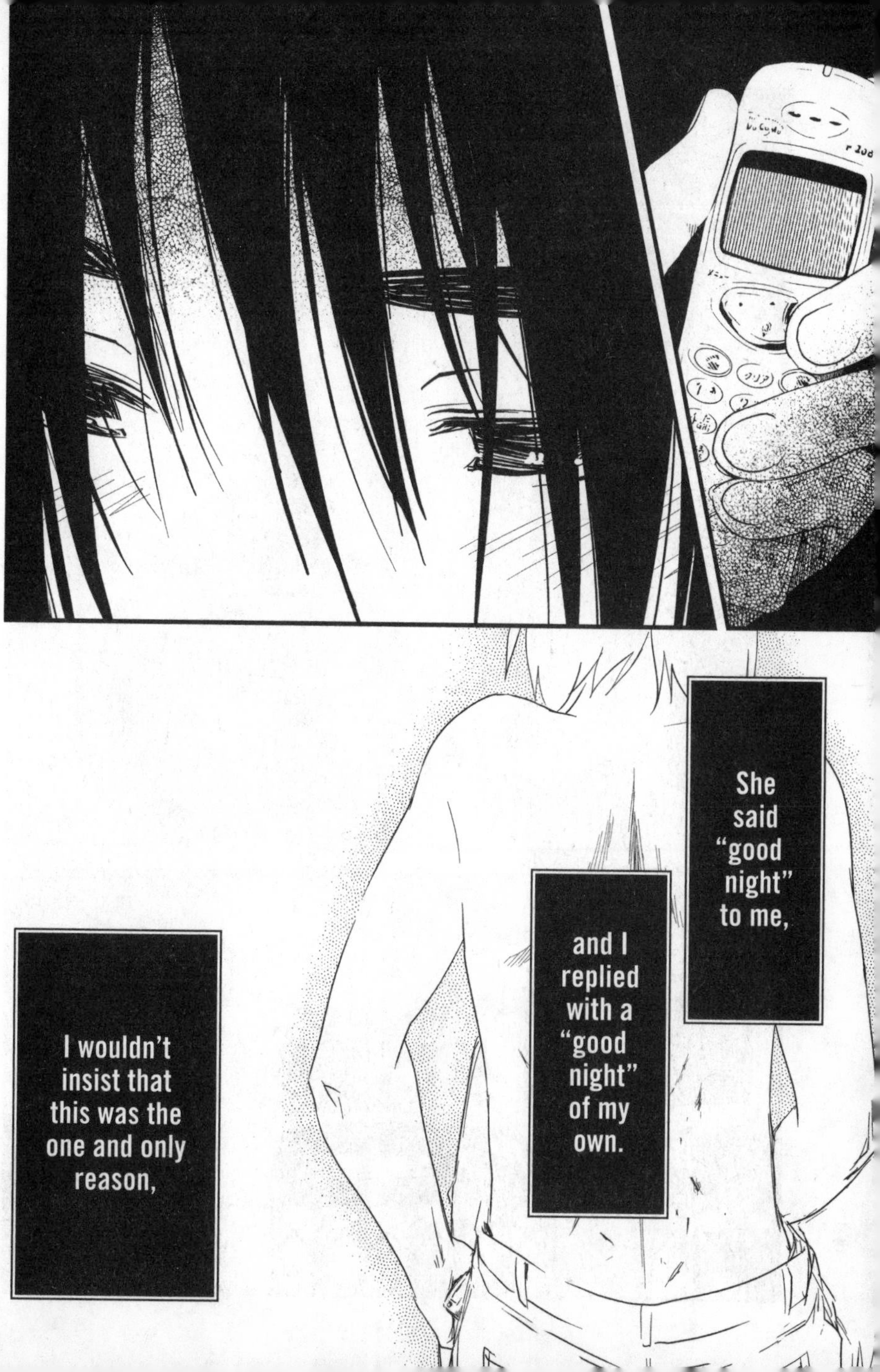
She said "good night" to me,
and I replied with a "good night" of my own.
I wouldn't insist that this was the one and only reason,

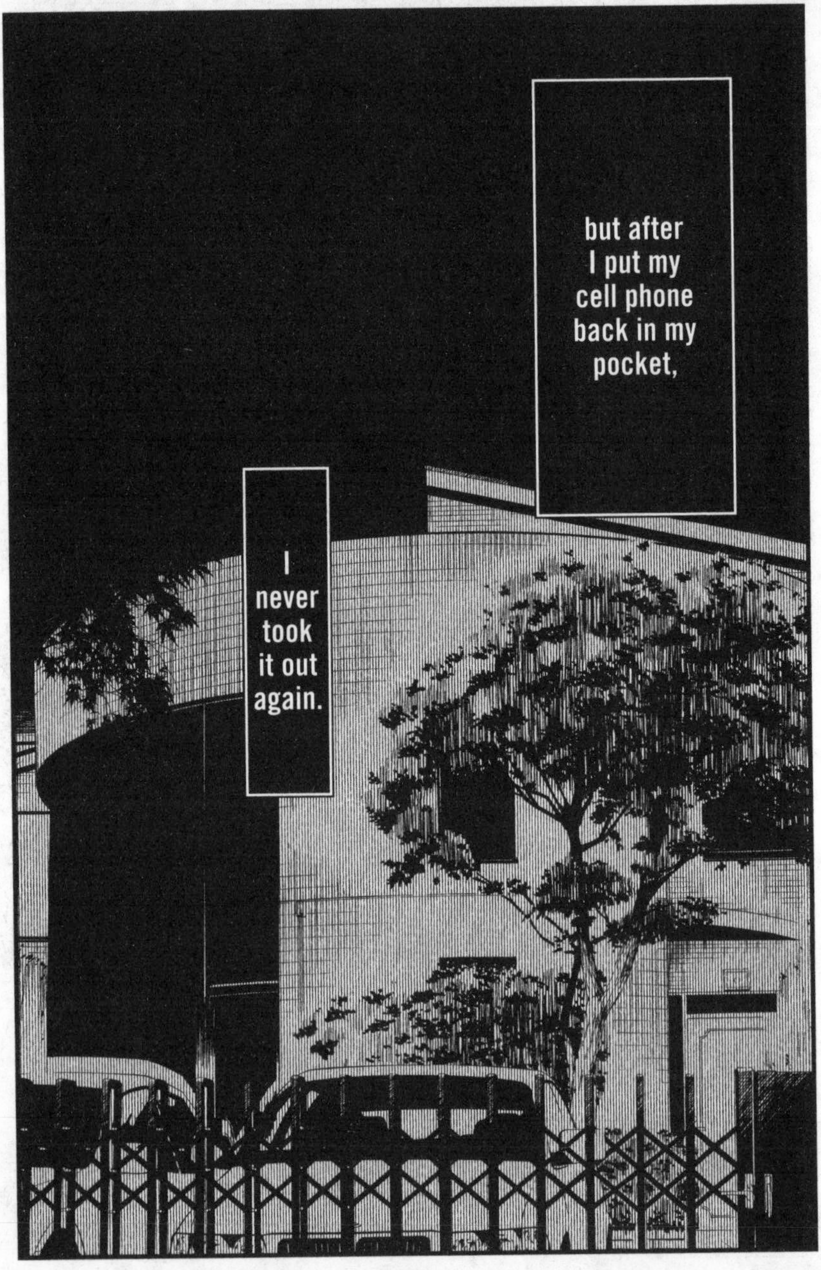
but after I put my cell phone back in my pocket,
I never took it out again.

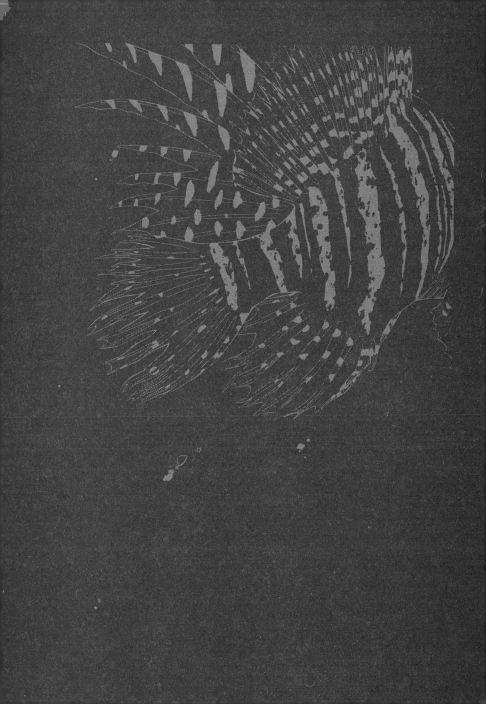

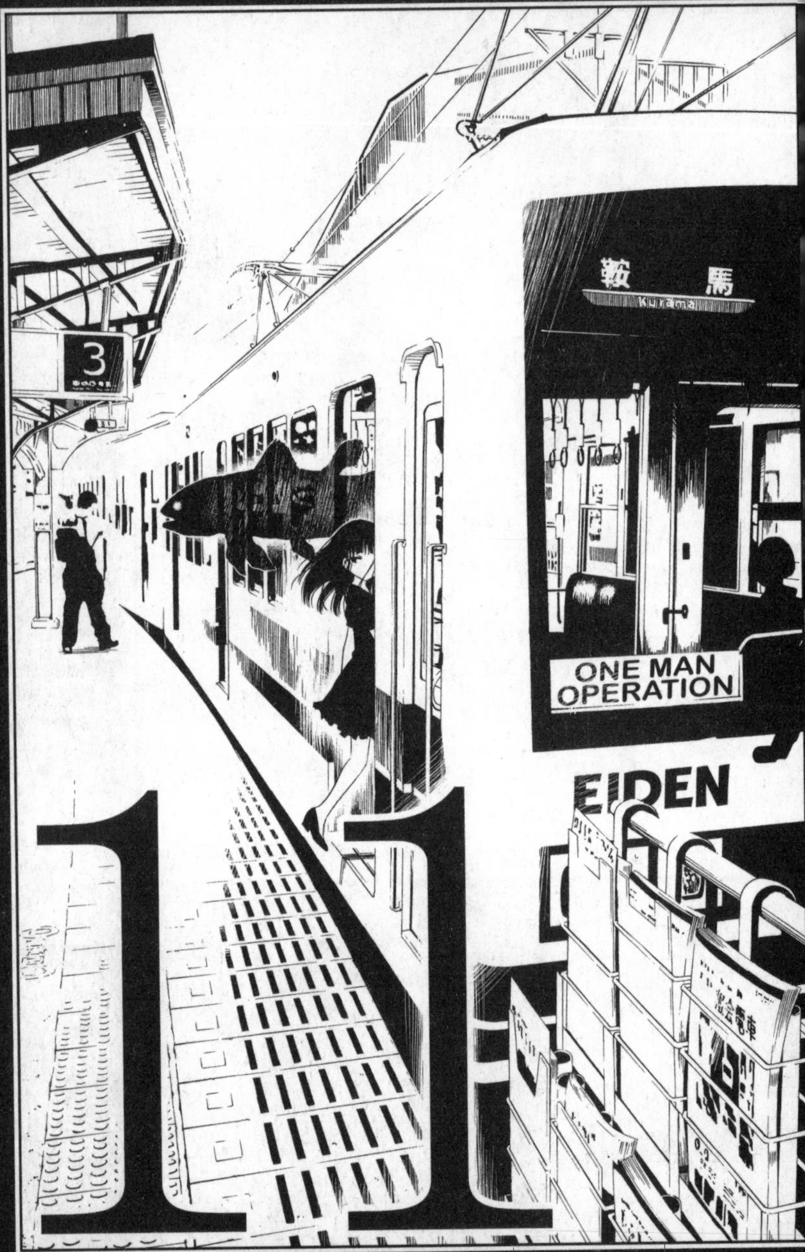
3
鞍　馬
Kurama
ONE MAN
OPERATION
EIDEN
11

Day 3 of Imprisonment

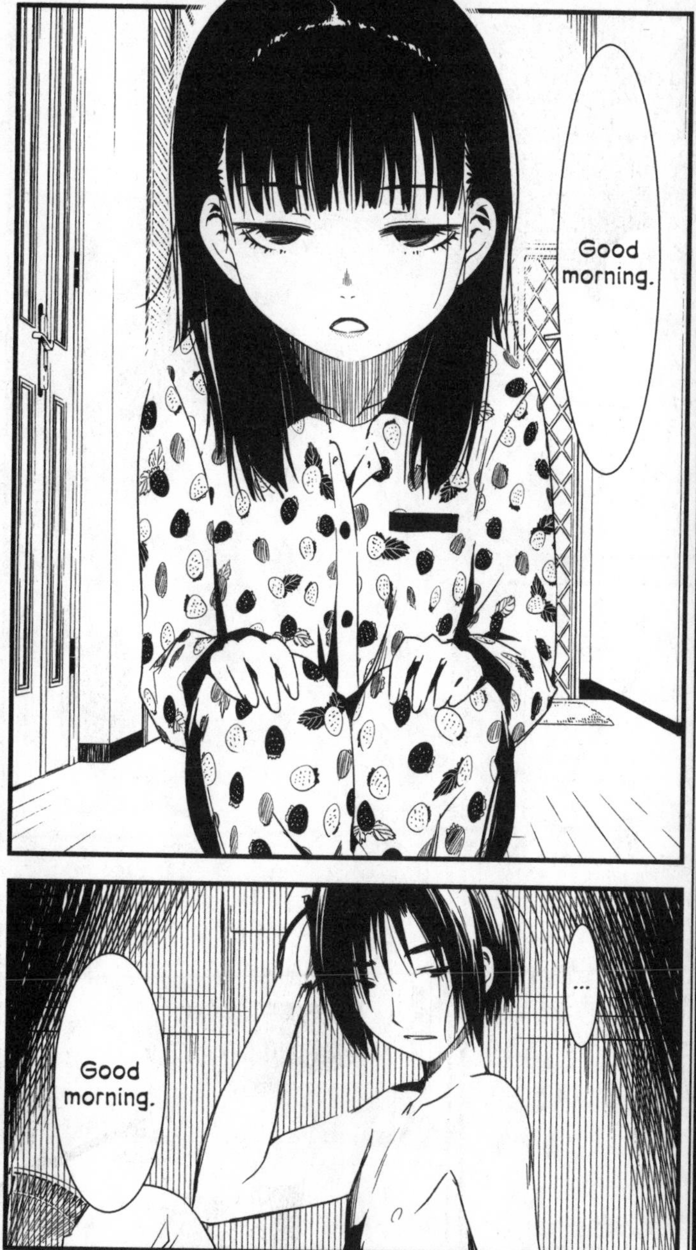
Good morning.
...
Good morning.

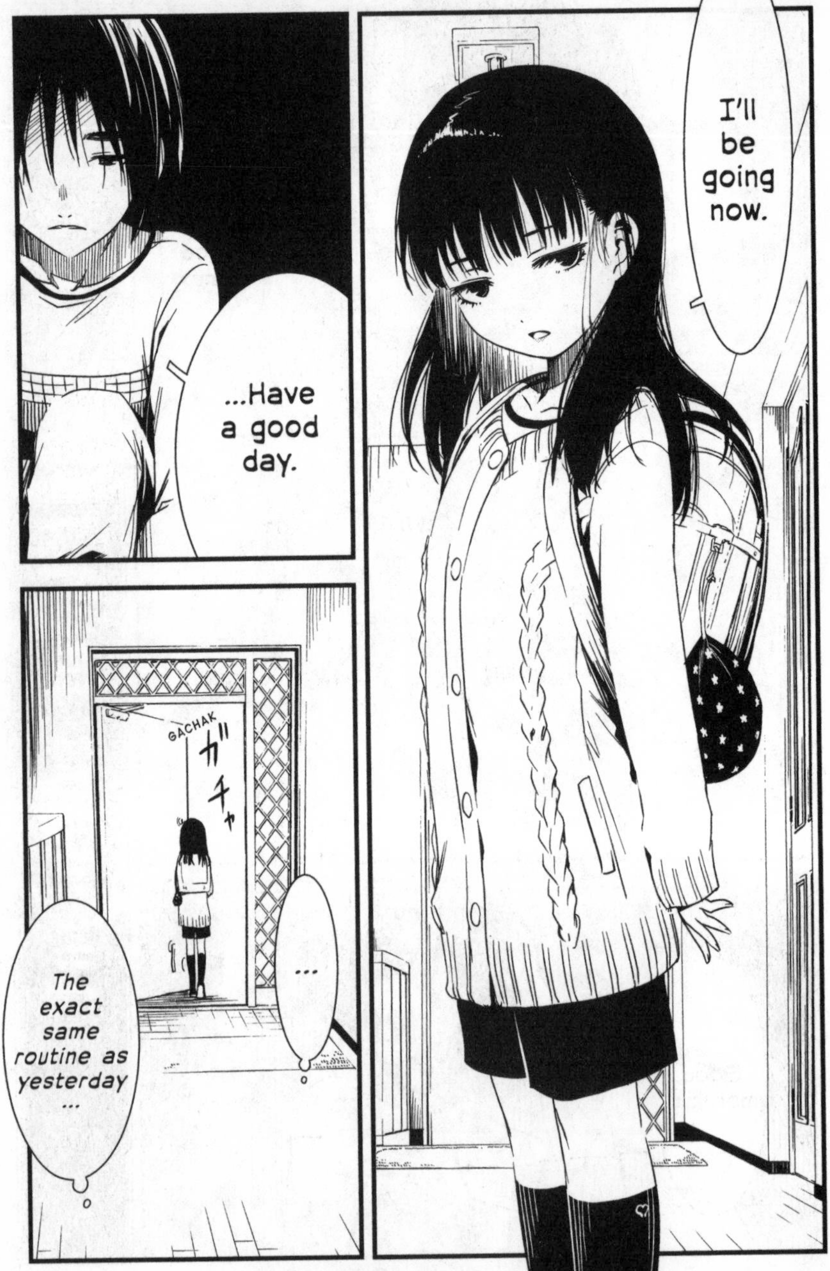
I'll be going now.
...Have a good day.
GACHAK
ガチャ
...
The exact same routine as yesterday...

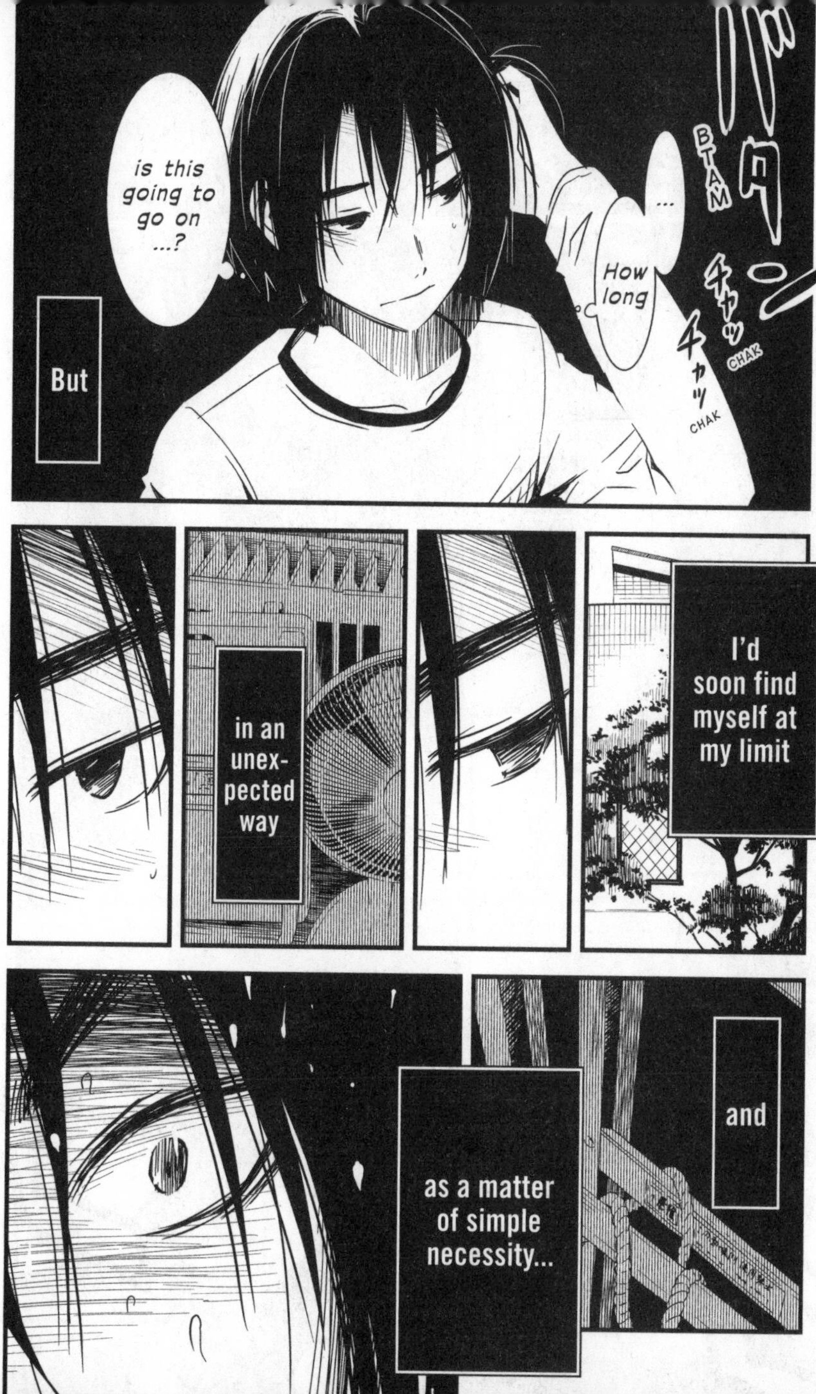

BTAM
... How long
is this going to go on ...?
チャッ
CHAK
チカッ
CHAK
But
I'd soon find myself at my limit
in an unex-pected way
and
as a matter of simple necessity...

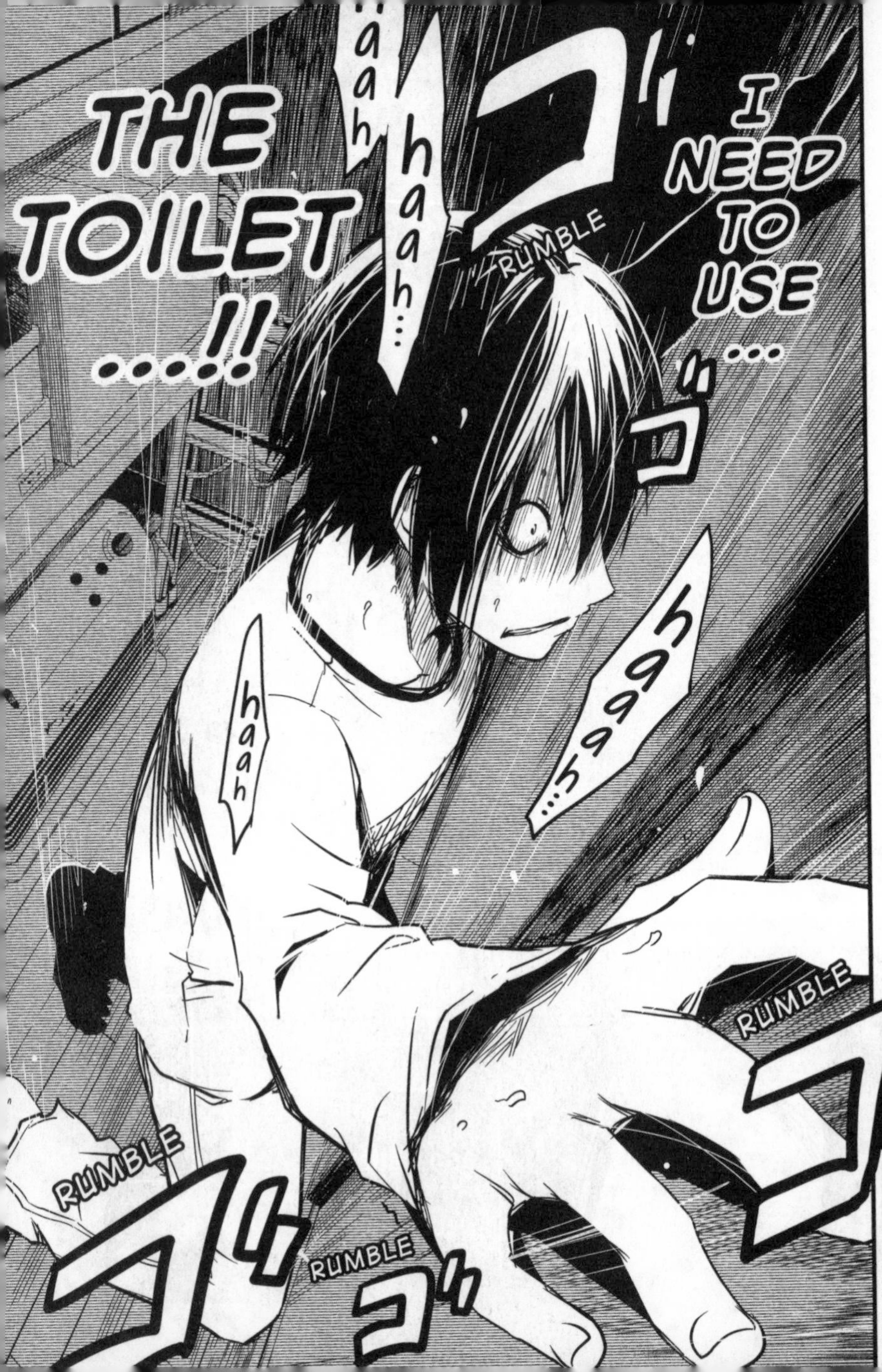
I NEED TO USE...
haah haah...
RUMBLE
THE TOILET ....!!
hgggh...
haah
RUMBLE
RUMBLE
RUMBLE

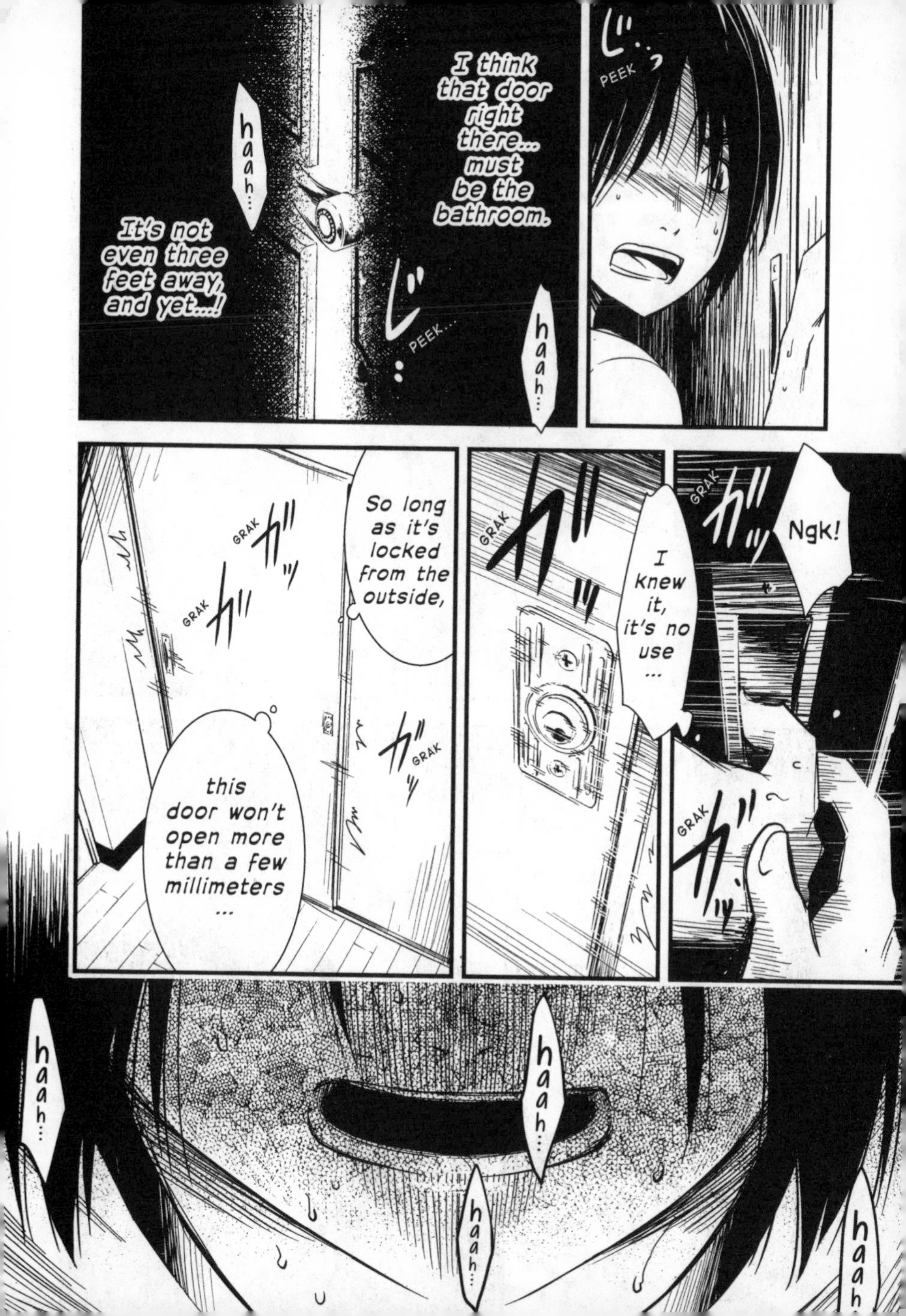
PEEK
haaah...
I think that door right there... must be the bathroom.
PEEK...
haaah...
It's not even three feet away, and yet...!
GRAK
Ngk!
GRAK
GRAK
I knew it, it's no use...
So long as it's locked from the outside,
GRAK
GRAK
GRAK
this door won't open more than a few millimeters...
haaah...
haaah...
haaah...
haaah...

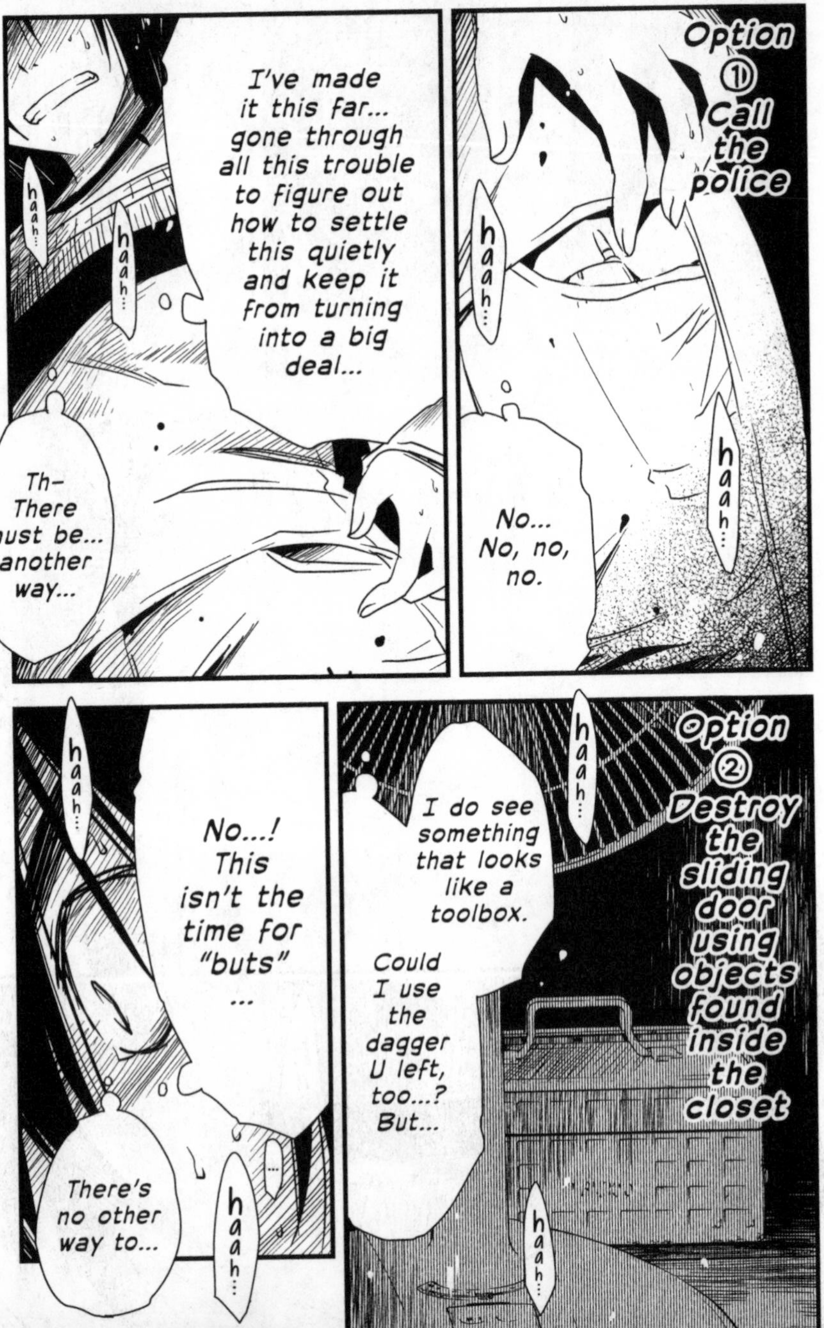
Option ① Call the police
haaah...
haaah...
No... No, no, no.
I've made it this far... gone through all this trouble to figure out how to settle this quietly and keep it from turning into a big deal...
haaah...
haaah...
Th- There must be... another way...
Option ② Destroy the sliding door using objects found inside the closet
haaah...
I do see something that looks like a toolbox.
Could I use the dagger U left, too...? But...
haaah...
haaah...
No...! This isn't the time for "buts" ...
...
haaah...
There's no other way to...

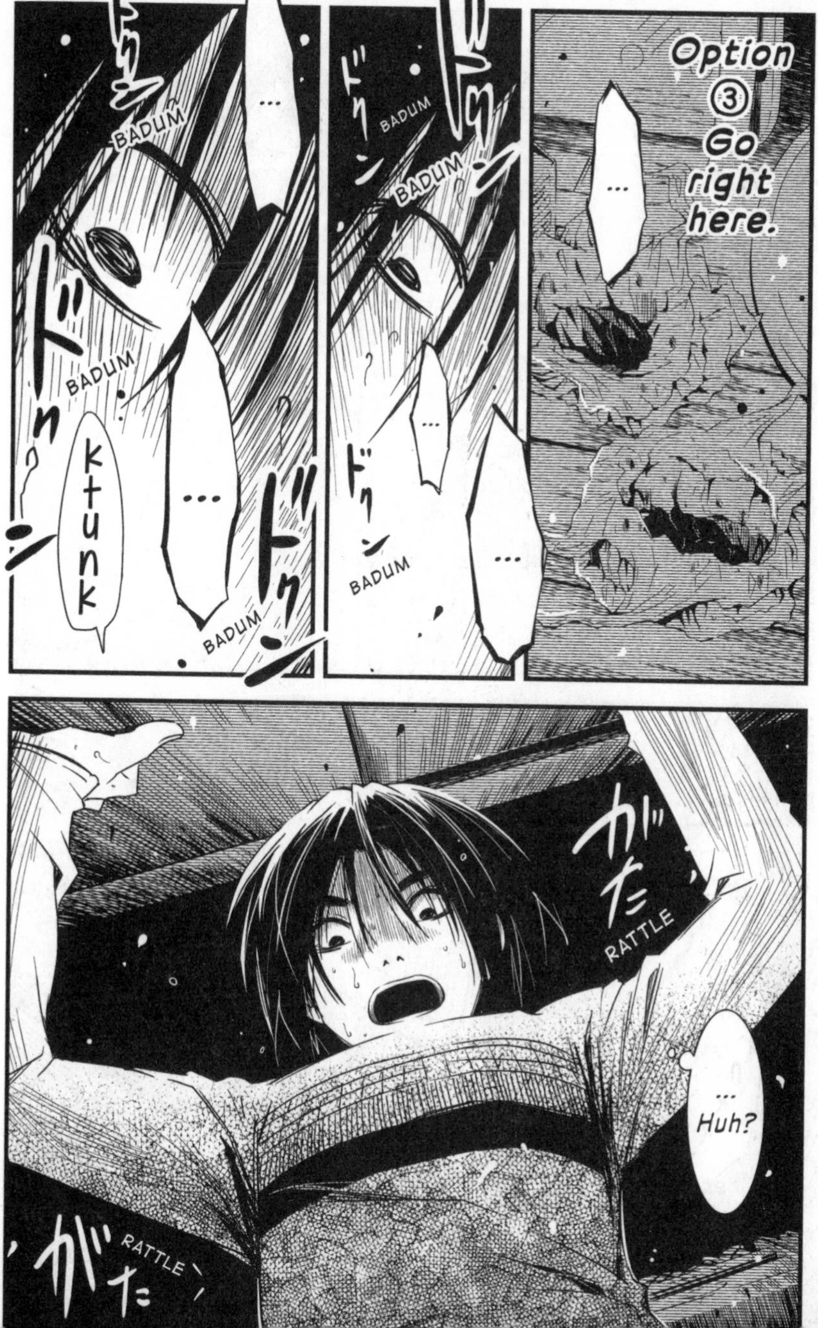
Option ③ Go right here.
...
BADUM
BADUM
...
...
BADUM
BADUM
...
BADUM
...
Ktunk
BADUM
RATTLE
... Huh?
RATTLE

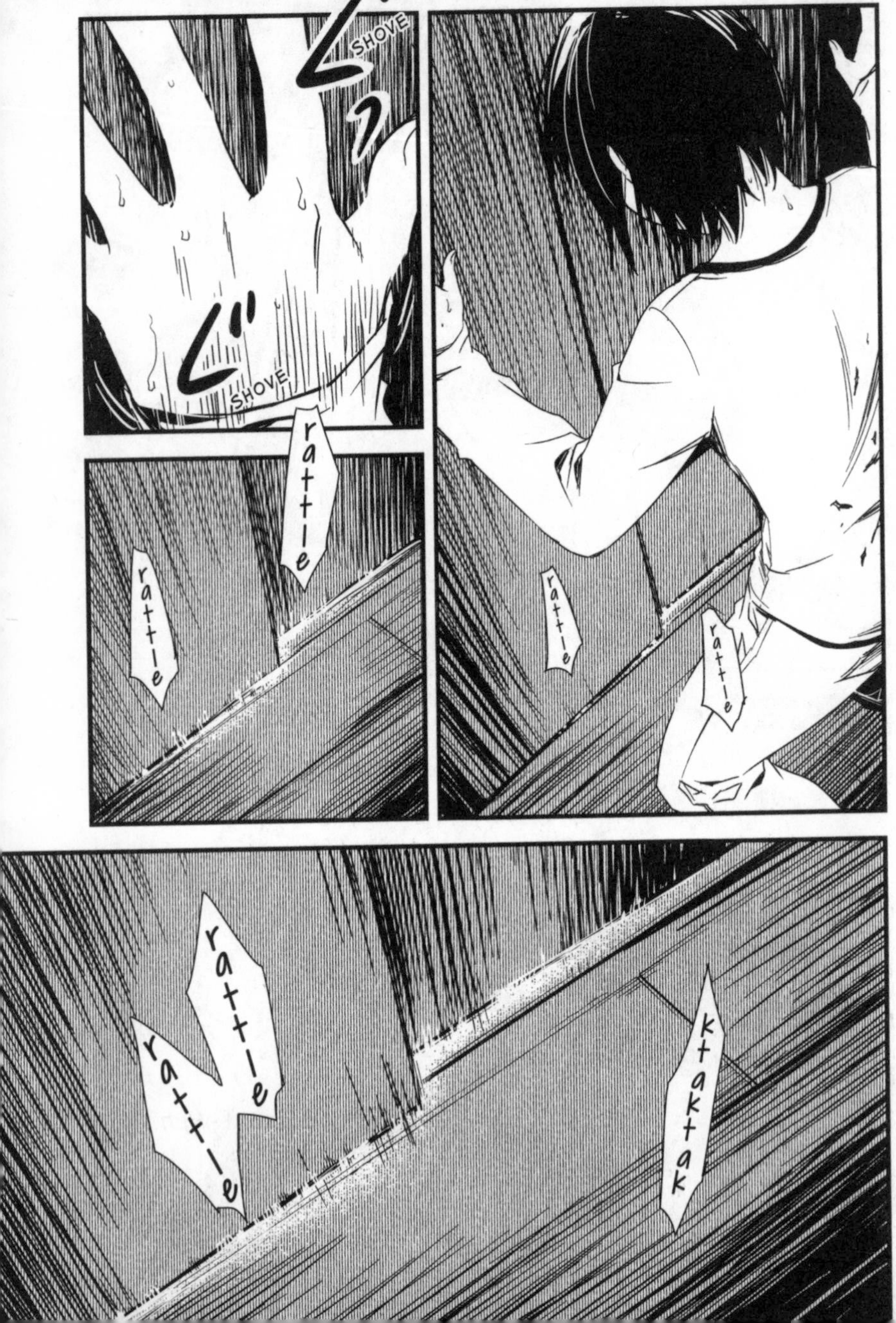
rattle
rattle
SHOVE
SHOVE
rattle
rattle
ktaktak
rattle
rattle

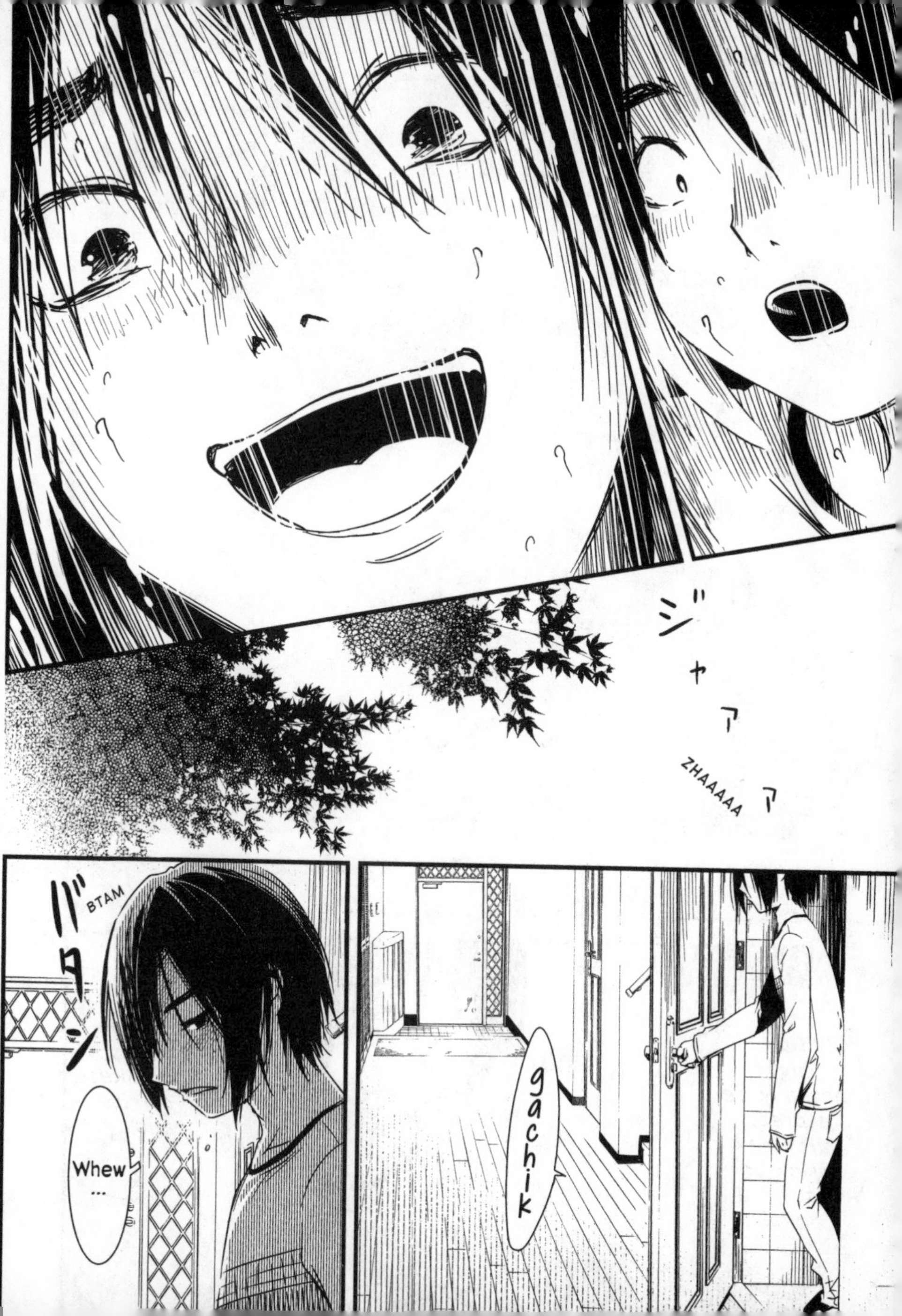
ジャアア
ZHAAAAA
gachik
バタ
BTAM
Whew...

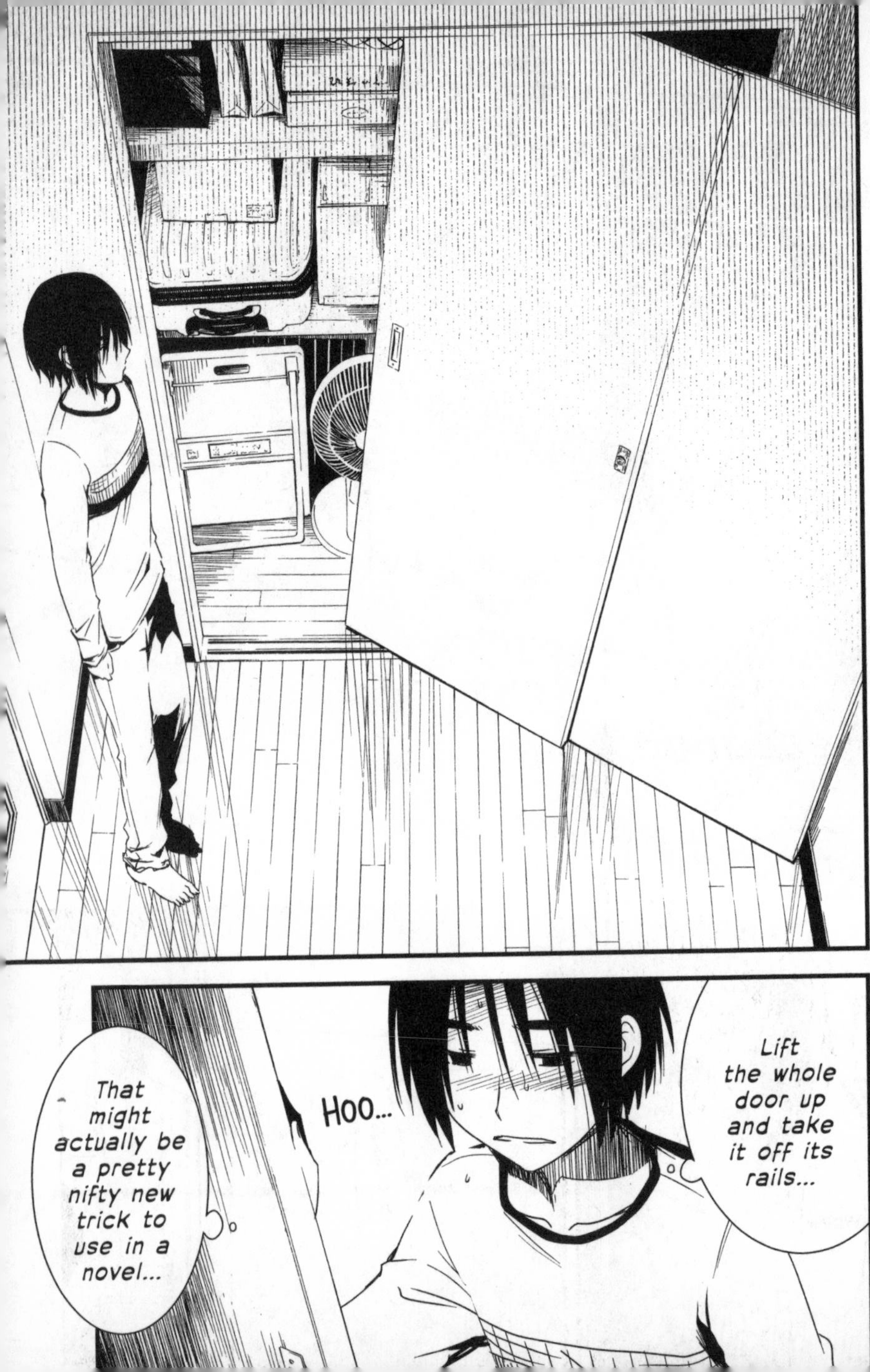
Lift the whole door up and take it off its rails...
HOO...
That might actually be a pretty nifty new trick to use in a novel...

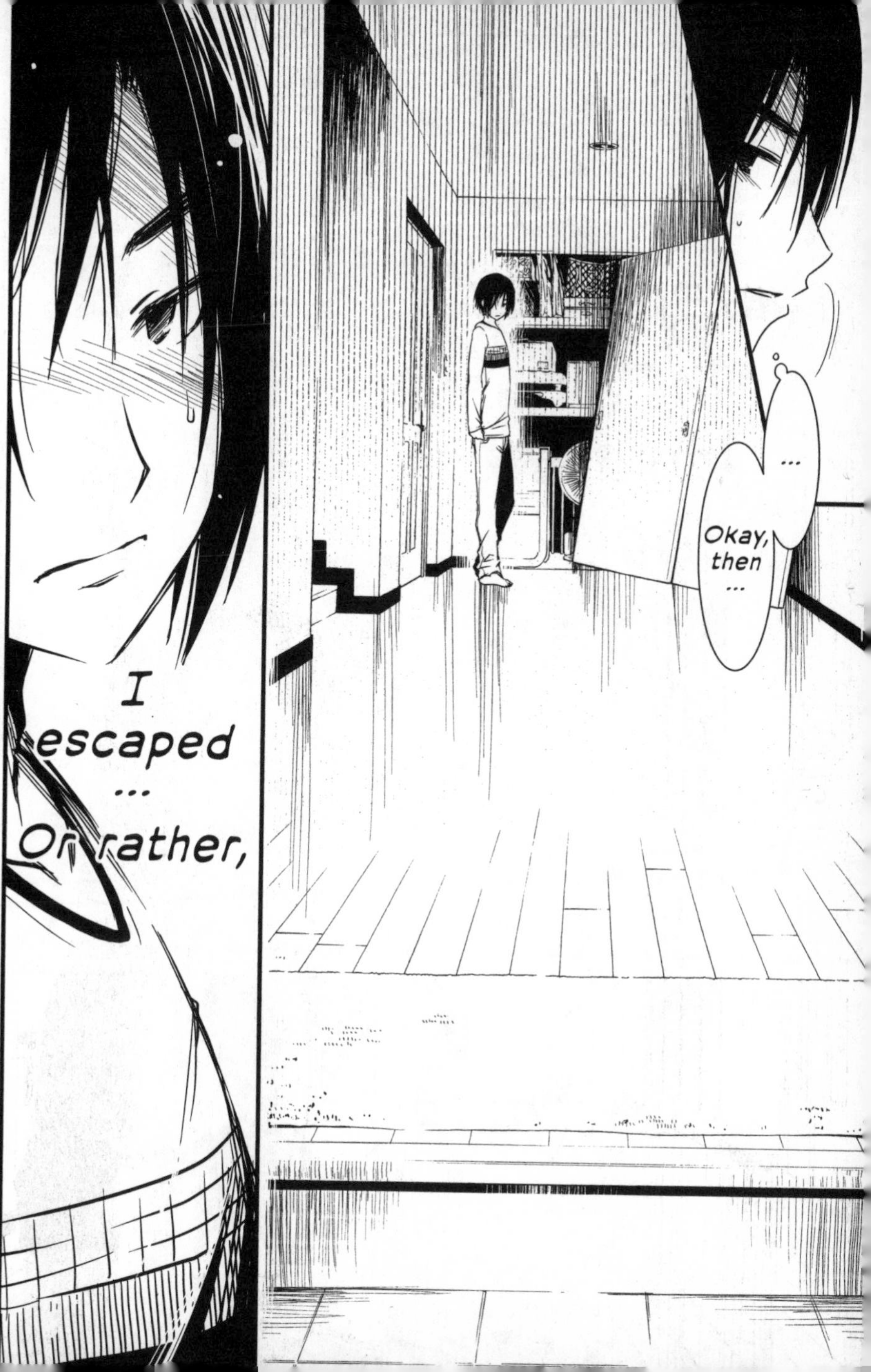
...
Okay, then ...
I escaped ...
Or rather,

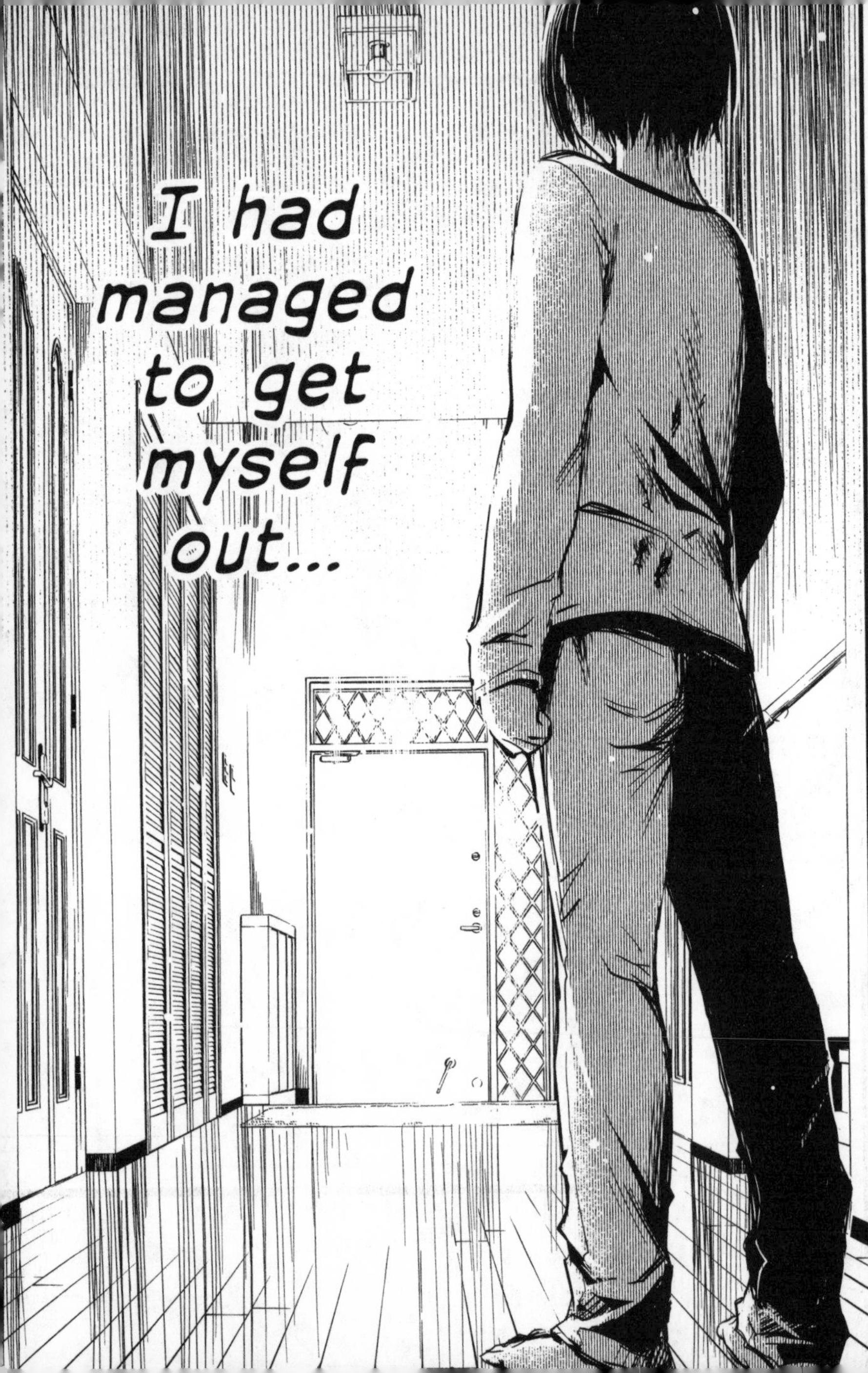
I had managed to get myself out...

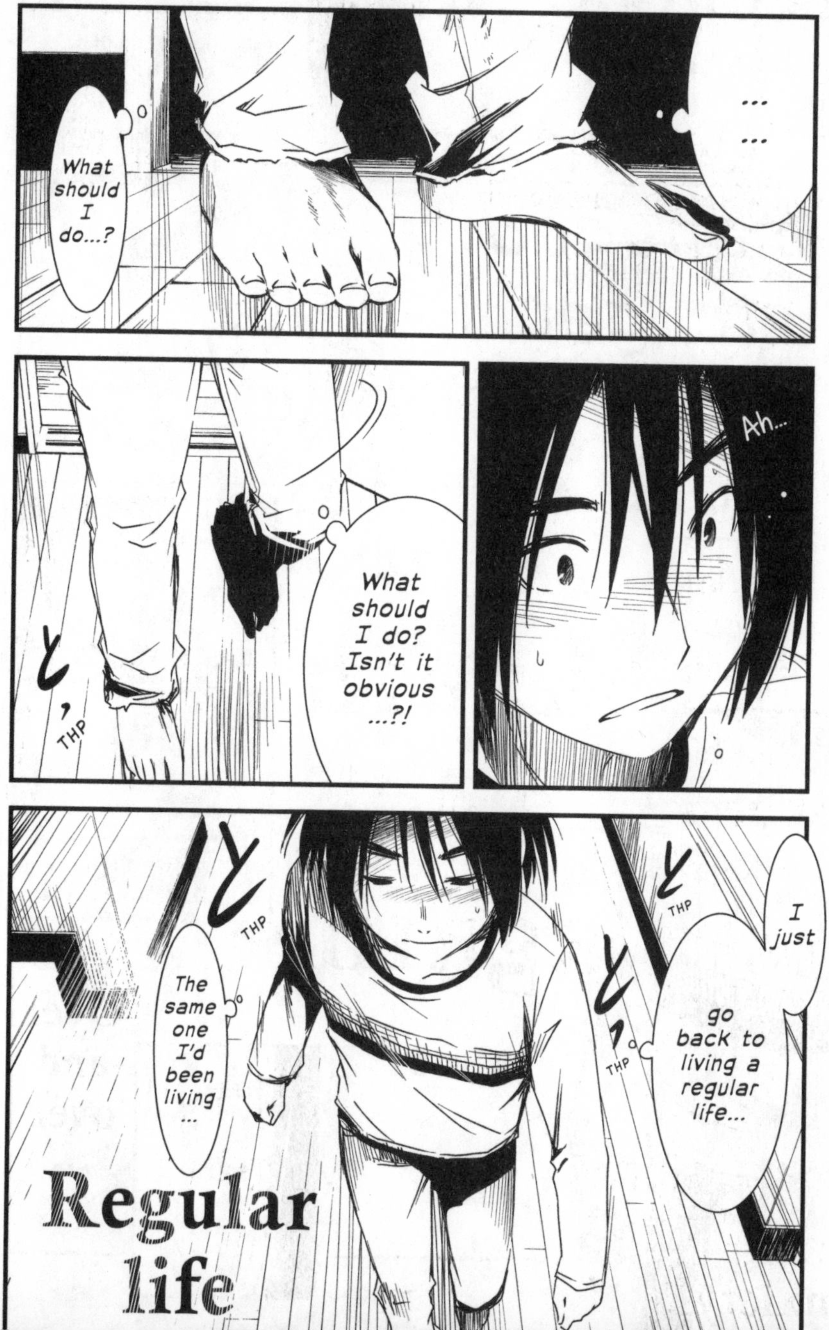
... ...
What should I do...?
Ah...
What should I do? Isn't it obvious ...?!
THP
I just go back to living a regular life...
THP
THP
The same one I'd been living ...
THP
Regular life

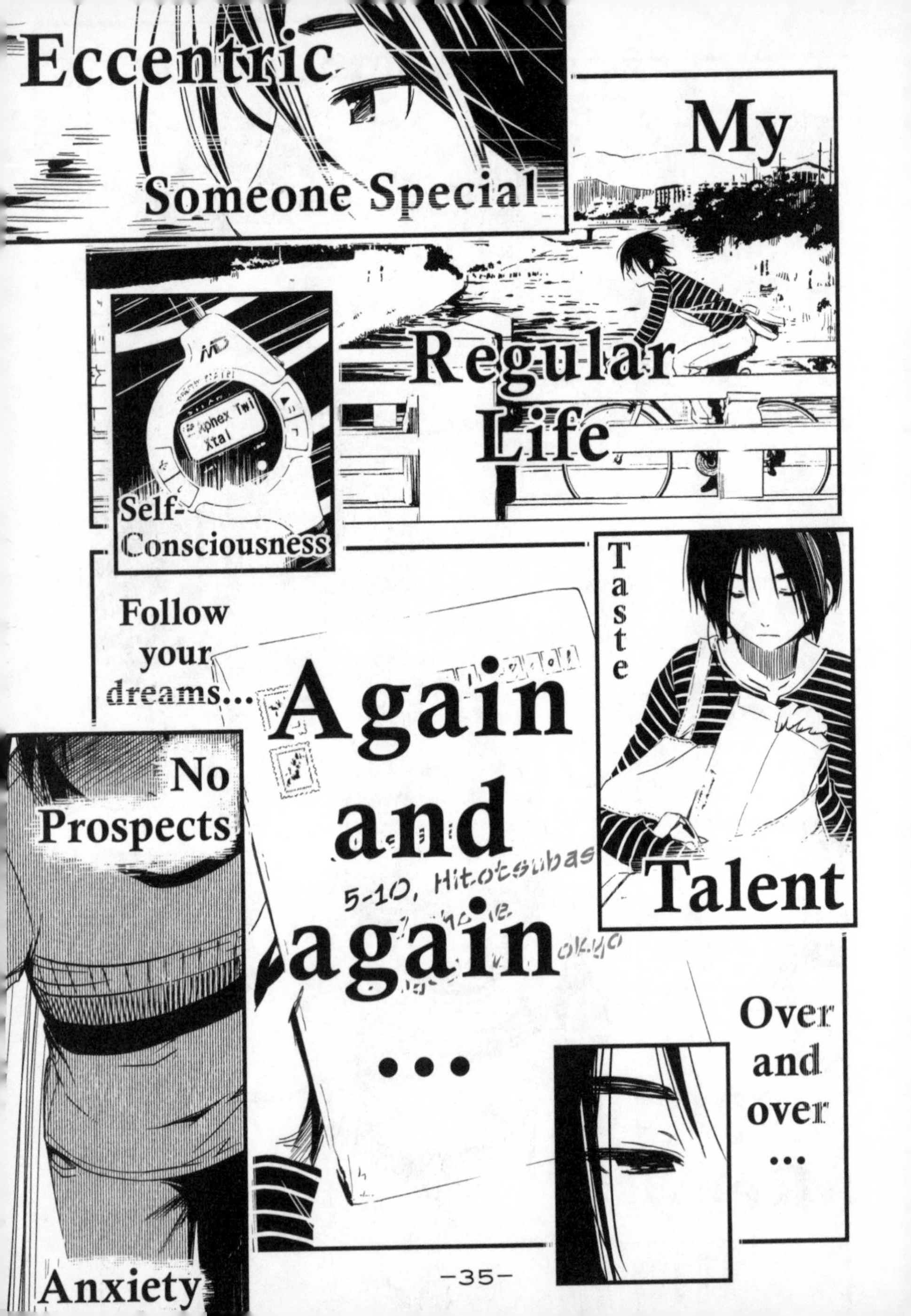

My
Regular Life
Eccentric
Someone Special
Aphex Twi
Xtal
Self-Consciousness
Taste
Talent
Again and again...
5-10, Hitotsubas
Follow your dreams...
No Prospects
Over and over...
Anxiety

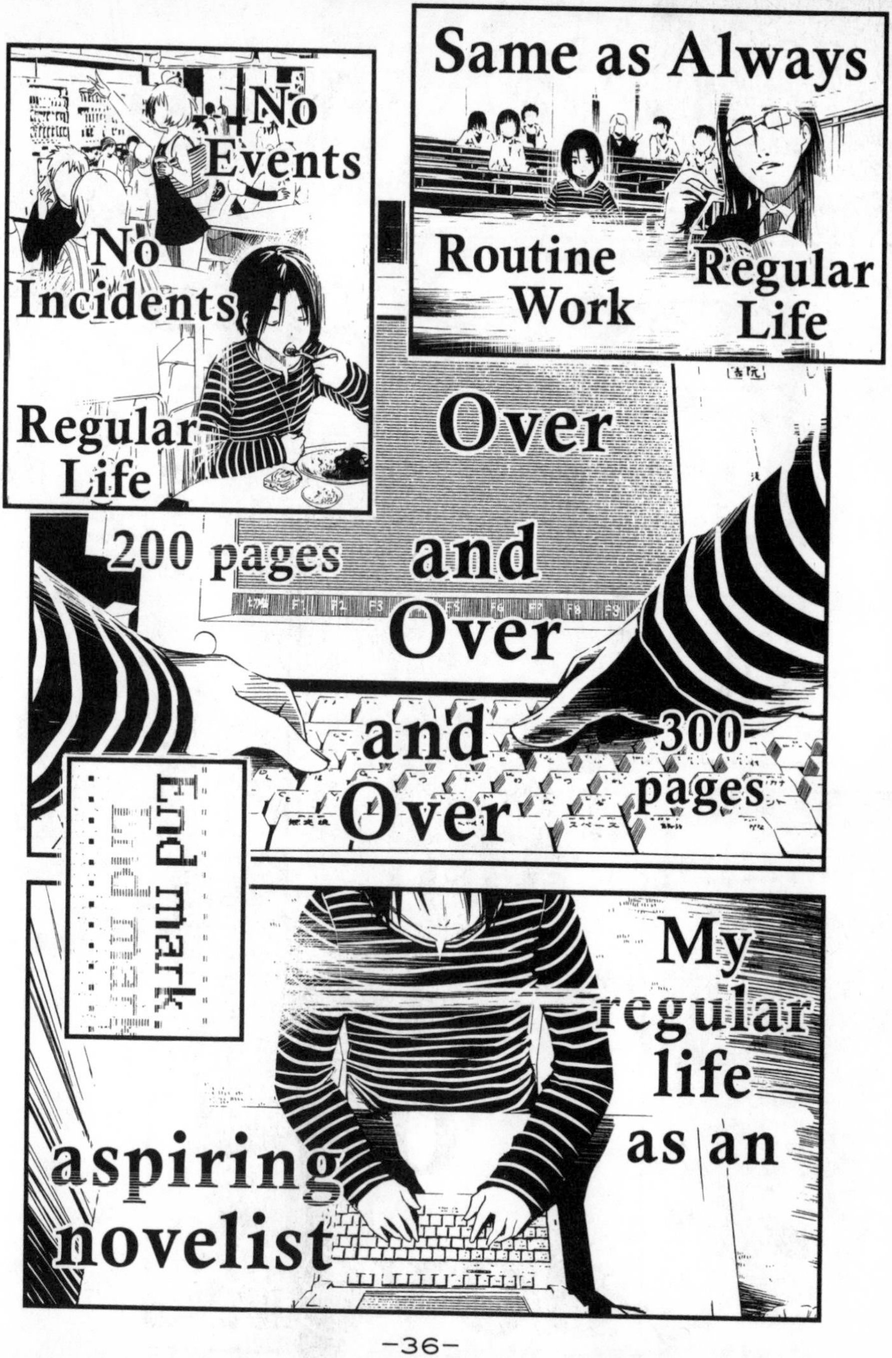
Same as Always
Regular Life
Routine Work
No Events
No Incidents
Regular Life
Over
and Over
and Over
300 pages
200 pages
End mark
My regular life as an
aspiring novelist

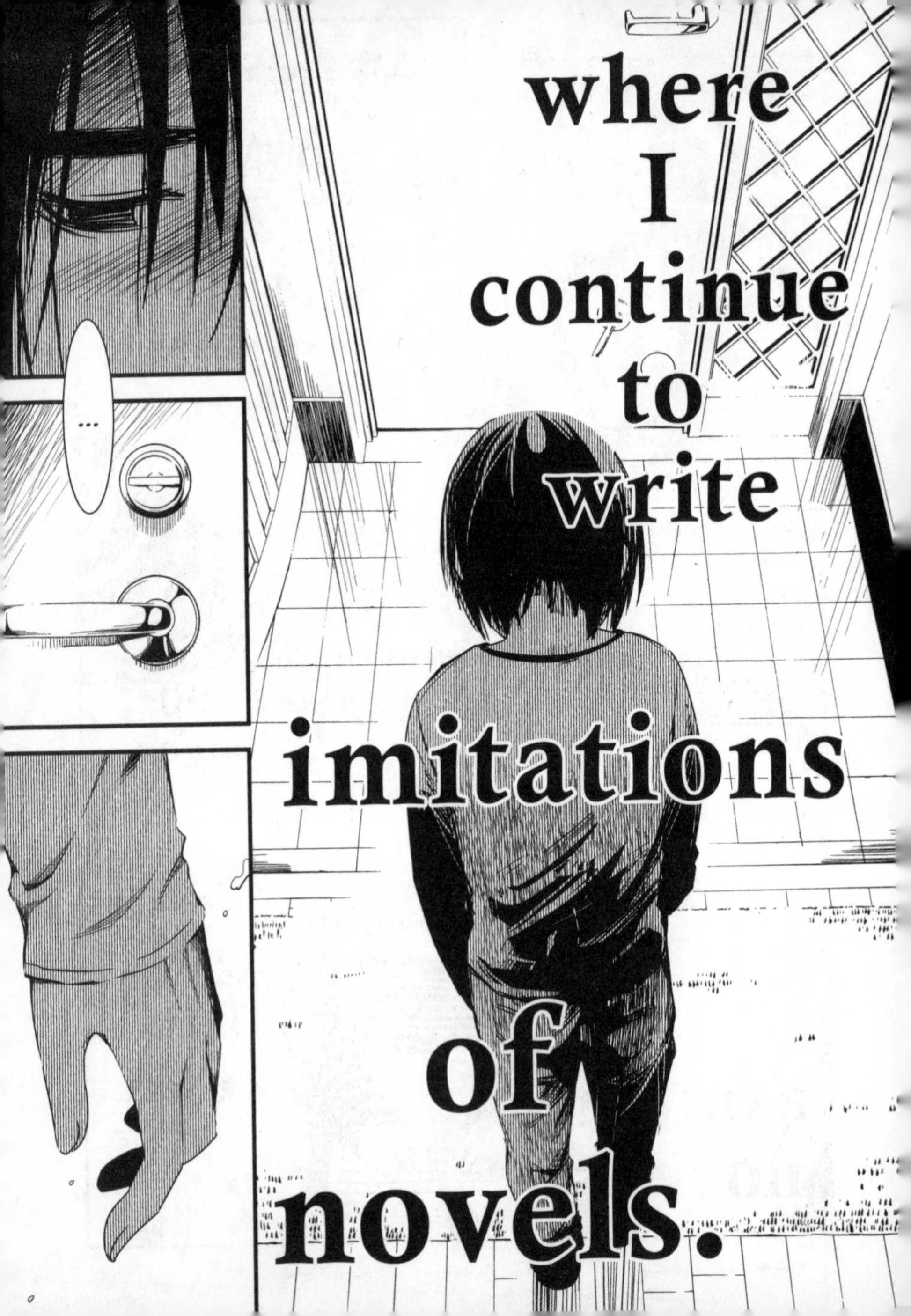
where I continue to write imitations of novels.
...

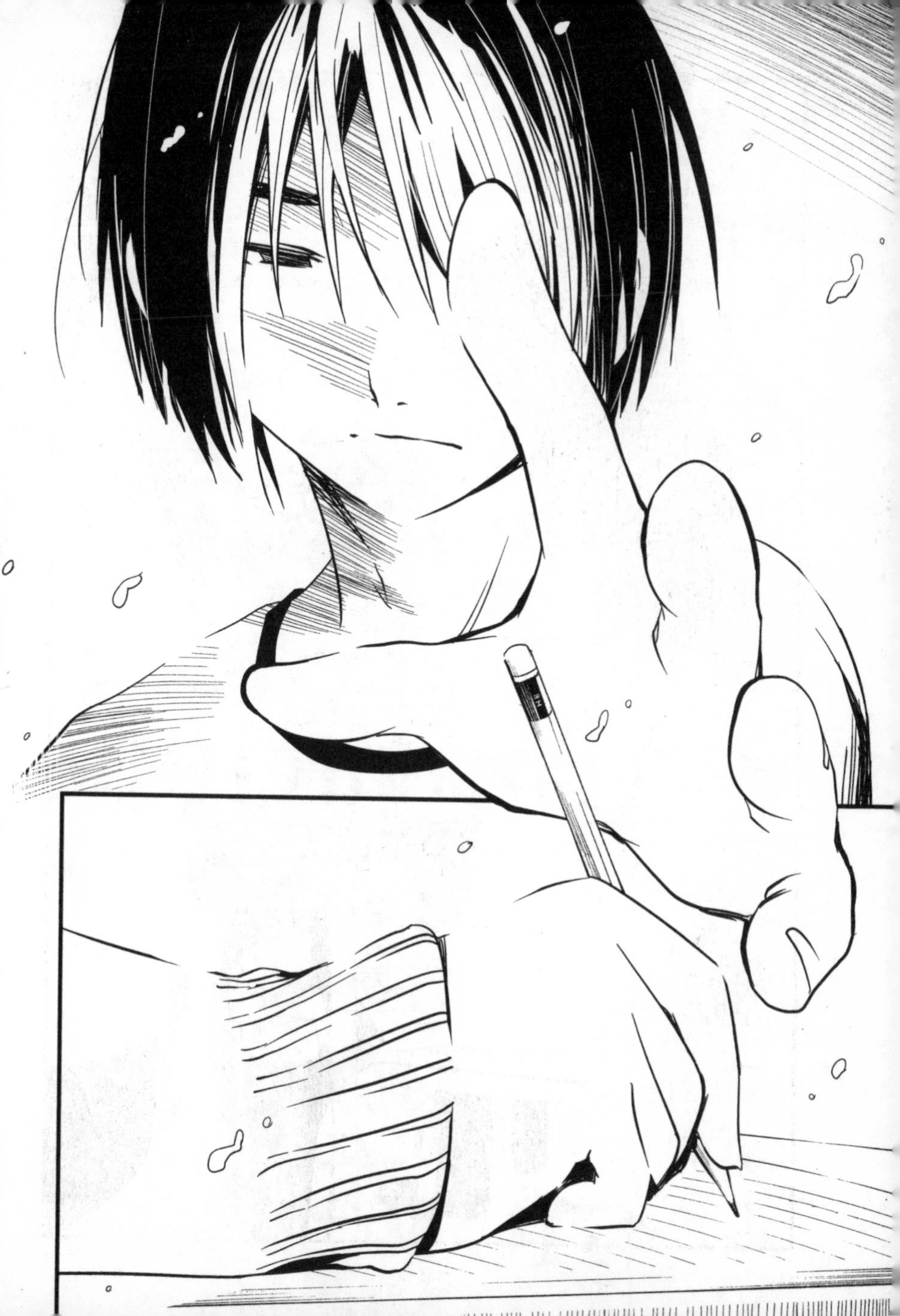

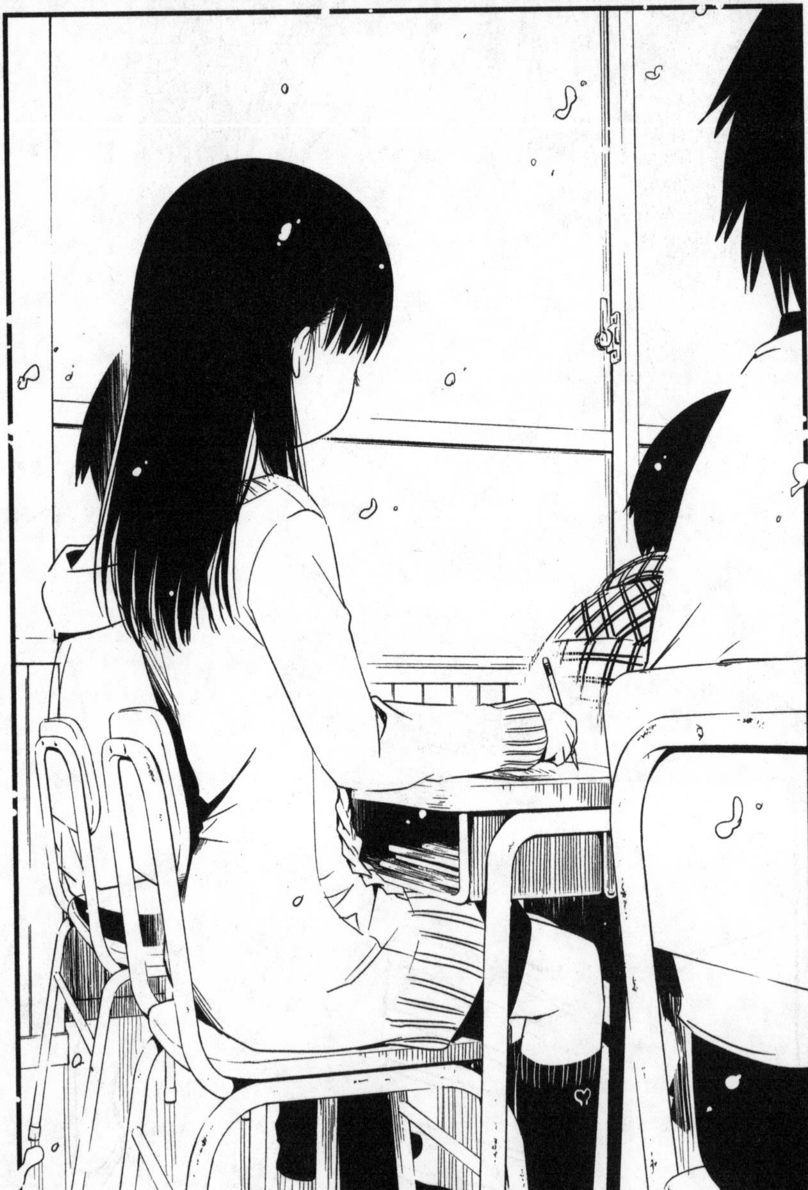

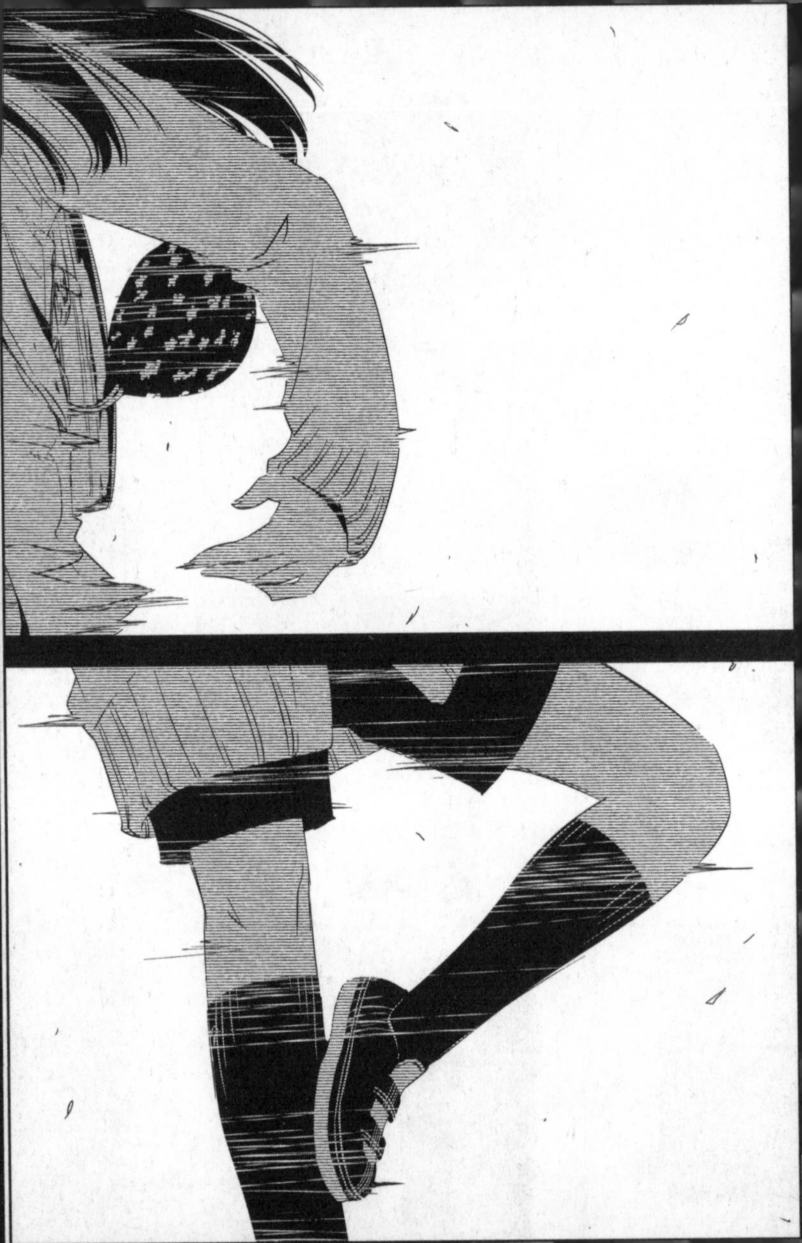

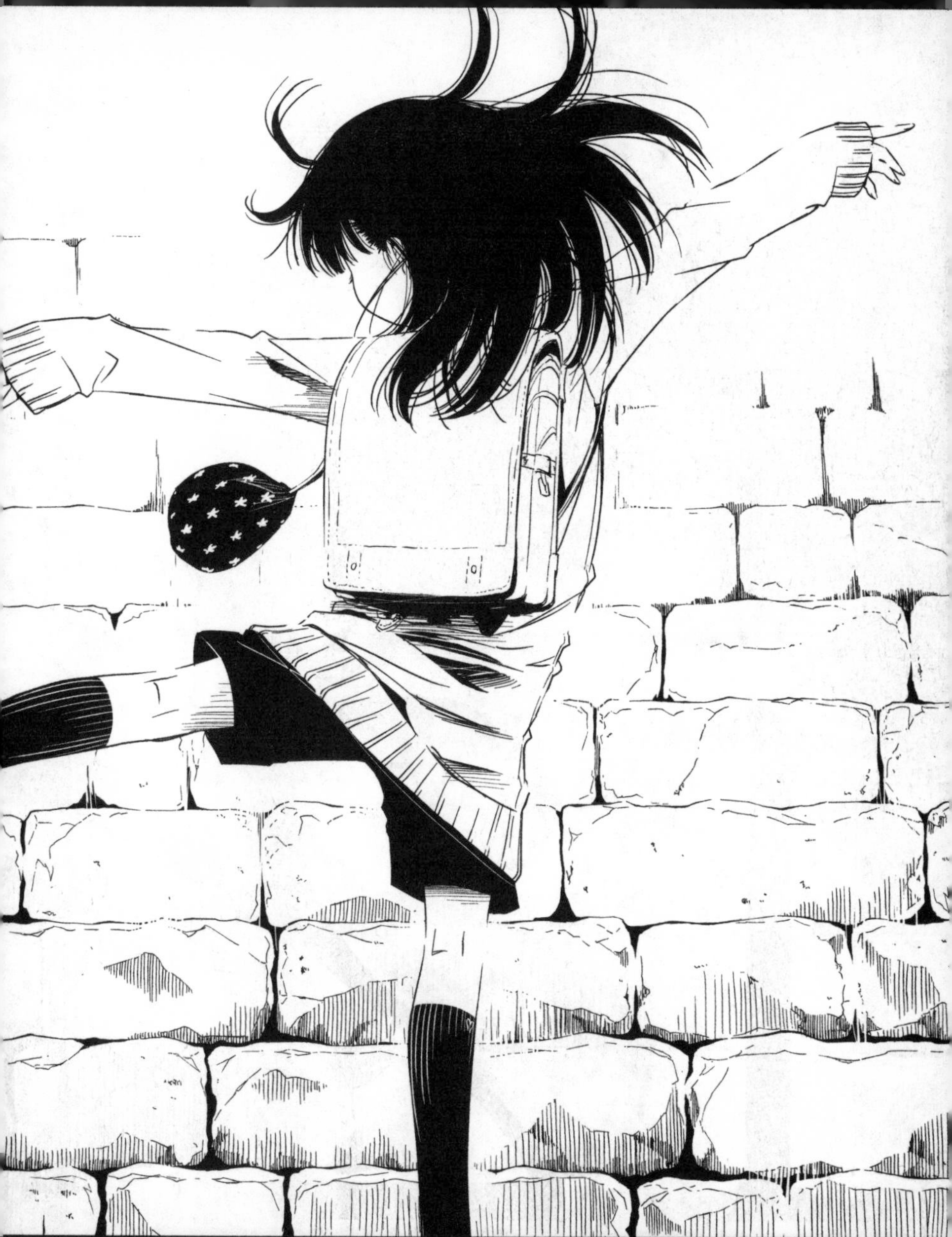

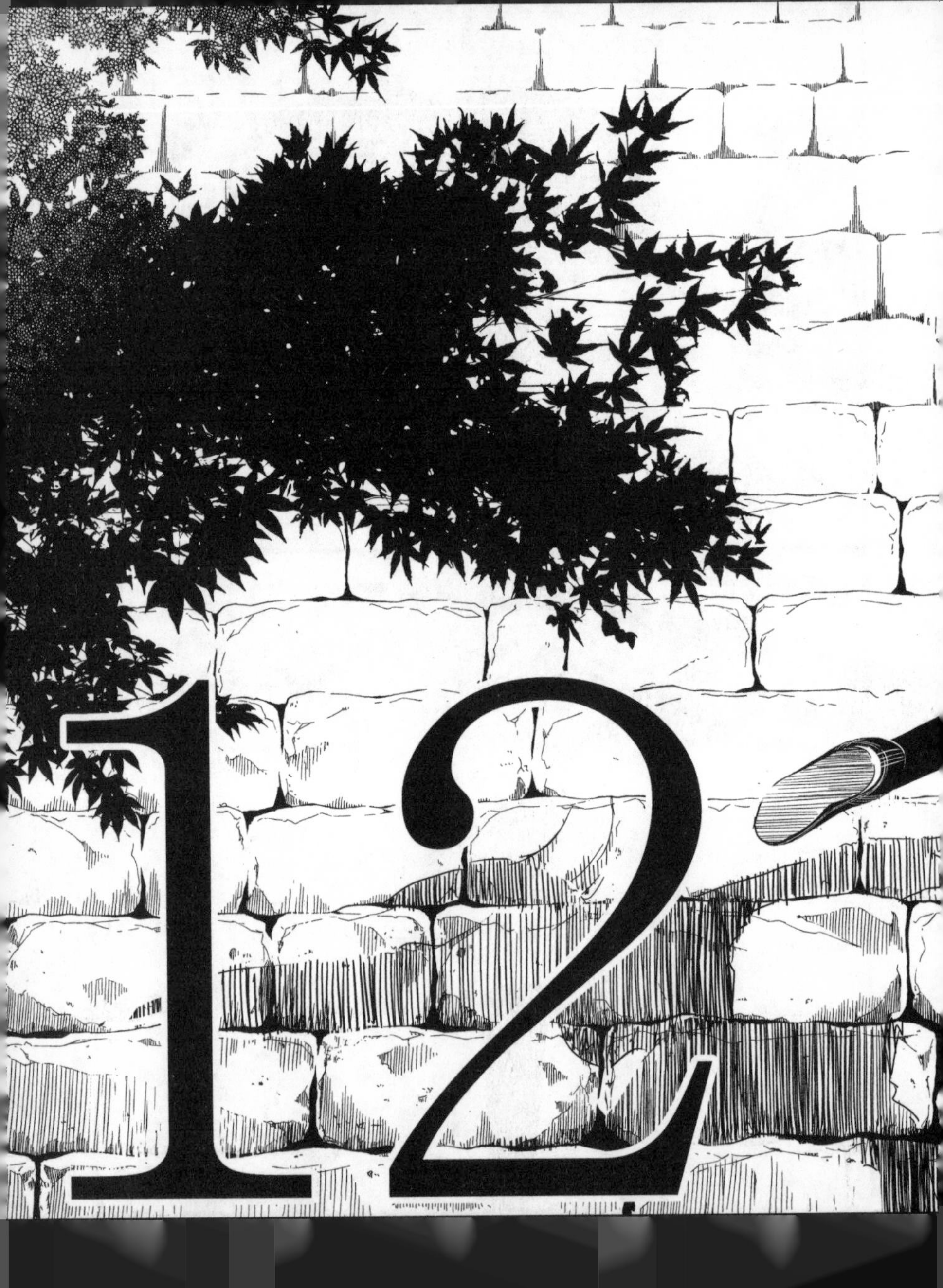
12

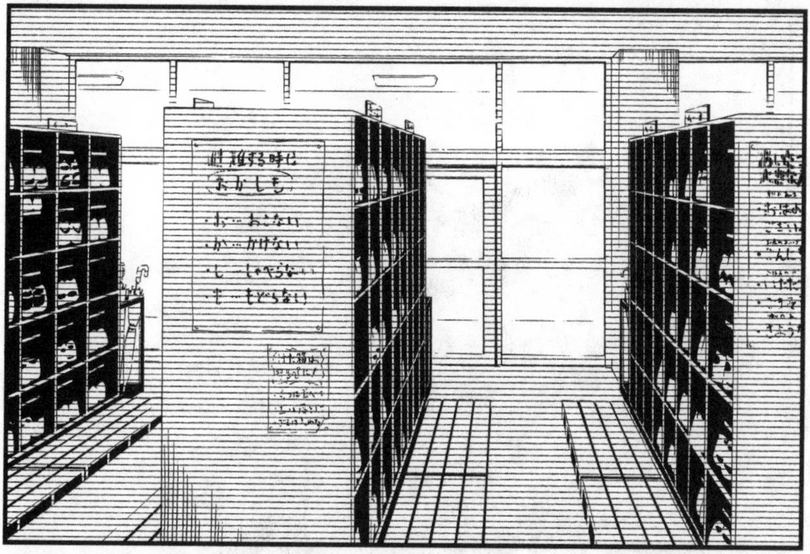
避難する時に
おかしも
・お…おさない
・か…かけない
・し…しゃべらない
・も…もどらない！
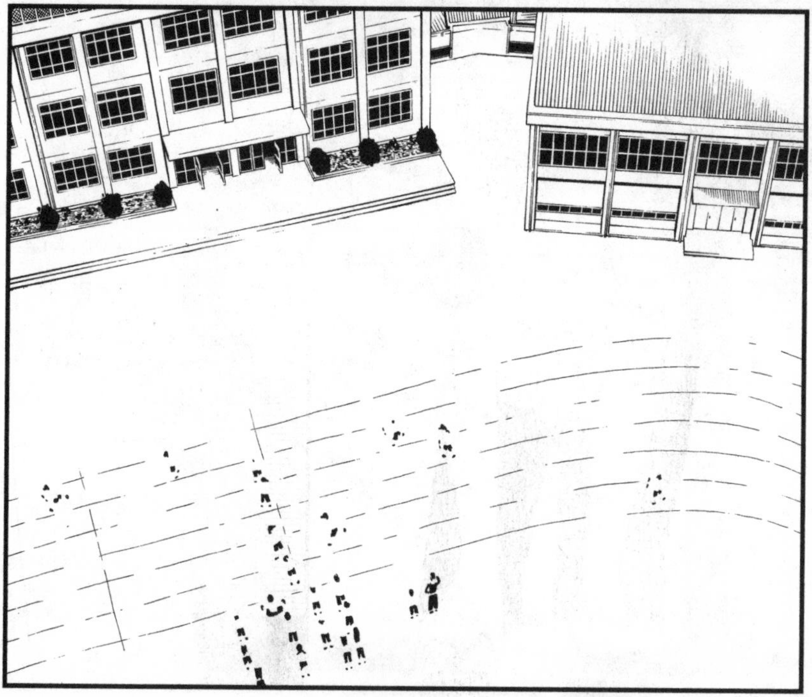

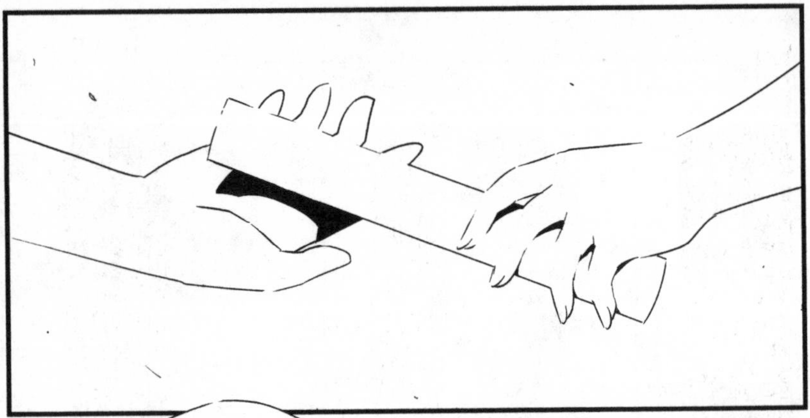

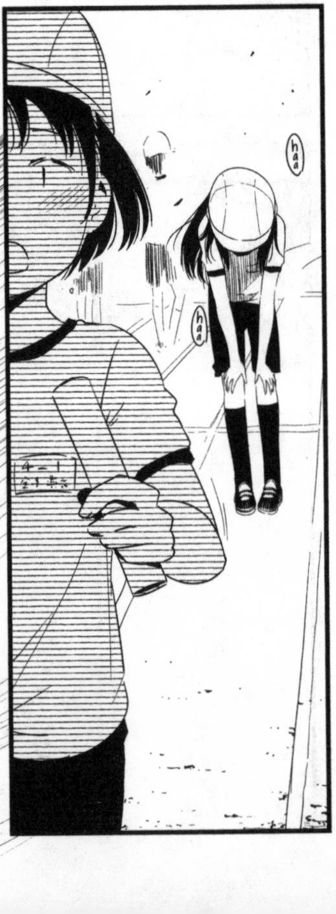
haa
haa

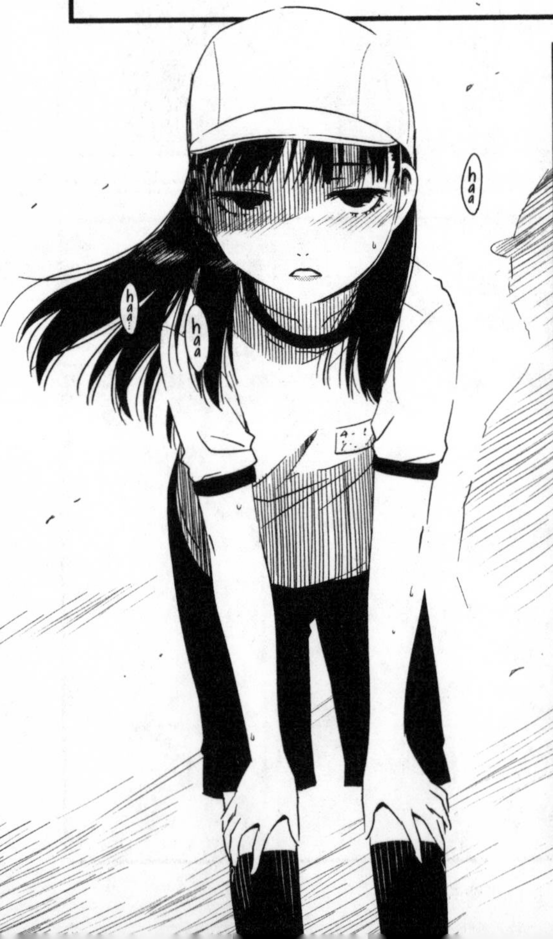
haa
haa
haa...

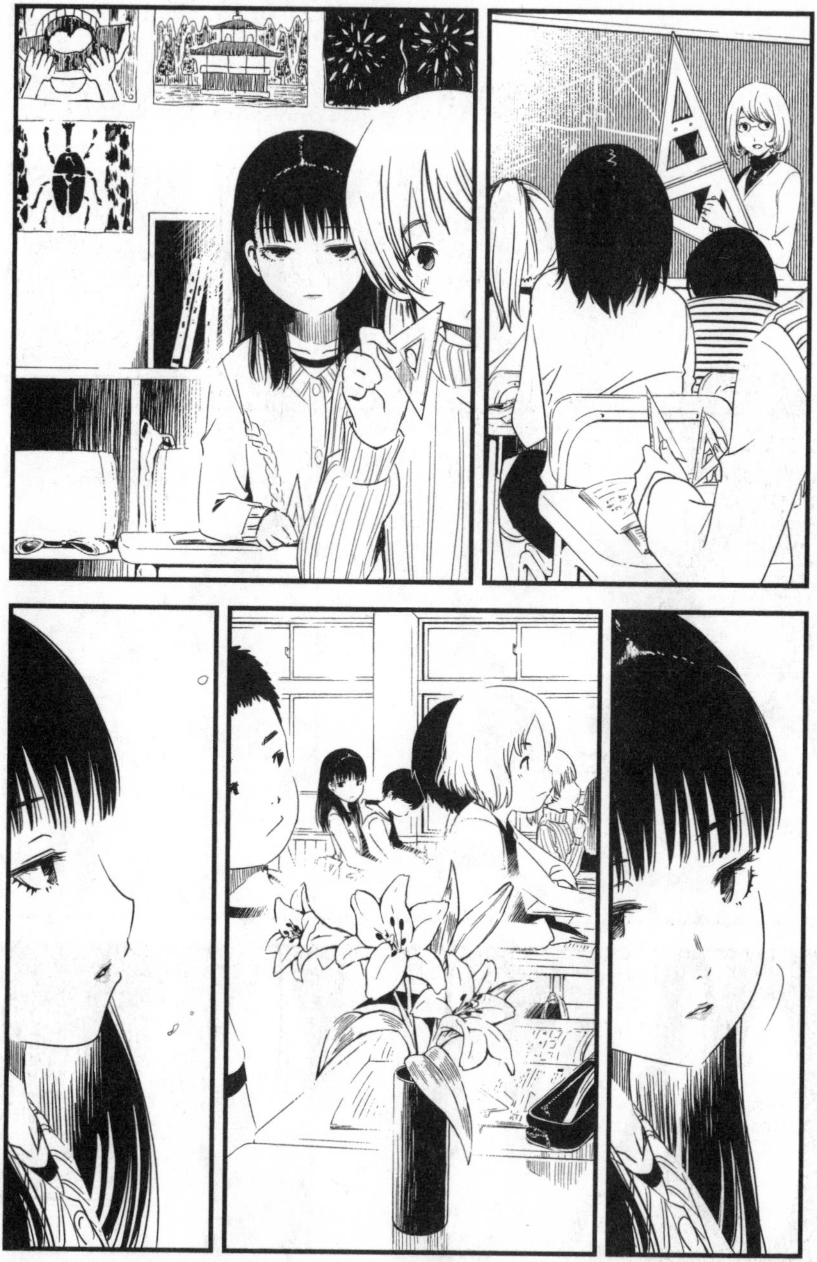

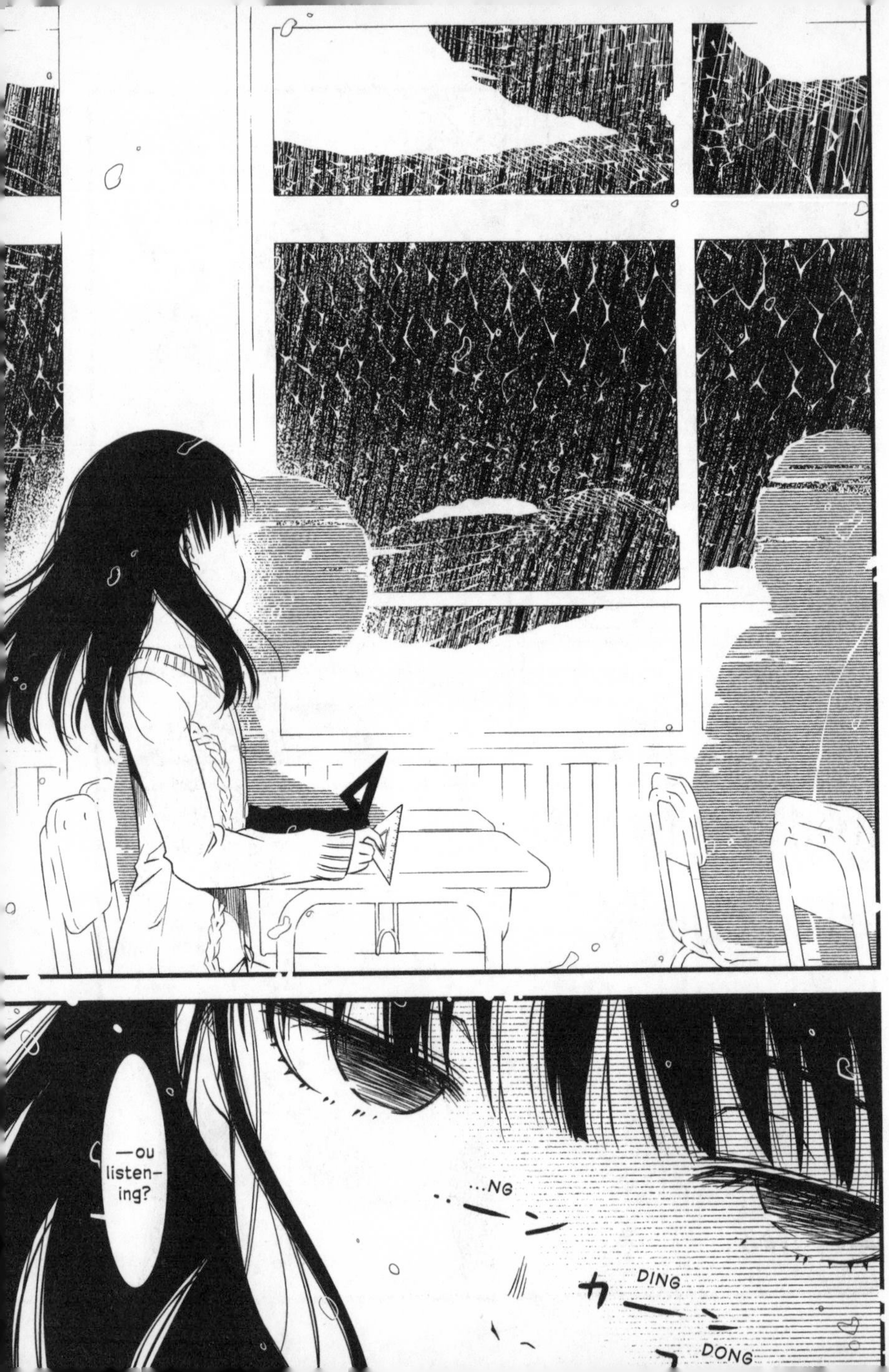
—ou listen-ing?
...NG
DING
DONG

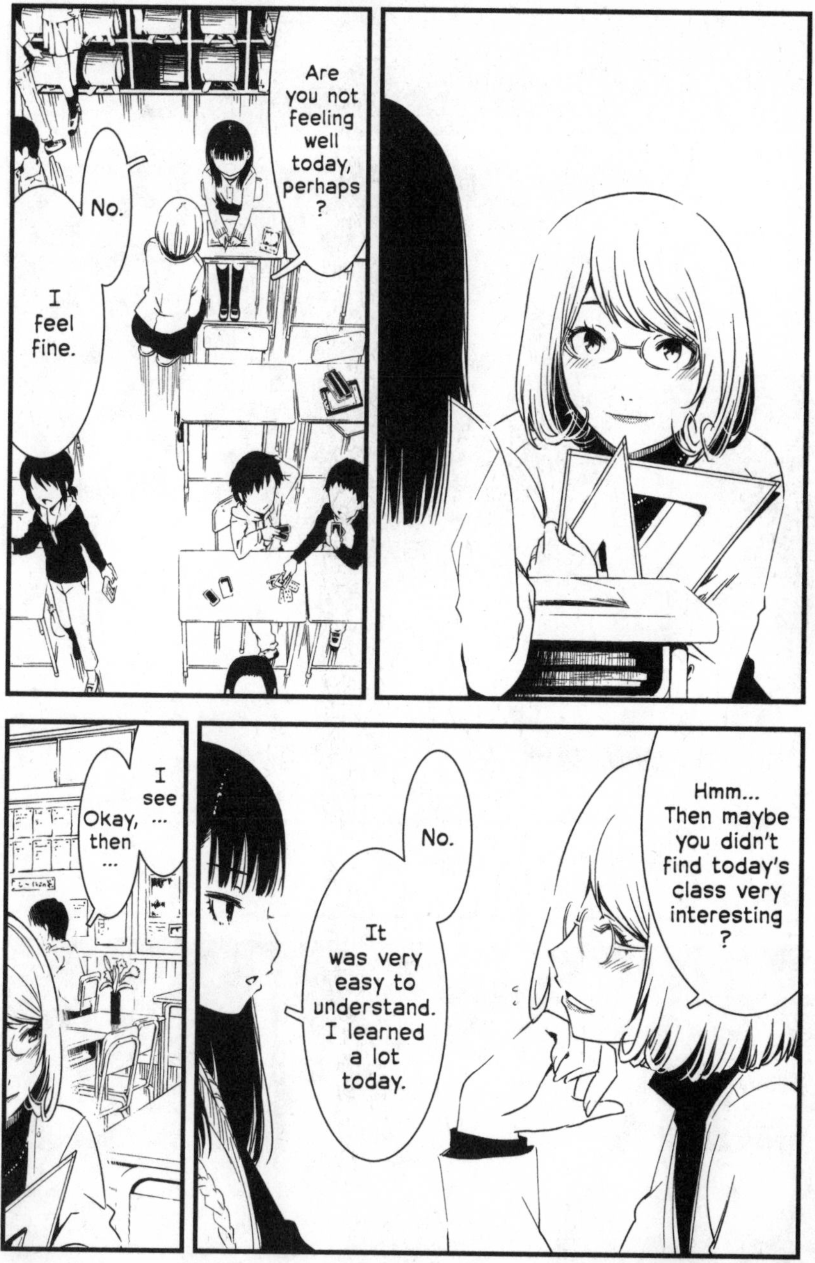
Are you not feeling well today, perhaps?
No.
I feel fine.
Hmm... Then maybe you didn't find today's class very interesting?
No.
It was very easy to understand. I learned a lot today.
I see ...
Okay, then ...

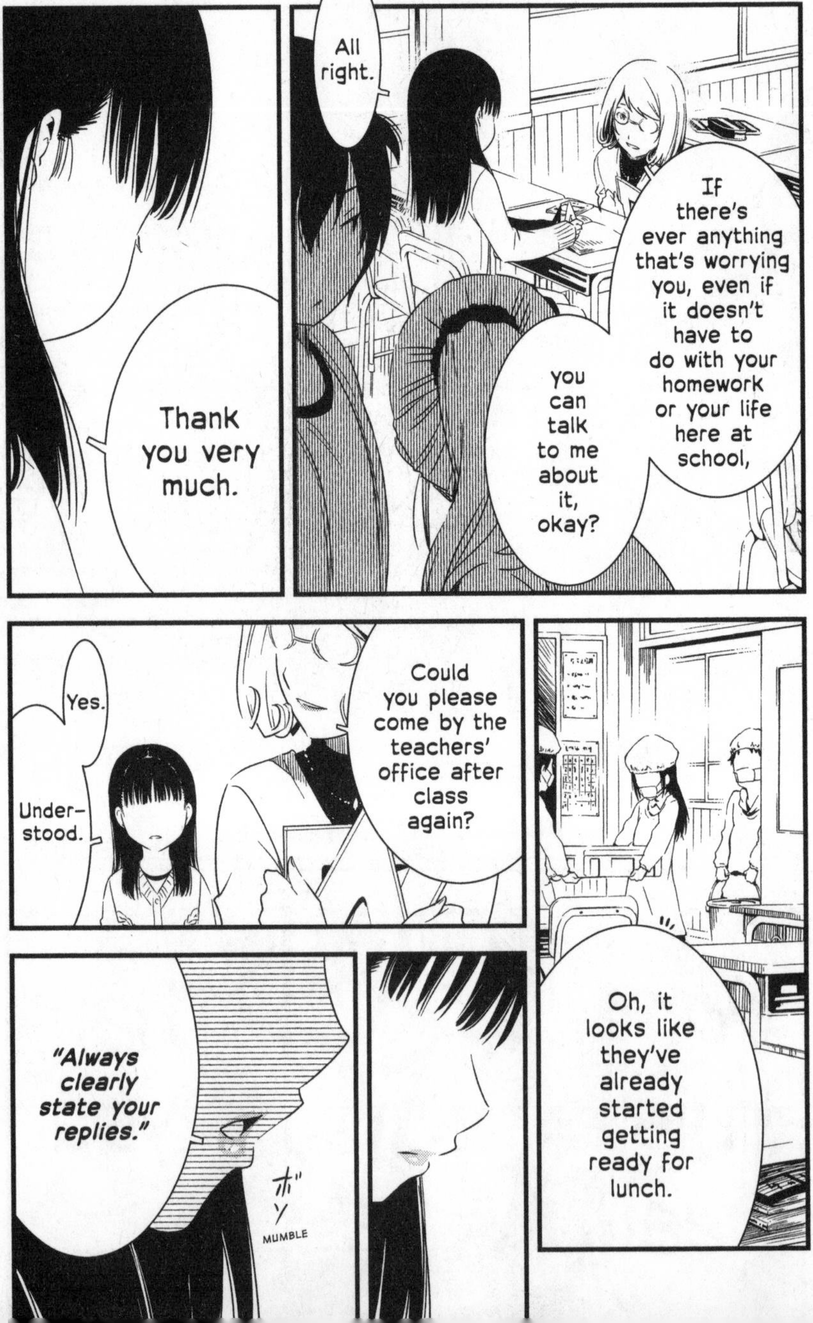
If there's ever anything that's worrying you, even if it doesn't have to do with your homework or your life here at school,
you can talk to me about it, okay?
All right.
Thank you very much.
Oh, it looks like they've already started getting ready for lunch.
Could you please come by the teachers' office after class again?
Yes.
Under-stood.
"Always clearly state your replies."
ボソ
MUMBLE

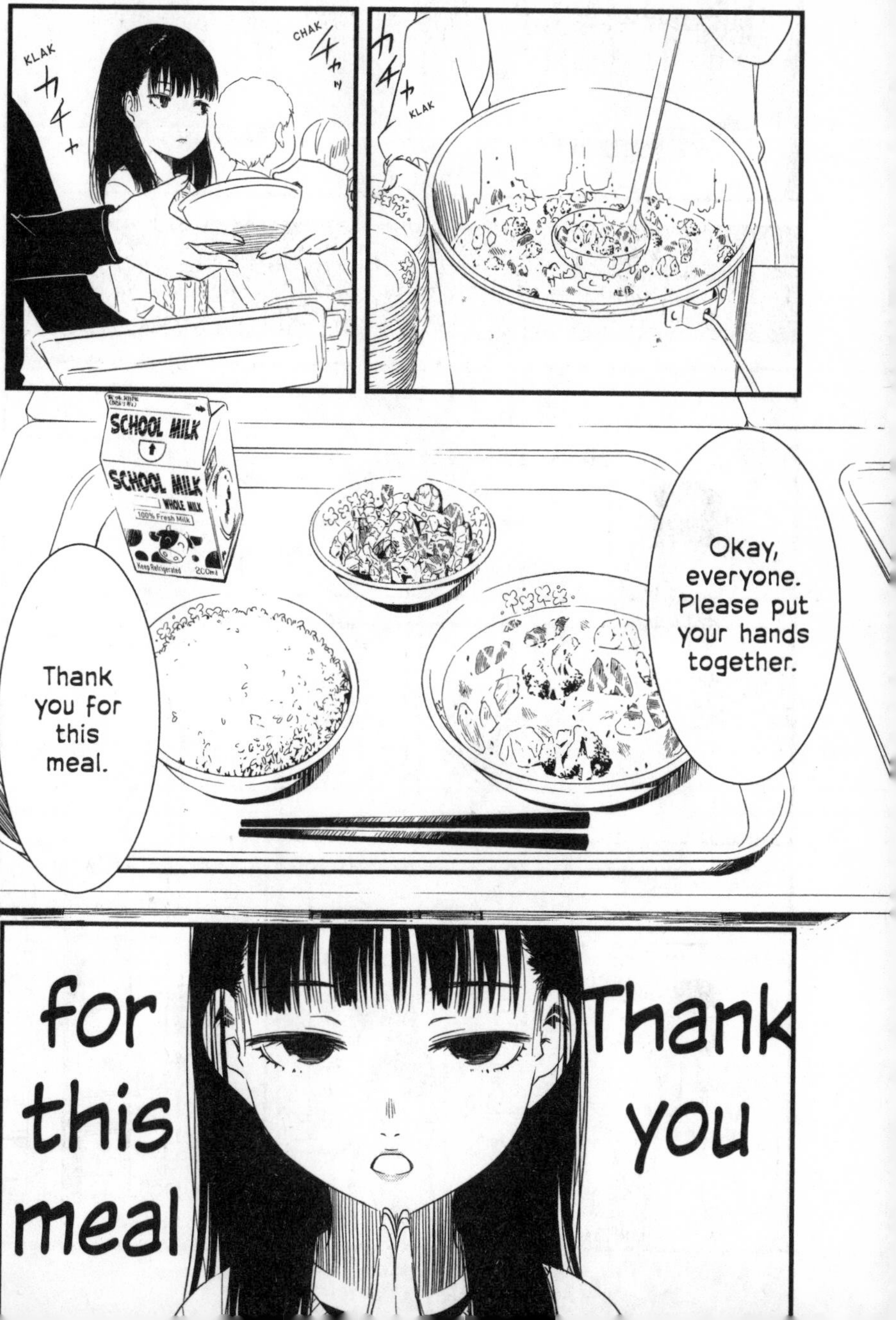
カチャ
KLAK
KLAK
カチャ
CHAK
チャッ
SCHOOL MILK
SCHOOL MILK
WHOLE MILK
100% Fresh Milk
Keep Refrigerated
200ml
Okay, everyone. Please put your hands together.
Thank you for this meal.
Thank you
for this meal

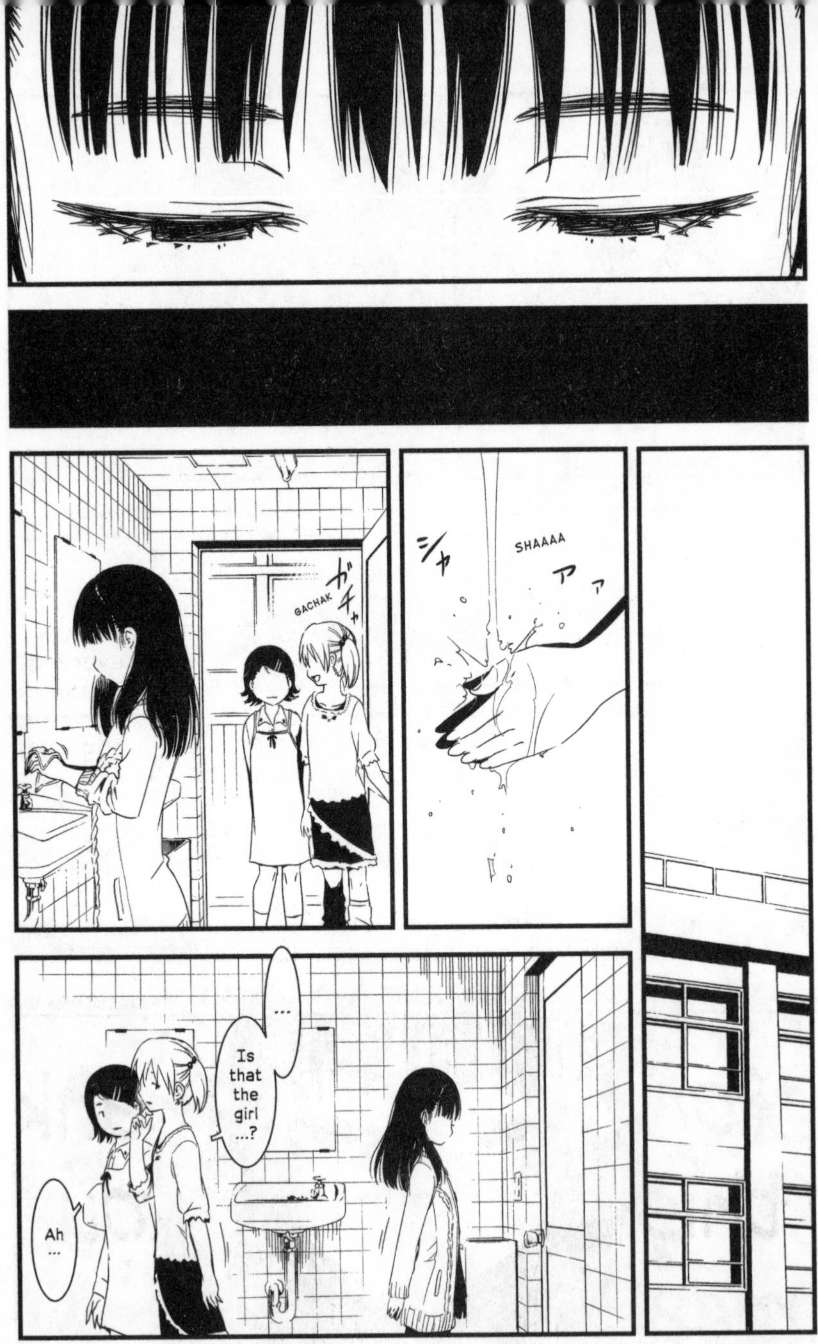

シャアァ
SHAAAA
ガチャ
GACHAK
...
Is that the girl ...?
Ah ...

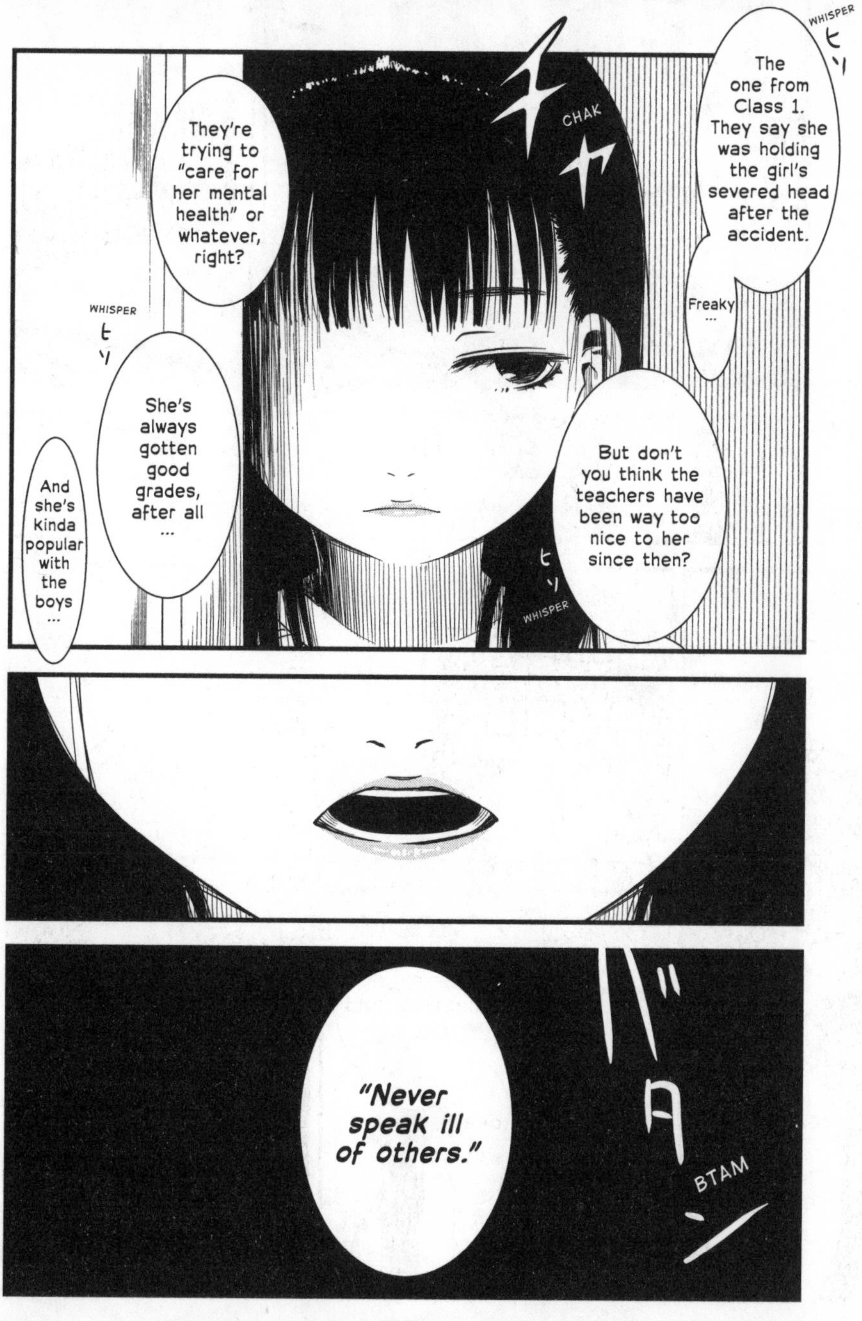
WHISPER
The one from Class 1. They say she was holding the girl's severed head after the accident.
Freaky ...
CHAK
They're trying to "care for her mental health" or whatever, right?
But don't you think the teachers have been way too nice to her since then?
WHISPER
WHISPER
She's always gotten good grades, after all ...
And she's kinda popular with the boys ...
BTAM
"Never speak ill of others."

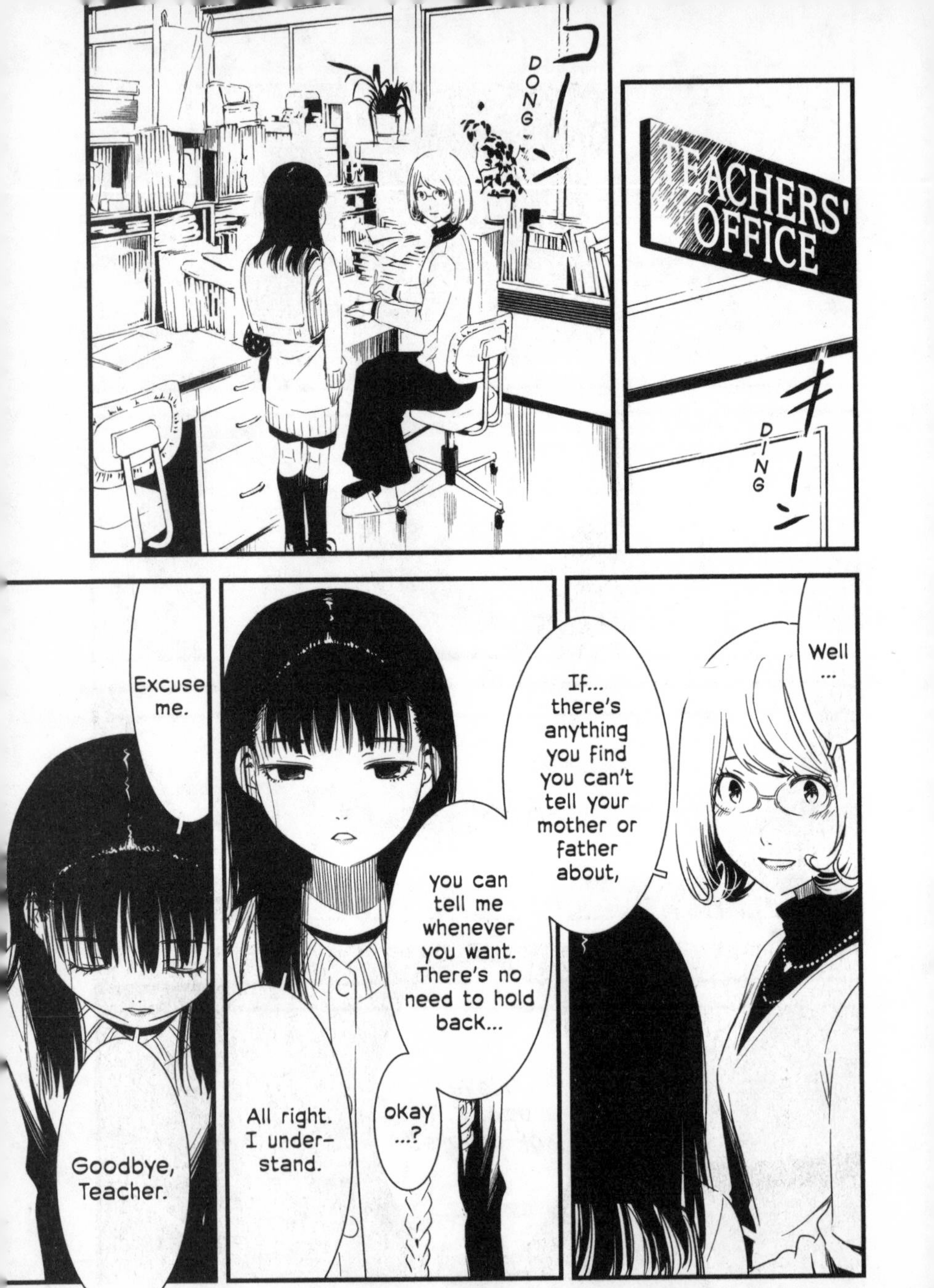
TEACHERS' OFFICE
キーン
DING
コーン
DONG
Well ...
If... there's anything you find you can't tell your mother or father about,
you can tell me whenever you want. There's no need to hold back...
okay ...?
All right. I under-stand.
Excuse me.
Goodbye, Teacher.

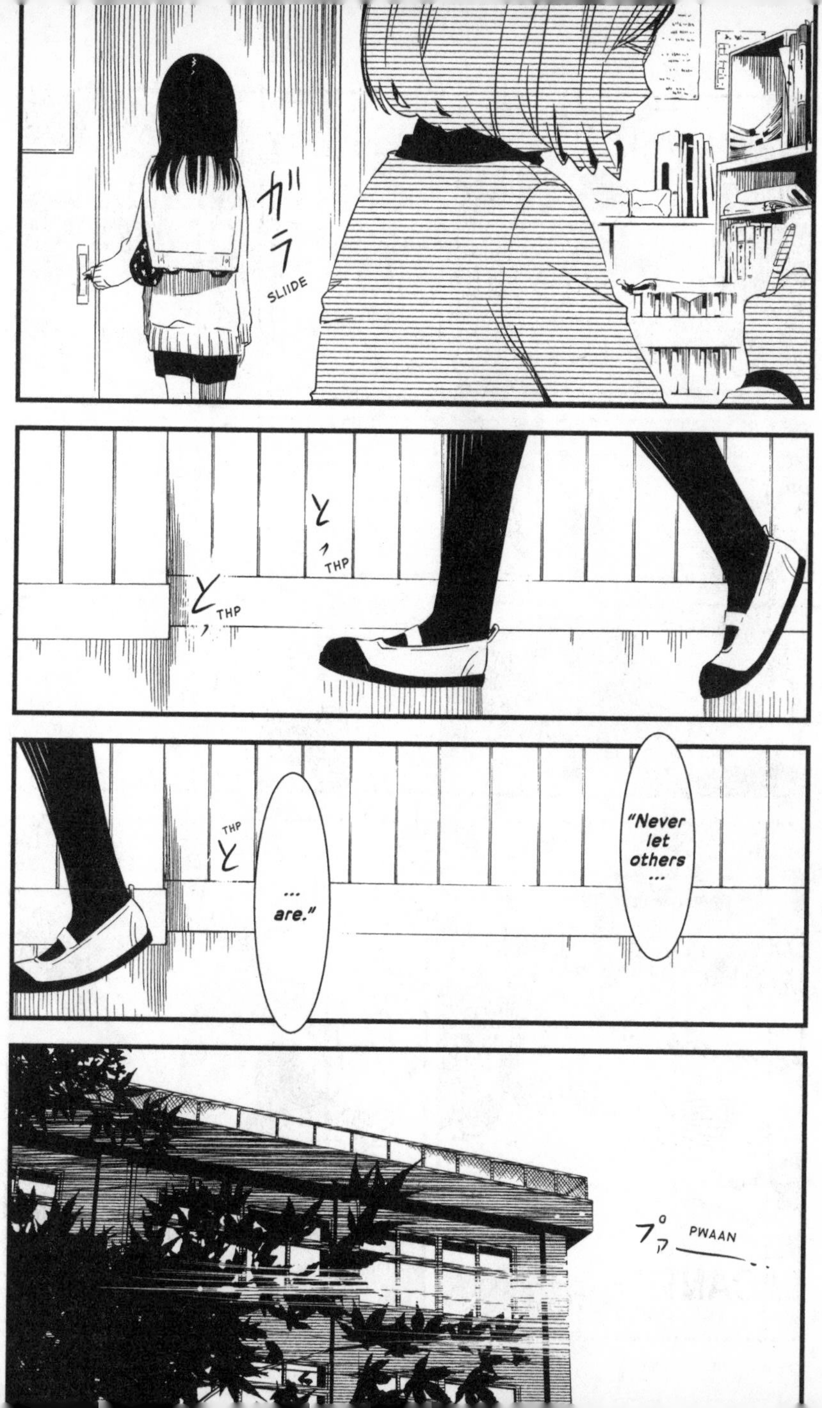
ガラ
SLIIDE
と
THP
と
THP
"Never let others ...
... are."
と
THP
プァ
PWAAN

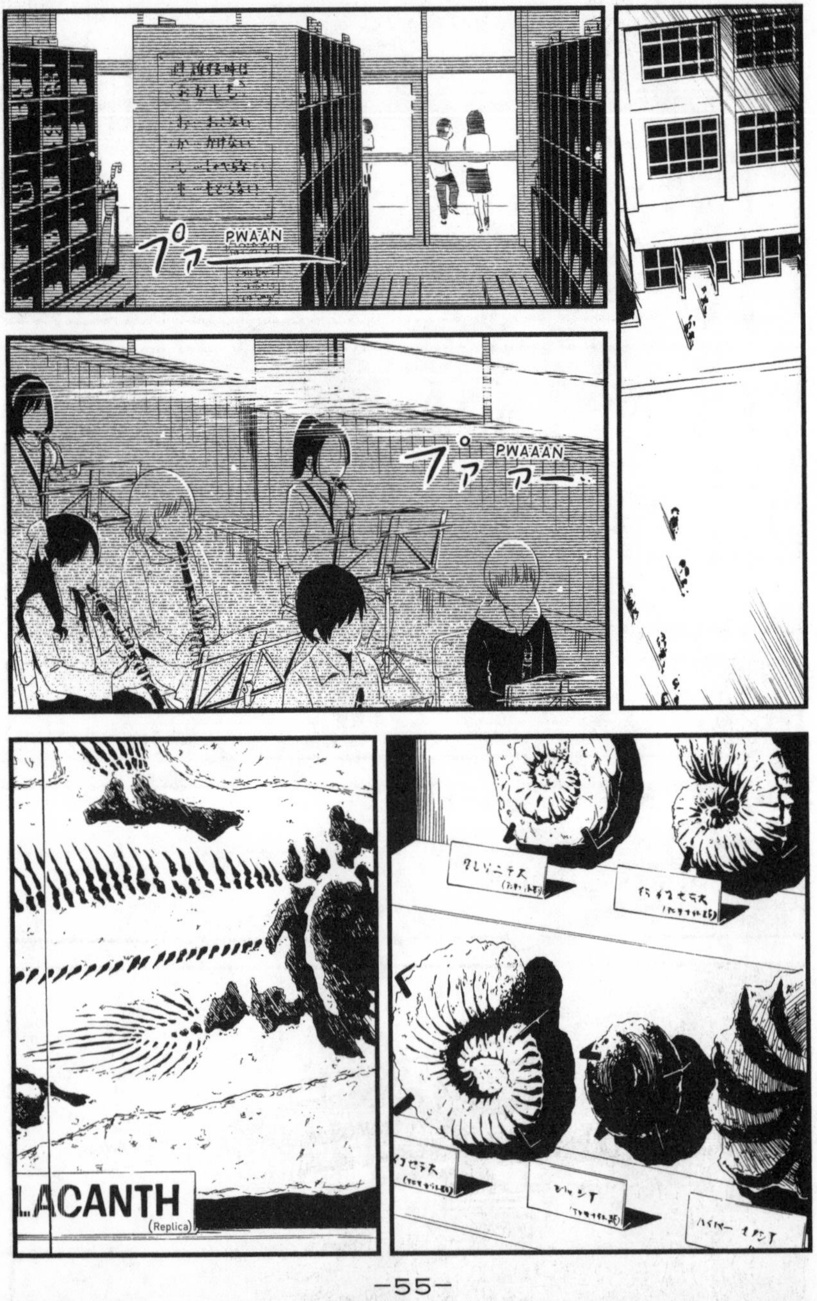

プァー
PWAAN
プァァー
PWAAAN
LACANTH
(Replica)

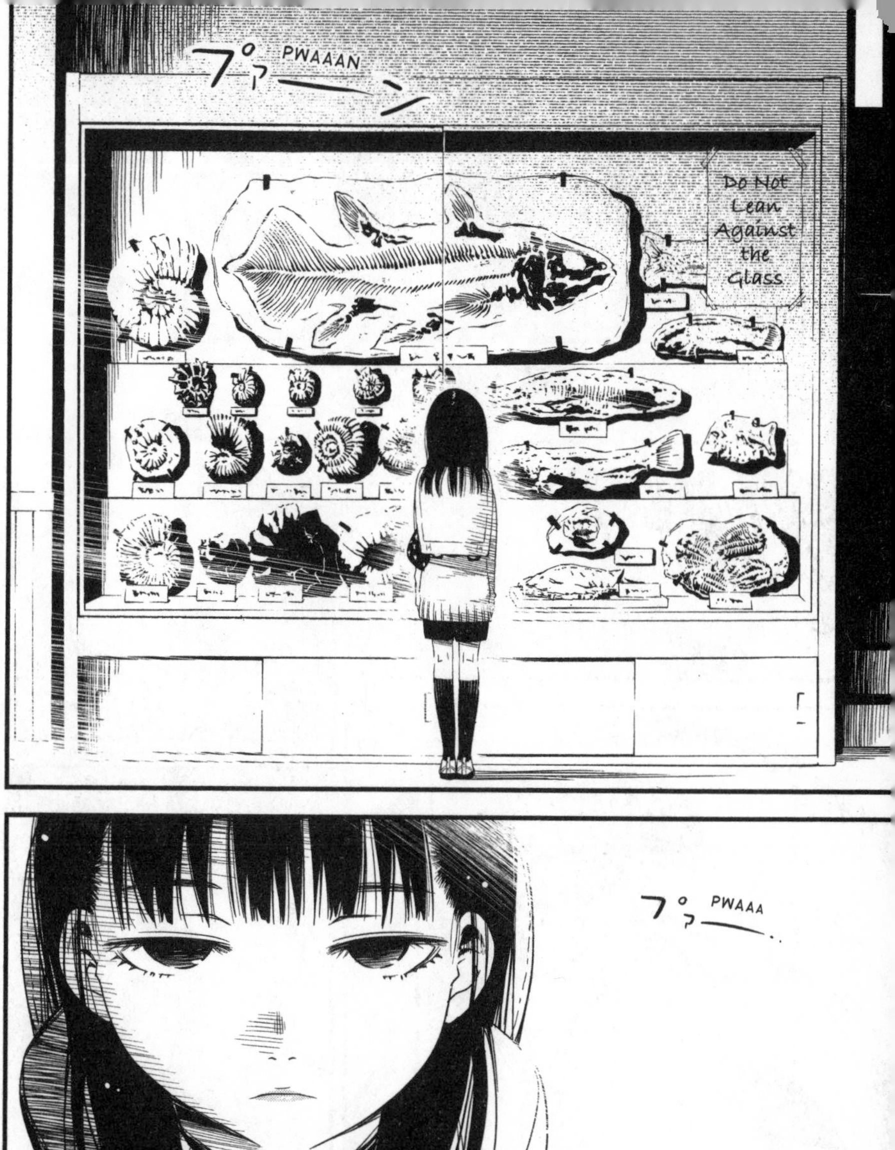
プァーン
PWAAAN
Do Not Lean Against the Glass
プァ
PWAAA

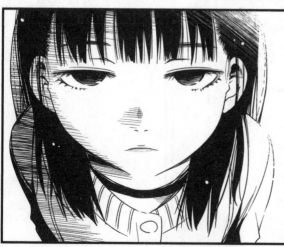

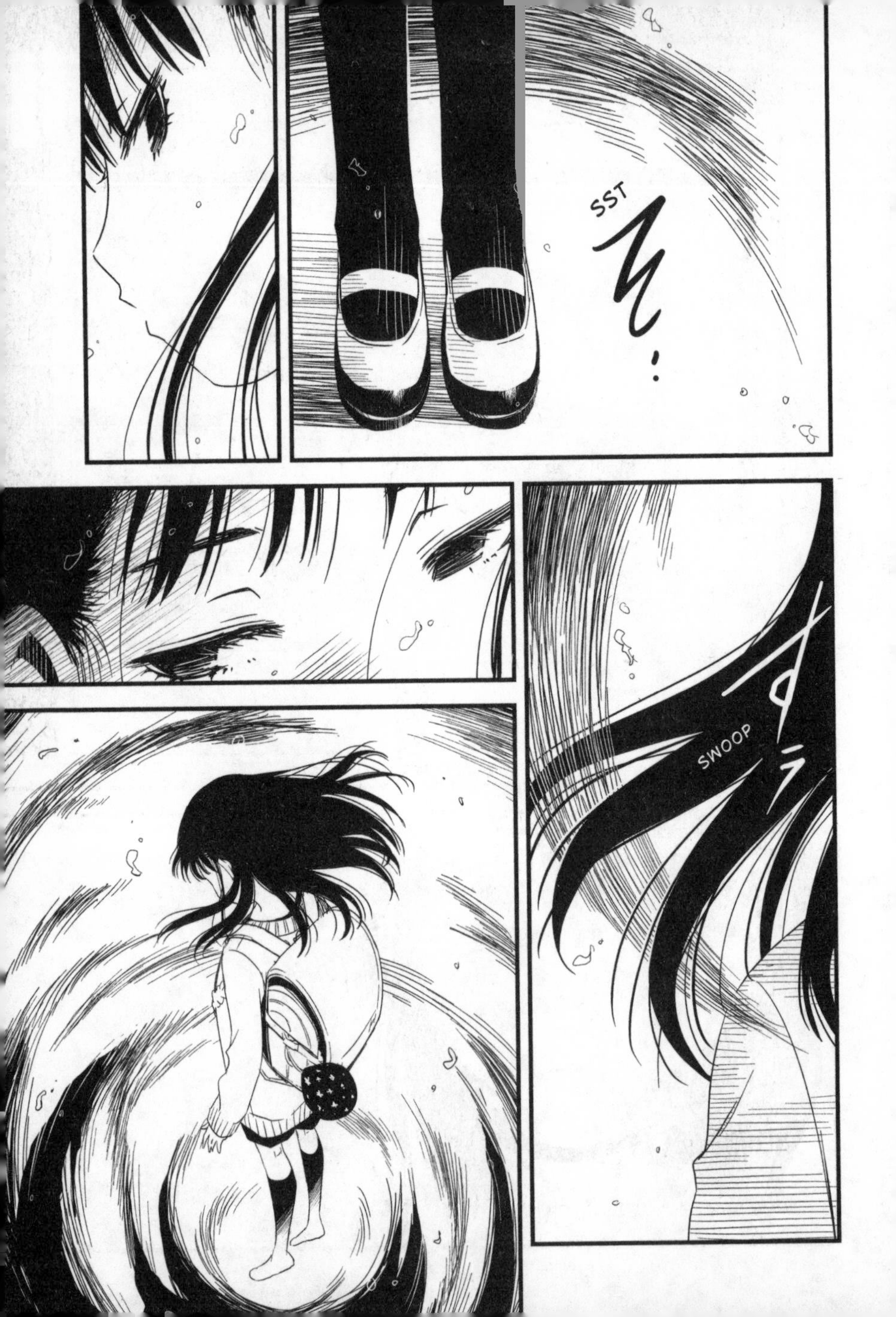
SST
SWOOP

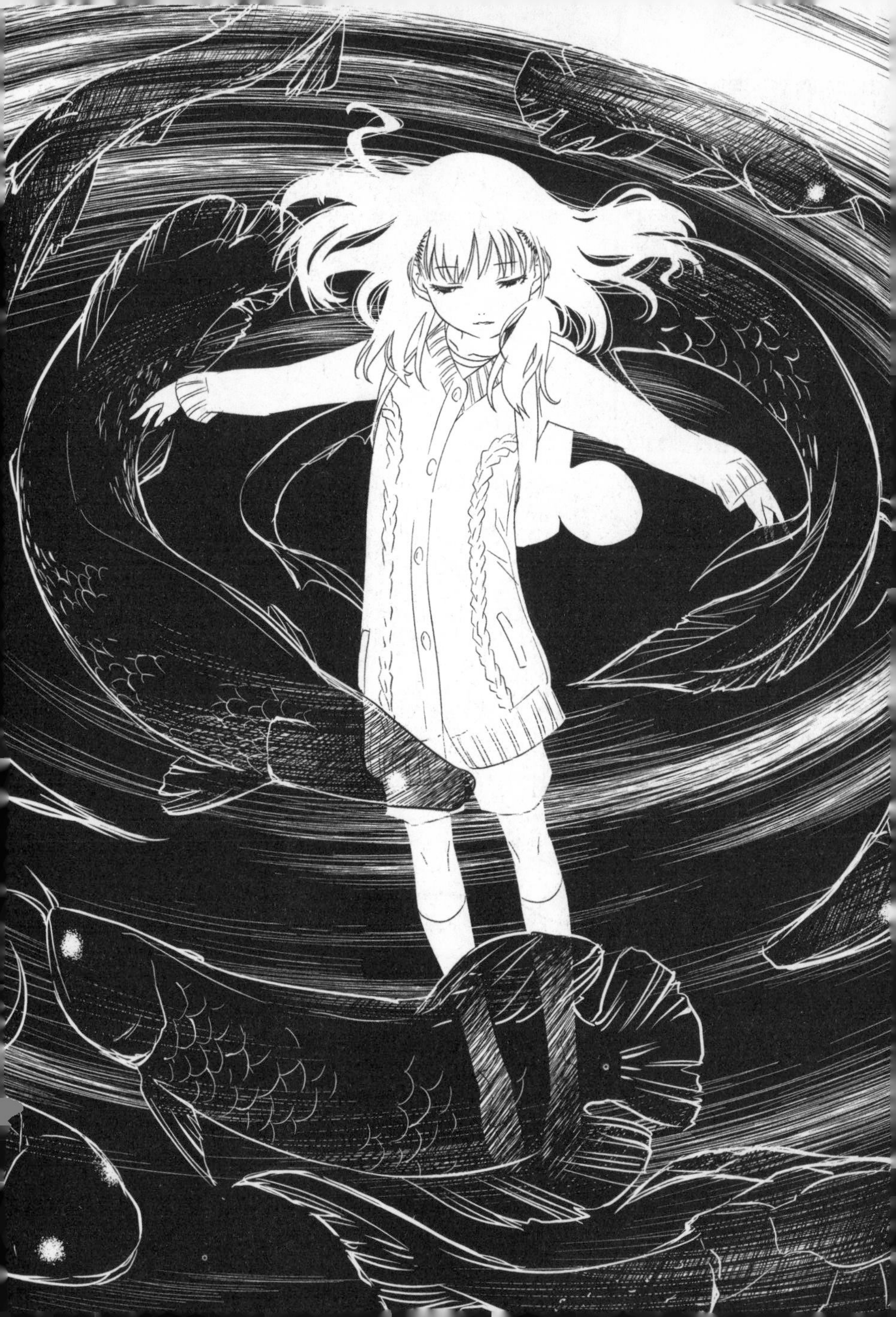

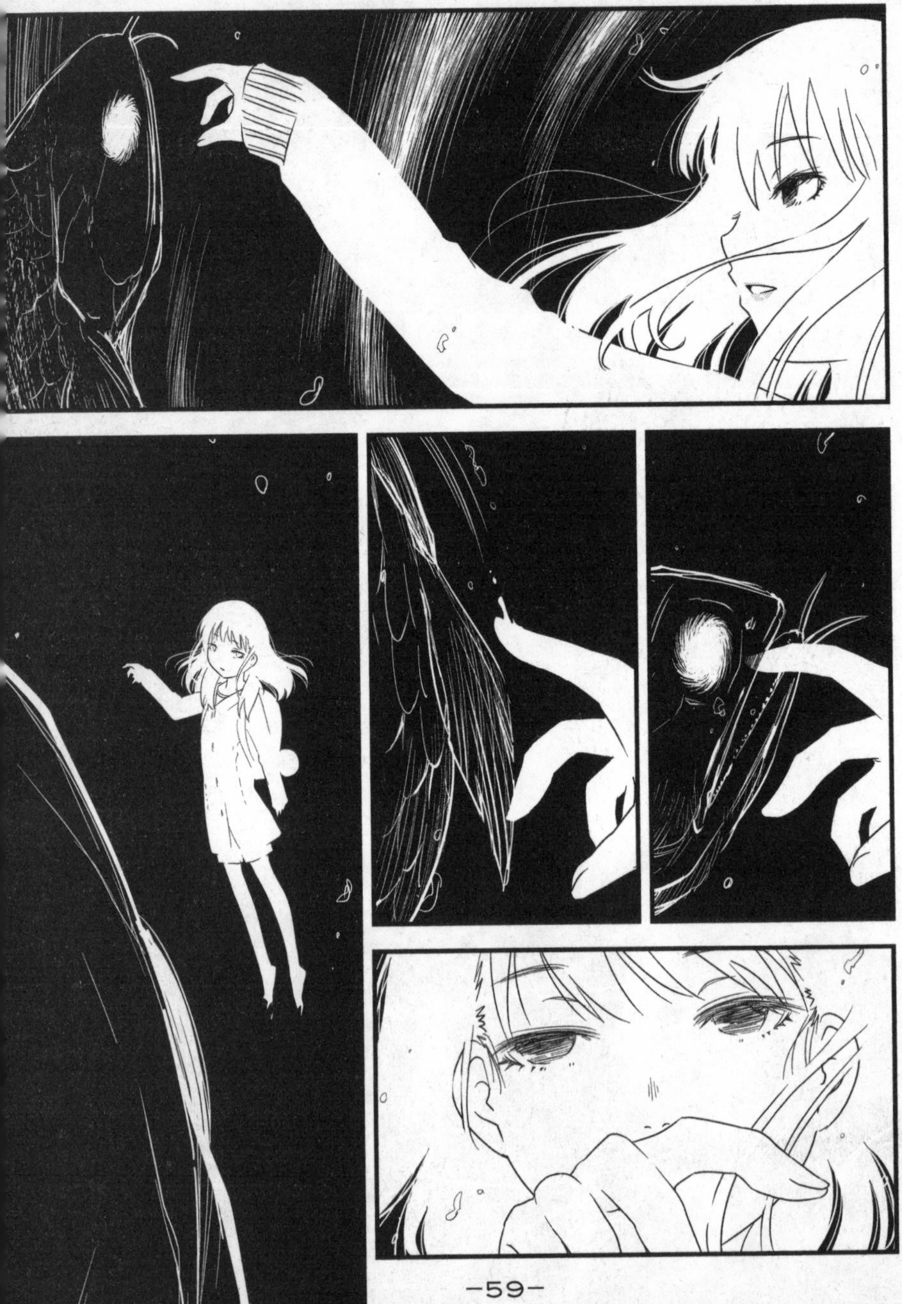

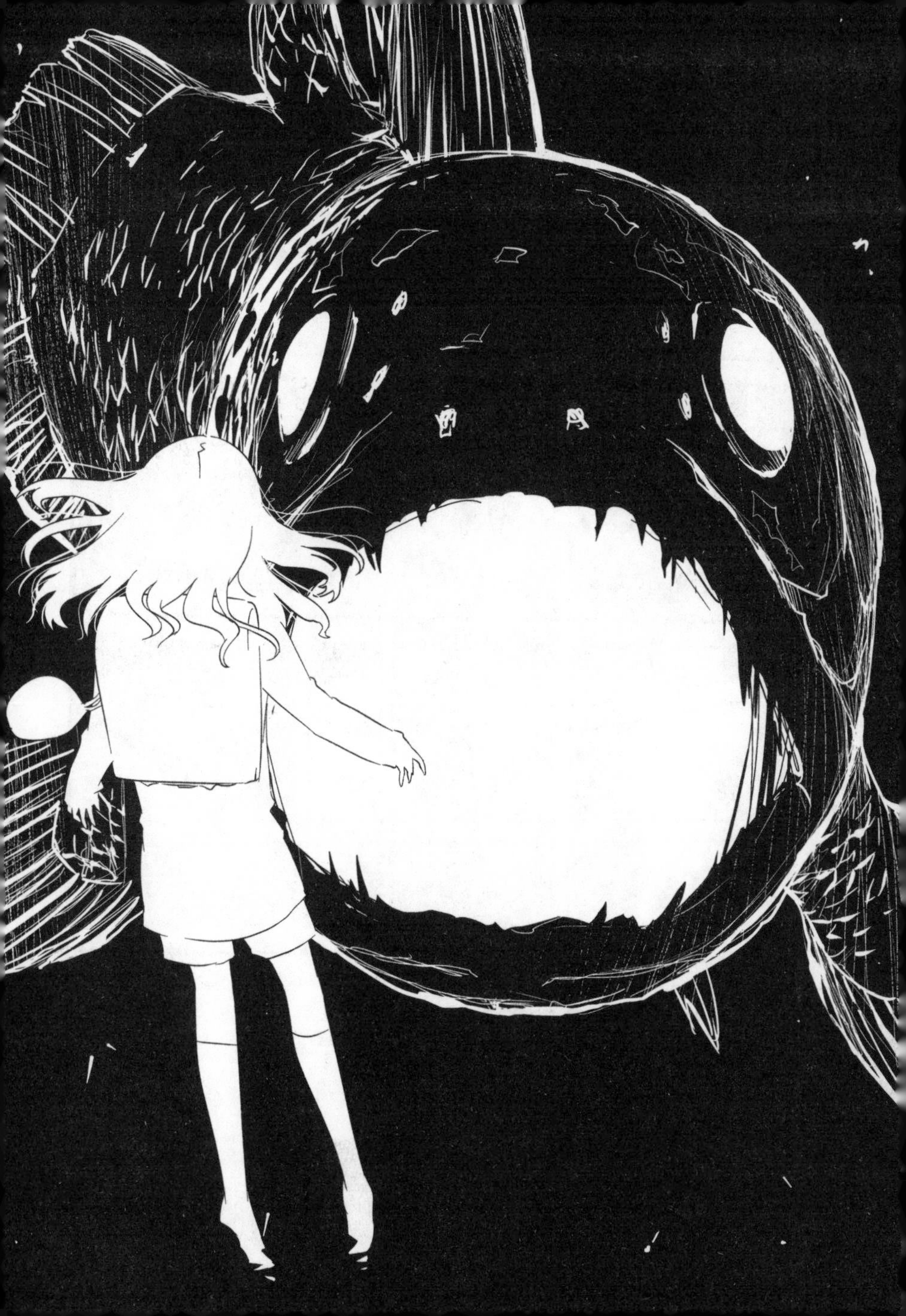

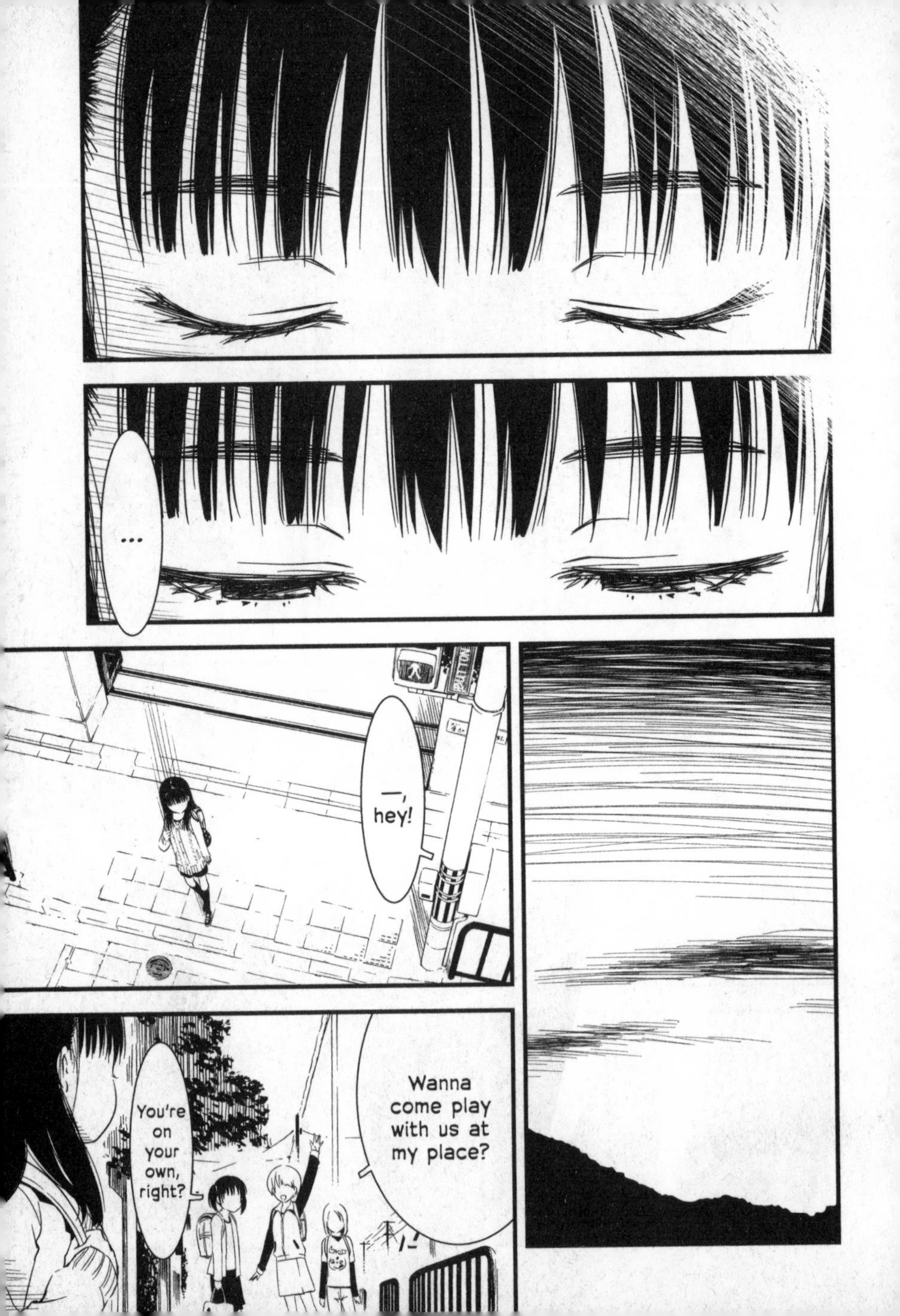
...
—, hey!
Wanna come play with us at my place?
You're on your own, right?

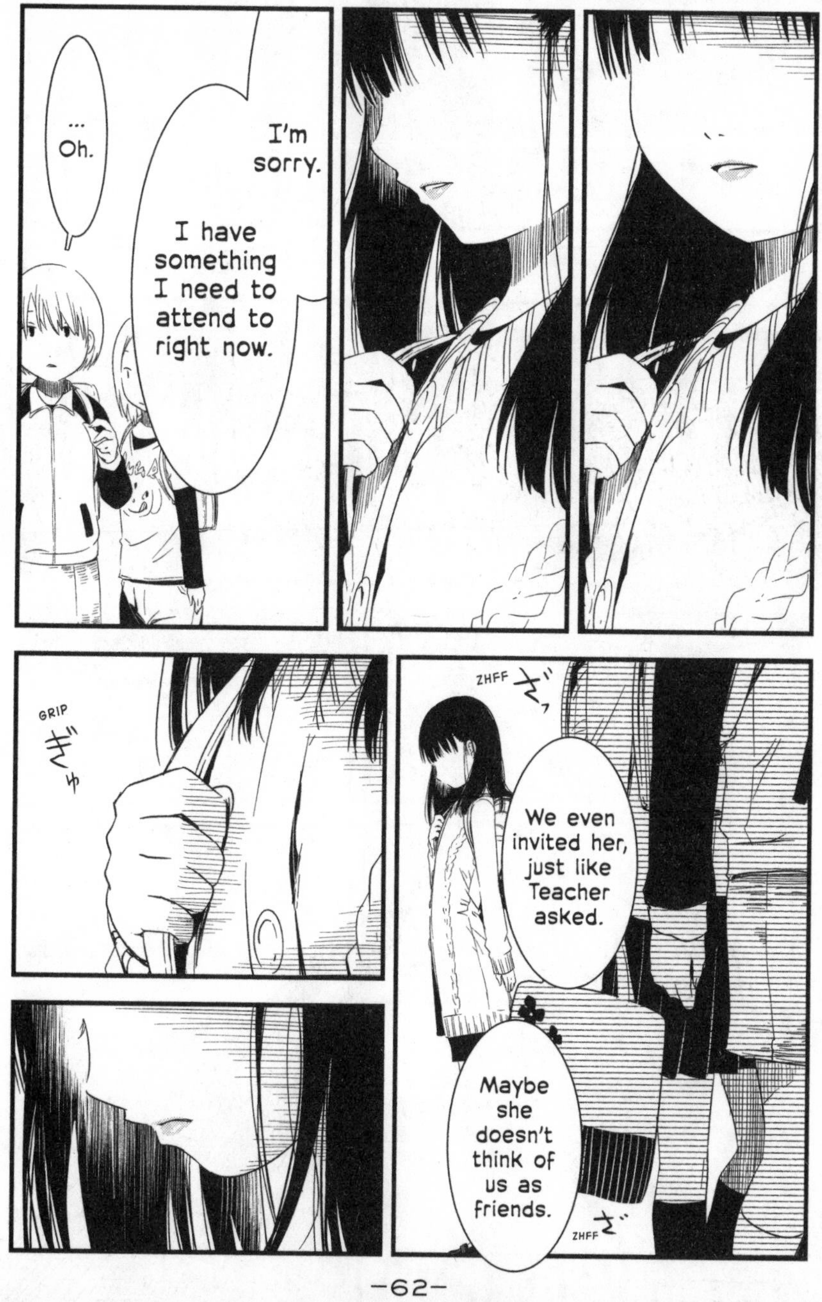
I'm sorry.
I have something I need to attend to right now.
... Oh.
ZHFF ざっ
We even invited her, just like Teacher asked.
Maybe she doesn't think of us as friends.
ZHFF ざ
GRIP ぎゅ

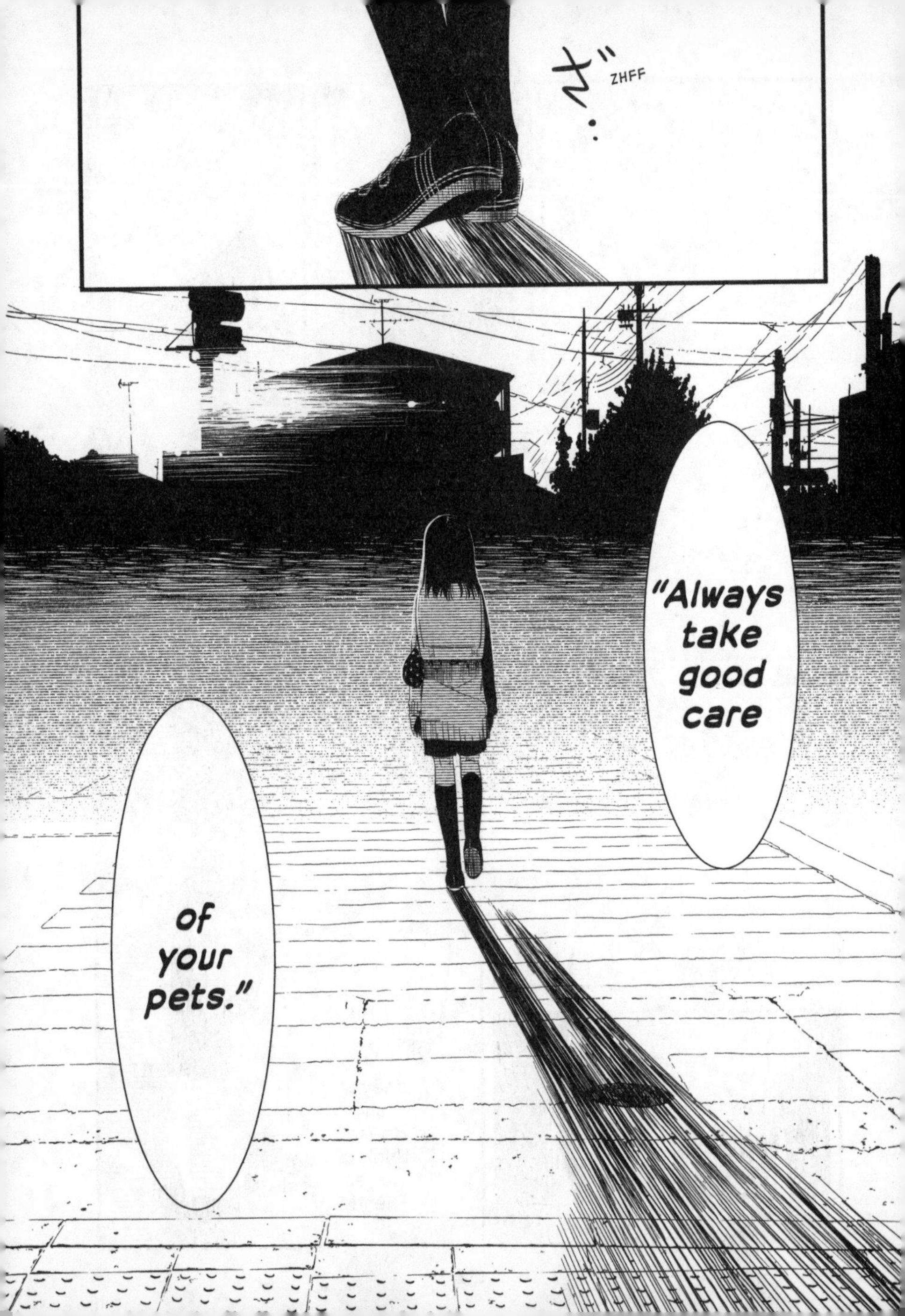
ざ ZHFF
"Always take good care
of your pets."

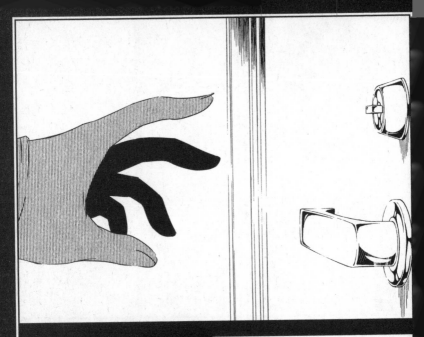

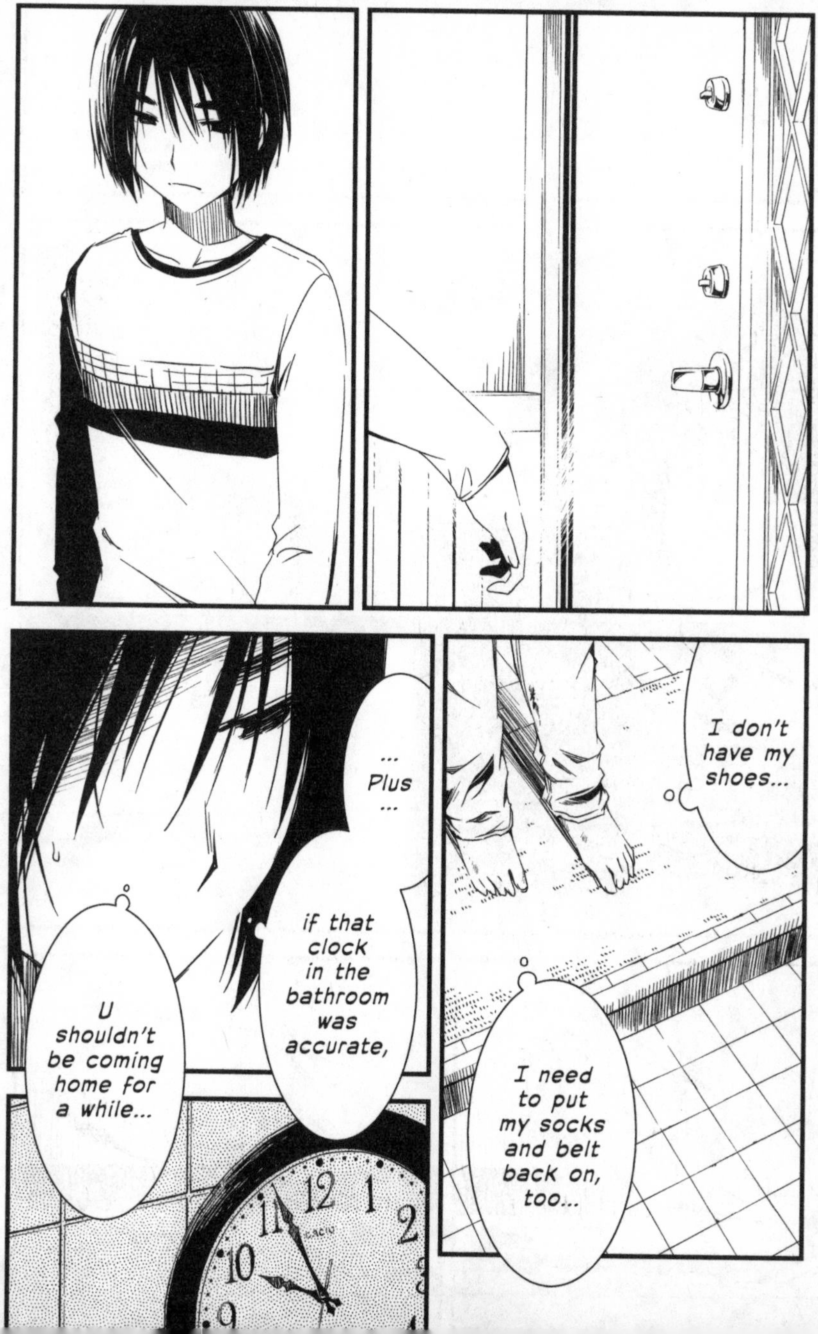
I don't have my shoes...
I need to put my socks and belt back on, too...
...Plus...
if that clock in the bathroom was accurate,
U shouldn't be coming home for a while...

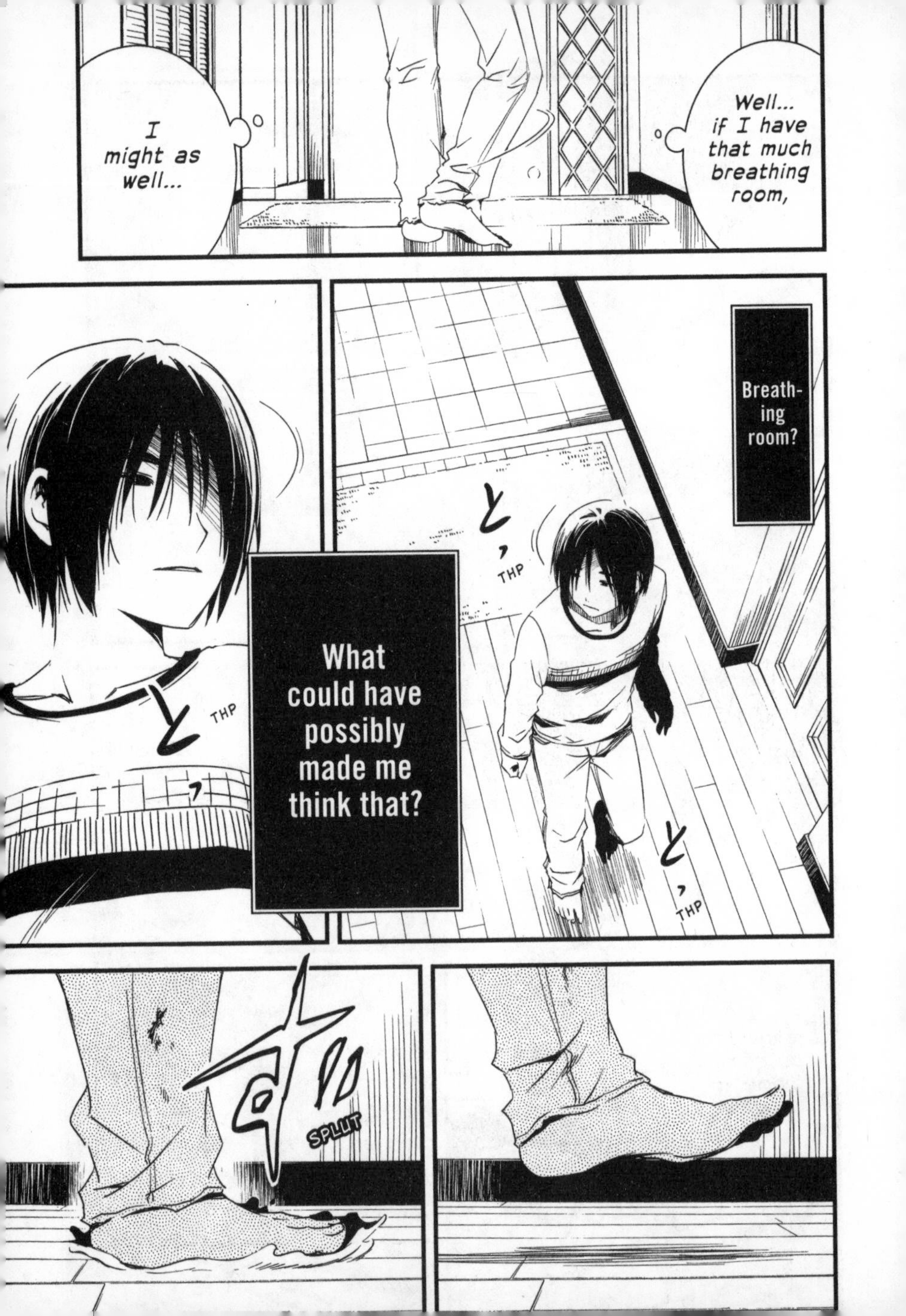

Well... if I have that much breathing room,
I might as well...
Breath-ing room?
THP
THP
What could have possibly made me think that?
THP
SPLUT

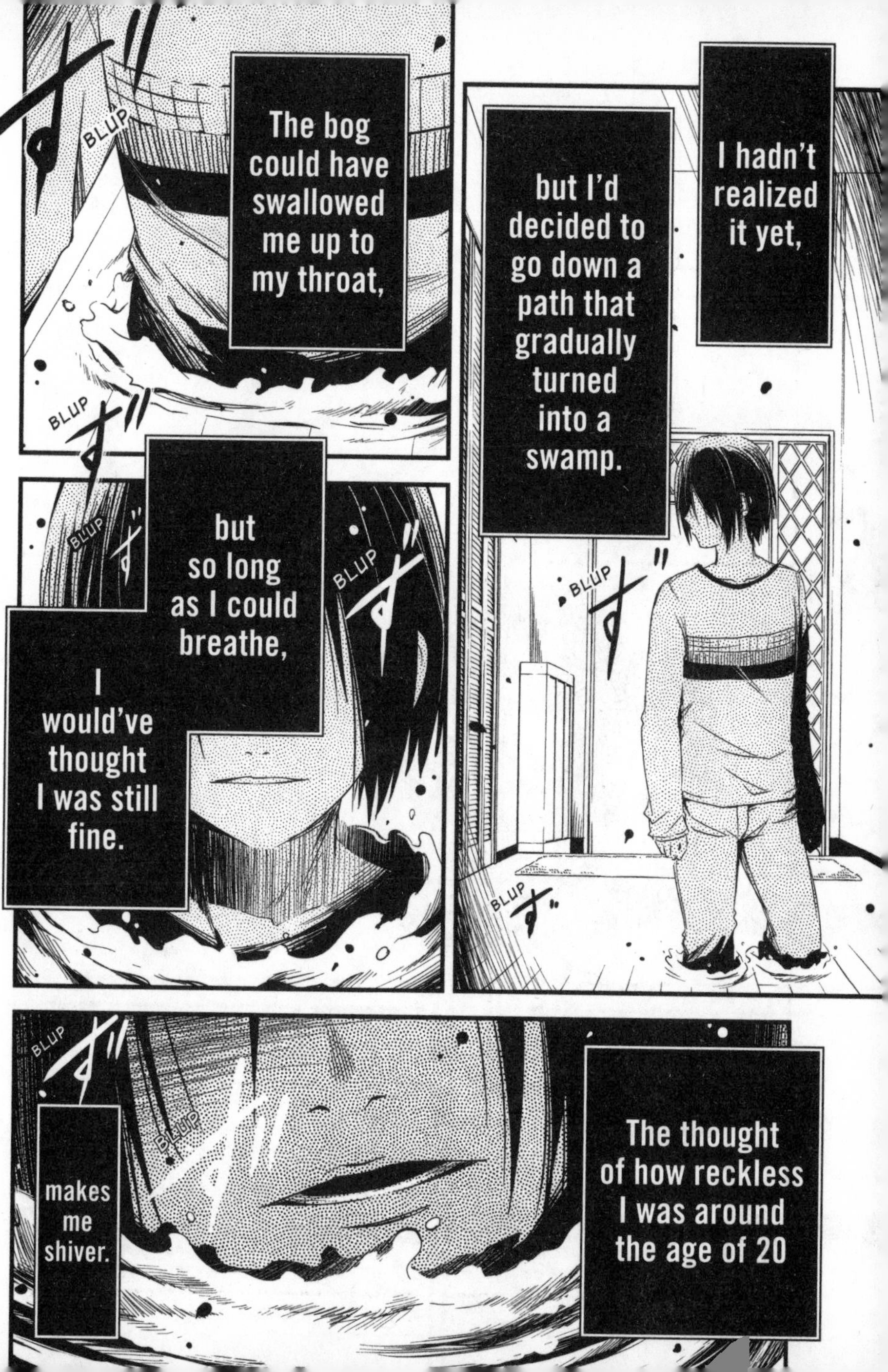
I hadn't realized it yet,
but I'd decided to go down a path that gradually turned into a swamp.
BLUP
ず
BLUP
ず
The bog could have swallowed me up to my throat,
BLUP
ず
BLUP
ず
but so long as I could breathe,
BLUP
ず
BLUP
ず
I would've thought I was still fine.
The thought of how reckless I was around the age of 20
BLUP
ず
BLUP
ず
makes me shiver.

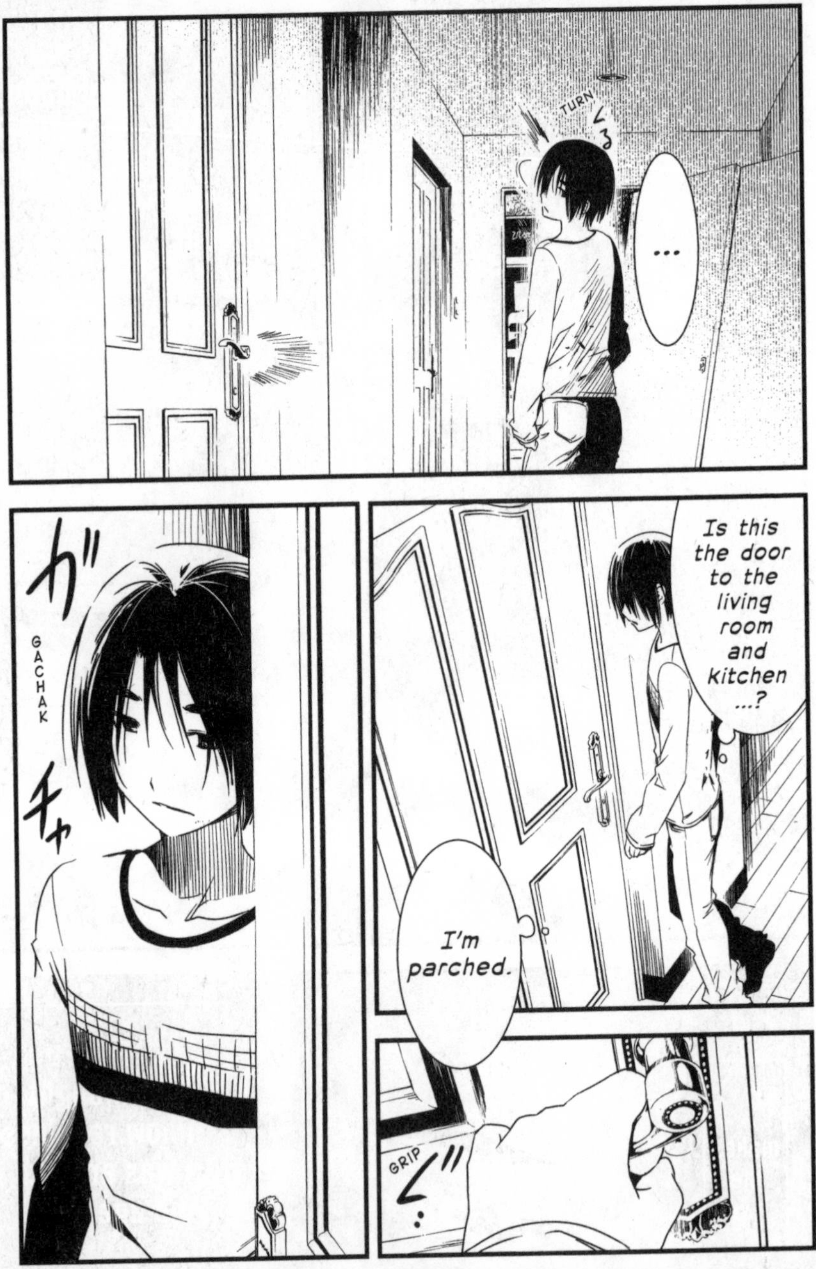
TURN
くる
...
Is this the door to the living room and kitchen ...?
I'm parched.
GRIP
ぐ
ガチャ
GACHAK

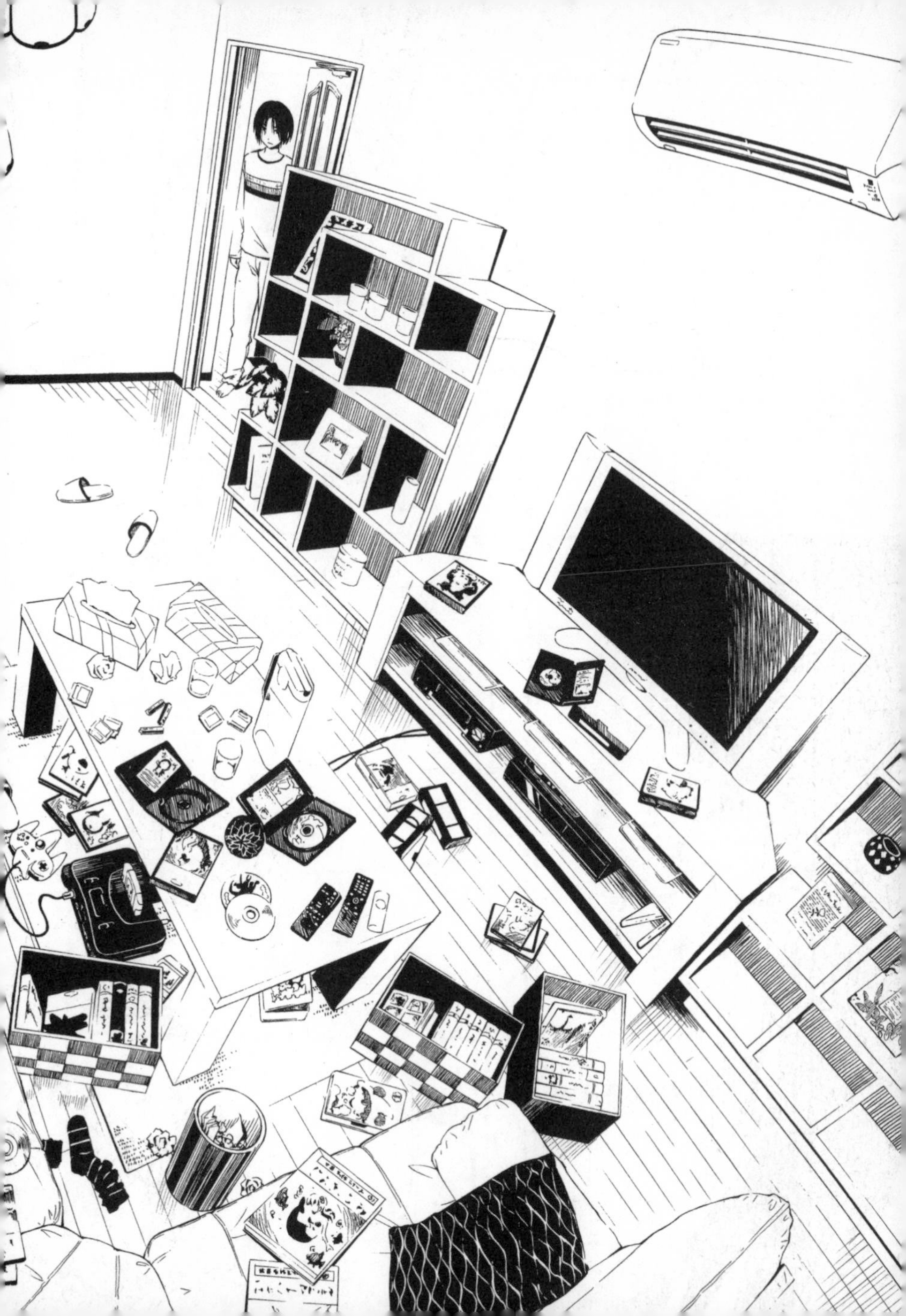

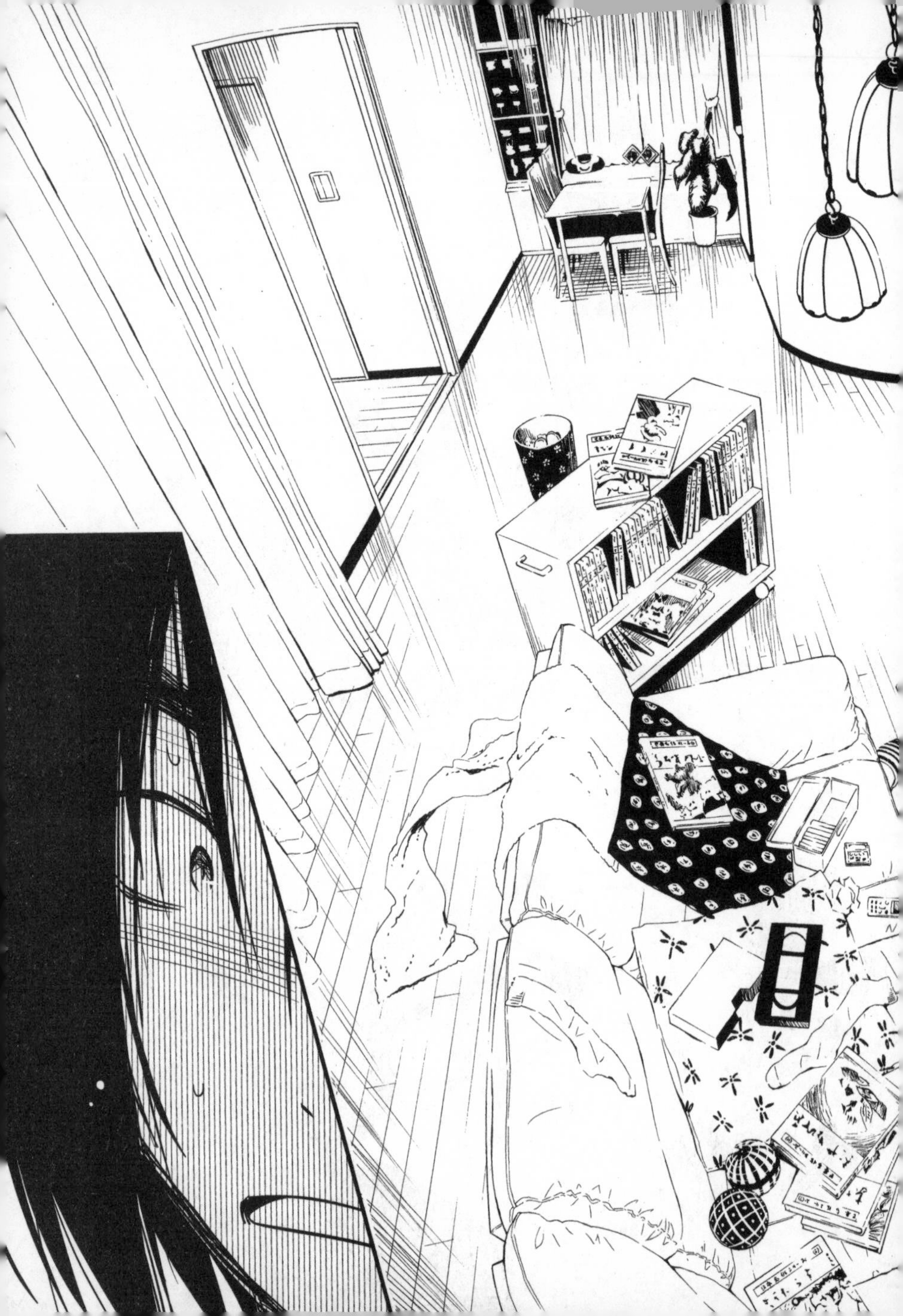

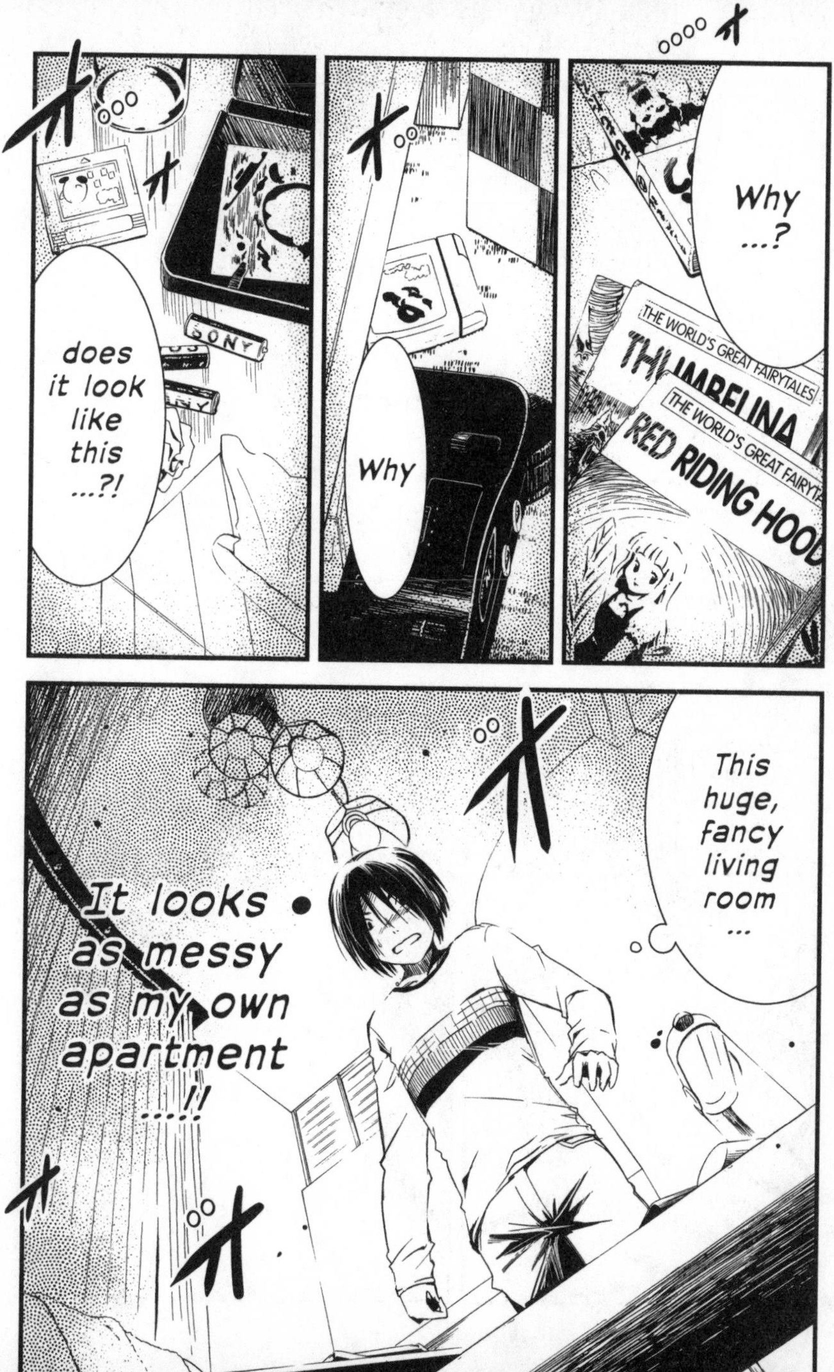
Why ...?
THE WORLD'S GREAT FAIRYTALES
THE WORLD'S GREAT FAIRYTALES
RED RIDING HOOD
Why
does it look like this ...?!
SONY
This huge, fancy living room ...
It looks as messy as my own apartment ...!!

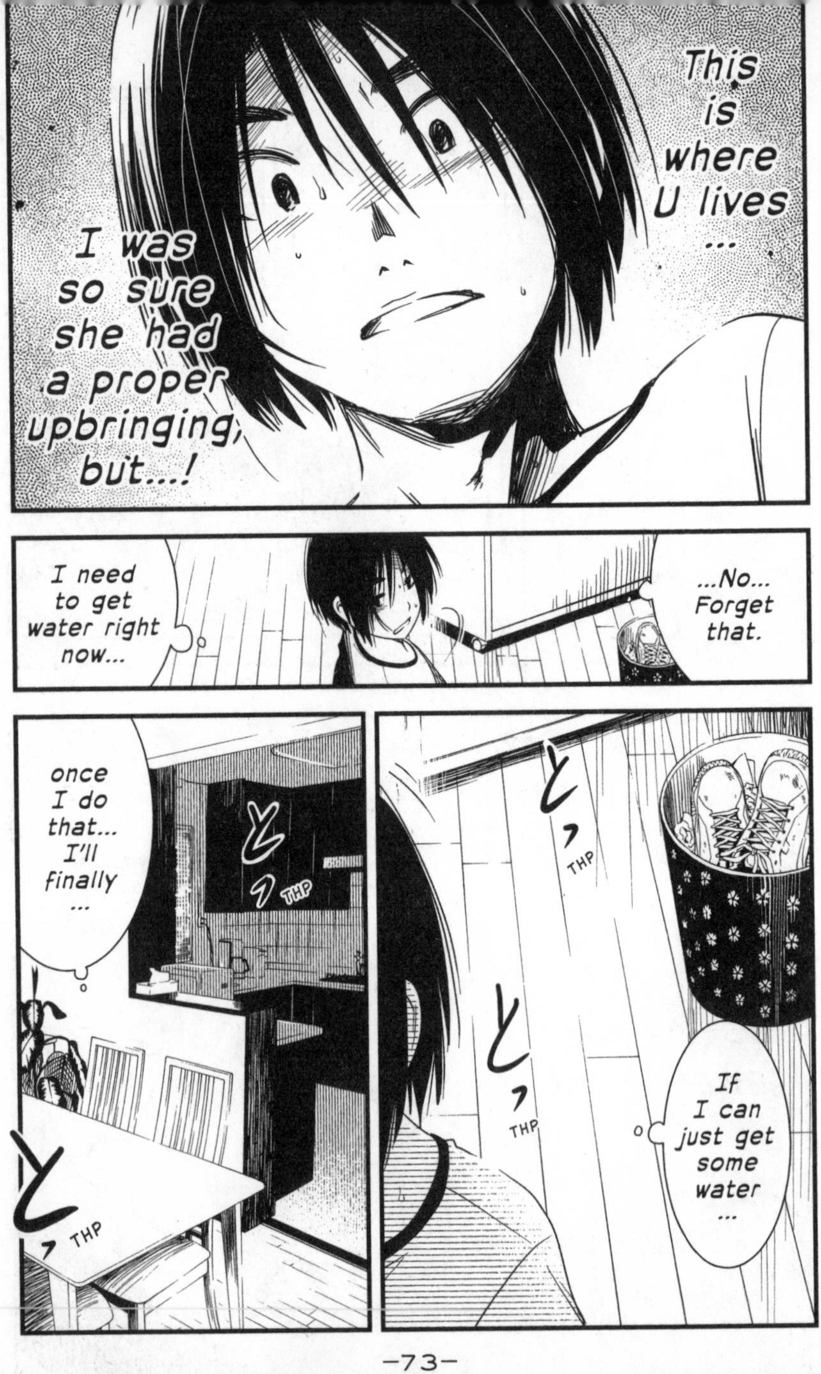
This is where U lives ...
I was so sure she had a proper upbringing, but...!
...No... Forget that.
I need to get water right now...
THP
THP
If I can just get some water ...
once I do that... I'll finally ...
THP
THP

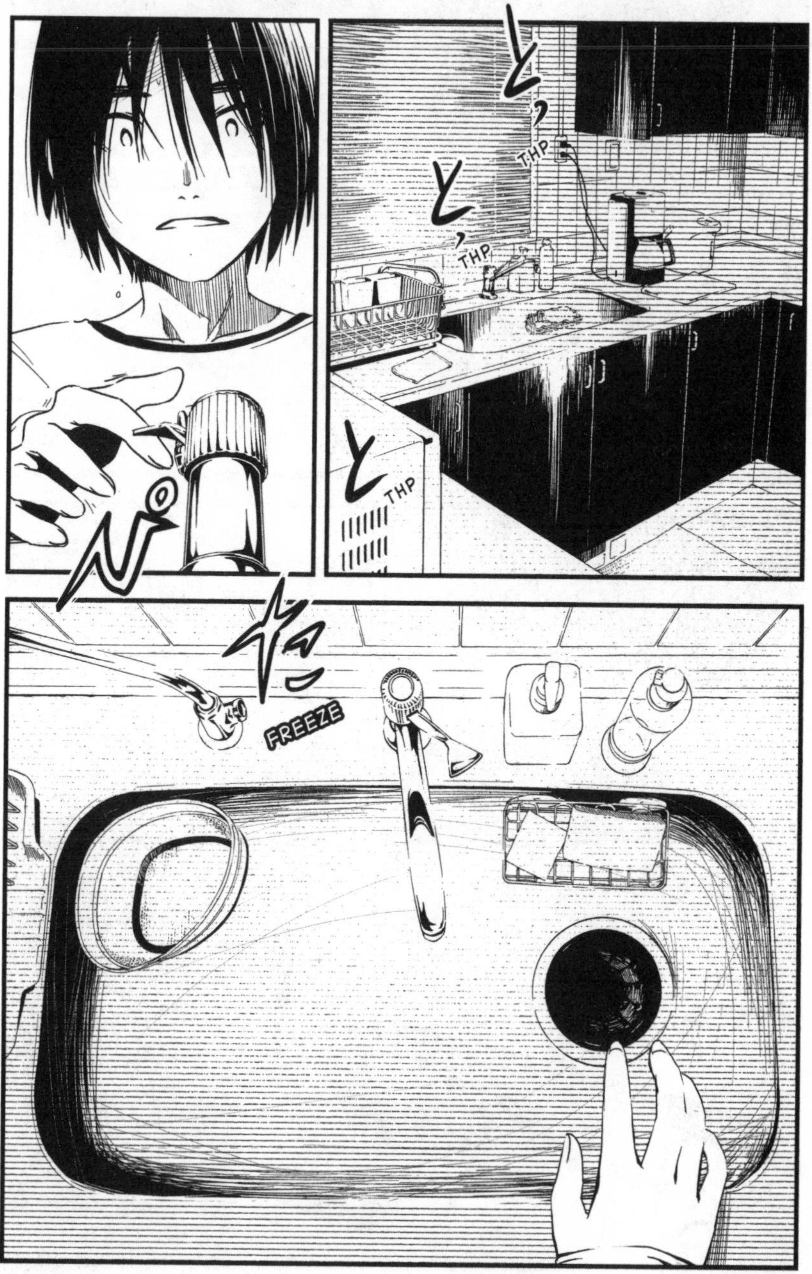
ど、
THP
ど、
THP
ど
THP
FREEZE

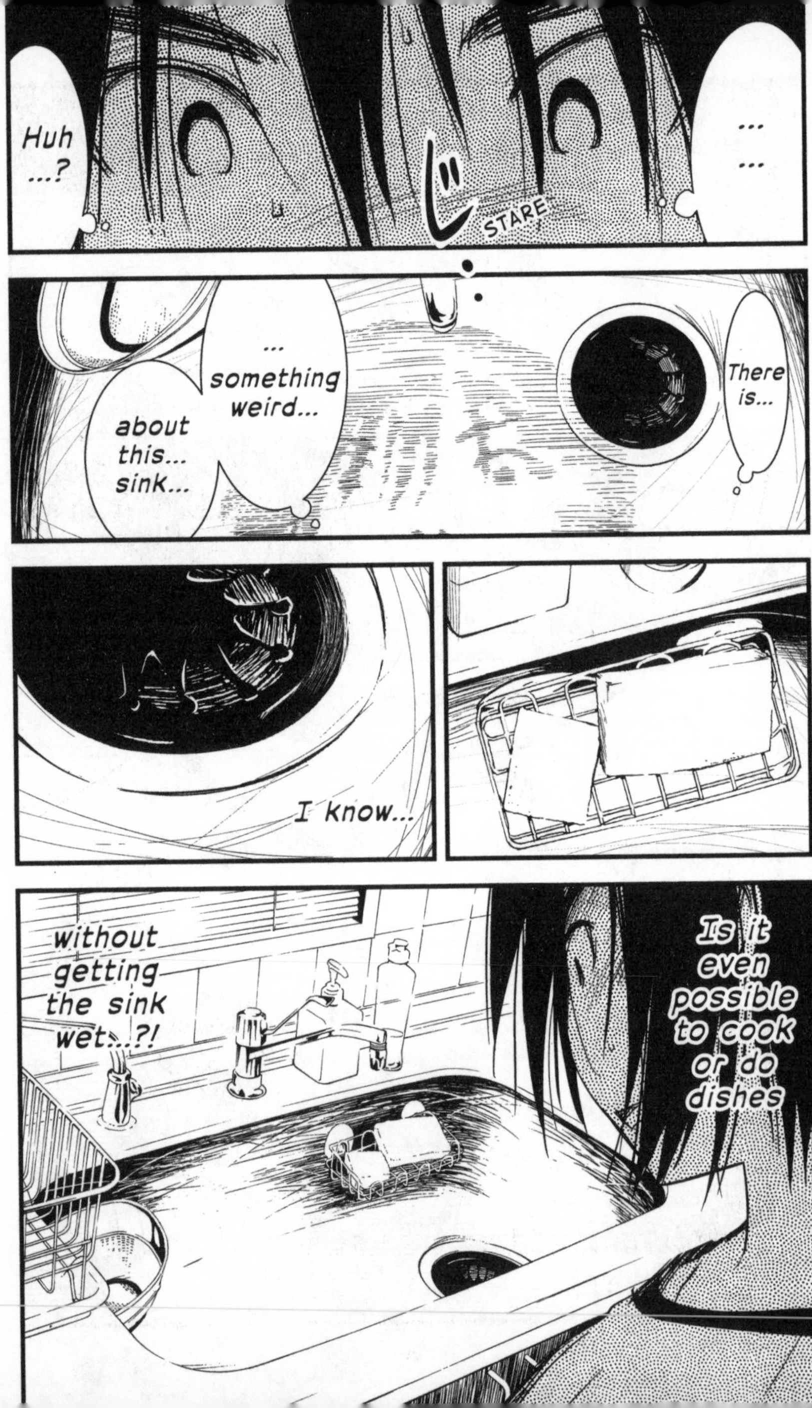
... ...
じ
STARE
Huh ...?
There is...
... something weird...
about this... sink...
I know...
Is it even possible to cook or do dishes
without getting the sink wet...?!

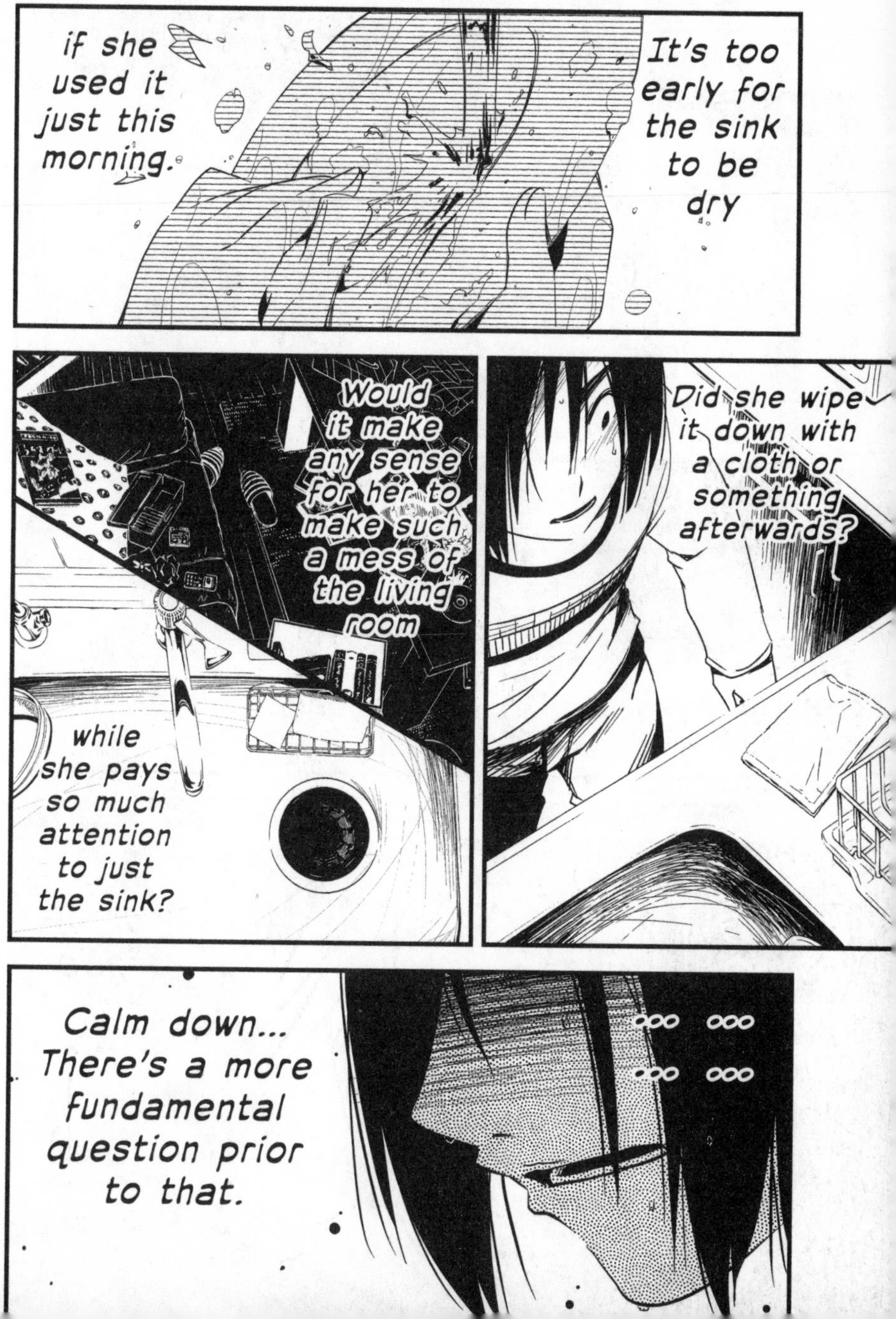
It's too early for the sink to be dry
if she used it just this morning.
Did she wipe it down with a cloth or something afterwards?
Would it make any sense for her to make such a mess of the living room
while she pays so much attention to just the sink?
Calm down... There's a more fundamental question prior to that.

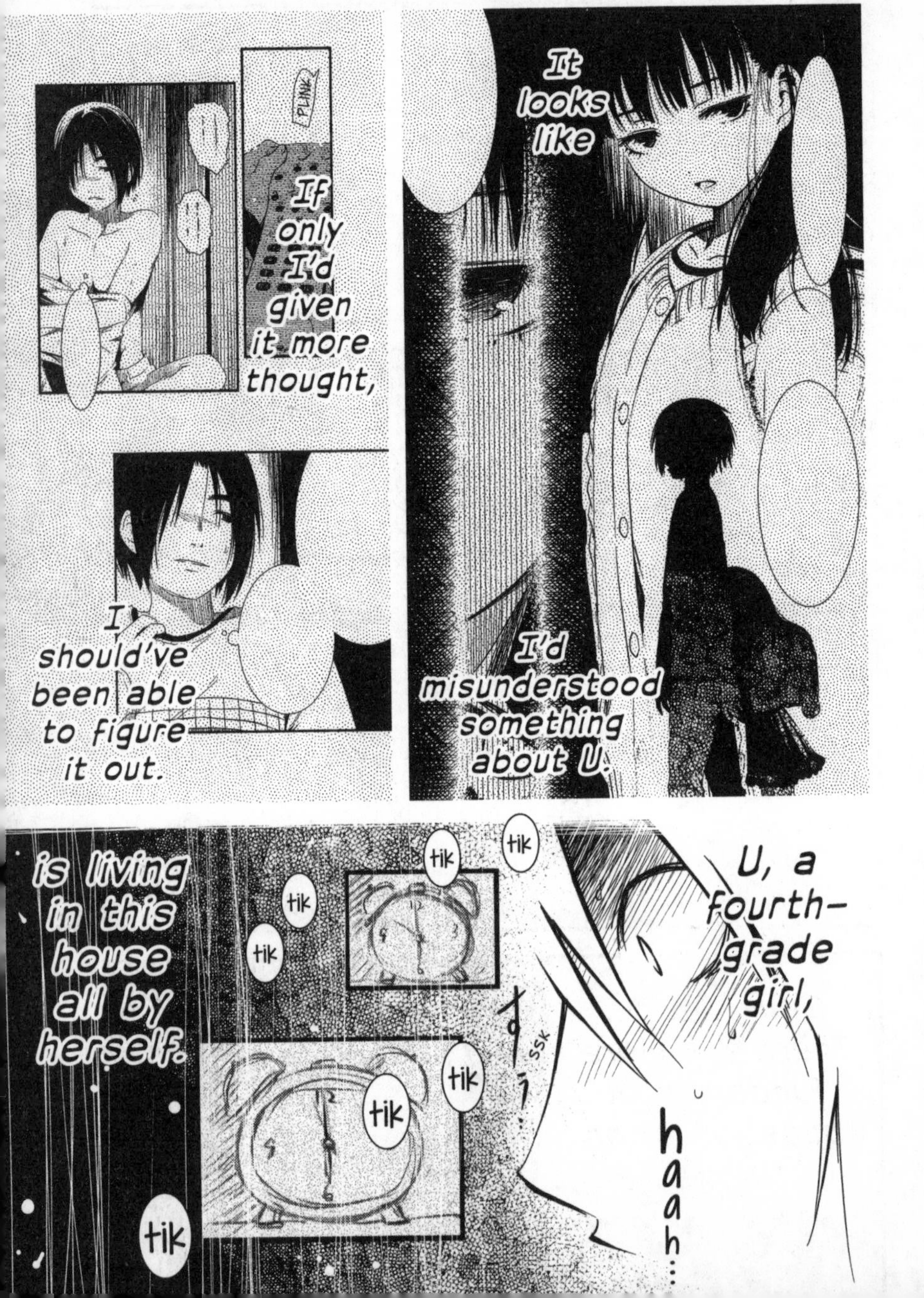
It looks like
I'd misunderstood something about U.
PLINK
If only I'd given it more thought,
I should've been able to figure it out.
U, a fourth-grade girl,
SSK
haaah...
tik
tik
tik
tik
tik
tik
tik
is living in this house all by herself.

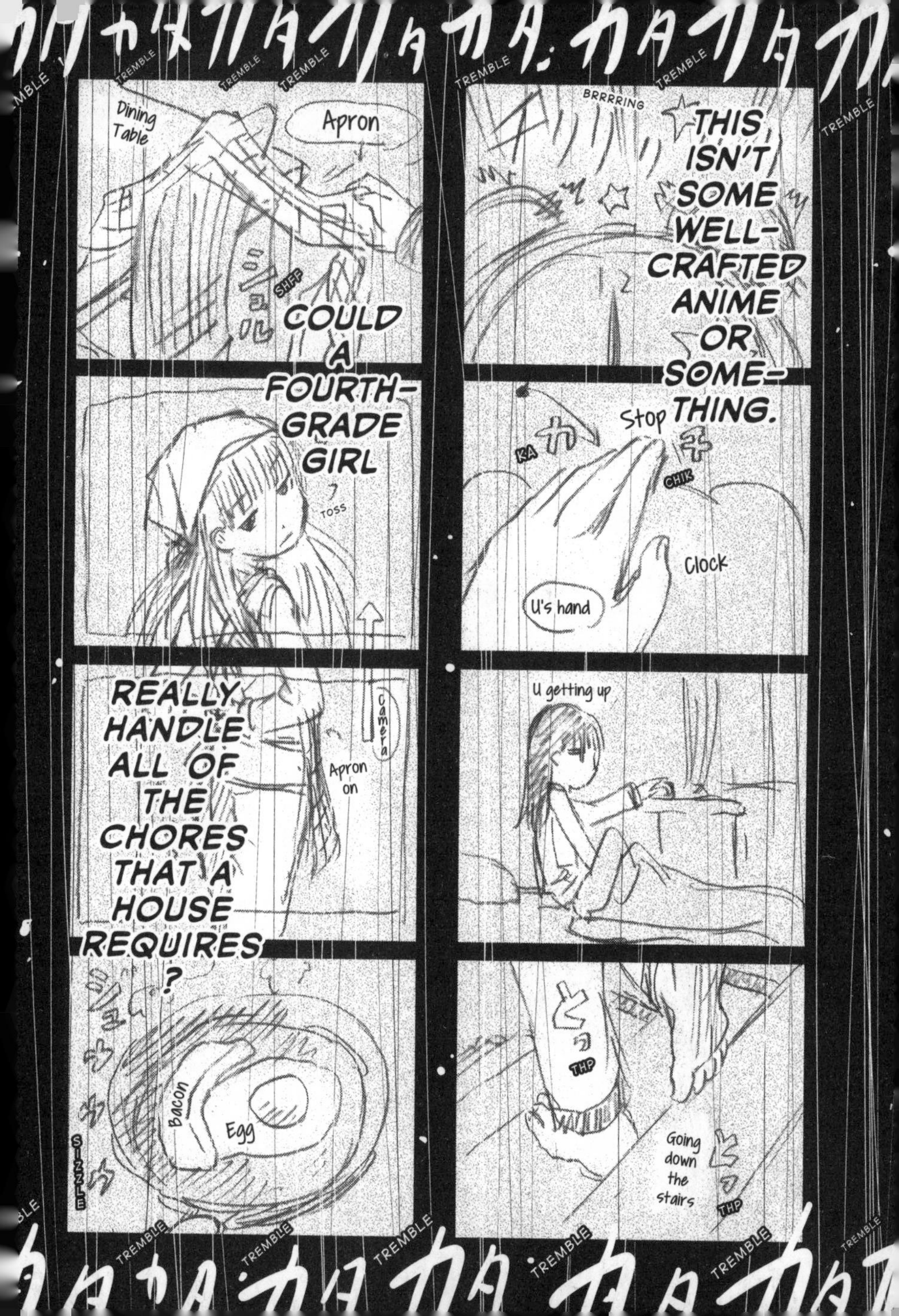
TREMBLE
BRRRRING
THIS ISN'T SOME WELL-CRAFTED ANIME OR SOME-THING.
Dining Table
Apron
SHFF
COULD A FOURTH-GRADE GIRL
Stop
KA
CHIK
Clock
U's hand
TOSS
U getting up
REALLY HANDLE ALL OF THE CHORES THAT A HOUSE REQUIRES?
Camera
Apron on
THP
Going down the stairs
THP
Bacon
Egg
SIZZLE
TREMBLE

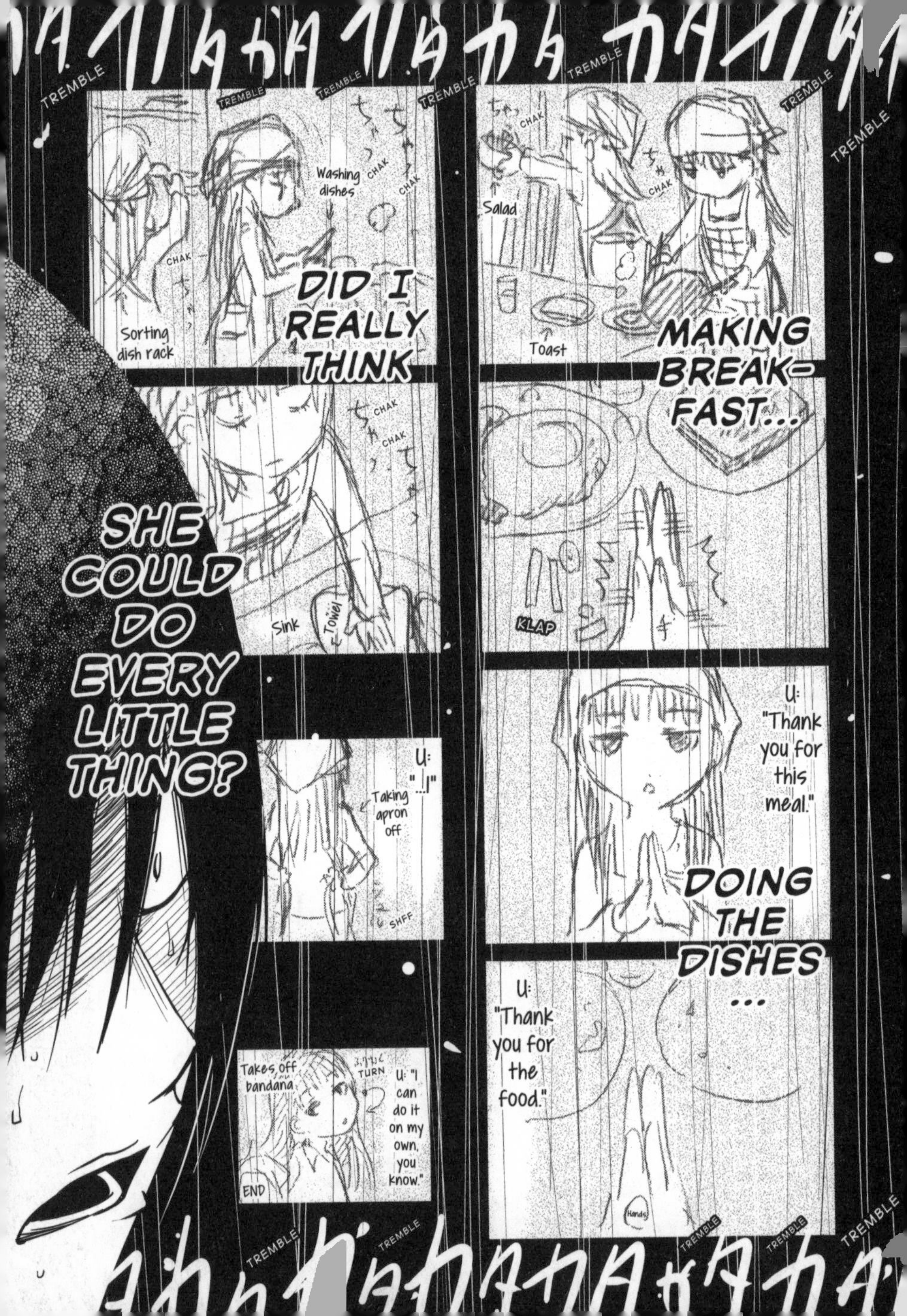
TREMBLE
Salad
CHAK
CHAK
Toast
MAKING BREAK-FAST...
Washing dishes
CHAK
CHAK
CHAK
Sorting dish rack
DID I REALLY THINK
KLAP
CHAK
CHAK
Sink
Towel
U: "Thank you for this meal."
DOING THE DISHES ...
U: "Thank you for the food."
Hands
U: "...!"
Taking apron off
SHFF
TURN
U: "I can do it on my own, you know."
Takes off bandana
END
SHE COULD DO EVERY LITTLE THING?
TREMBLE

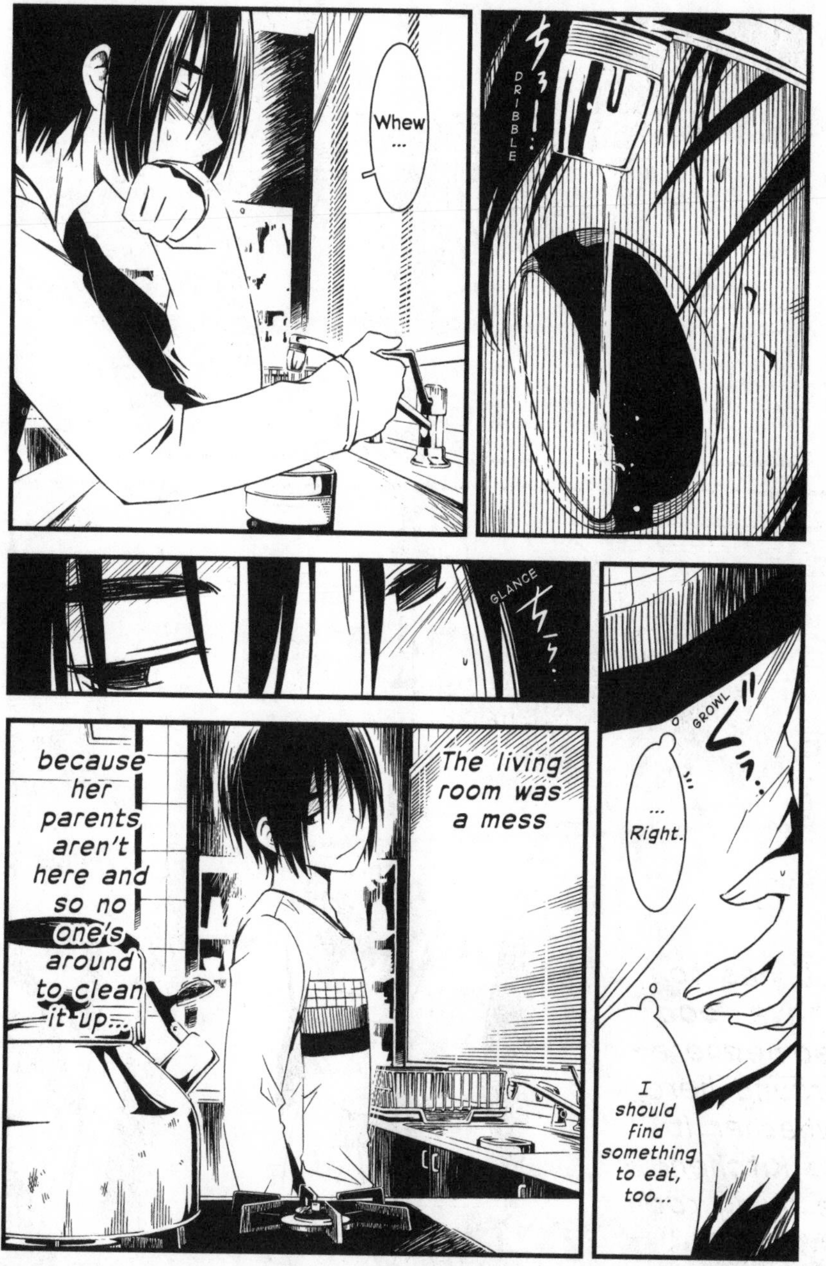
DRIBBLE
Whew ...
GROWL
... Right.
I should find something to eat, too...
GLANCE
The living room was a mess
because her parents aren't here and so no one's around to clean it up...

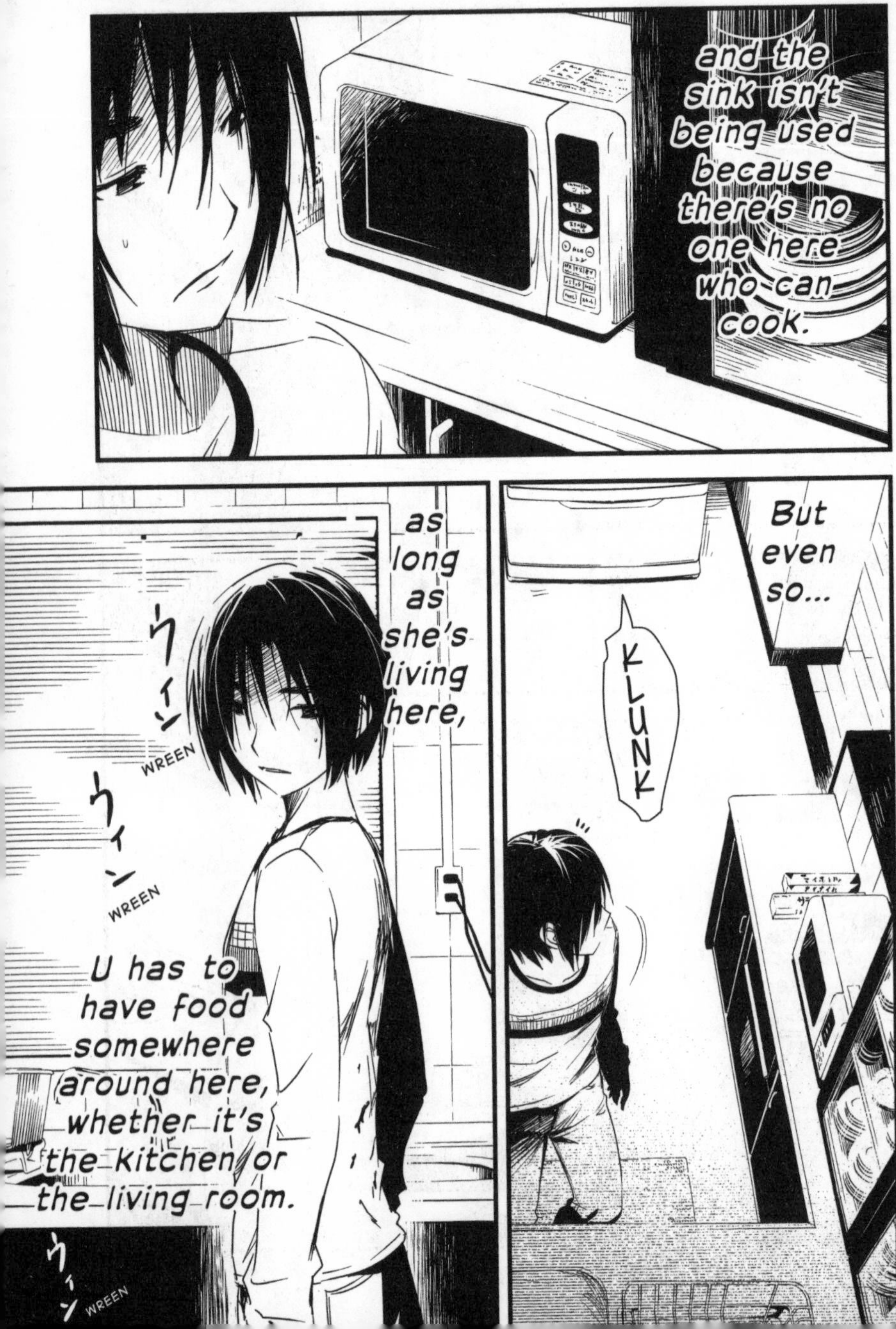
and the sink isn't being used because there's no one here who can cook.
But even so...
KLUNK
as long as she's living here,
ウィン
WREEN
ウィン
WREEN
U has to have food somewhere around here, whether it's the kitchen or the living room.
ウィン
WREEN

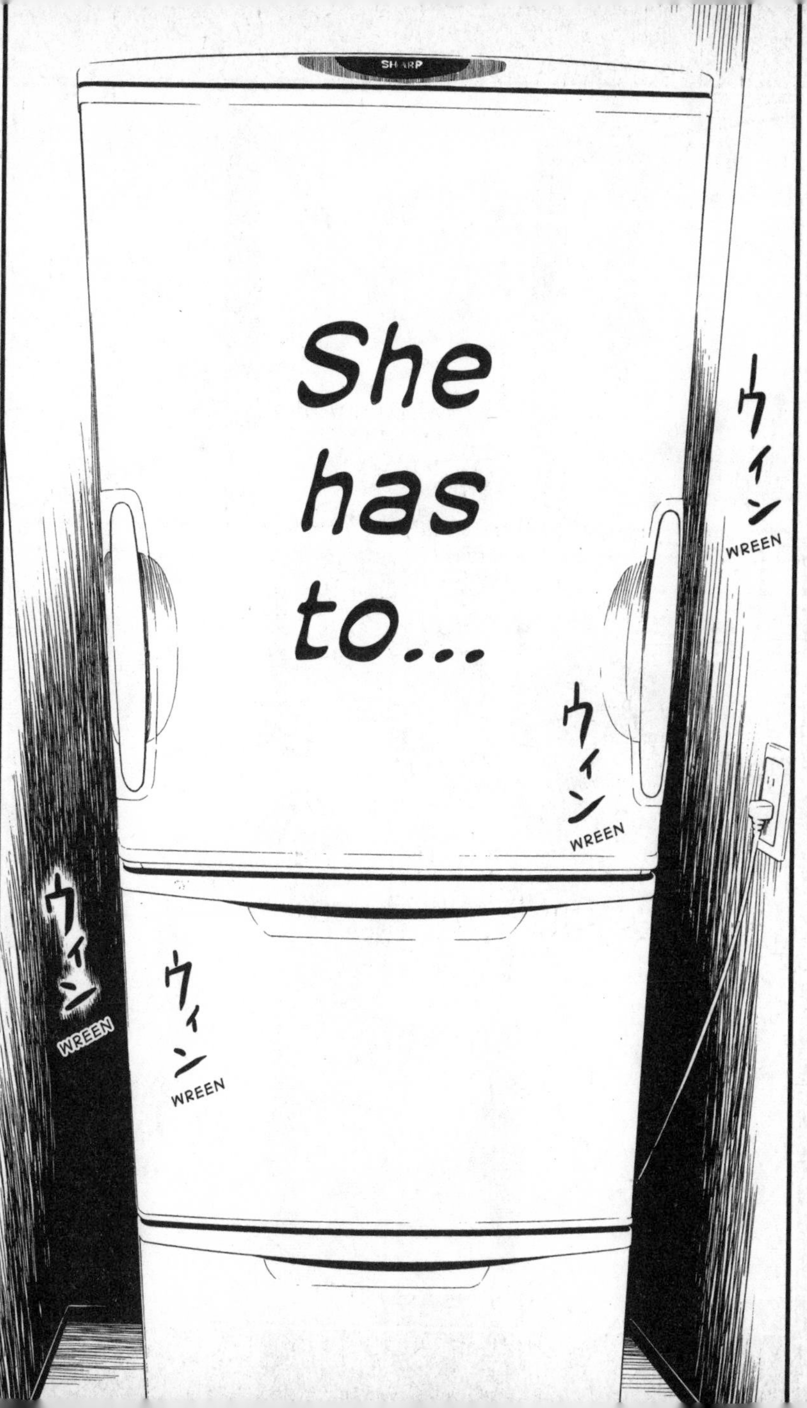
SHARP
She has to...
ウィン
WREEN
ウィン
WREEN
ウィン
WREEN
ウィン
WREEN

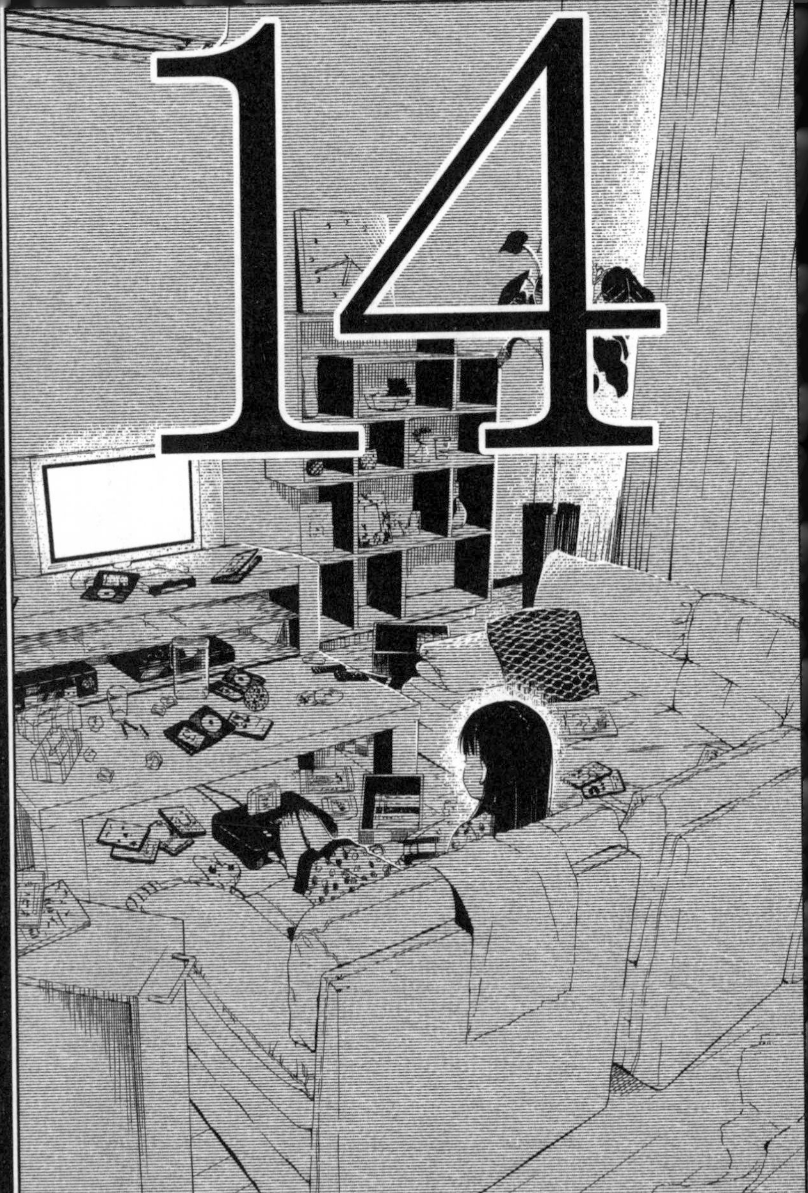
14

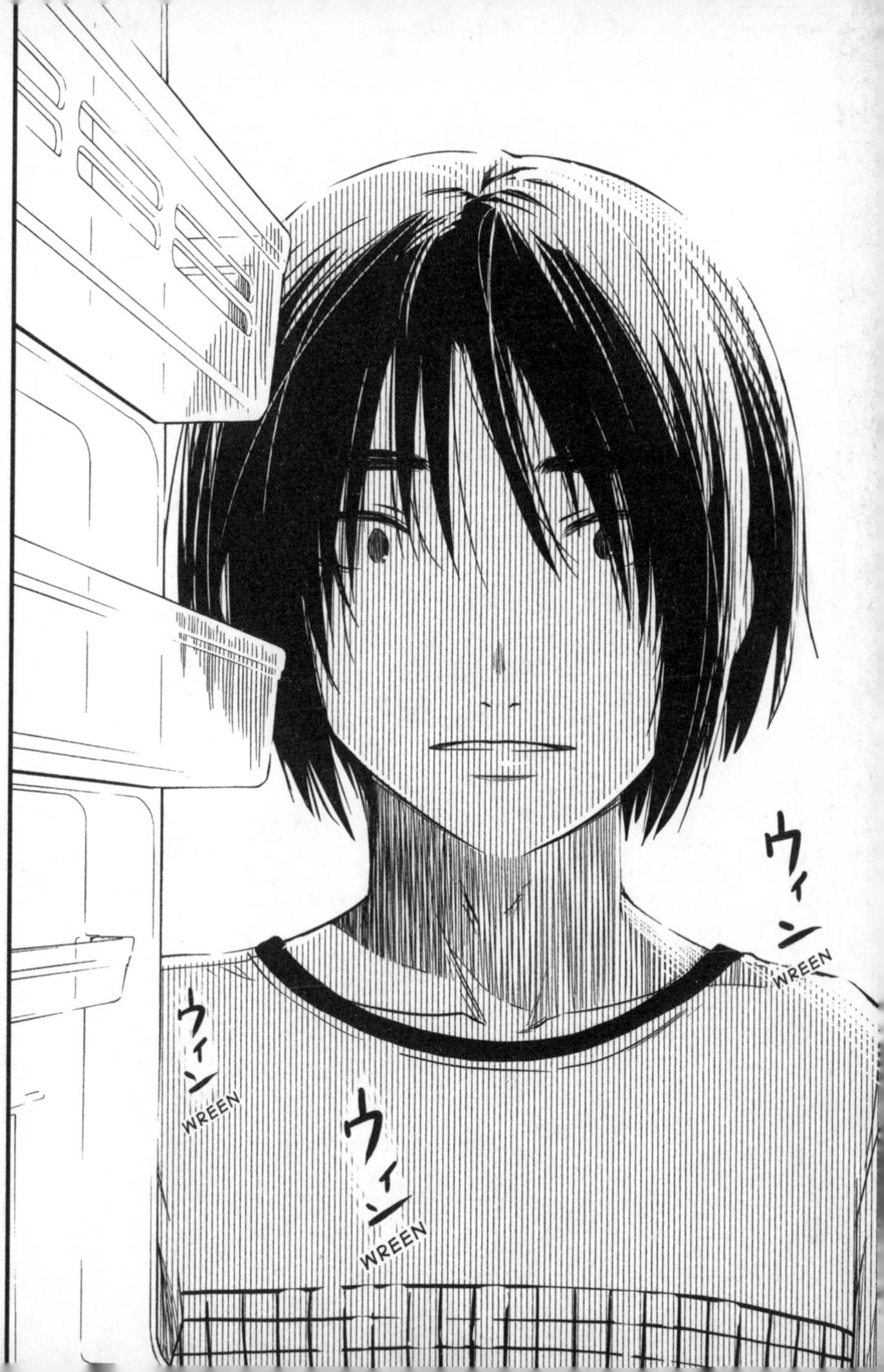
ウィン
WREEN
ウィン
WREEN
ウィン
WREEN

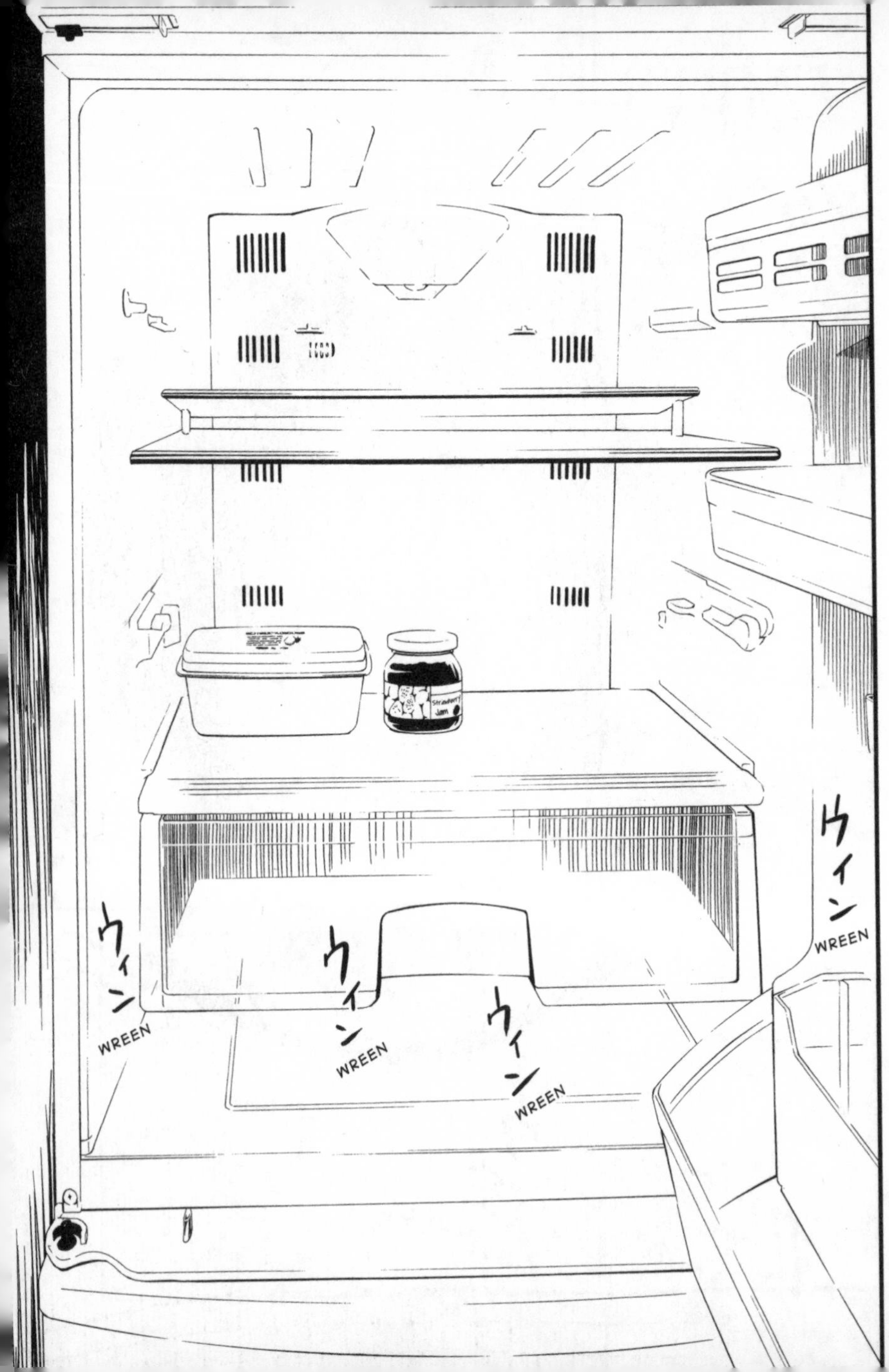
Strawberry Jam
ウィン
WREEN
ウィン
WREEN
ウィン
WREEN
ウィン
WREEN

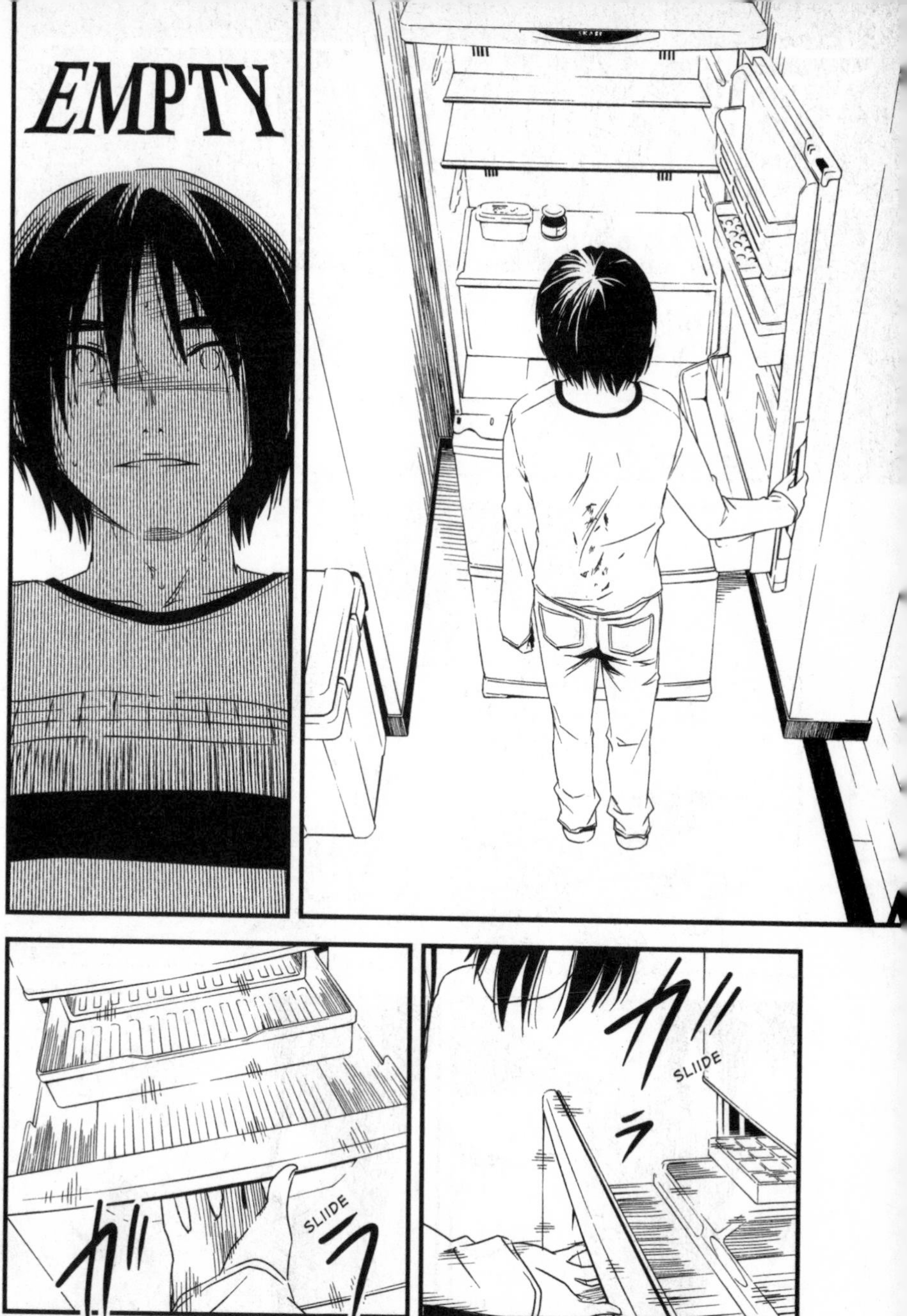
EMPTY
ガラ
SLIIDE
ガラ
SLIIDE

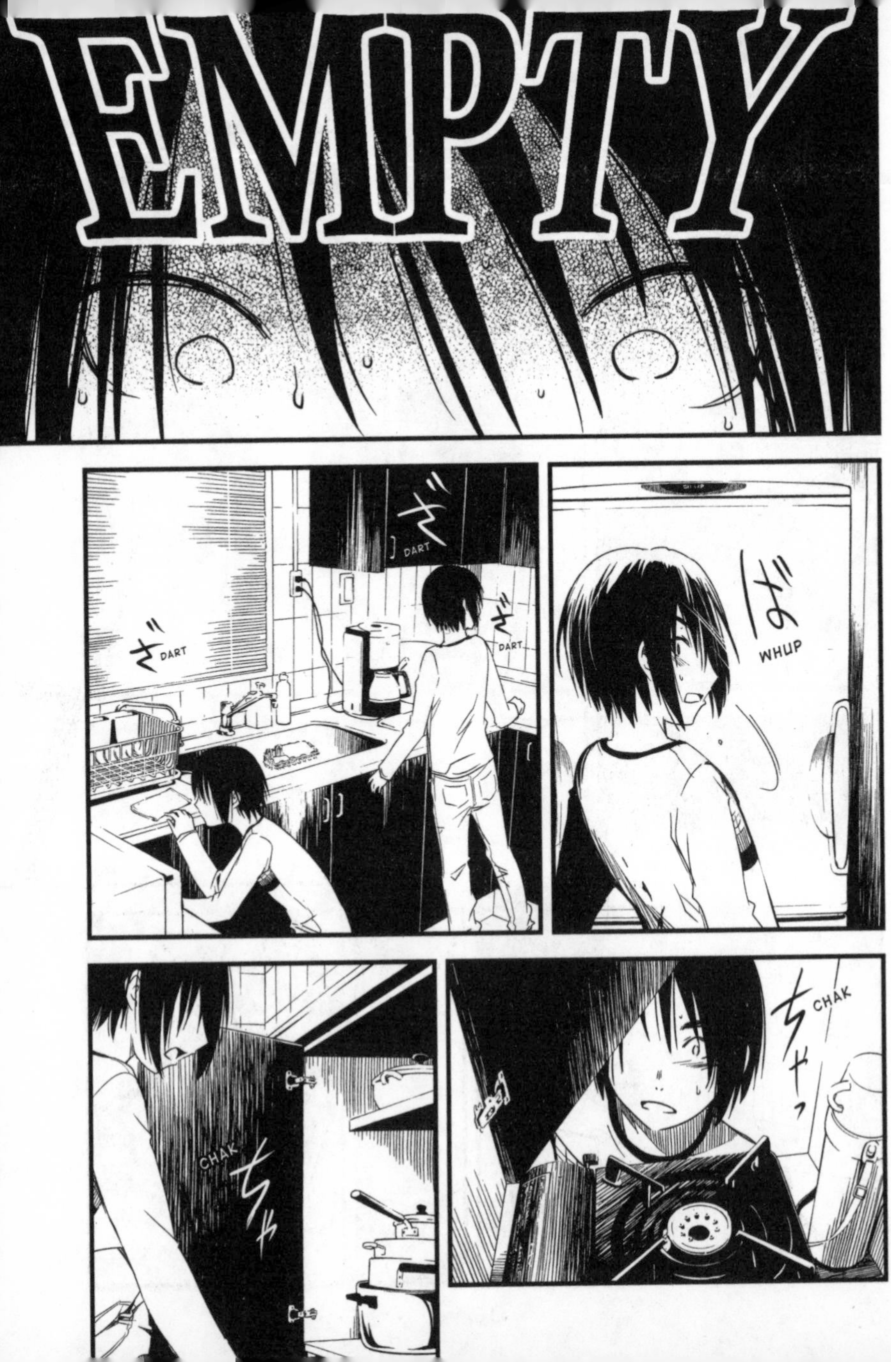
EMPTY
ぼ
WHUP
ざ
DART
ざ
DART
ざ
DART
ちゃっ
CHAK
ちゃ
CHAK

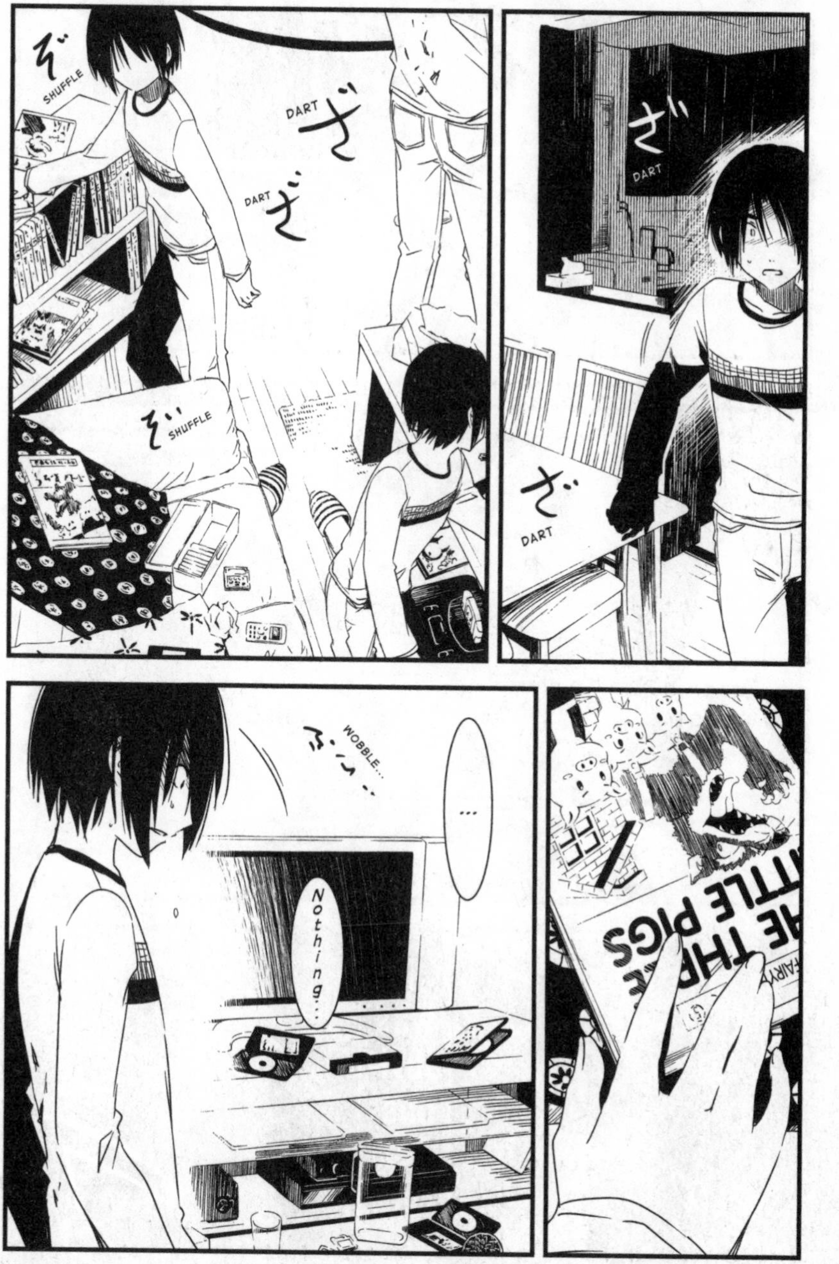
ざ
DART
ざ
DART
ぞ
SHUFFLE
ざ
DART
ざ
DART
ぞい
SHUFFLE
HE THREE
TTLE PIGS
FAIRY
...
Nothing...
ふら..
WOBBLE...

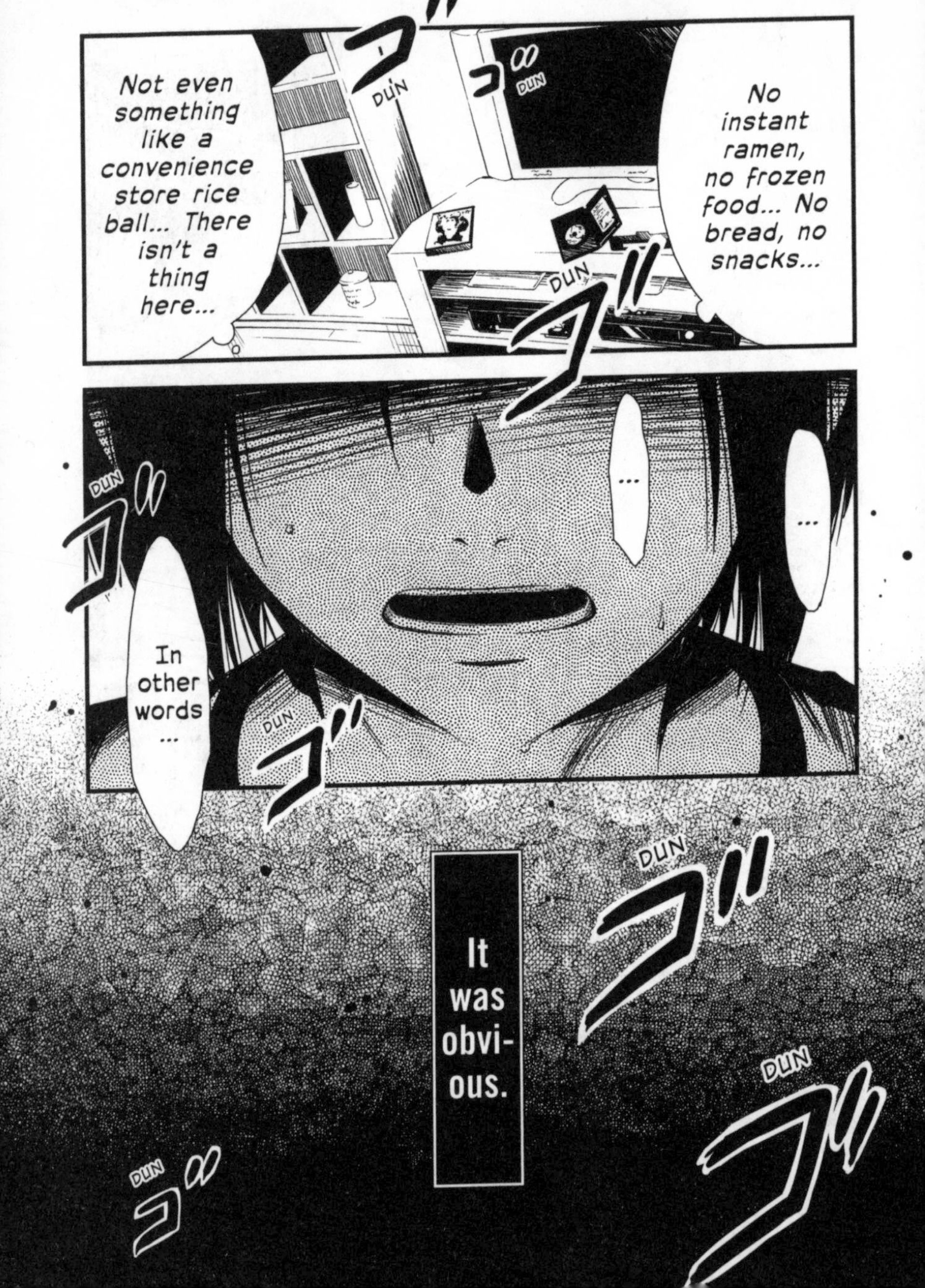
DUN
DUN
No instant ramen, no frozen food... No bread, no snacks...
Not even something like a convenience store rice ball... There isn't a thing here...
DUN
...
...
DUN
In other words ...
DUN
DUN
It was obvi-ous.
DUN
DUN

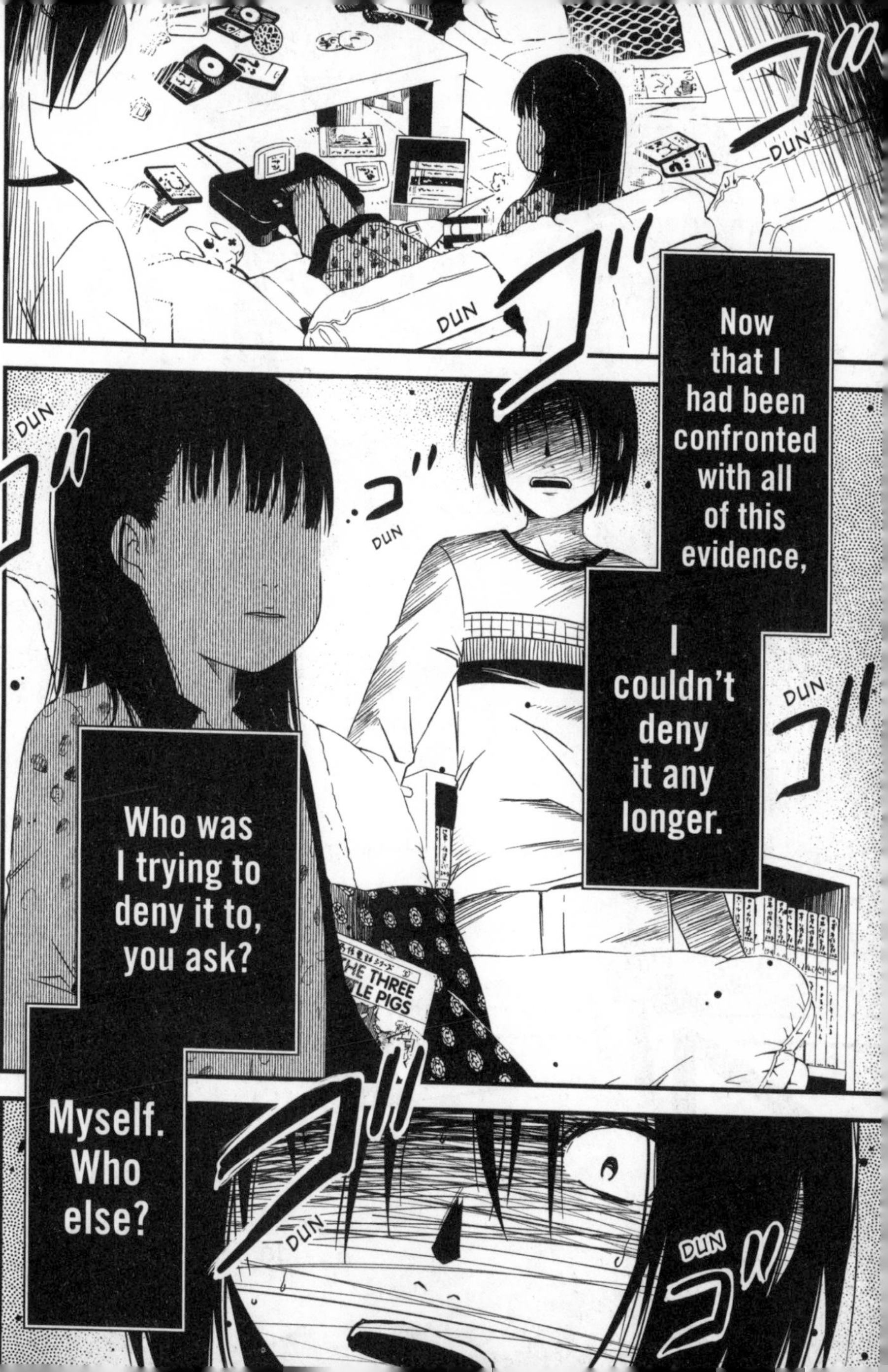
ゴ
DUN
ゴ
DUN
Now that I had been confronted with all of this evidence,
I couldn't deny it any longer.
ゴ
DUN
ゴ
DUN
ゴ
DUN
THE THREE
LE PIGS
Who was I trying to deny it to, you ask?
ゴ
DUN
Myself. Who else?
ゴ
DUN

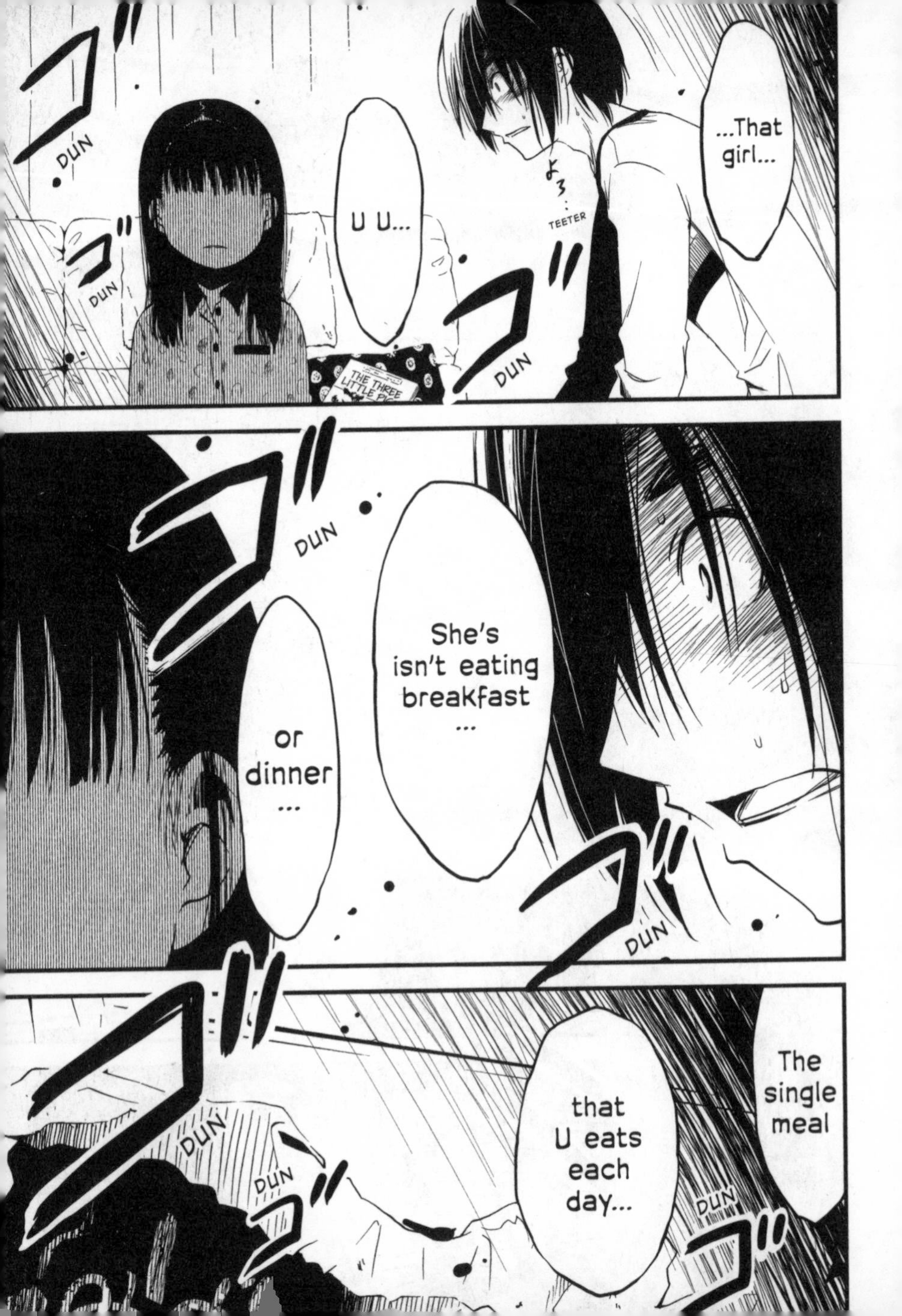
...That girl...
よろ…
TEETER
ゴ
DUN
U U...
ゴ
DUN
ゴ
DUN
She's isn't eating breakfast ...
DUN
ゴ
or dinner ...
ゴ
DUN
The single meal
that U eats each day...
ゴ
DUN
ゴ
DUN
ゴ
DUN

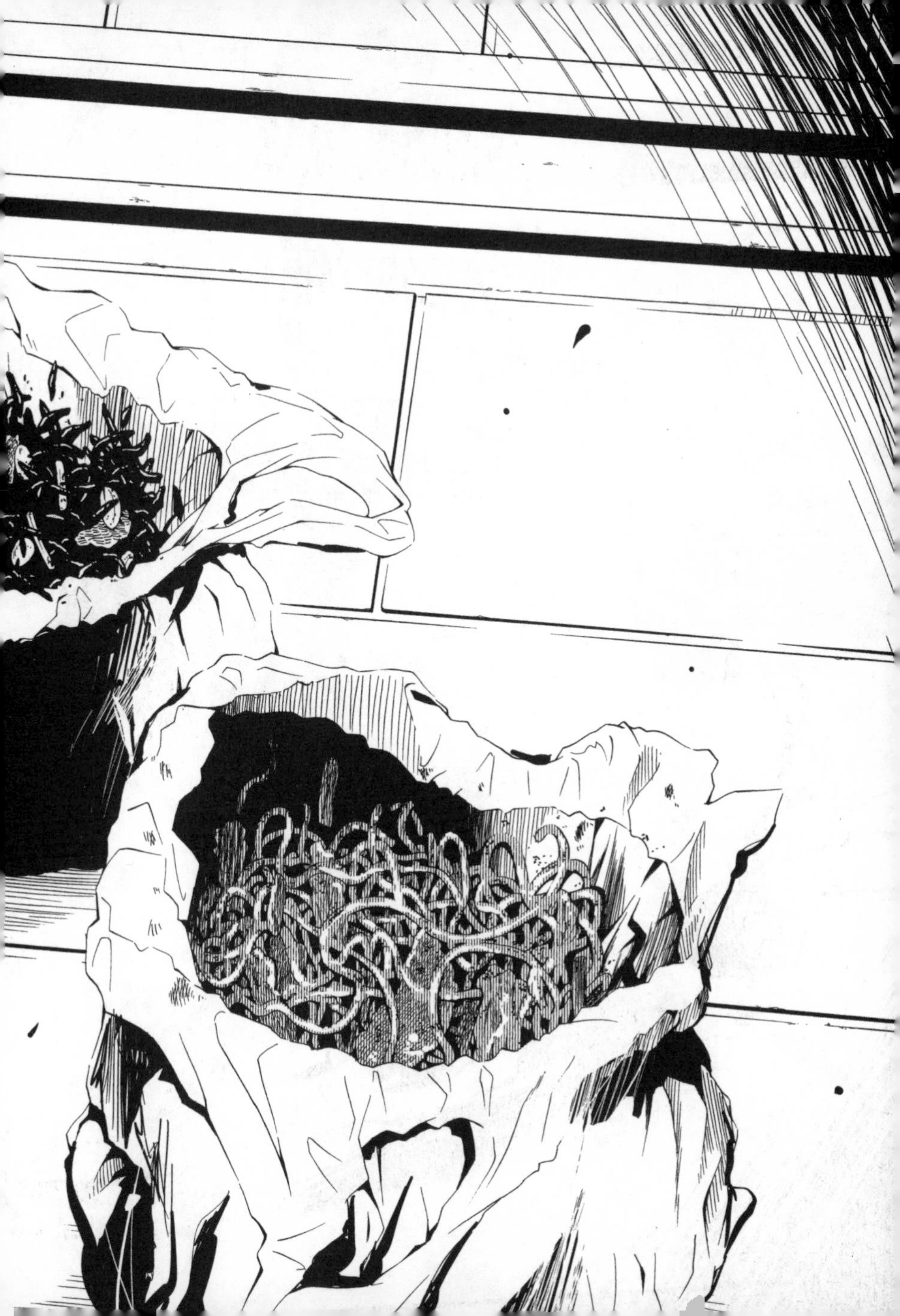

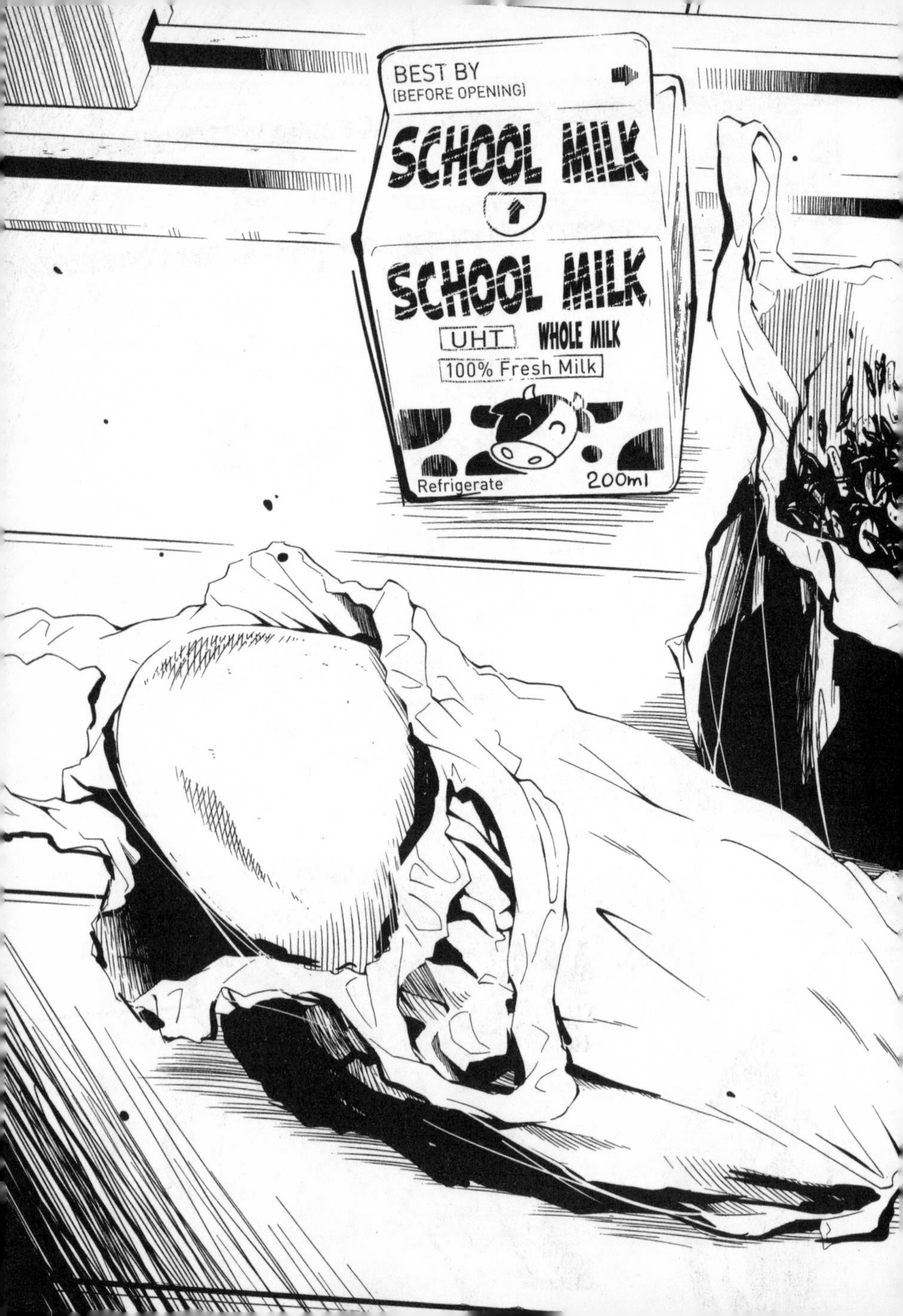
BEST BY
(BEFORE OPENING)
SCHOOL MILK
SCHOOL MILK
UHT
WHOLE MILK
100% Fresh Milk
Refrigerate
200ml

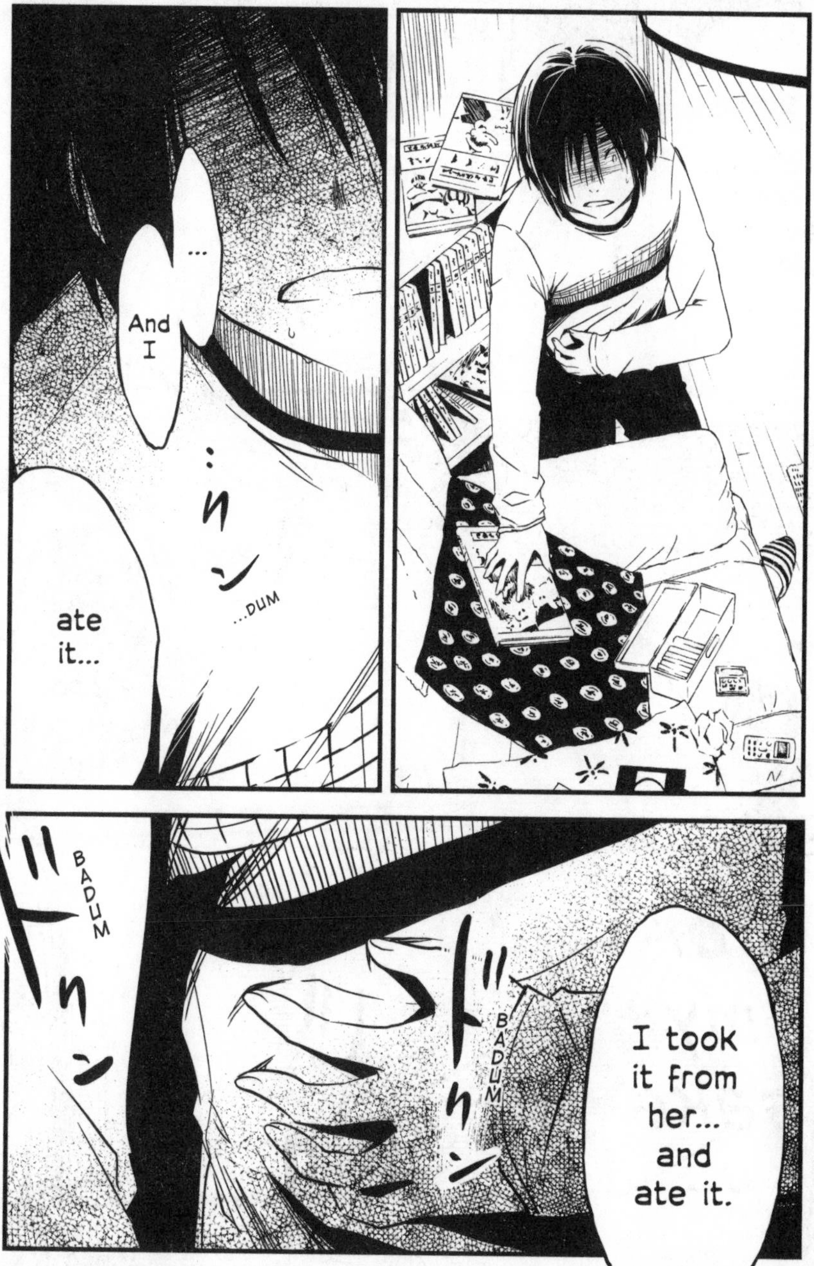
... And I
...DUM
ate it...
I took it from her... and ate it.
BADUM
BADUM

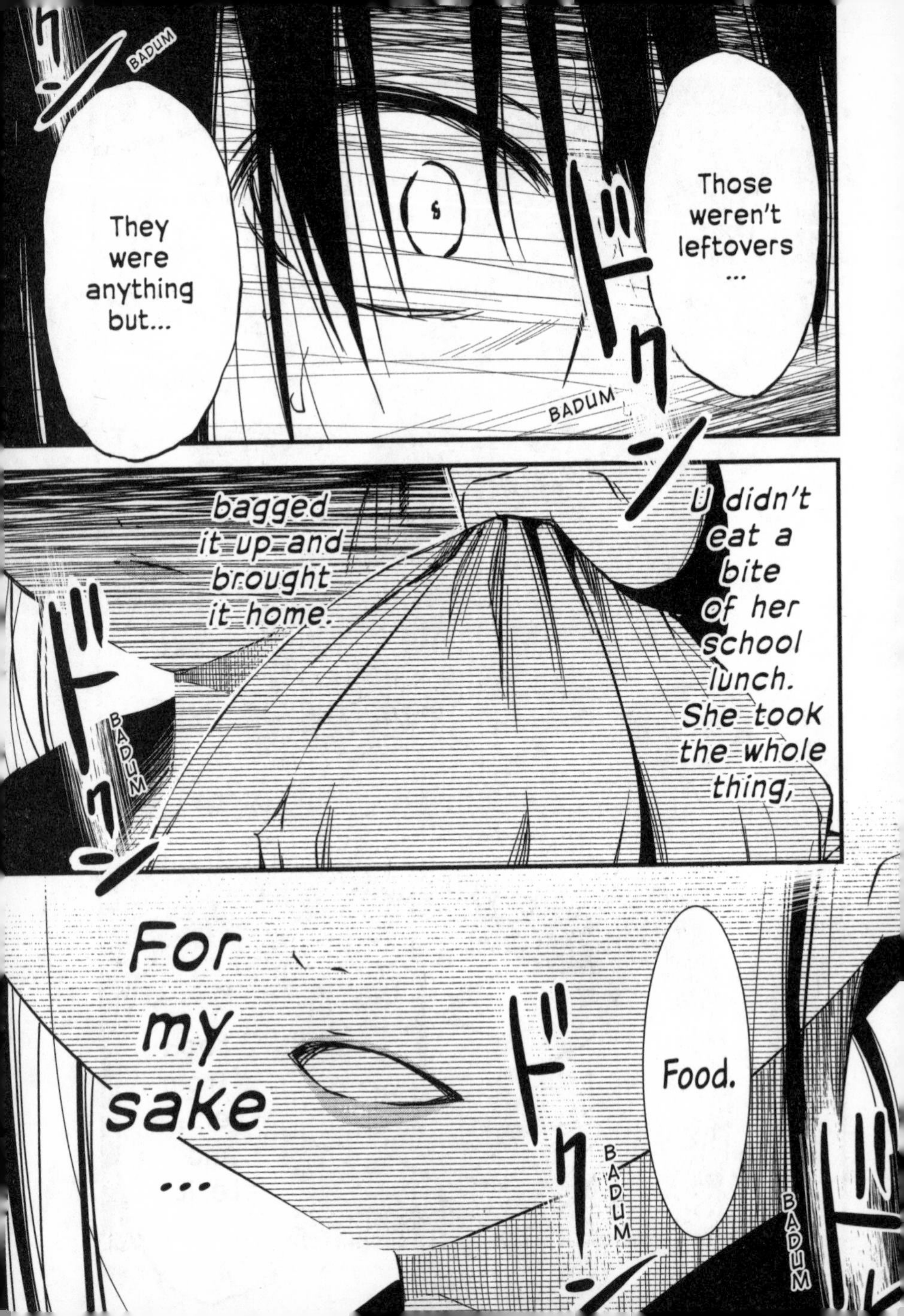
BADUM
Those weren't leftovers ...
They were anything but...
BADUM
U didn't eat a bite of her school lunch. She took the whole thing,
bagged it up and brought it home.
BADUM
BADUM
Food.
BADUM
For my sake ...

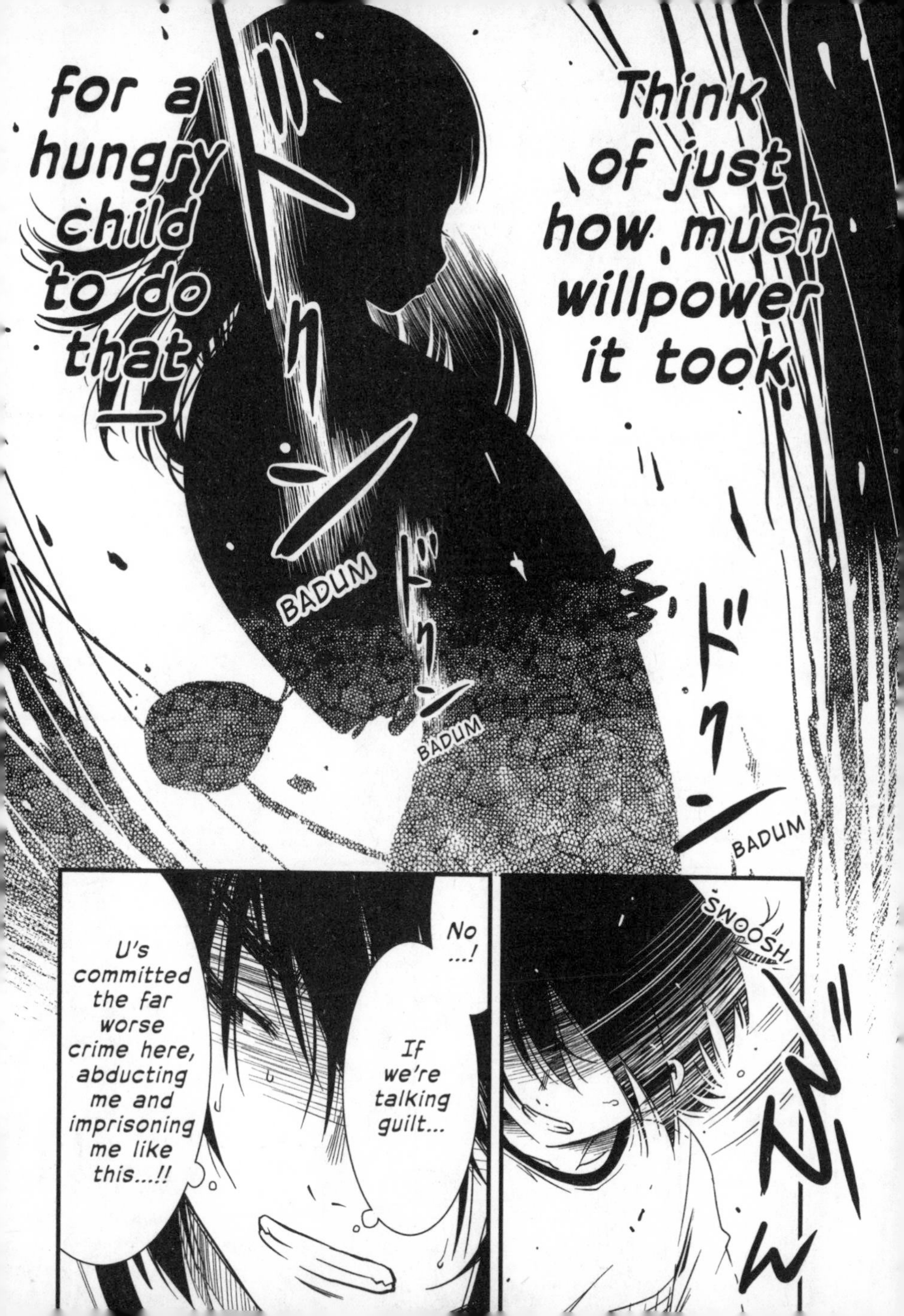

Think of just how much willpower it took.
for a hungry child to do that—
BADUM
BADUM
BADUM
SWOOSH
No ...!
If we're talking guilt...
U's committed the far worse crime here, abducting me and imprisoning me like this...!!

GOONG

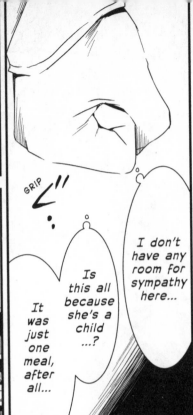

GRIP

I don't have any room for sympathy here...

Is this all because she's a child ...?

It was just one meal, after all...

Ah

what if it turns into two meals...?

GOONG

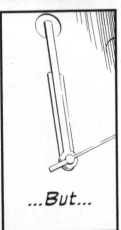

...But...

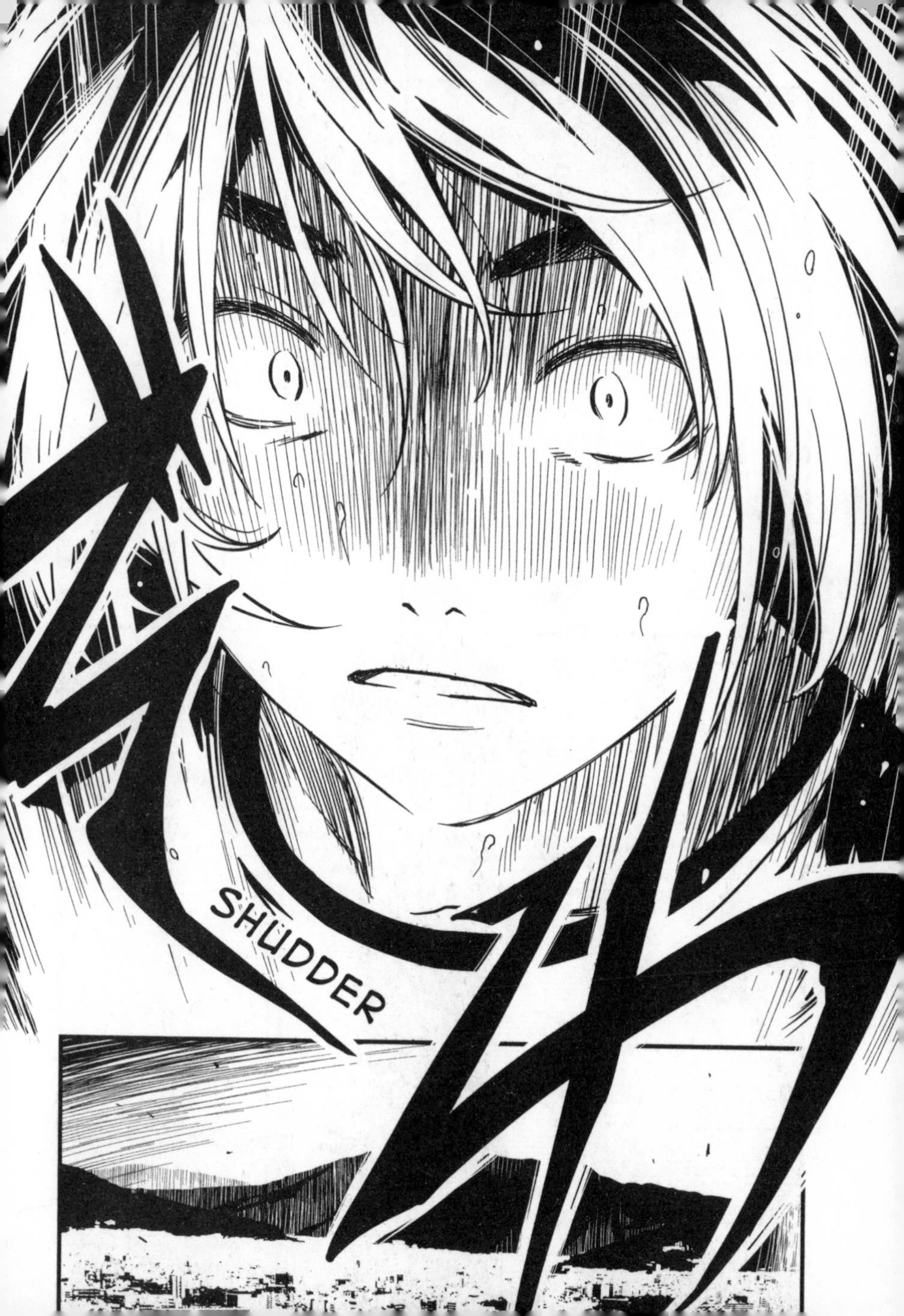
SHUDDER

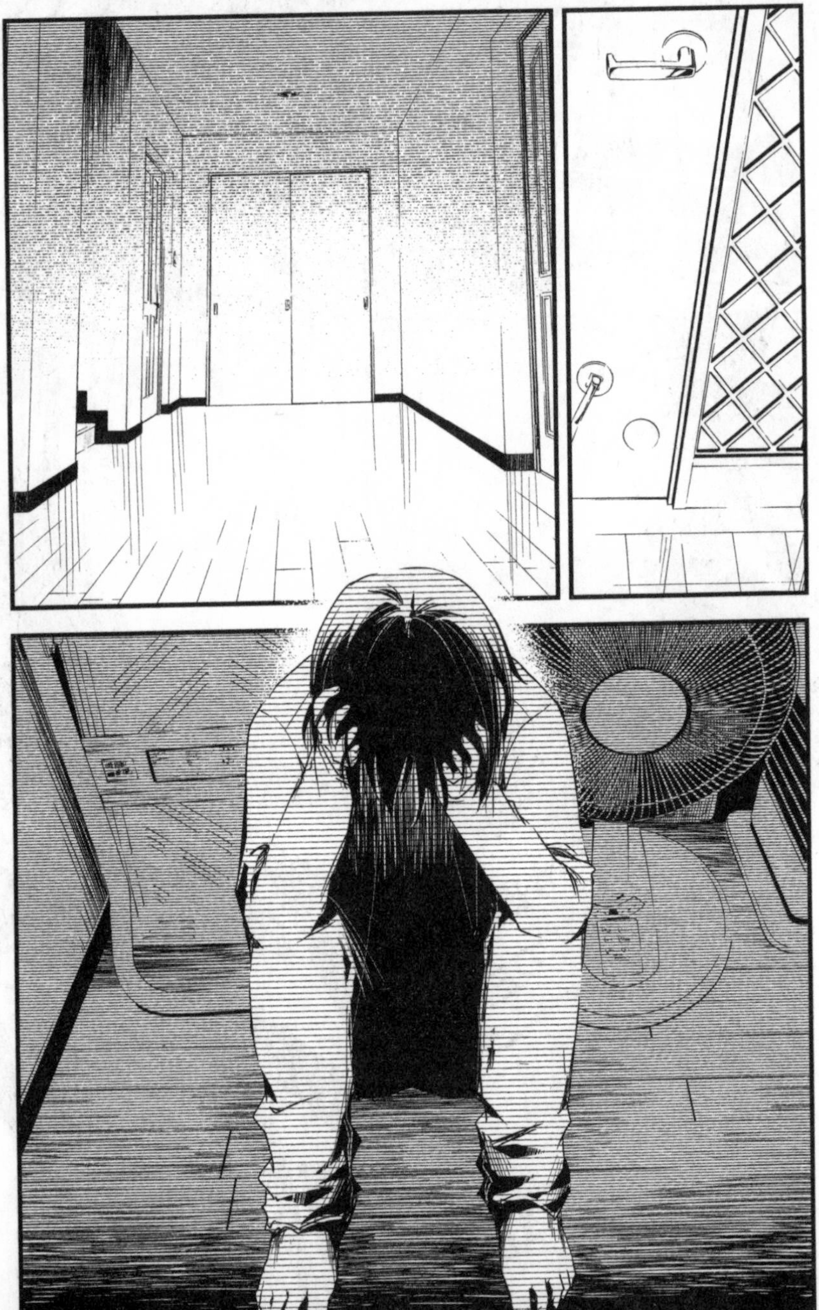

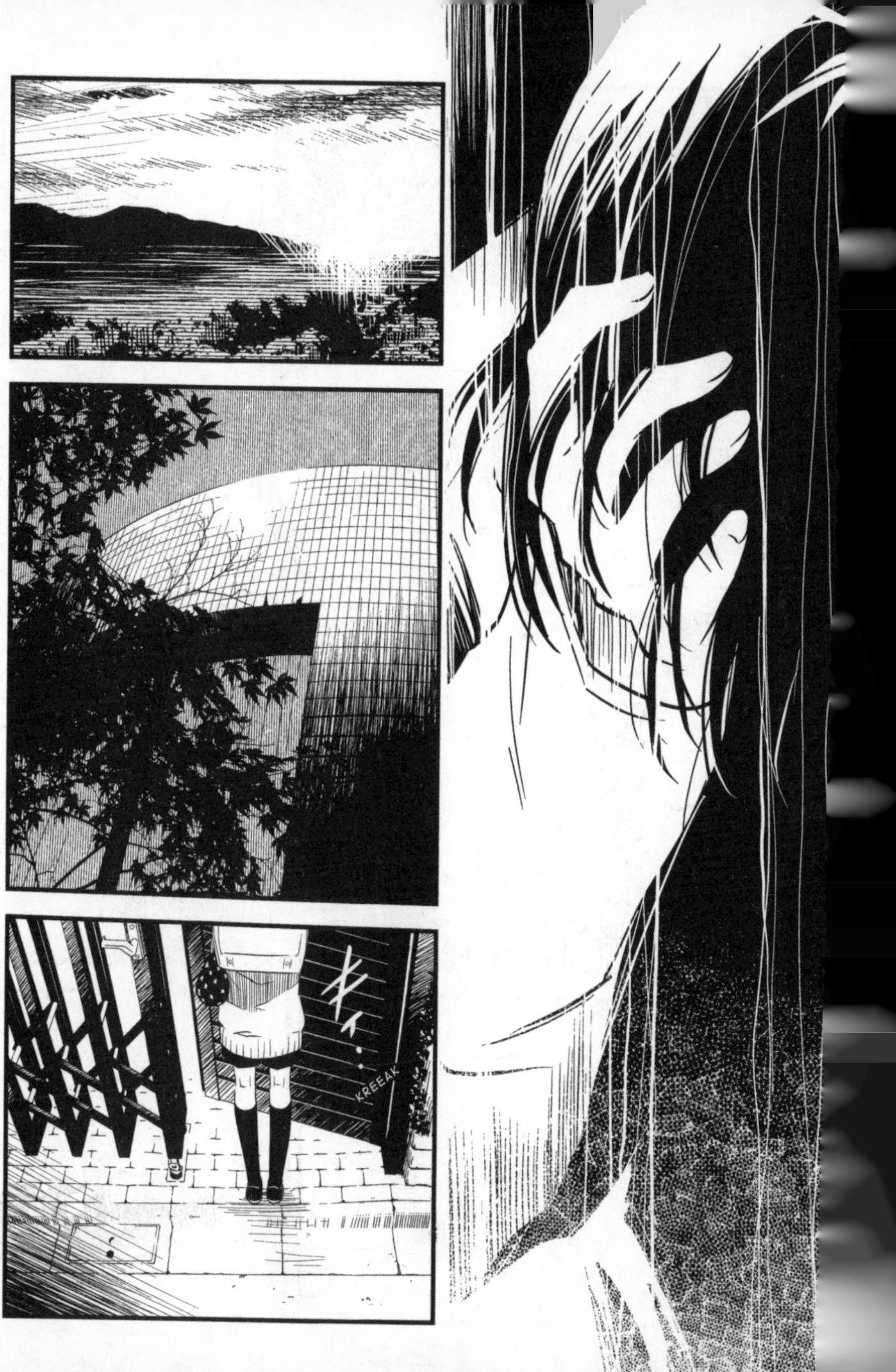
KREEAK

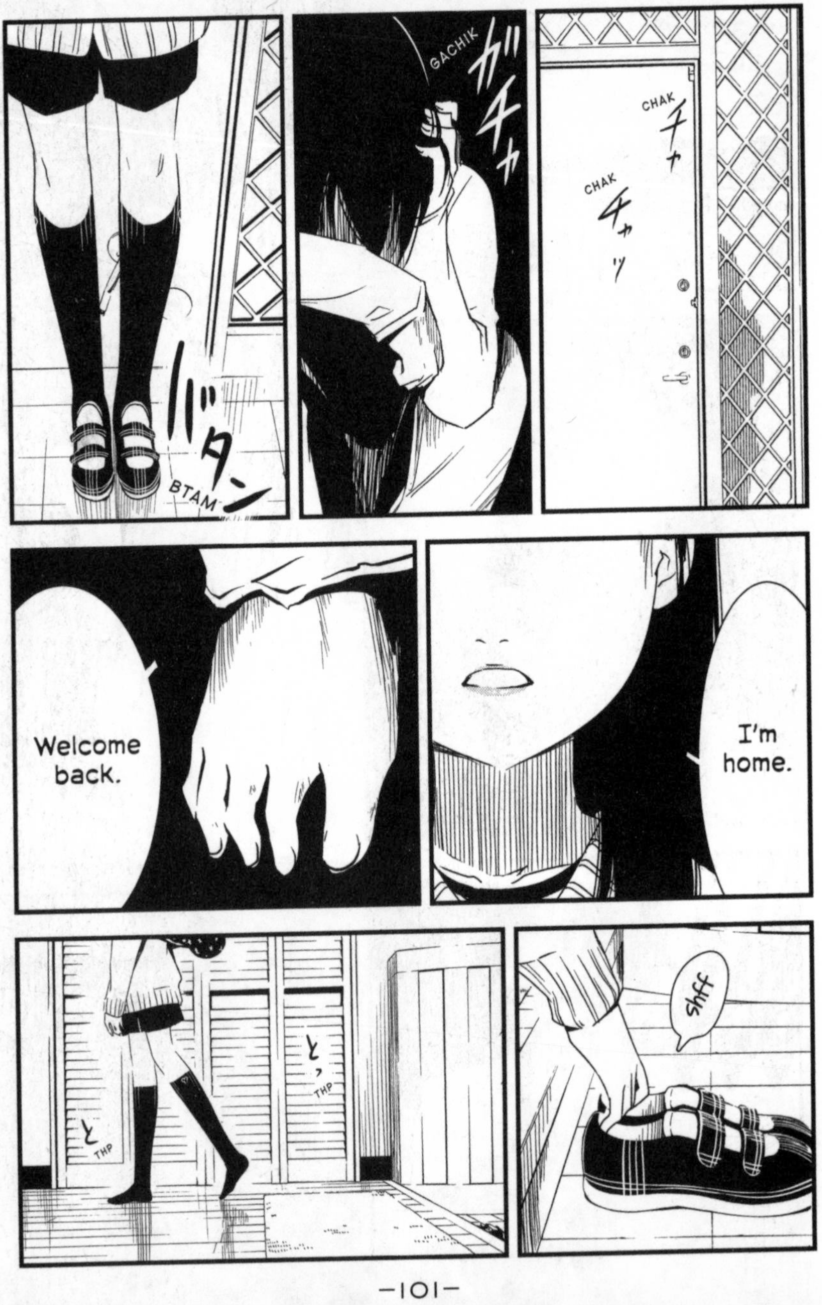
CHAK
チャ
CHAK
チャッ
GACHIK
ガチャ
バタン
BTAM
I'm home.
Welcome back.
shff
と
THP
と
THP

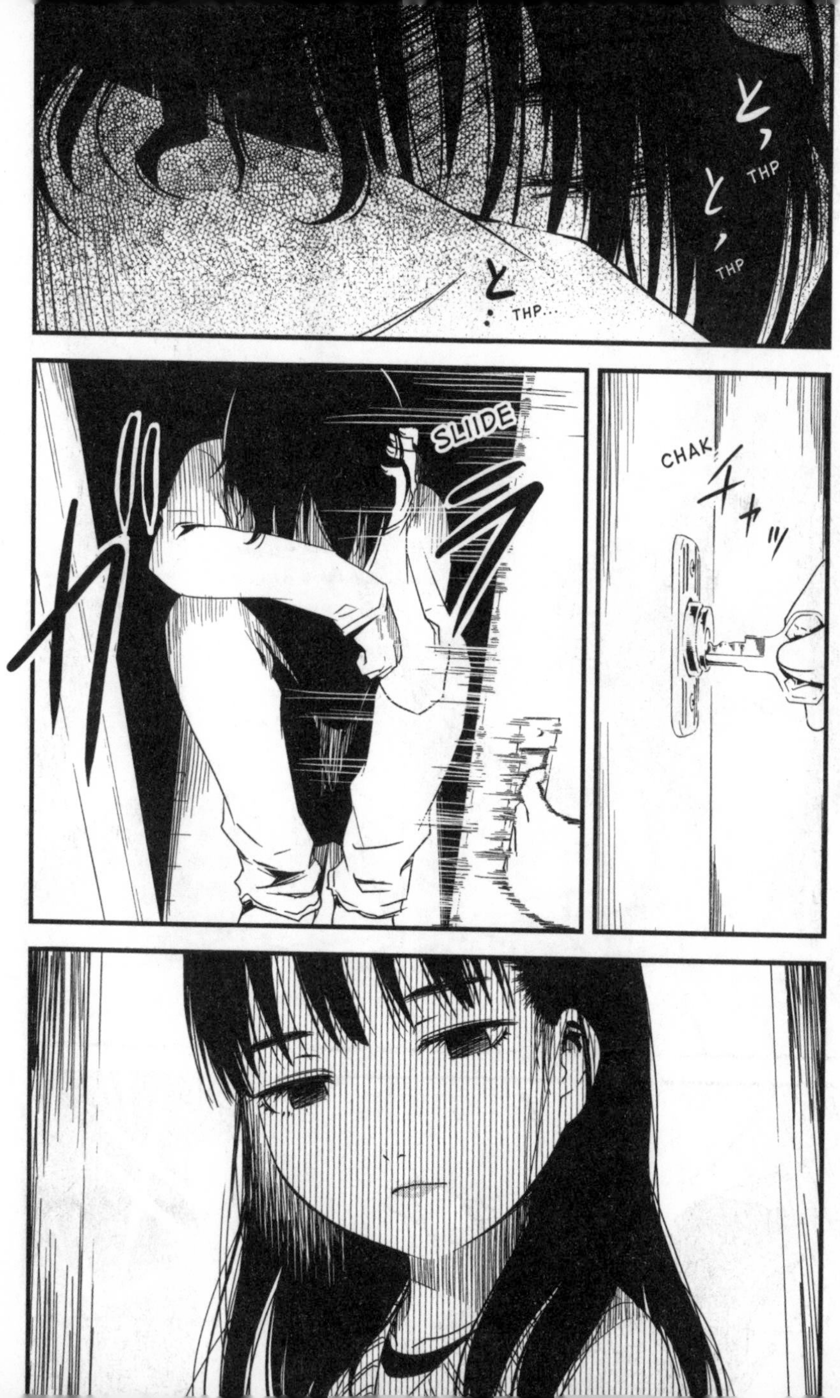

とっ
THP
と、
THP
と…
THP...
CHAK
チャッ
SLIIDE
ガラ

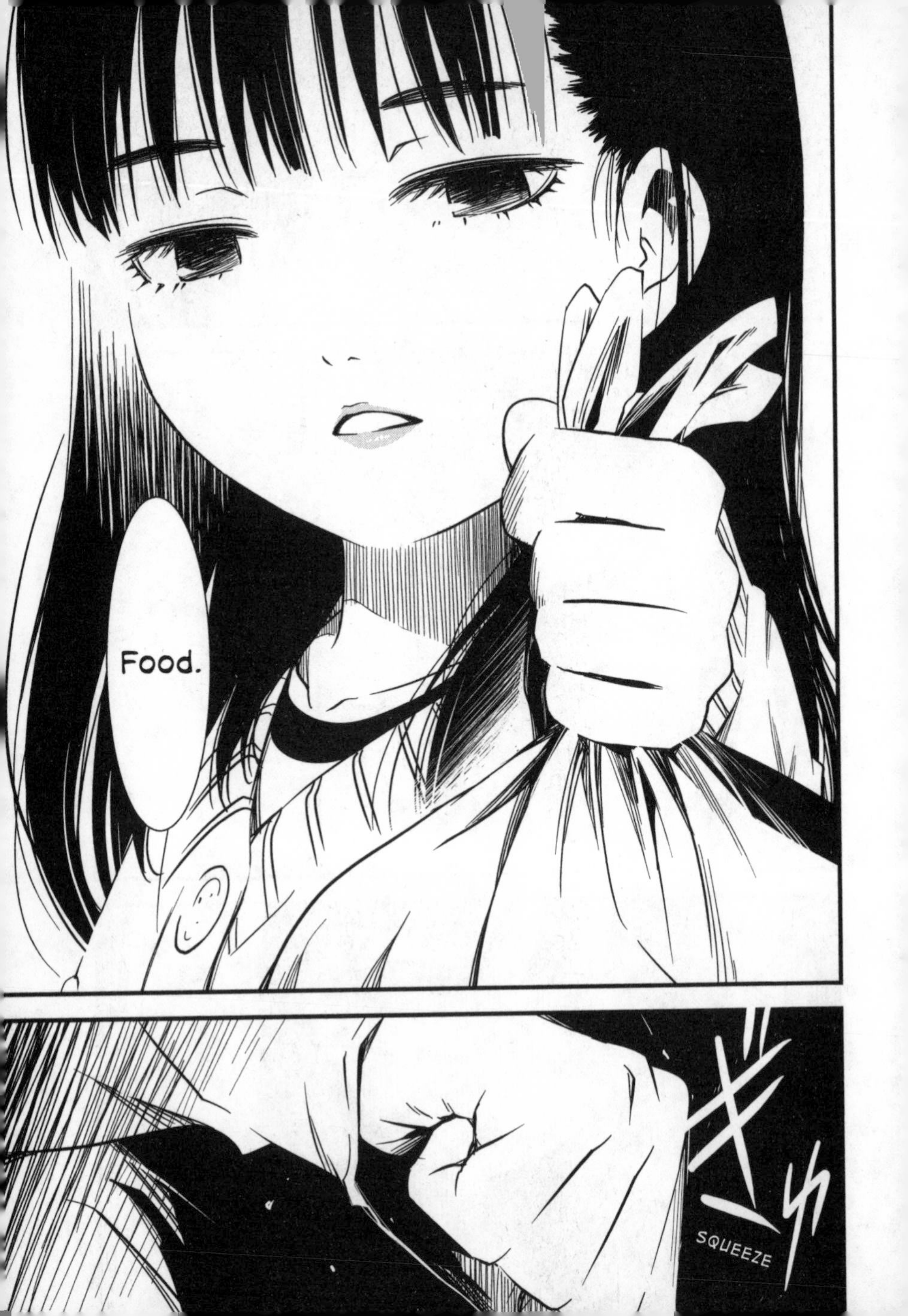
Food.
SQUEEZE

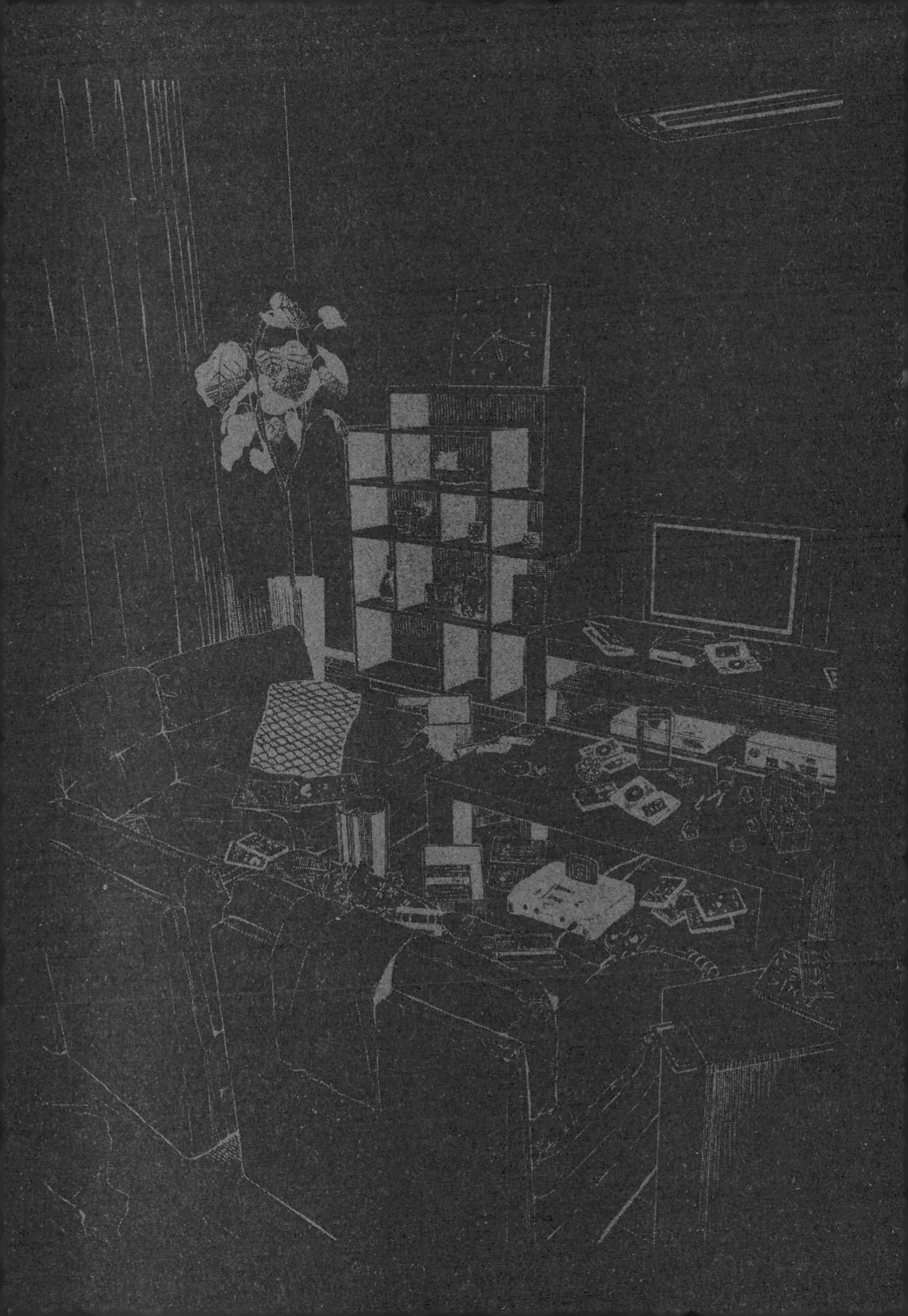

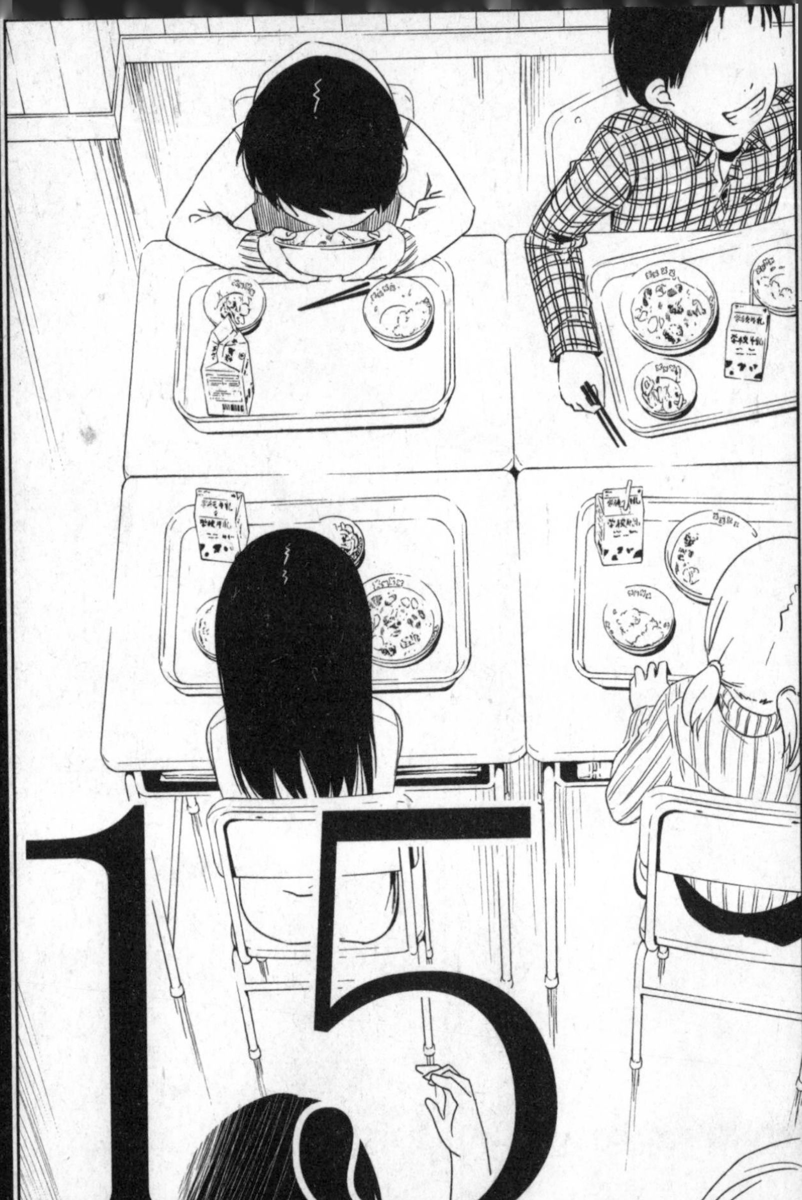
15

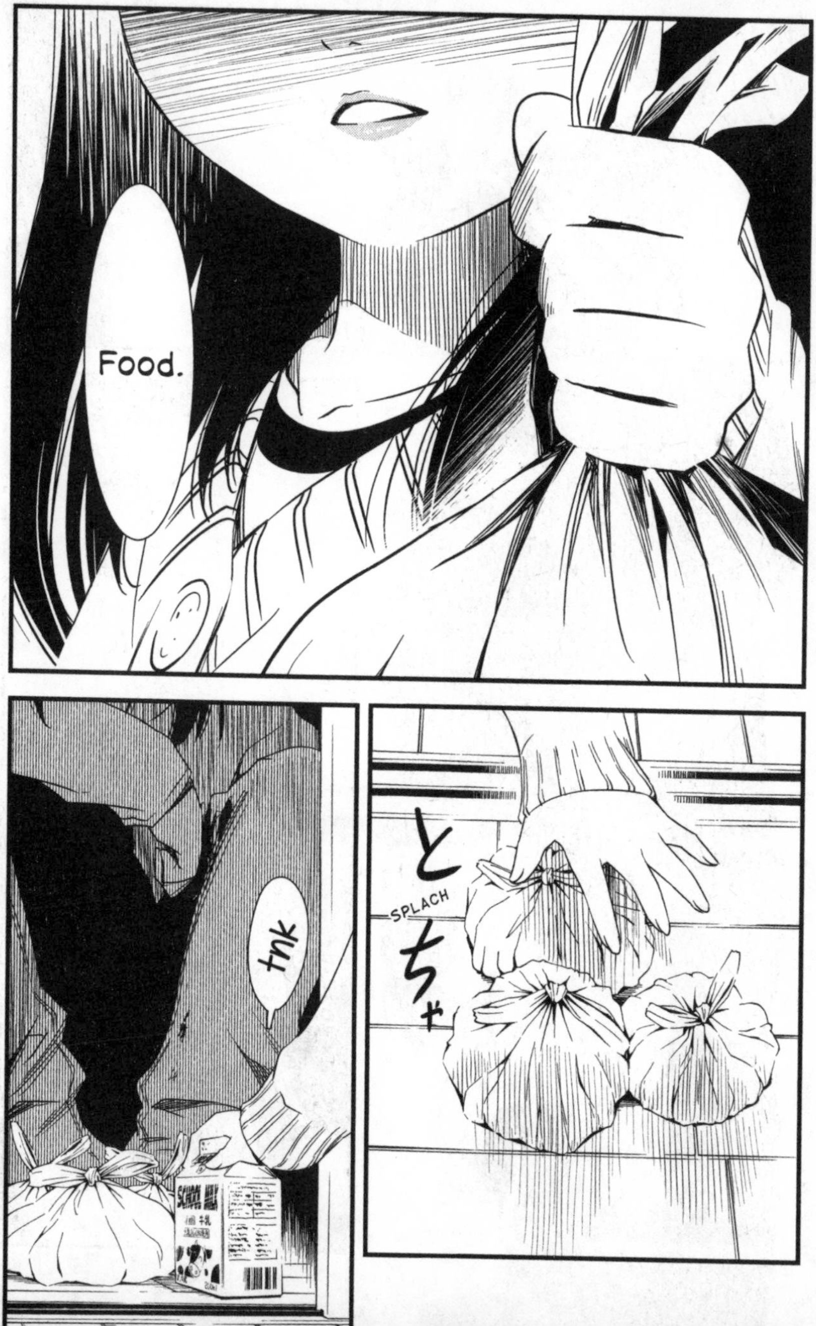
Food.
とちゃ
SPLACH
tnk

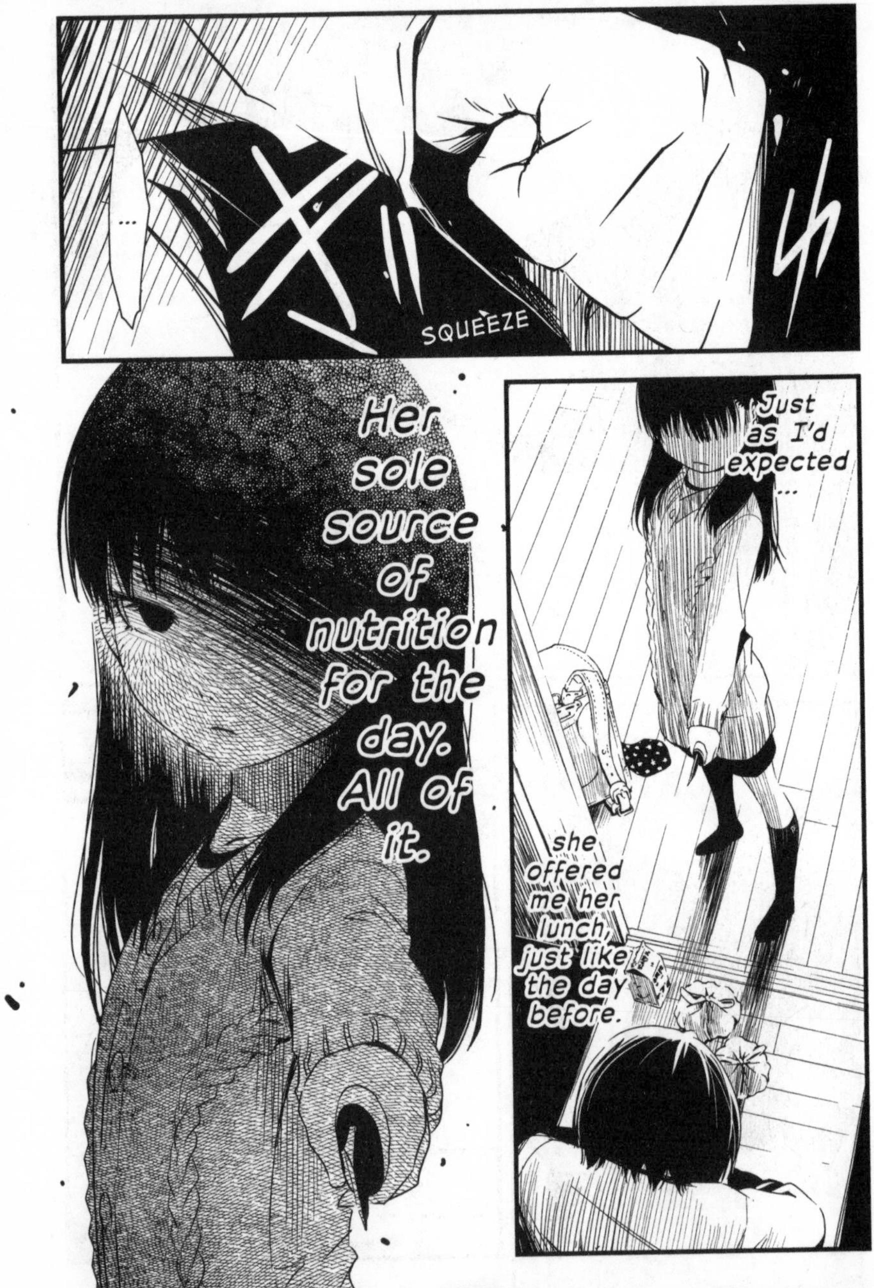
SQUEEZE
...
Just as I'd expected...
she offered me her lunch, just like the day before.
Her sole source of nutrition for the day. All of it.

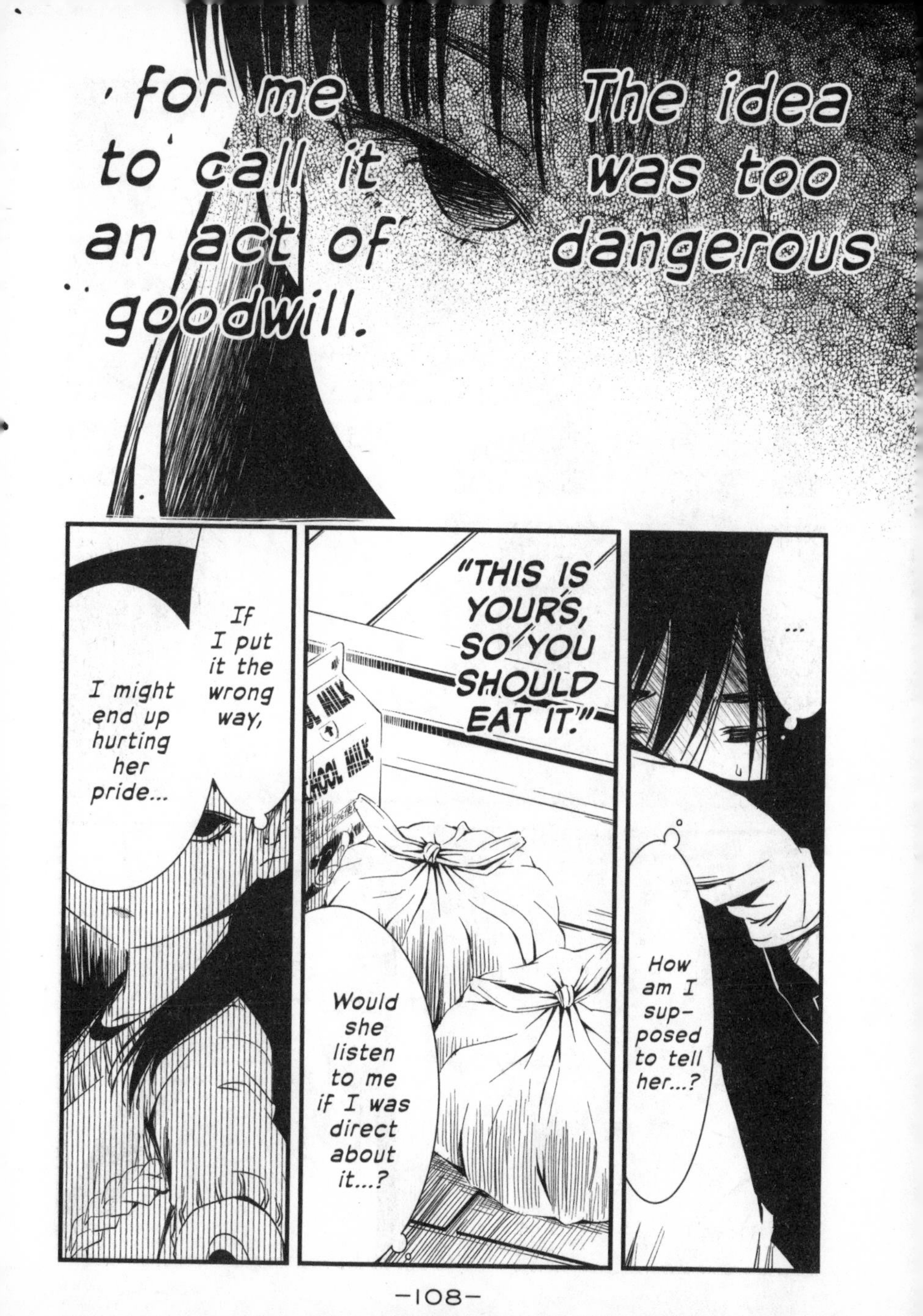
The idea was too dangerous
for me to call it an act of goodwill.
...
How am I sup-posed to tell her...?
"THIS IS YOURS, SO YOU SHOULD EAT IT."
Would she listen to me if I was direct about it...?
If I put it the wrong way,
I might end up hurting her pride...

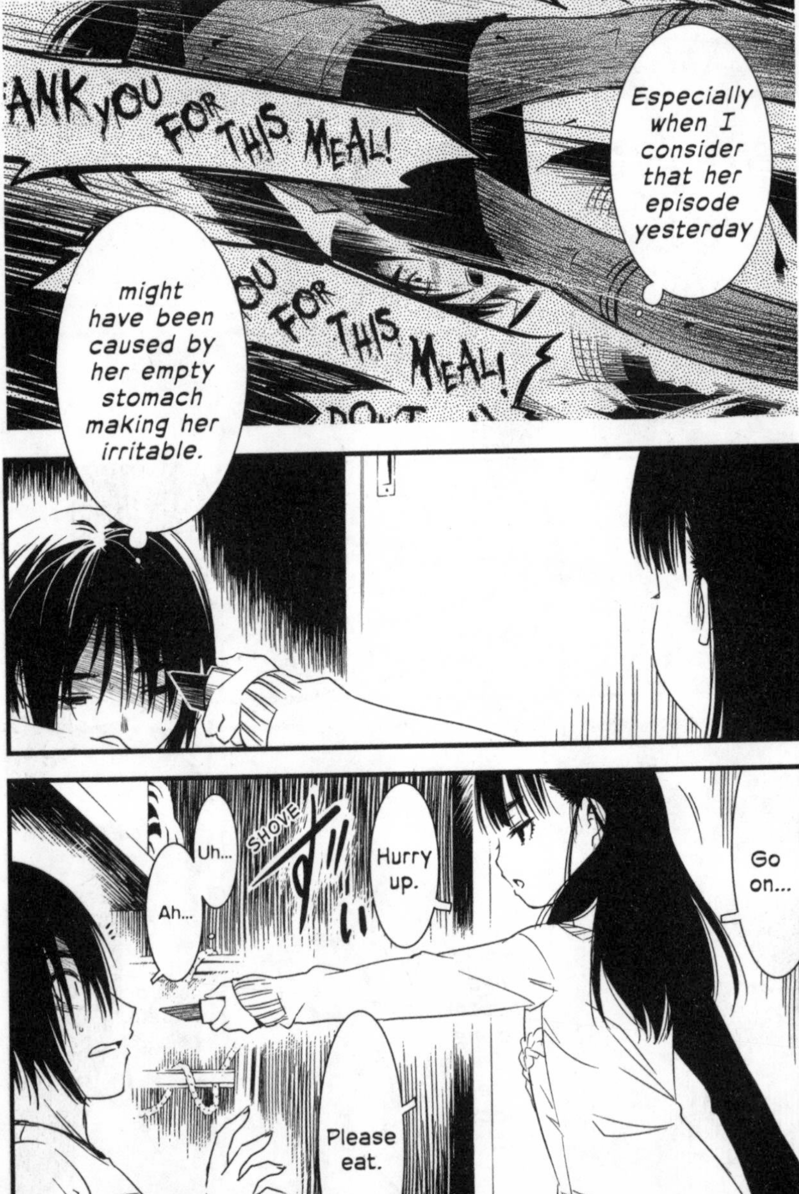
Especially when I consider that her episode yesterday
ANK YOU FOR THIS MEAL!
YOU FOR THIS MEAL!
might have been caused by her empty stomach making her irritable.
Go on...
Hurry up.
SHOVE
Uh...
Ah...
Please eat.

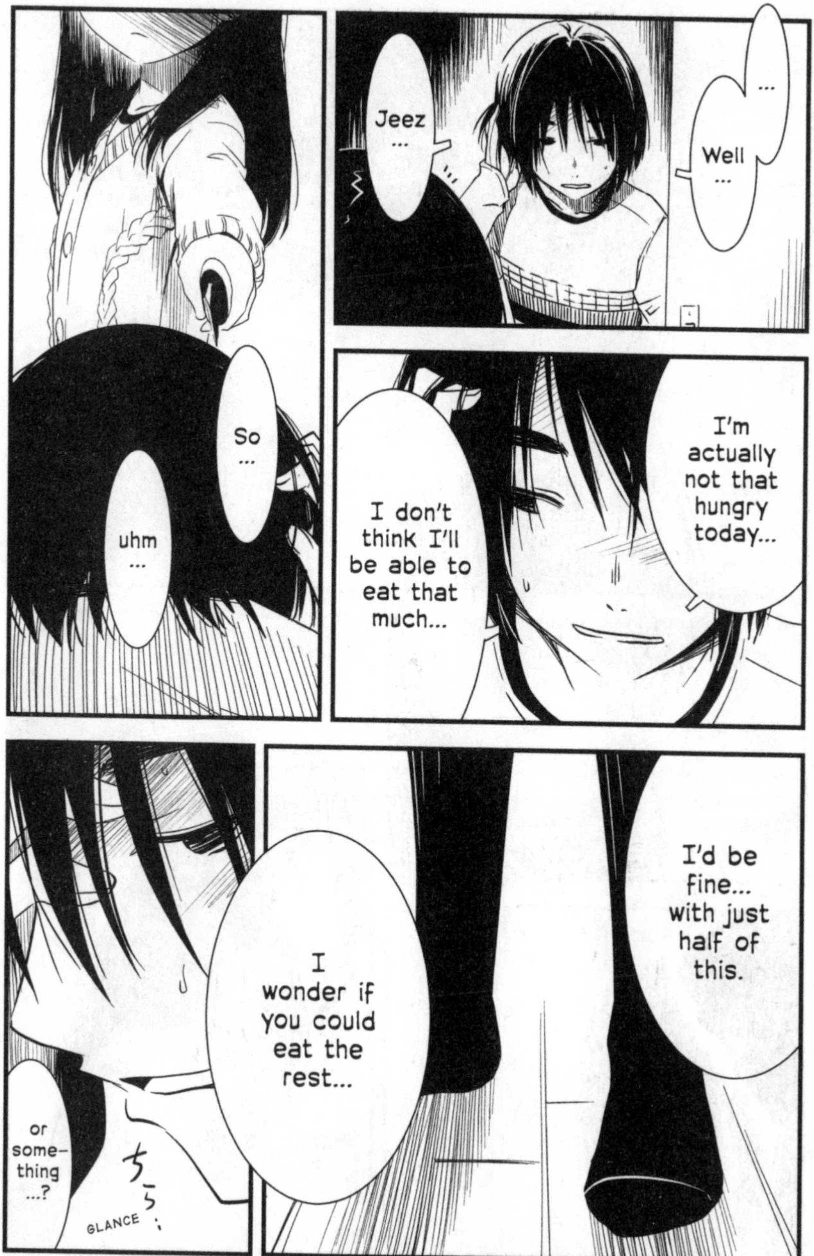
...
Well ...
Jeez ...
I'm actually not that hungry today...
I don't think I'll be able to eat that much...
So ...
uhm ...
I'd be fine... with just half of this.
I wonder if you could eat the rest...
or some-thing ...?
ちら
GLANCE

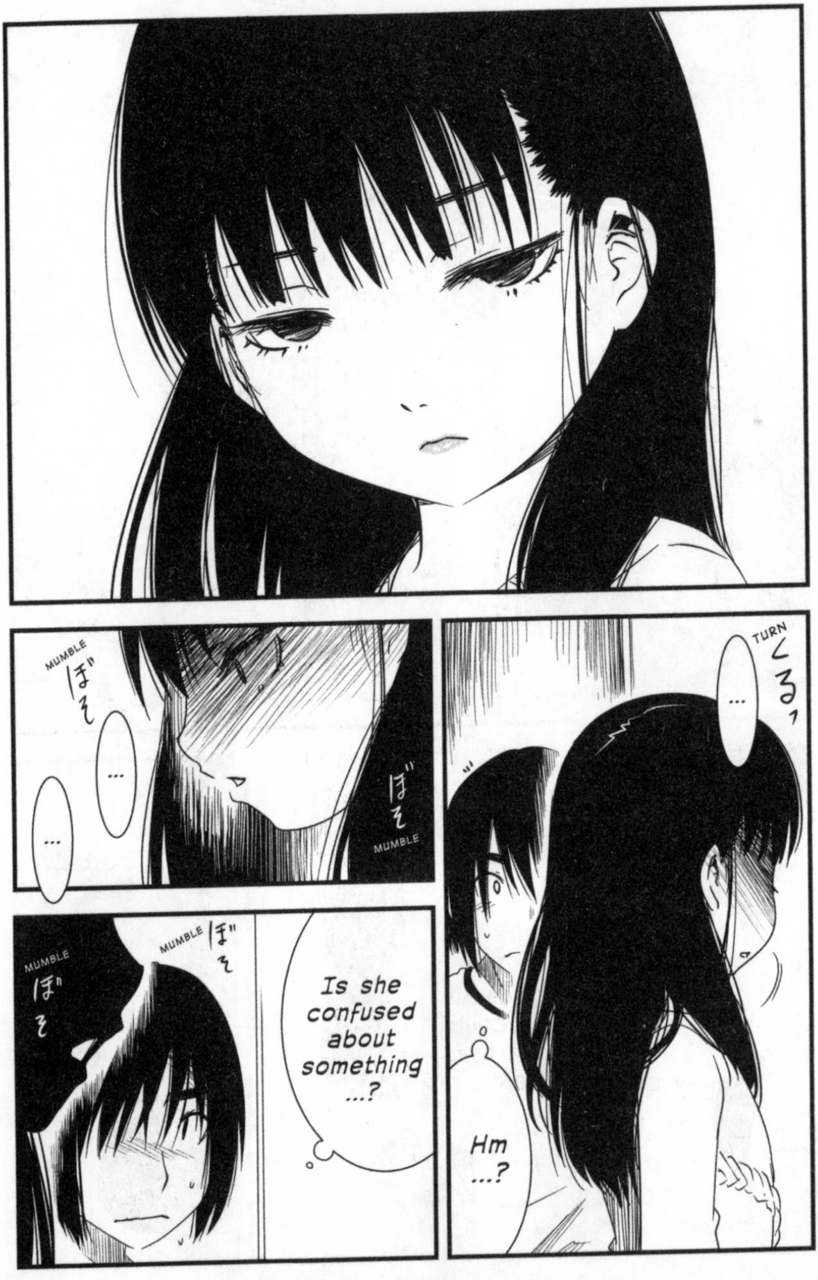
TURN
くる
...
Hm ...?
ぼそ
MUMBLE
...
...
MUMBLE
ぼそ
Is she confused about something ...?
MUMBLE
ぼそ
MUMBLE
ぼそ

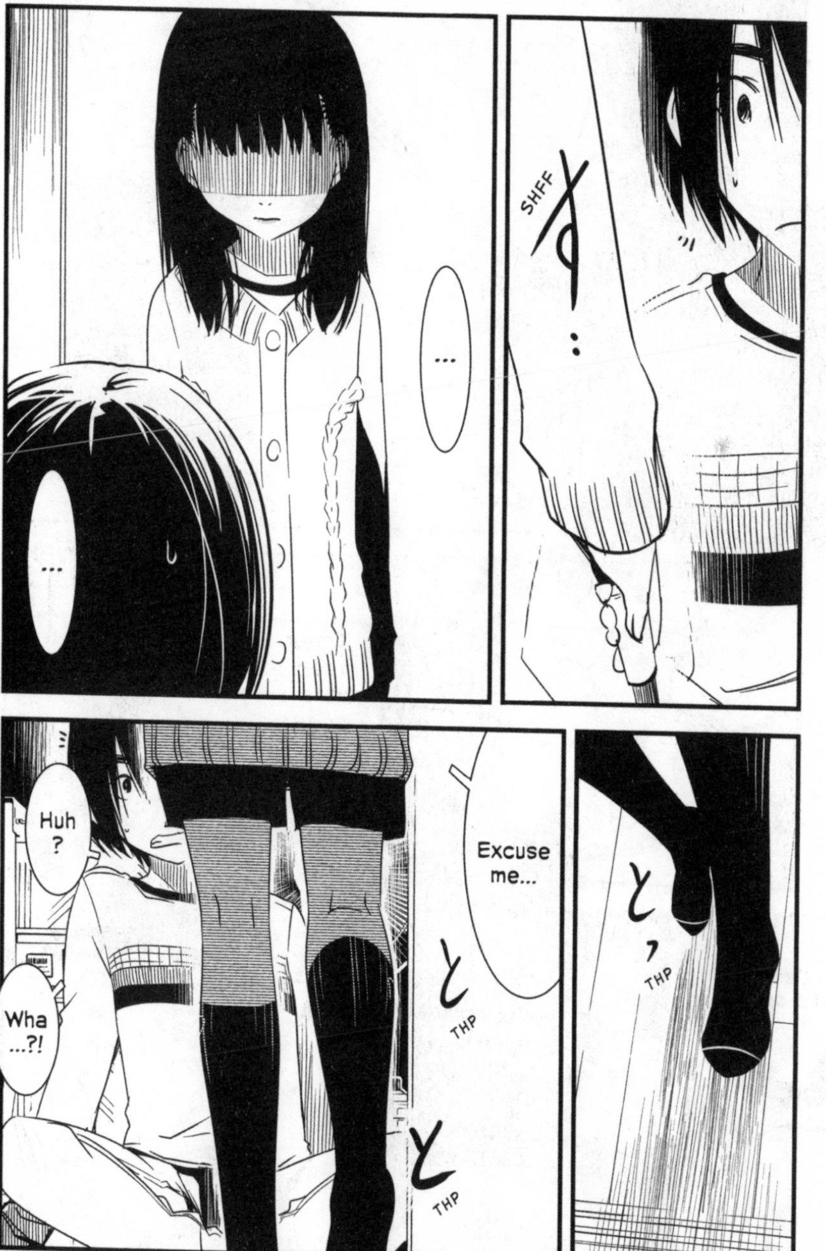

す
SHFF
...
...
と
THP
Excuse me...
と
THP
と
THP
Huh?
Wha...?!

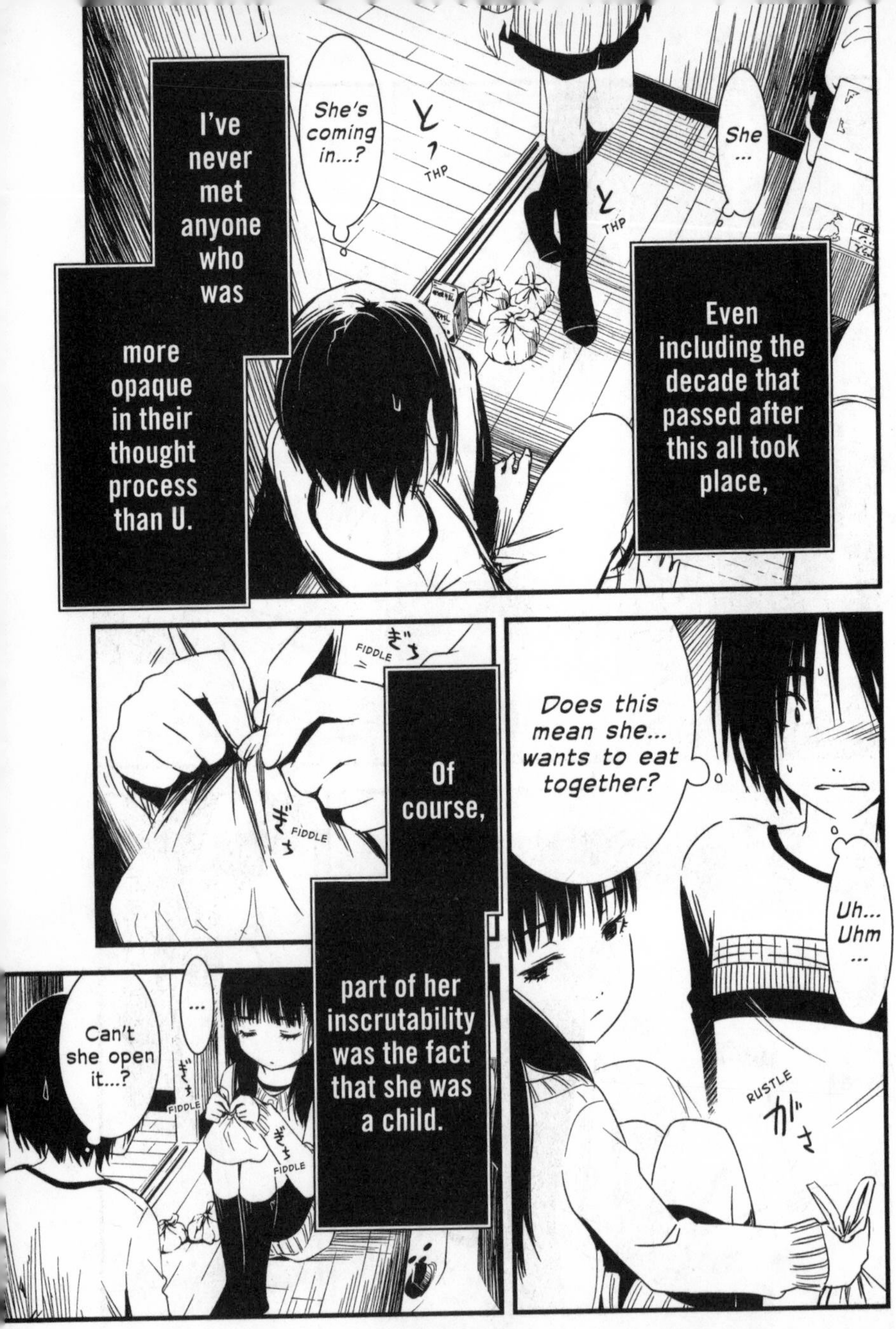
She ...
Even including the decade that passed after this all took place,
THP
She's coming in...?
THP
I've never met anyone who was more opaque in their thought process than U.
Does this mean she... wants to eat together?
Uh... Uhm ...
RUSTLE
FIDDLE
Of course,
FIDDLE
part of her inscrutability was the fact that she was a child.
...
FIDDLE
FIDDLE
Can't she open it...?

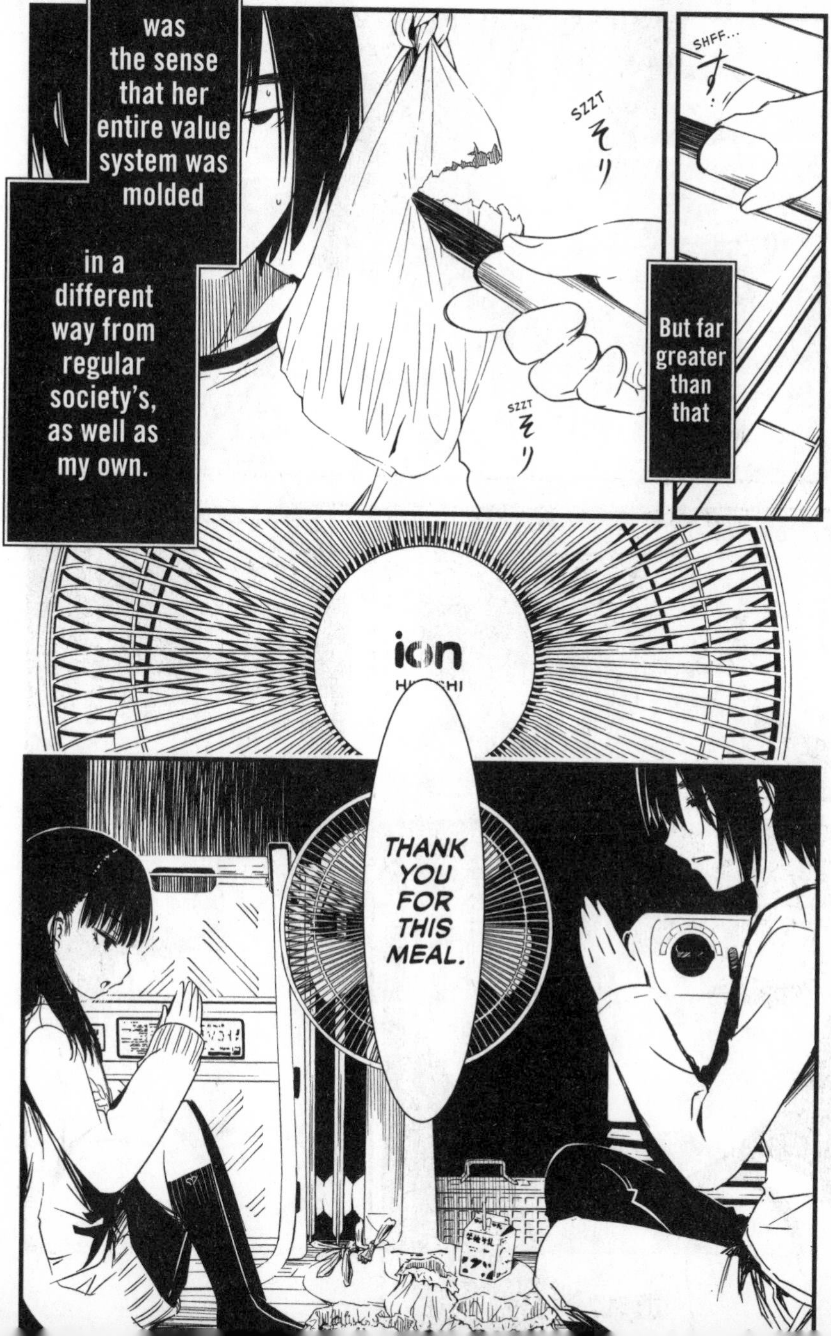
SHFF...
す
But far greater than that
SZZT
そり
was the sense that her entire value system was molded
in a different way from regular society's, as well as my own.
SZZT
そり
THANK YOU FOR THIS MEAL.

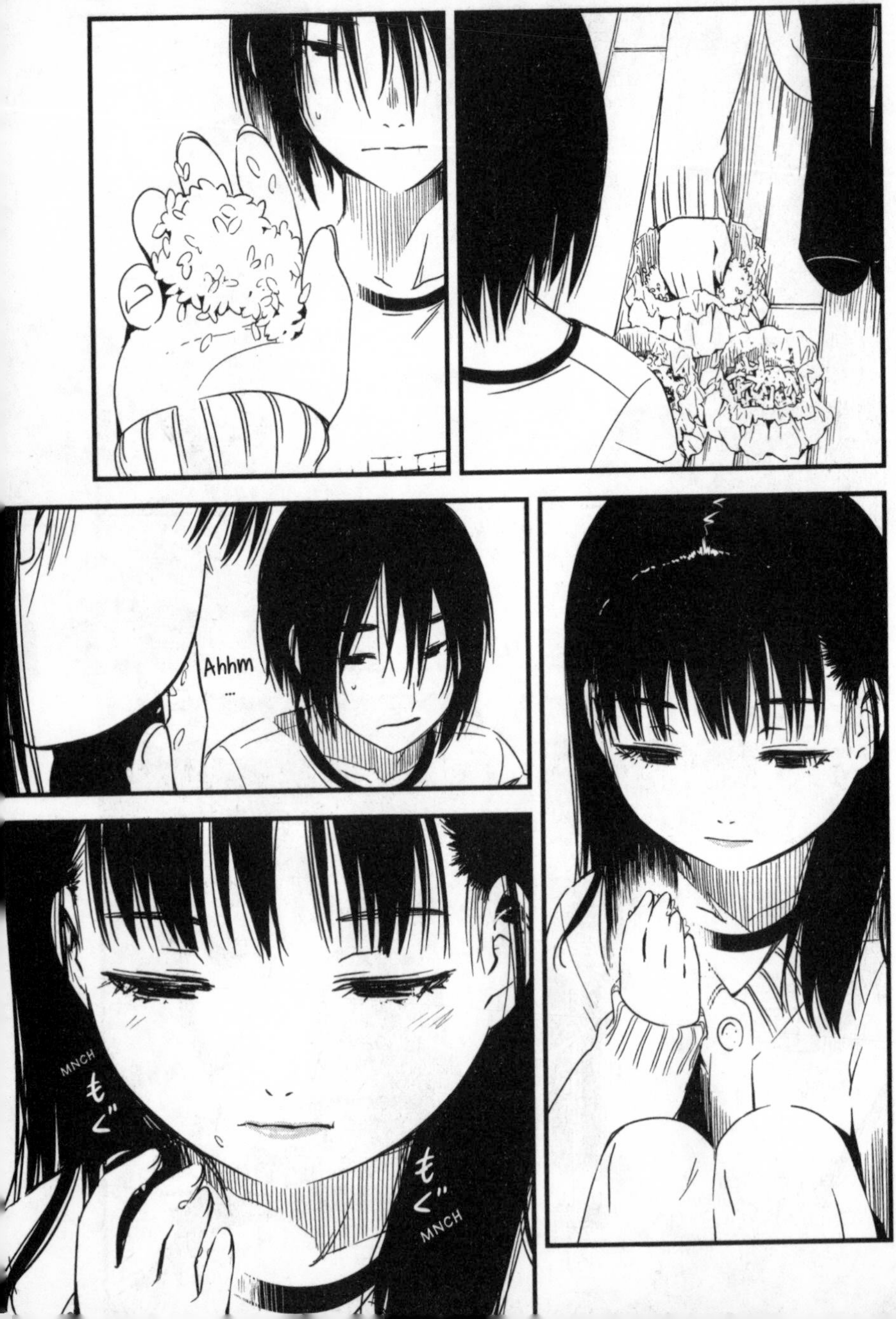
Ahhm
...
MNCH
もぐ
もぐ
MNCH

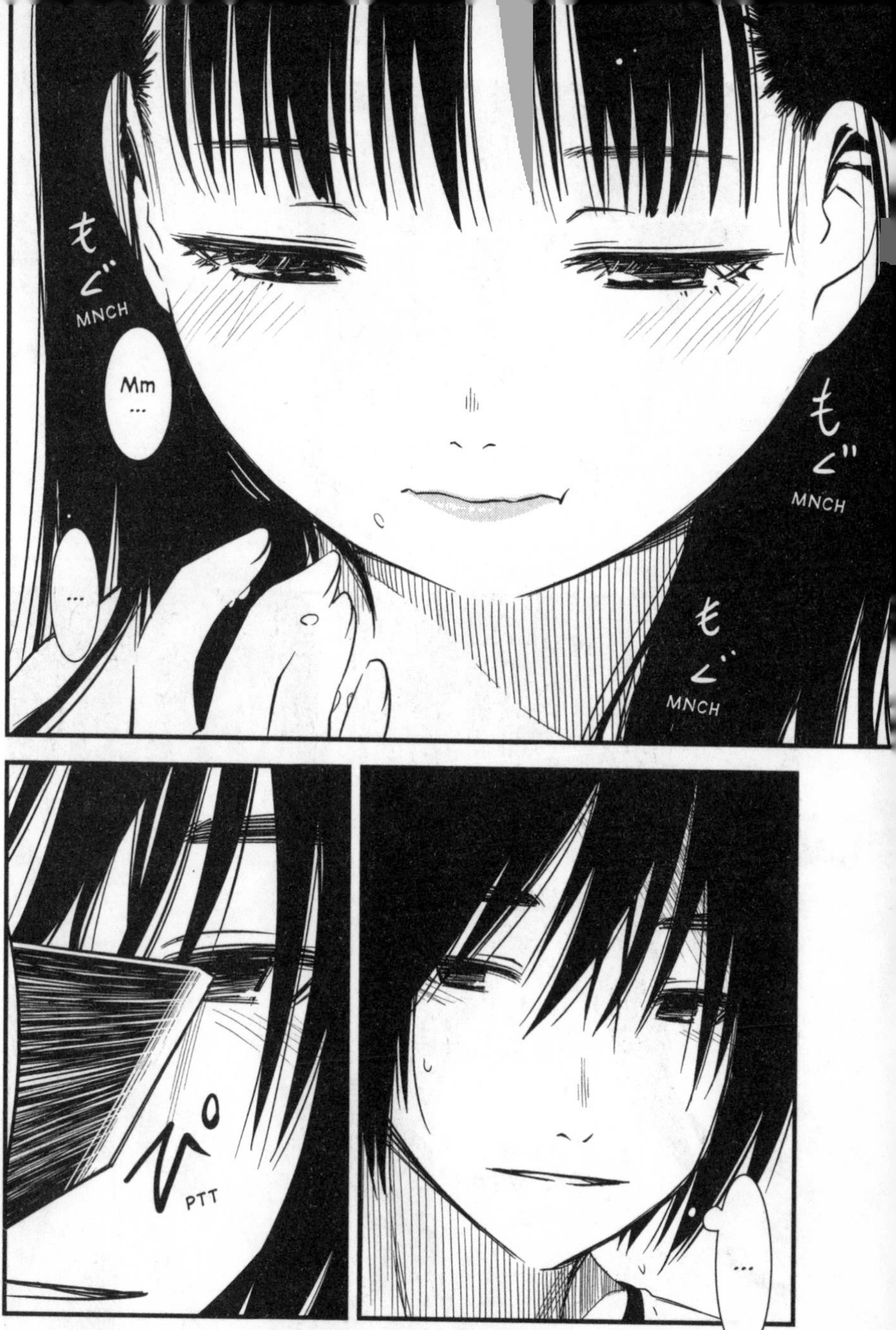

もぐ
MNCH
もぐ
MNCH
もぐ
MNCH
Mm ...
...
...
ぴ
PTT

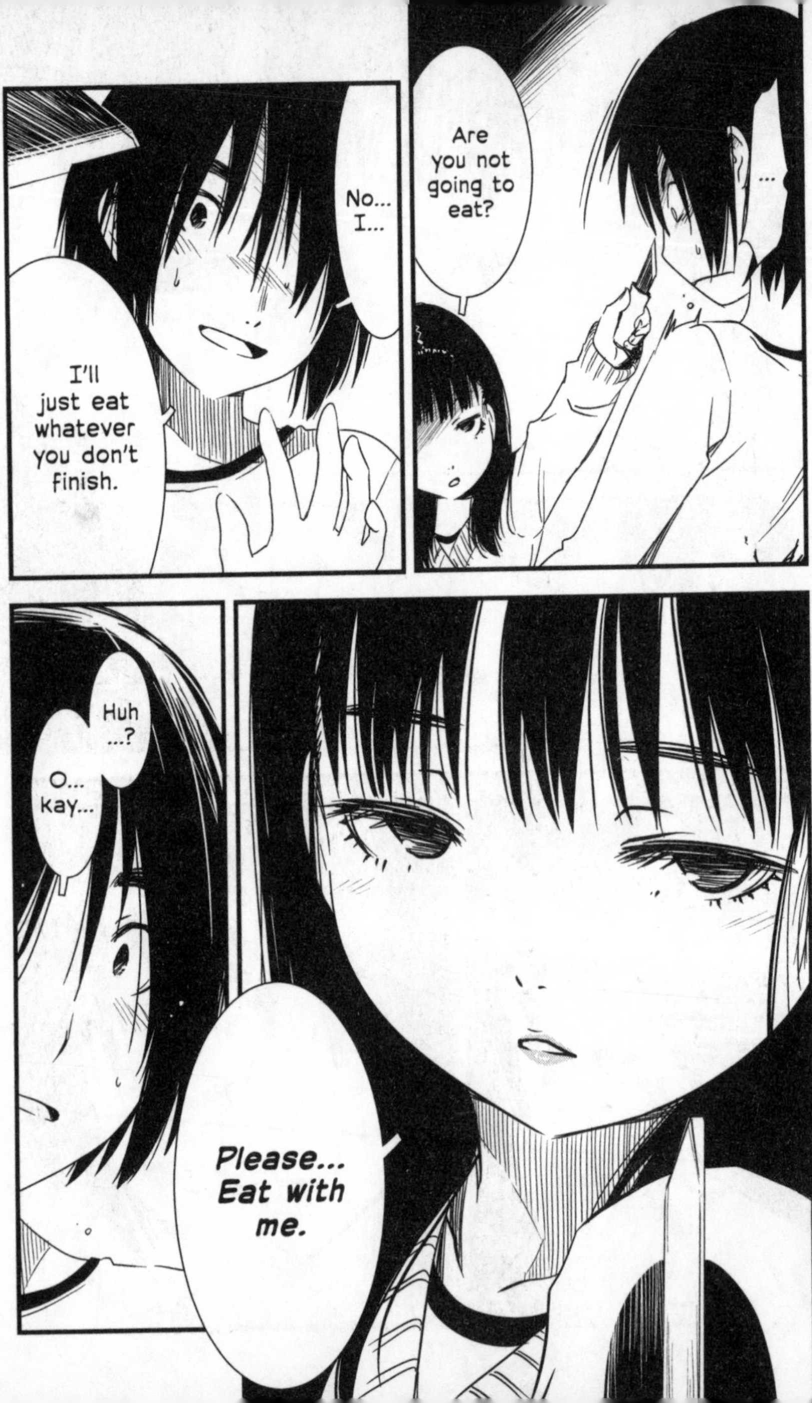
...
Are you not going to eat?
No... I...
I'll just eat whatever you don't finish.
Please... Eat with me.
Huh ...?
O... kay...

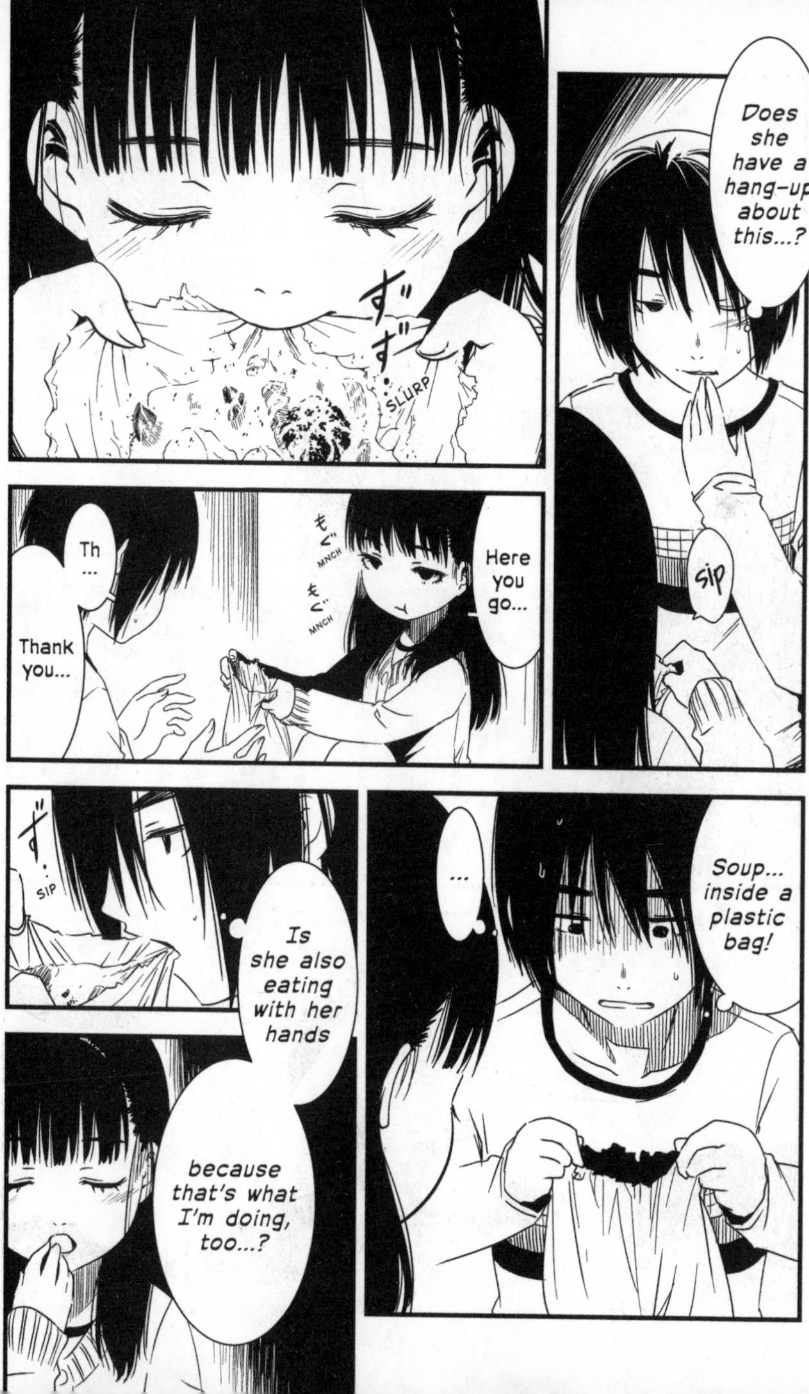
Does she have a hang-up about this...?
sip
ずず
SLURP
Here you go...
もぐ
MNCH
もぐ
MNCH
Th...
Thank you...
Soup... inside a plastic bag!
...
ず
SIP
Is she also eating with her hands
because that's what I'm doing, too...?

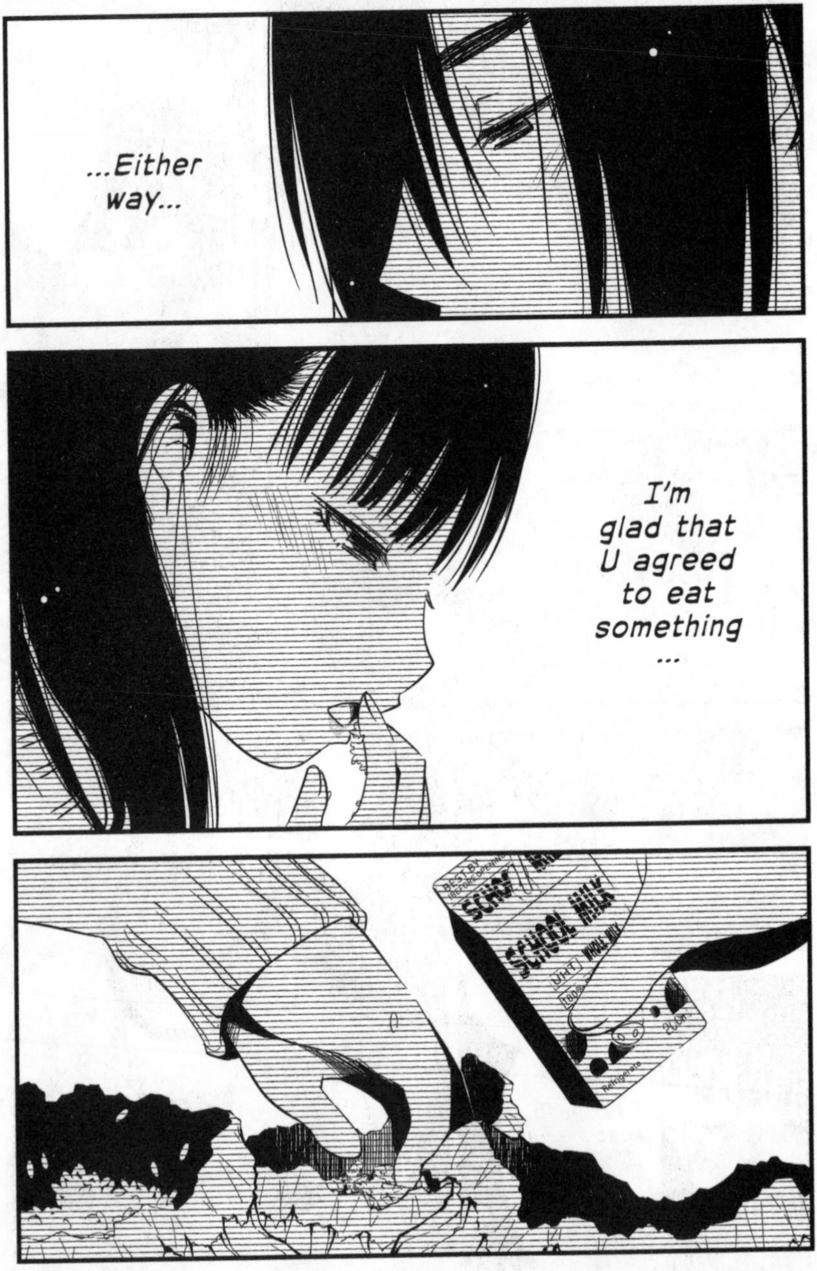
...Either way...
I'm glad that U agreed to eat something ...
SCHOOL MILK

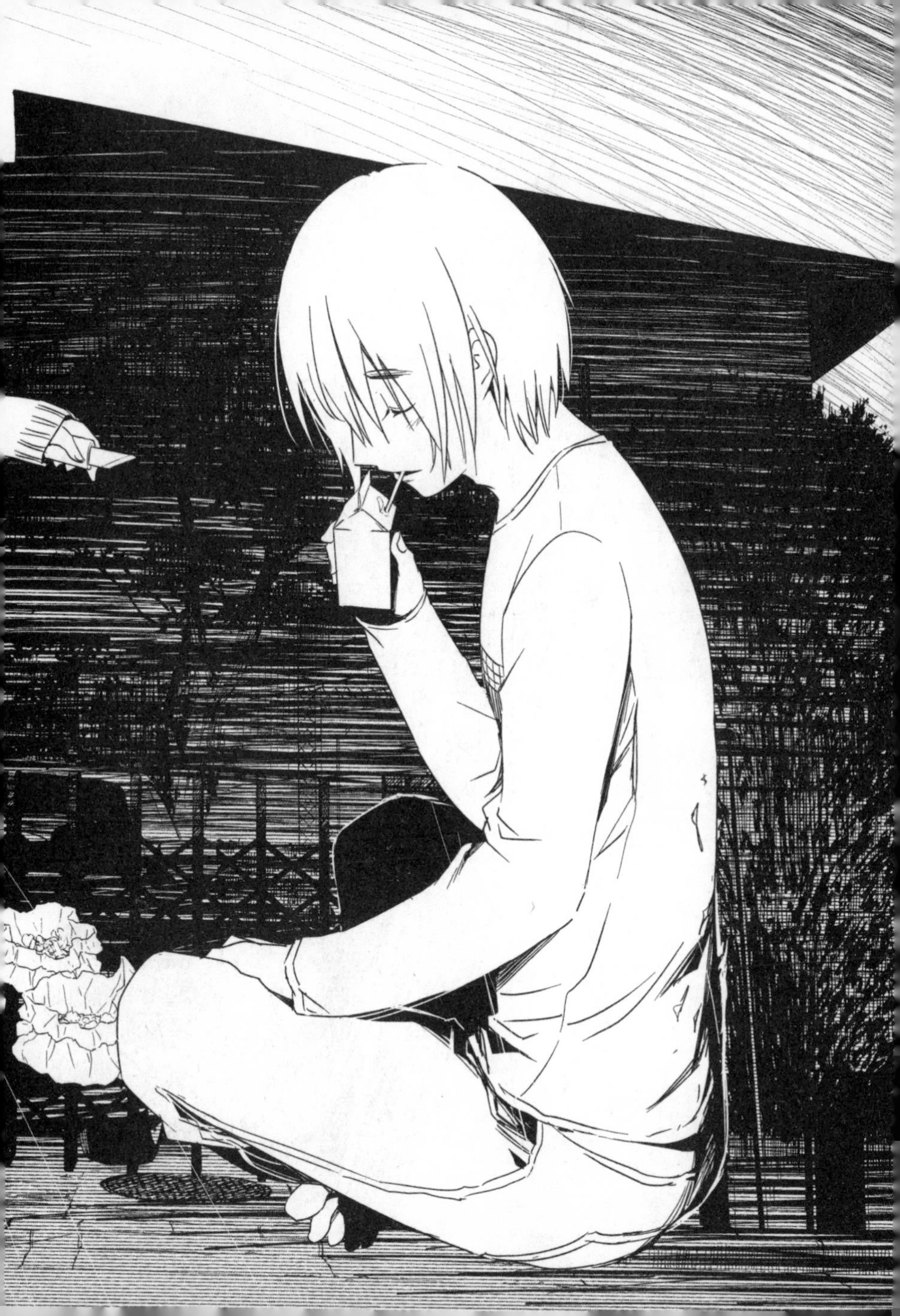

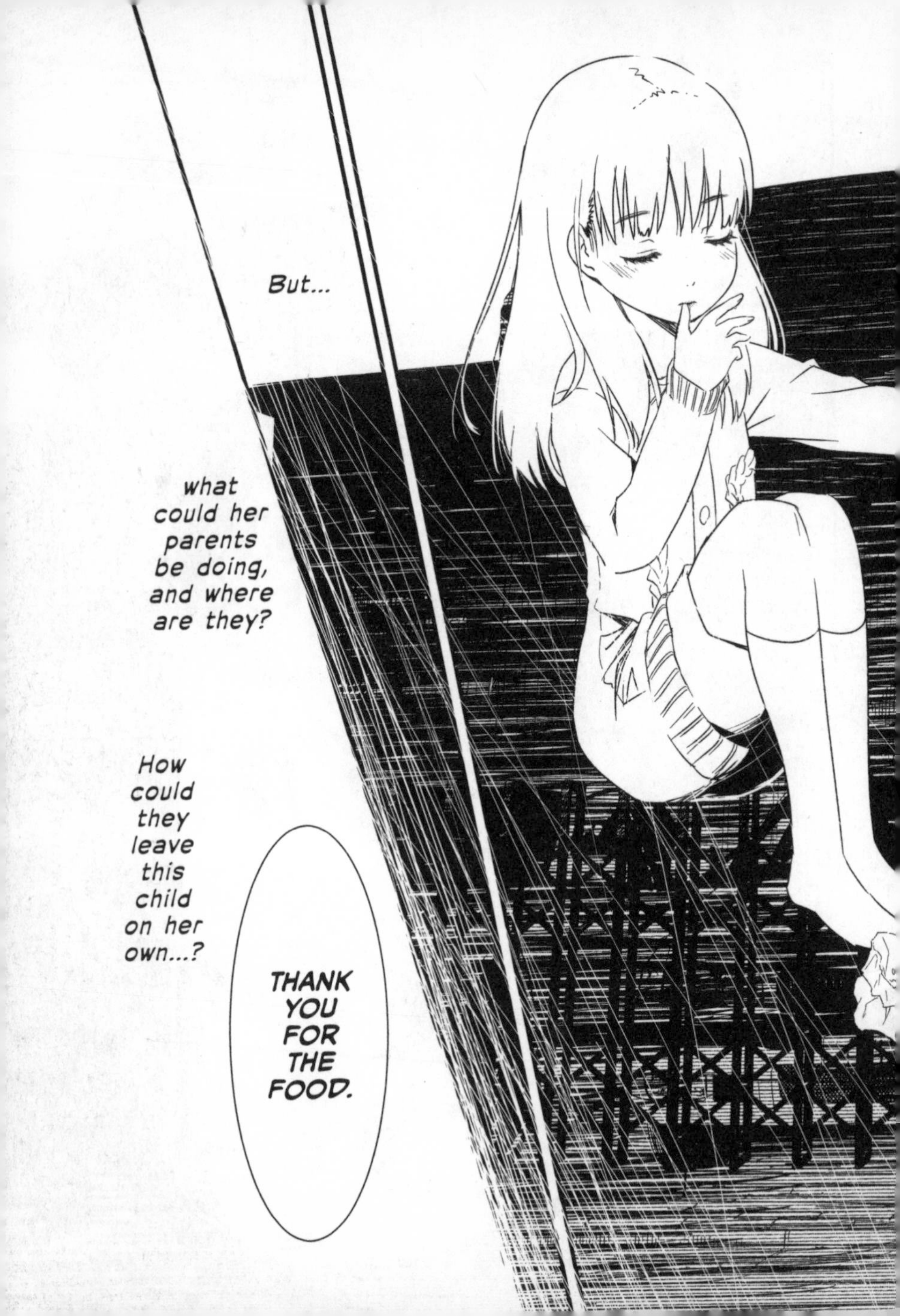
But...
what could her parents be doing, and where are they?
How could they leave this child on her own...?
THANK YOU FOR THE FOOD.

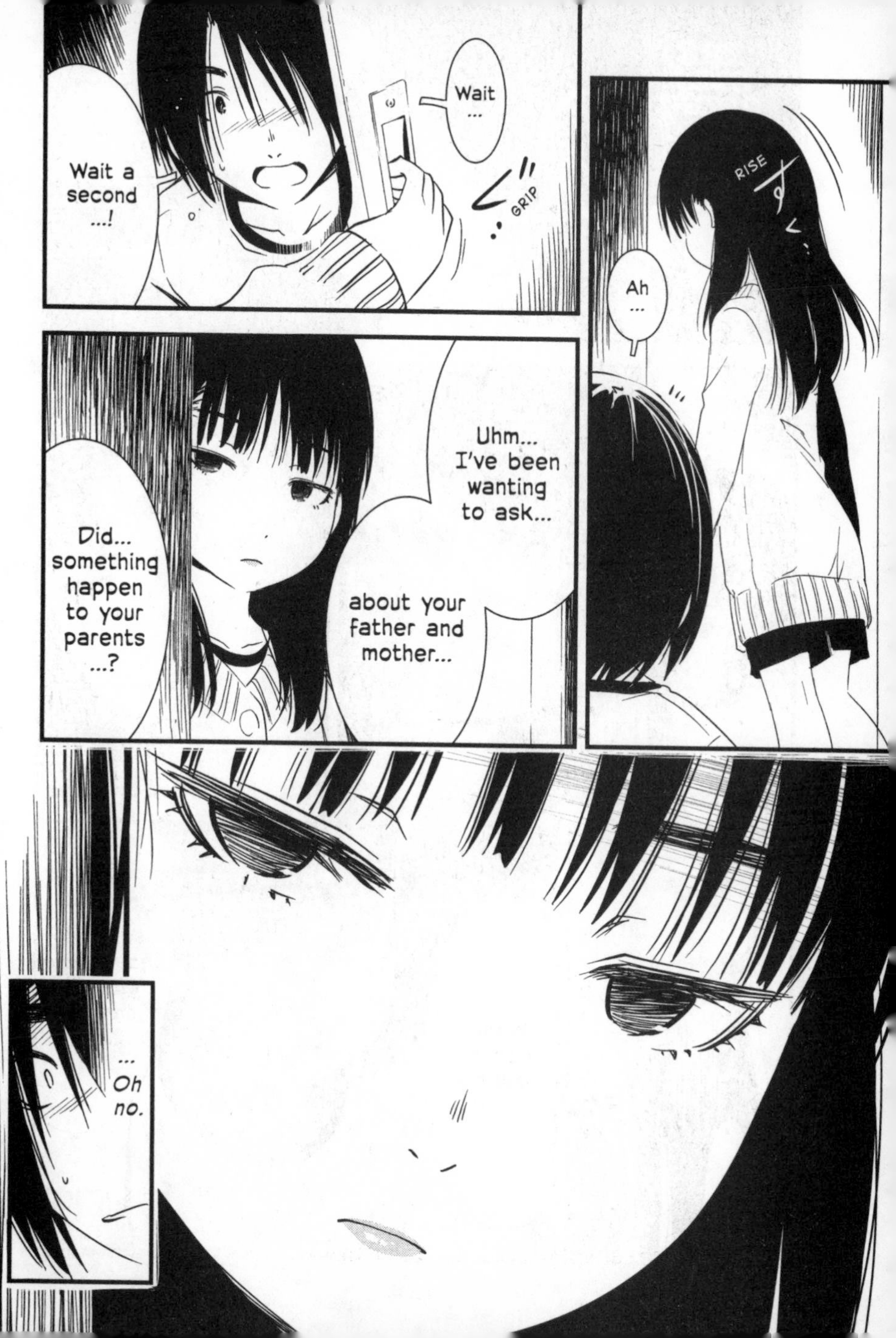
RISE
Ah ...
Wait ...
GRIP
Wait a second ...!
Uhm... I've been wanting to ask...
about your father and mother...
Did... something happen to your parents ...?
... Oh no.

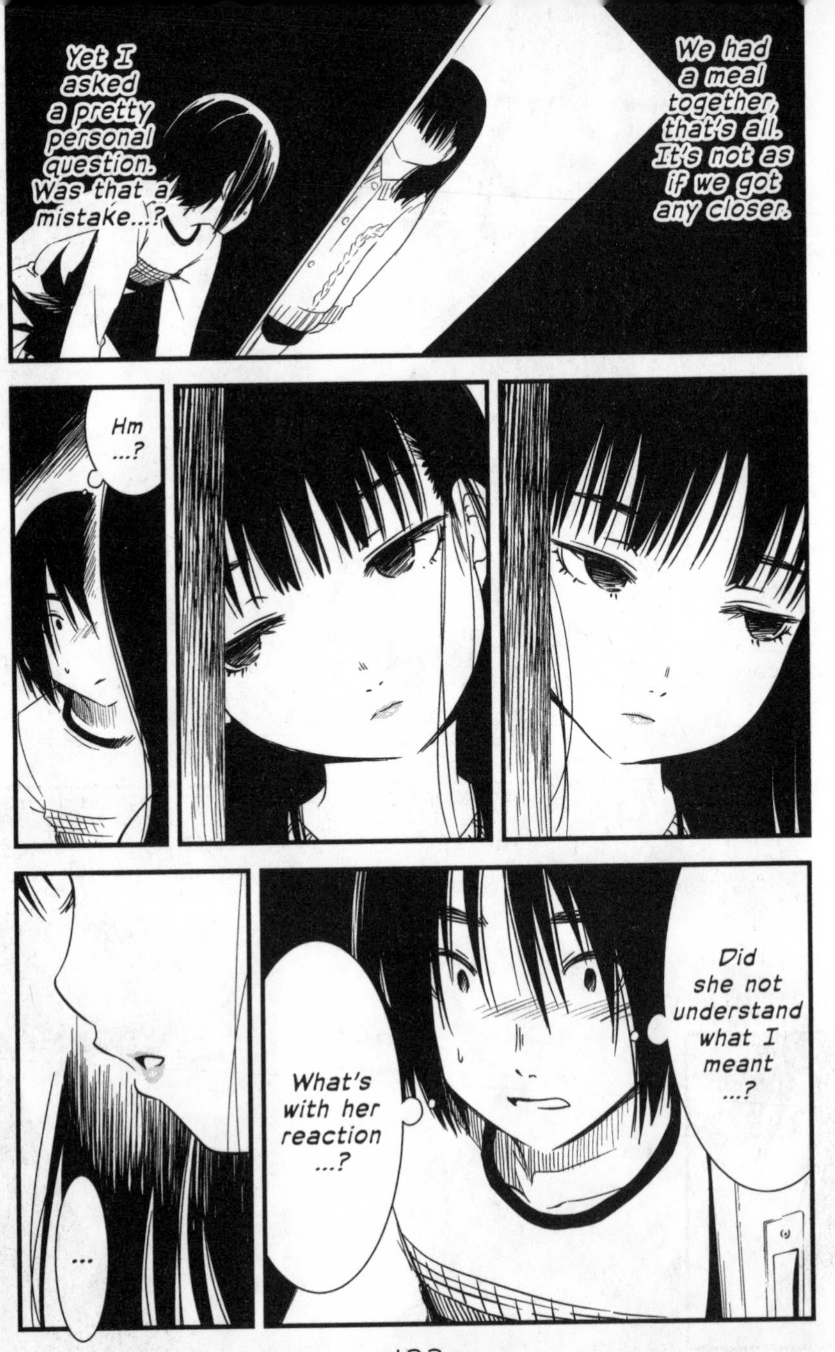
We had a meal together, that's all. It's not as if we got any closer.
Yet I asked a pretty personal question. Was that a mistake...?
Hm ...?
Did she not understand what I meant ...?
What's with her reaction ...?
...

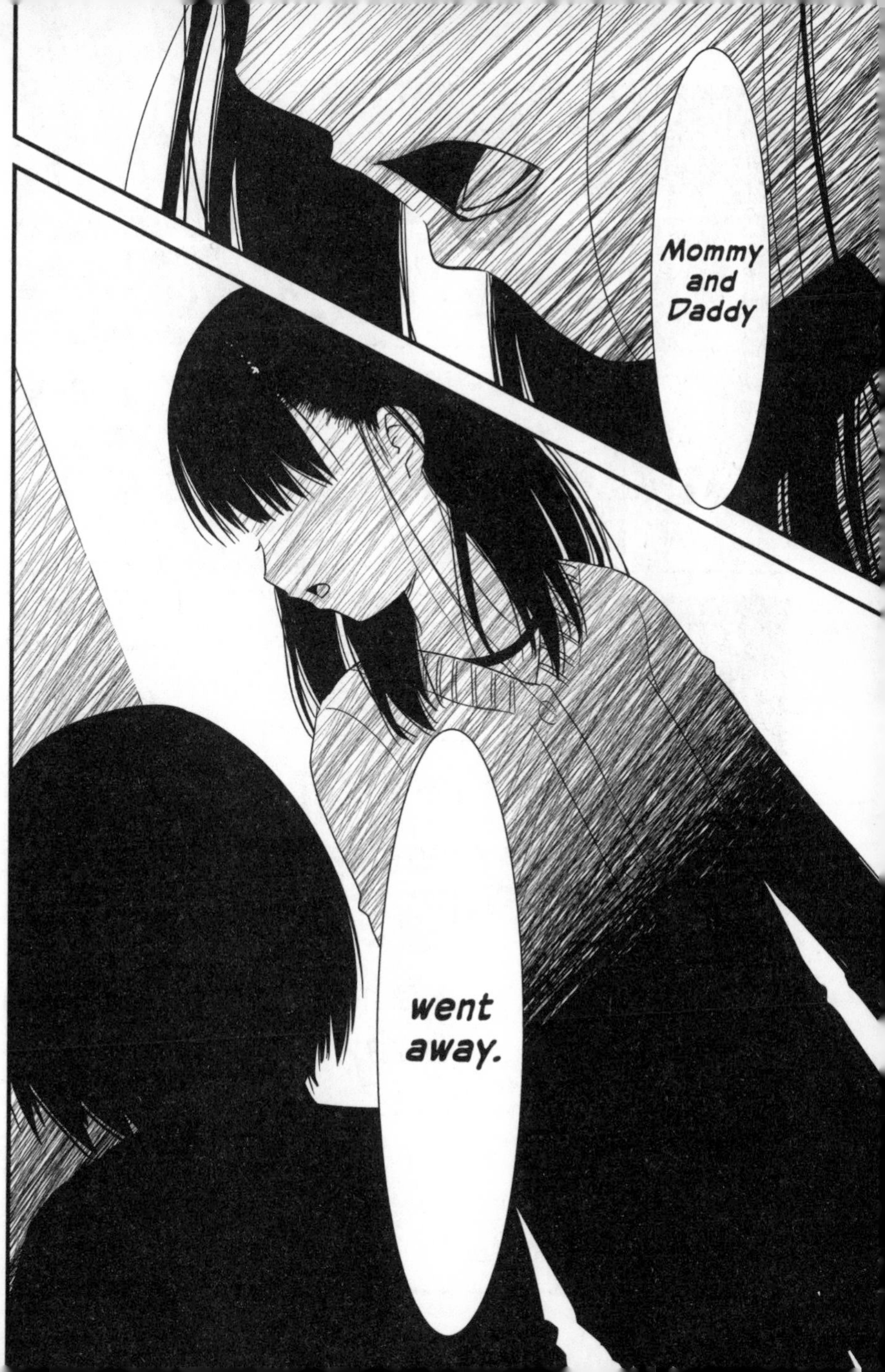

Mommy and Daddy
went away.

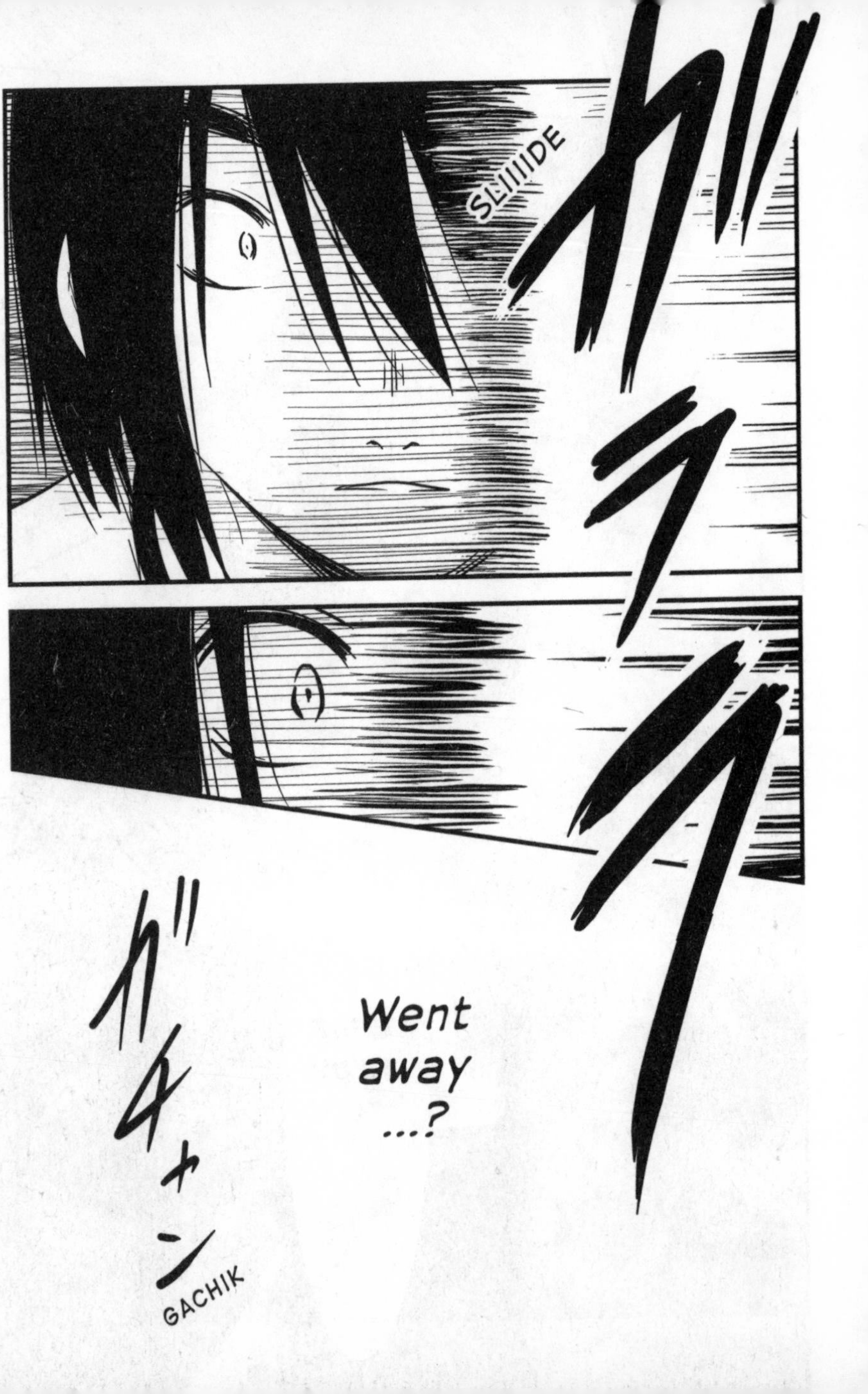
SLIIIIDE
Went away ...?
GACHIK

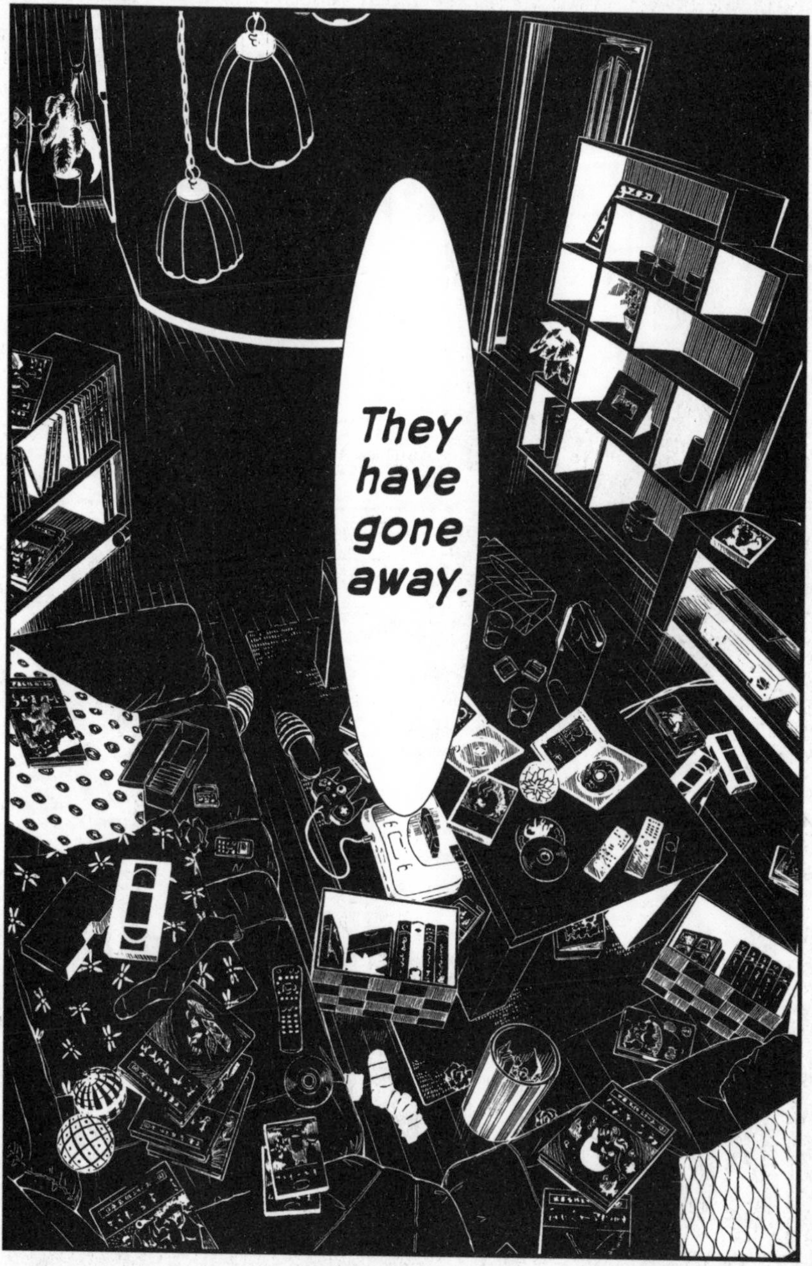
They have gone away.

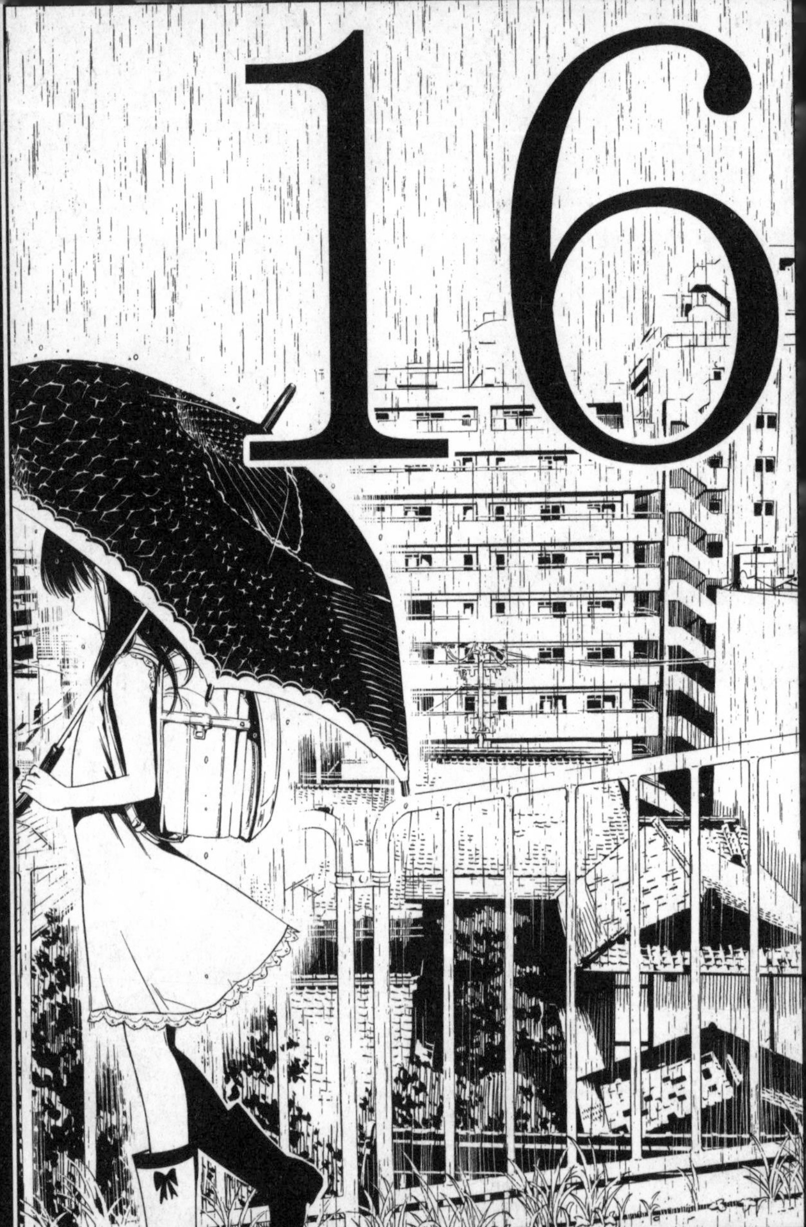
16

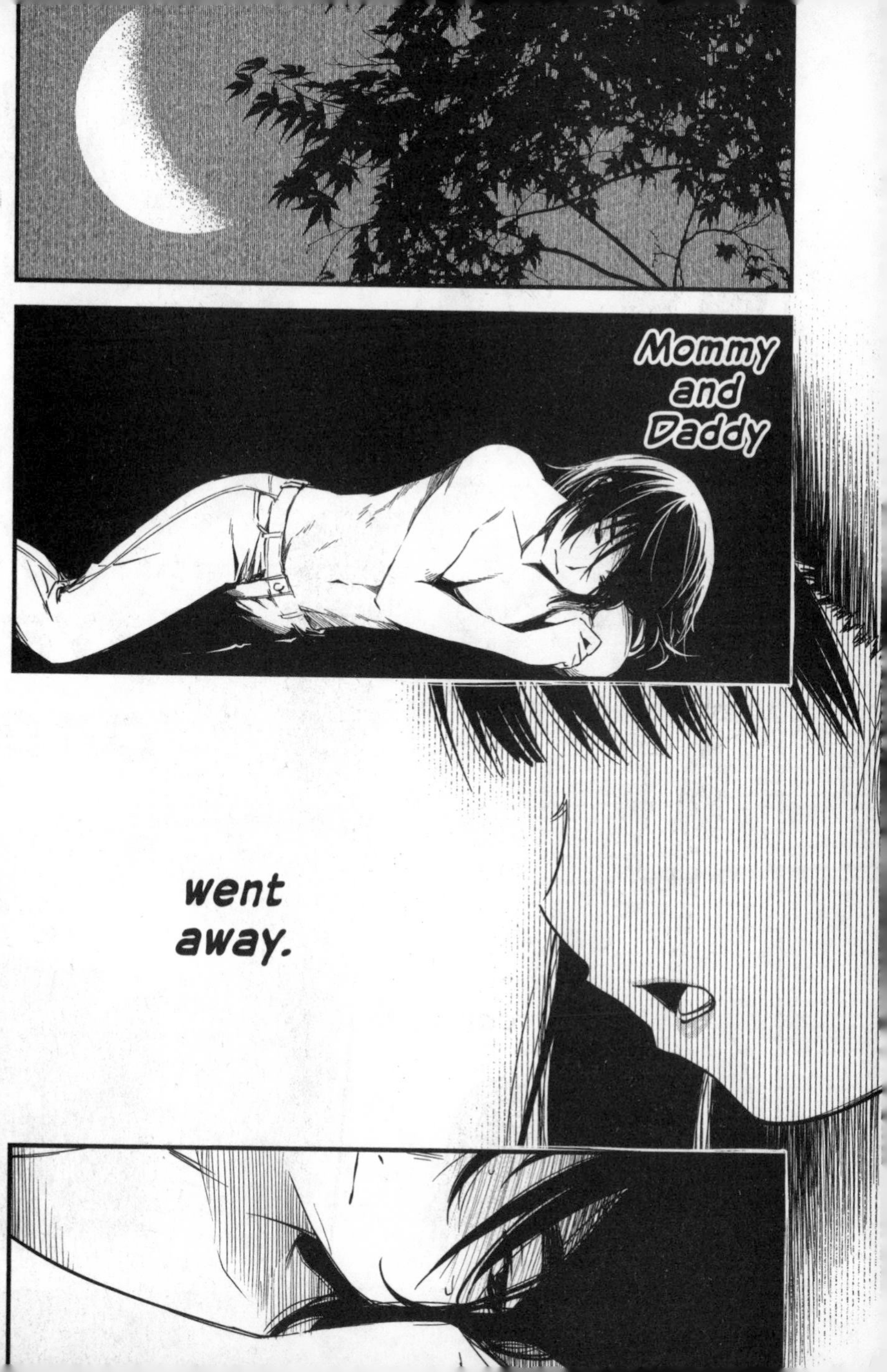
Mommy and Daddy
went away.

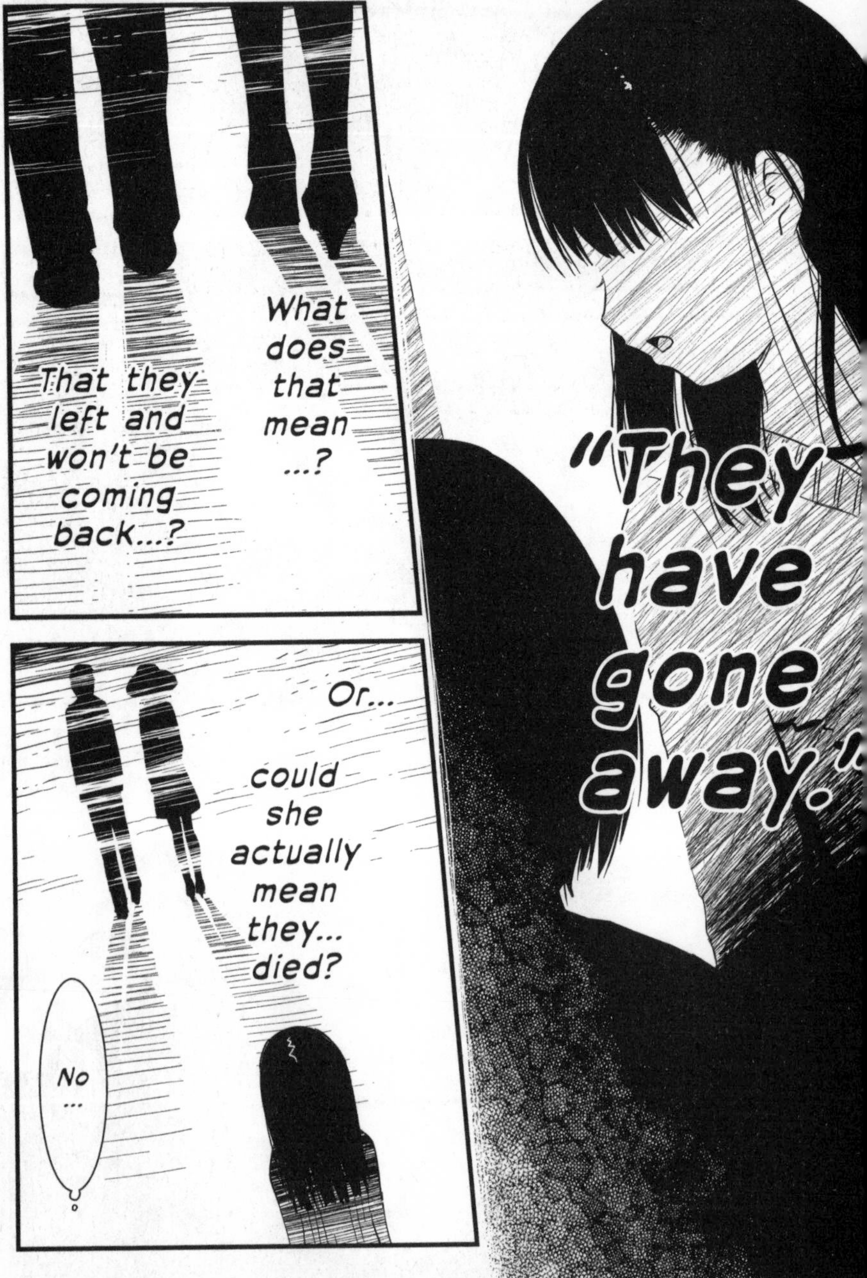
"They have gone away."
What does that mean ...?
That they left and won't be coming back...?
Or...
could she actually mean they... died?
No ...

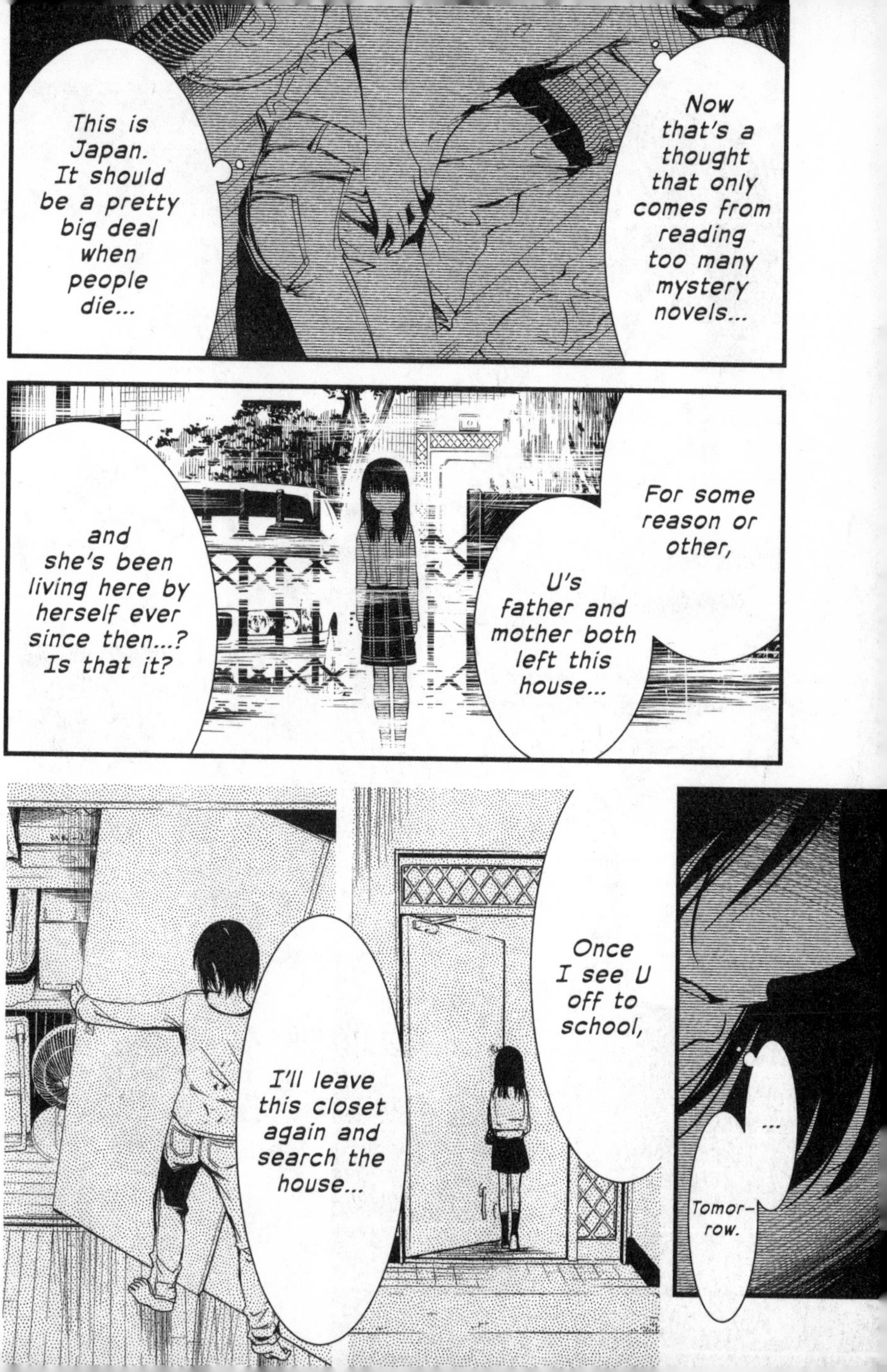

Now that's a thought that only comes from reading too many mystery novels...
This is Japan. It should be a pretty big deal when people die...
For some reason or other,
U's father and mother both left this house...
and she's been living here by herself ever since then...? Is that it?
...
Tomor-row.
Once I see U off to school,
I'll leave this closet again and search the house...

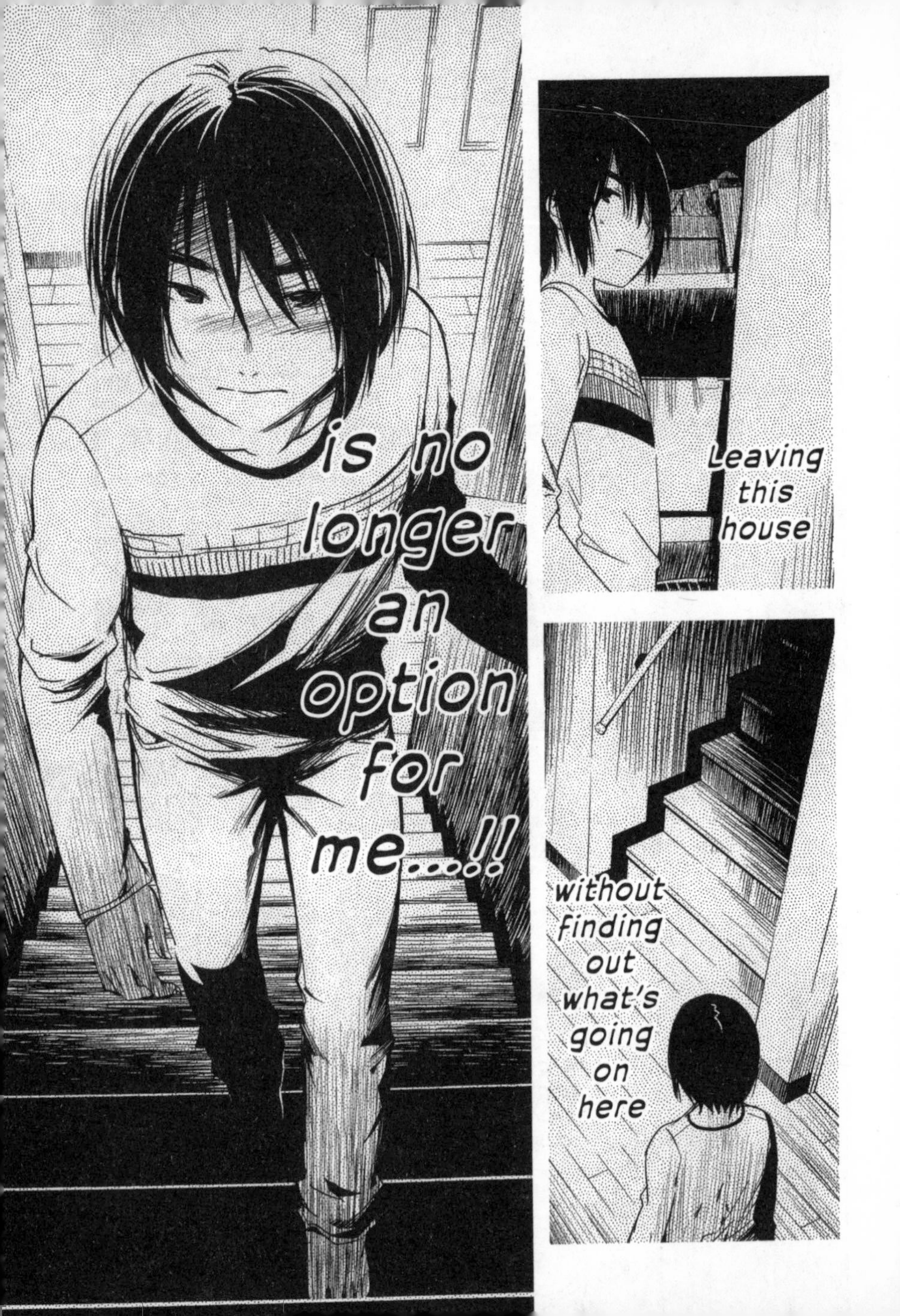
Leaving this house
without finding out what's going on here
is no longer an option for me...!!

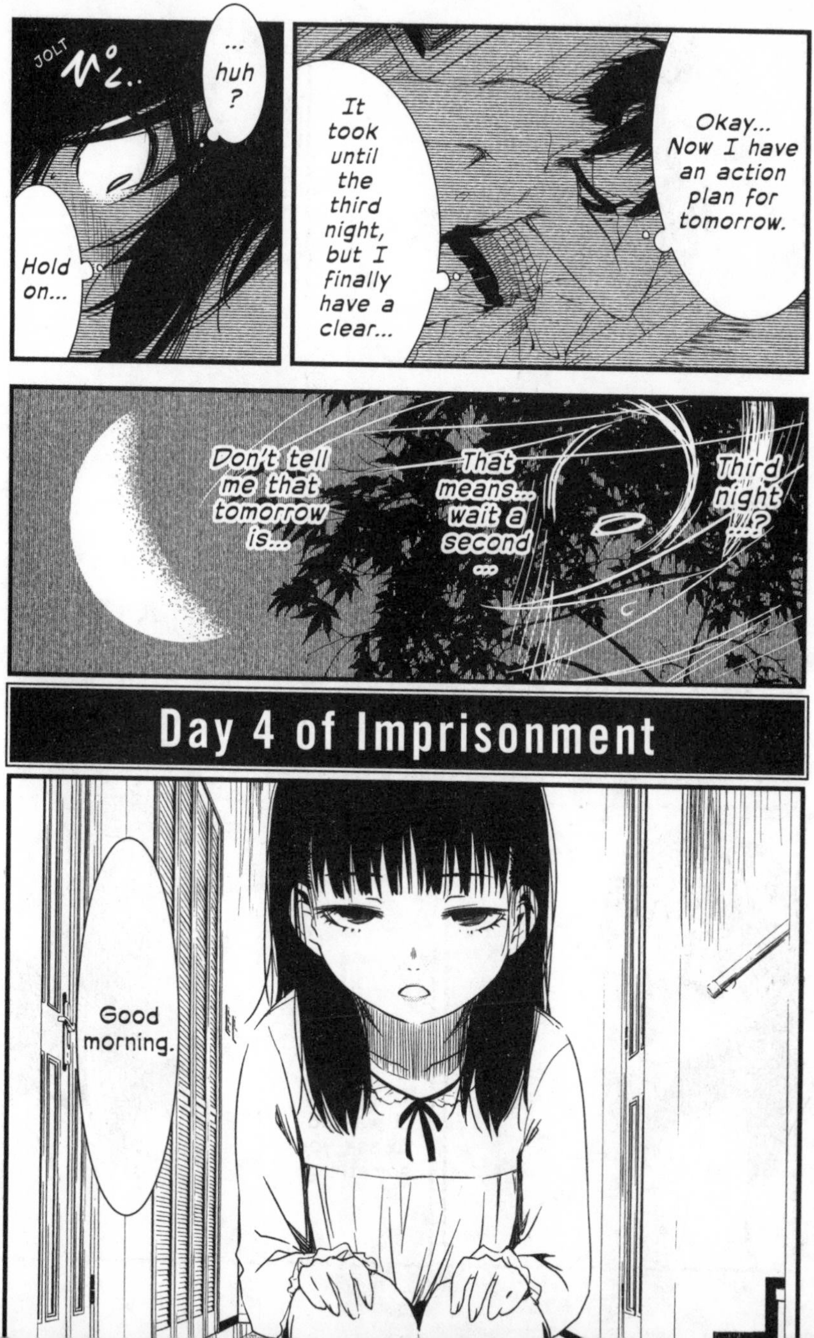
Okay... Now I have an action plan for tomorrow.
It took until the third night, but I finally have a clear...
... huh?
JOLT
Hold on...
Third night ...?
That means... wait a second ...
Don't tell me that tomorrow is...
Day 4 of Imprisonment
Good morning.

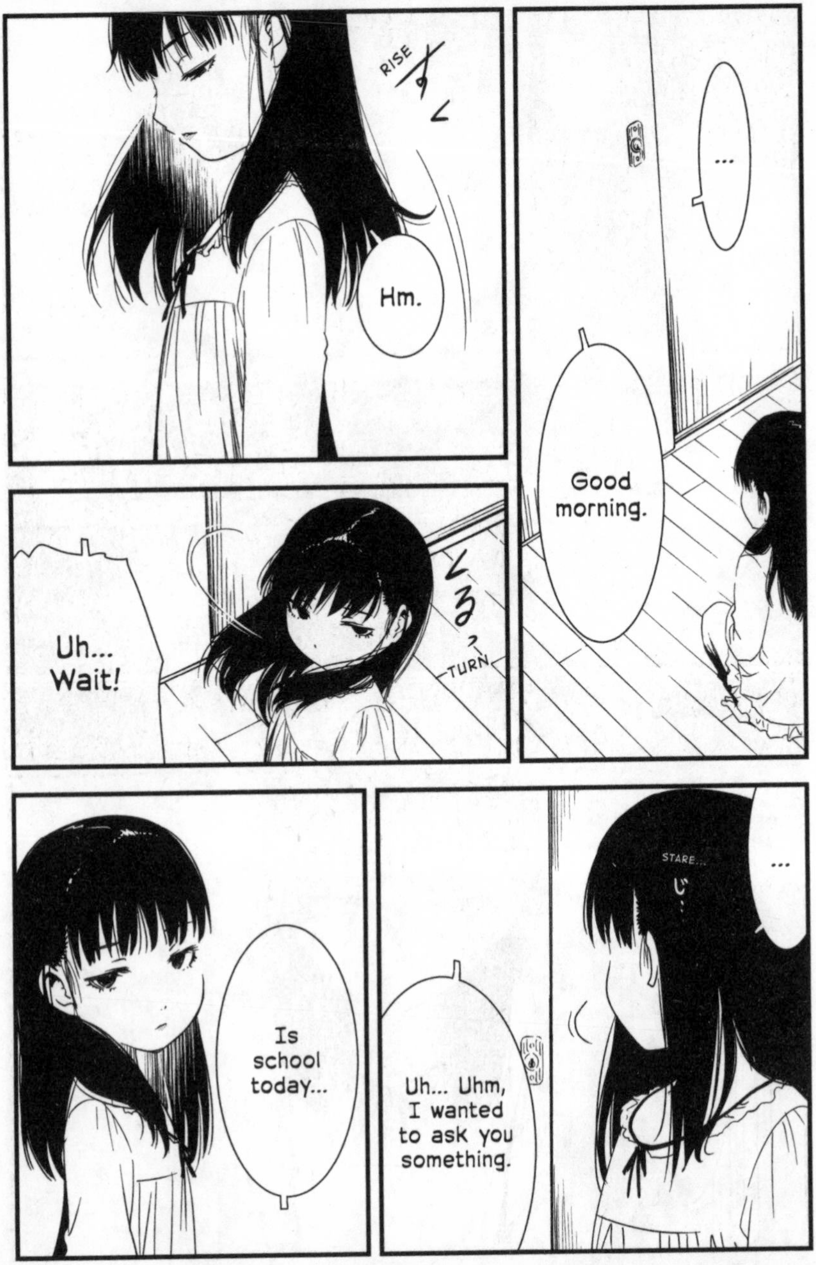
...
Good morning.
RISE
すく
Hm.
くるっ
TURN
Uh... Wait!
STARE...
じ…
...
Uh... Uhm, I wanted to ask you something.
Is school today...

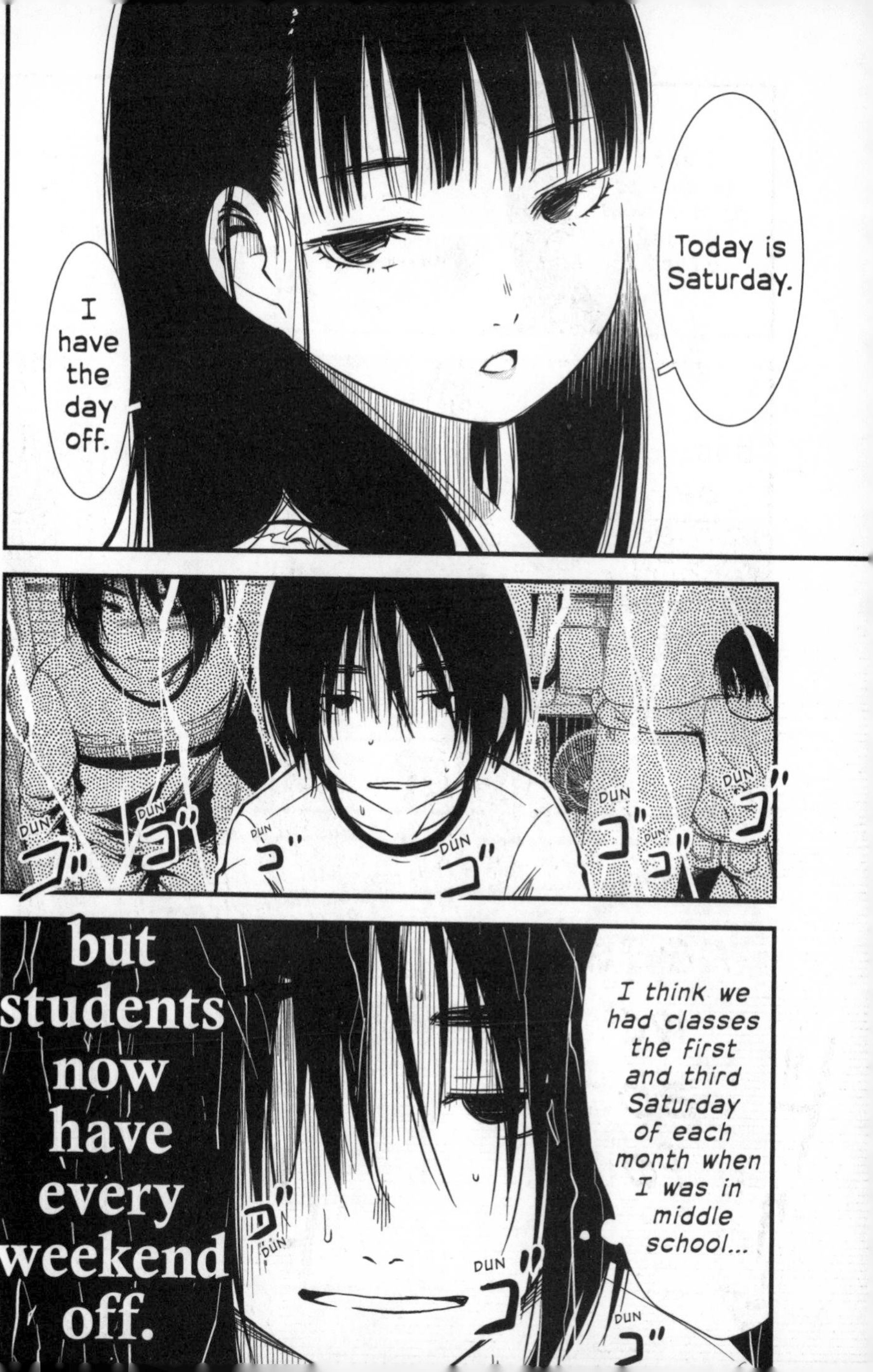
Today is Saturday.
I have the day off.
ゴ DUN
ゴ DUN
ゴ DUN
ゴ DUN
ゴ DUN
ゴ DUN
ゴ DUN
ゴ DUN
I think we had classes the first and third Saturday of each month when I was in middle school...
ゴ DUN
ゴ DUN
ゴ DUN
but students now have every weekend off.

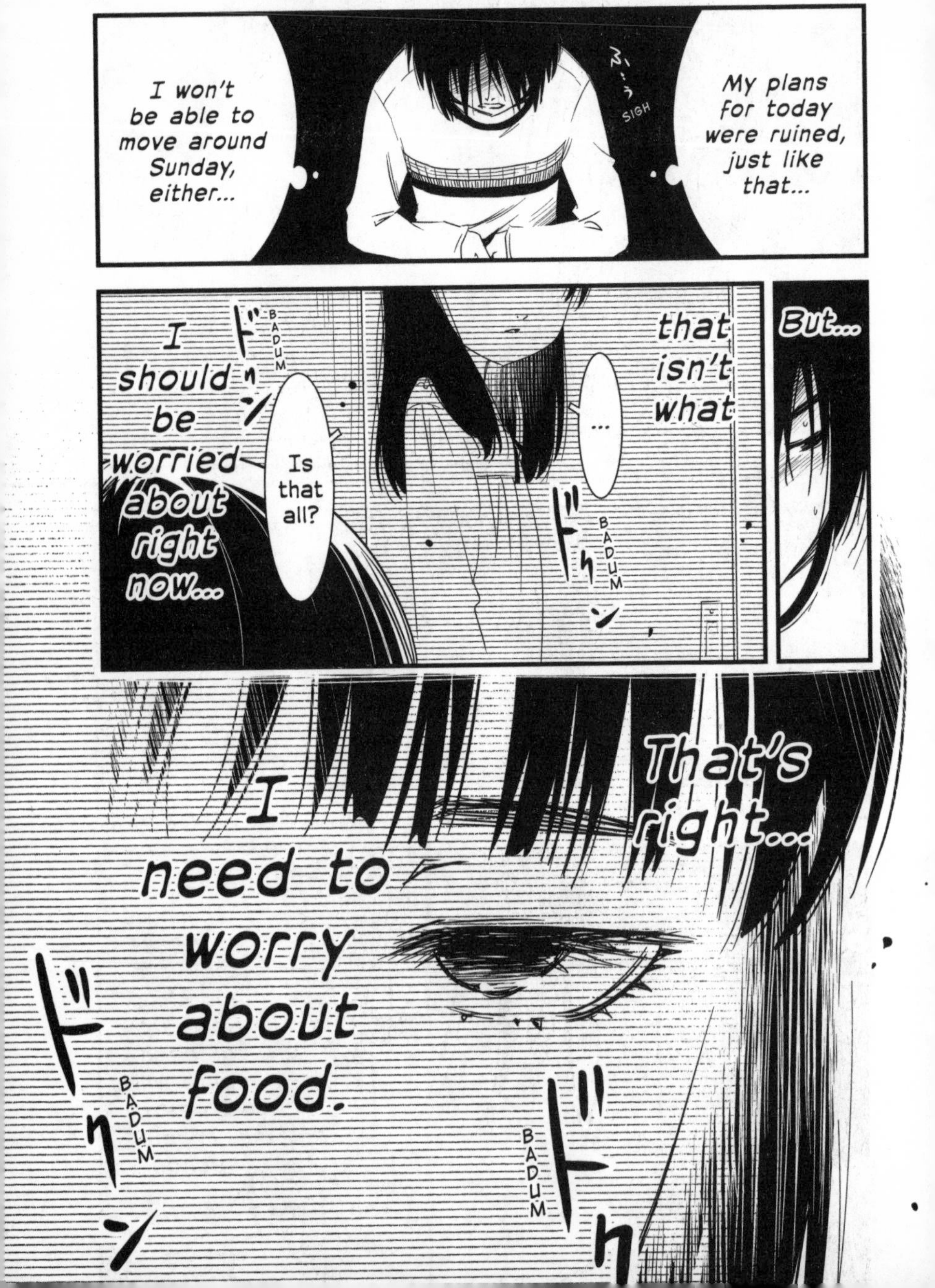
My plans for today were ruined, just like that...
SIGH
I won't be able to move around Sunday, either...
But...
that isn't what
...
BADUM
Is that all?
BADUM
I should be worried about right now...
That's right...
I need to worry about food.
BADUM
BADUM

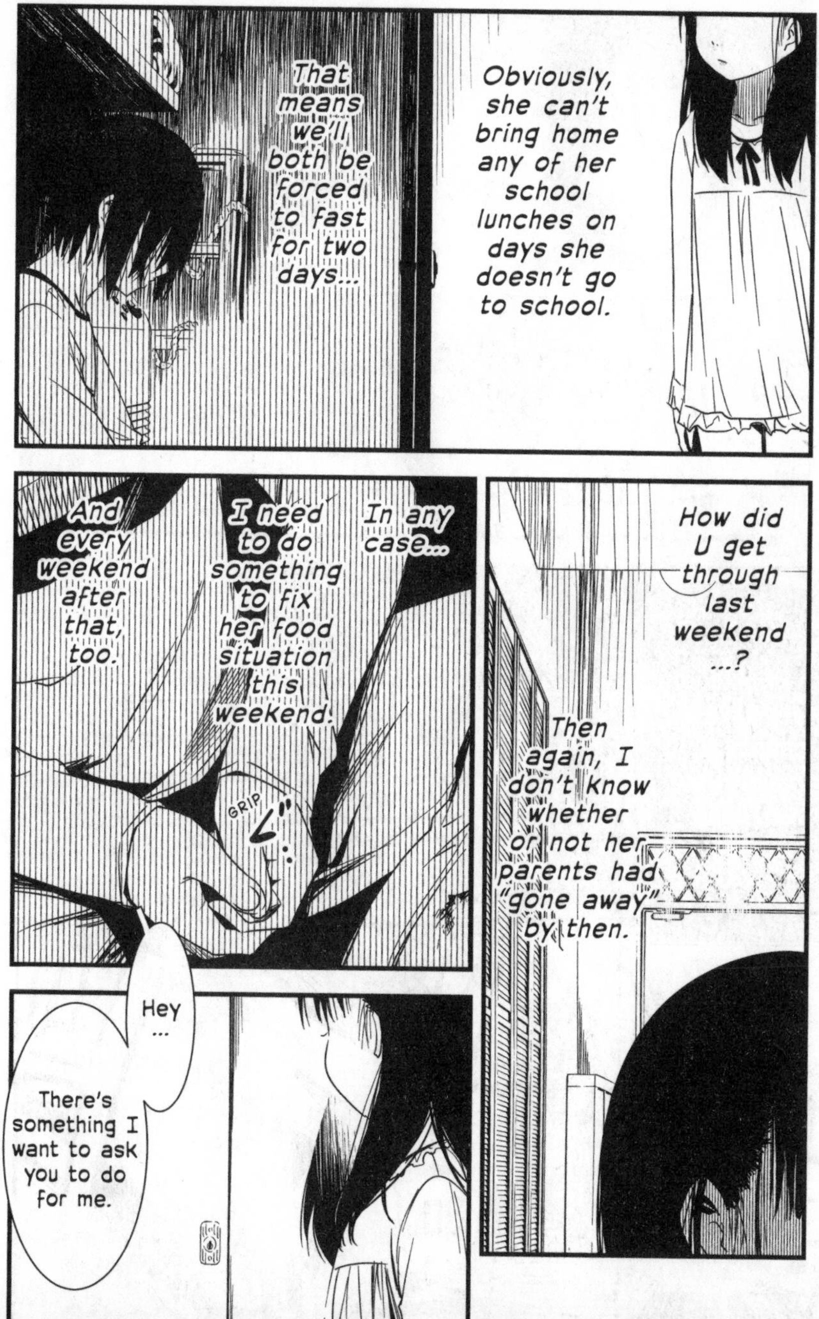
Obviously, she can't bring home any of her school lunches on days she doesn't go to school.
That means we'll both be forced to fast for two days...
How did U get through last weekend ...?
Then again, I don't know whether or not her parents had "gone away" by then.
In any case...
I need to do something to fix her food situation this weekend.
And every weekend after that, too.
GRIP
Hey ...
There's something I want to ask you to do for me.

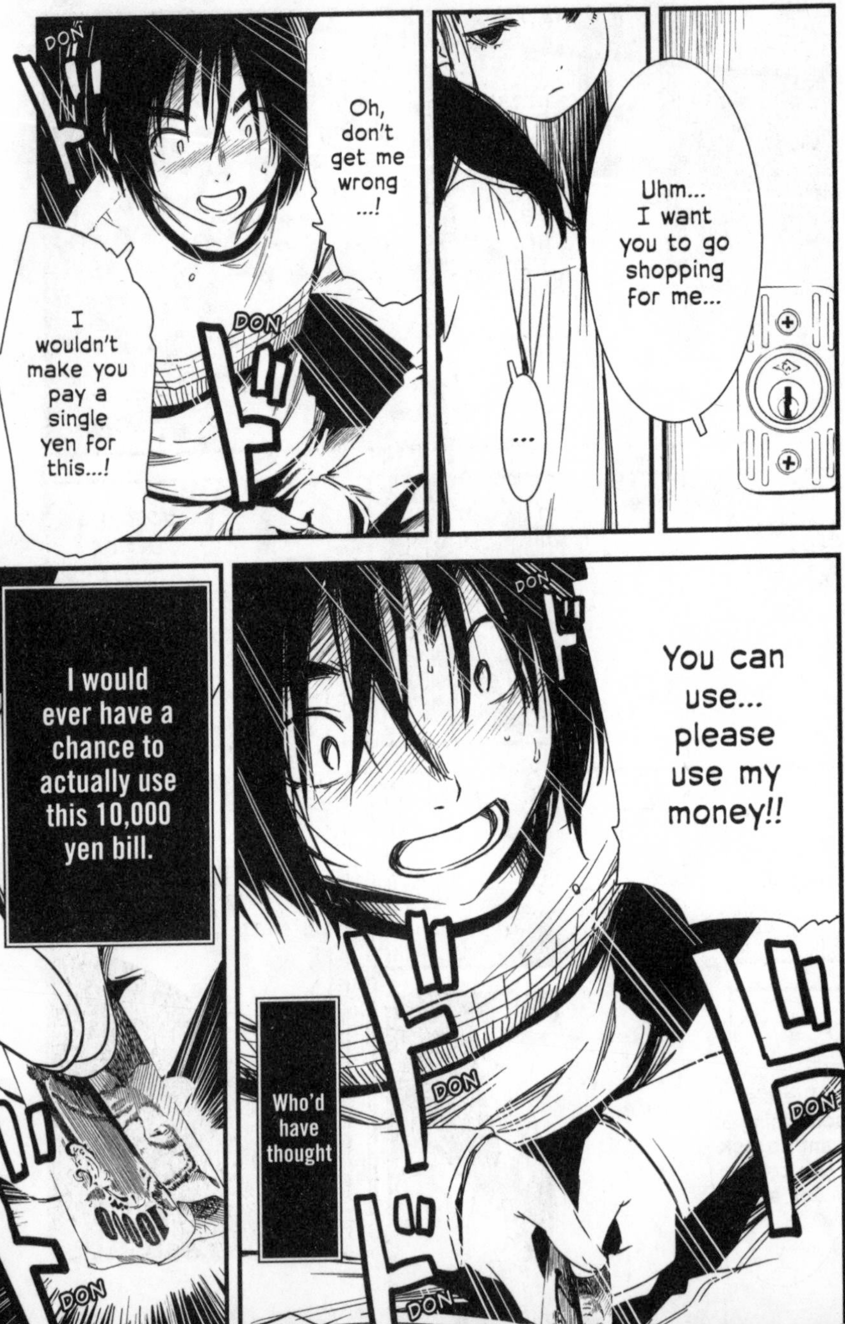
Uhm... I want you to go shopping for me...
...
DON
Oh, don't get me wrong ...!
I wouldn't make you pay a single yen for this...!
DON
DON
You can use... please use my money!!
DON
DON
Who'd have thought
DON
I would ever have a chance to actually use this 10,000 yen bill.
DON

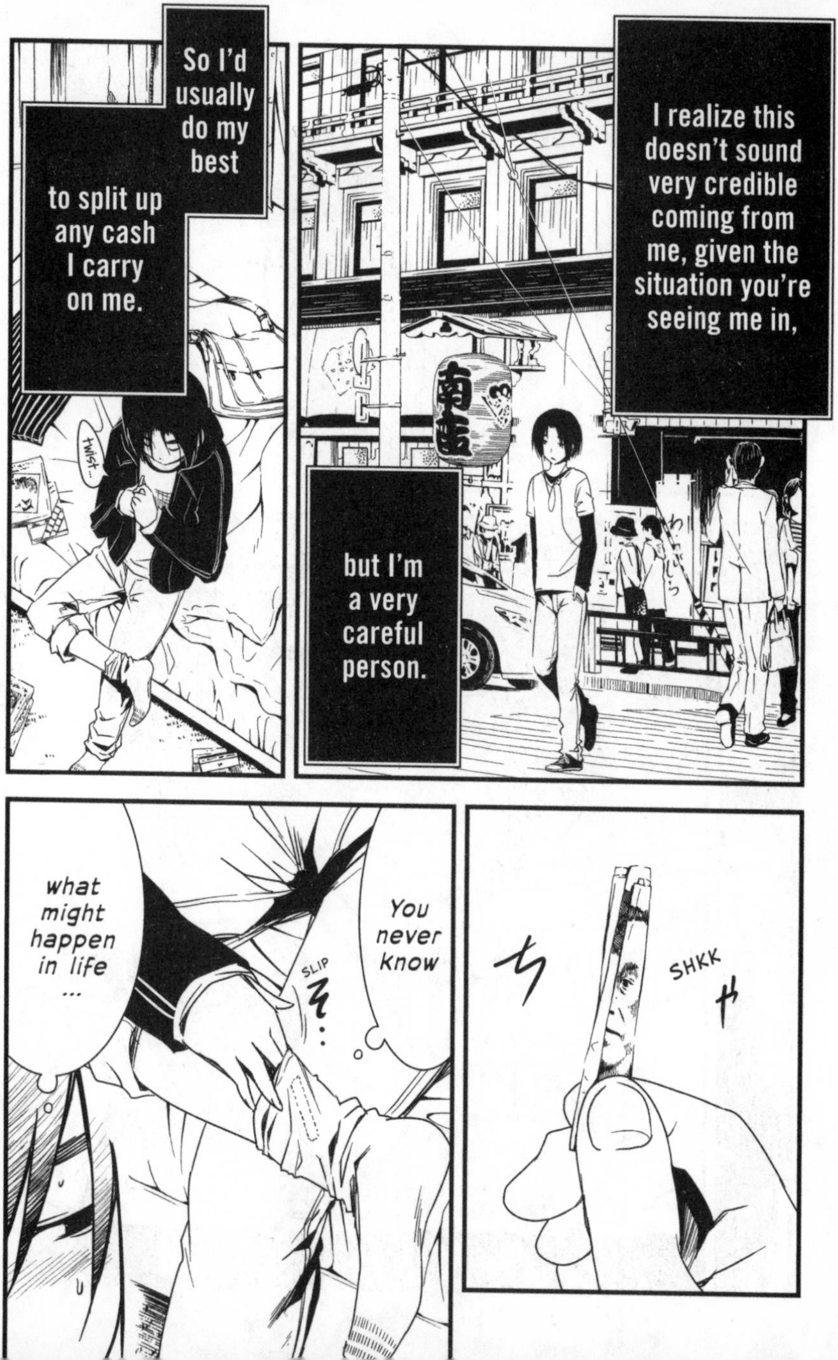
I realize this doesn't sound very credible coming from me, given the situation you're seeing me in,
but I'm a very careful person.
So I'd usually do my best
to split up any cash I carry on me.
twist...
SHKK
You never know
what might happen in life ...
SLIP

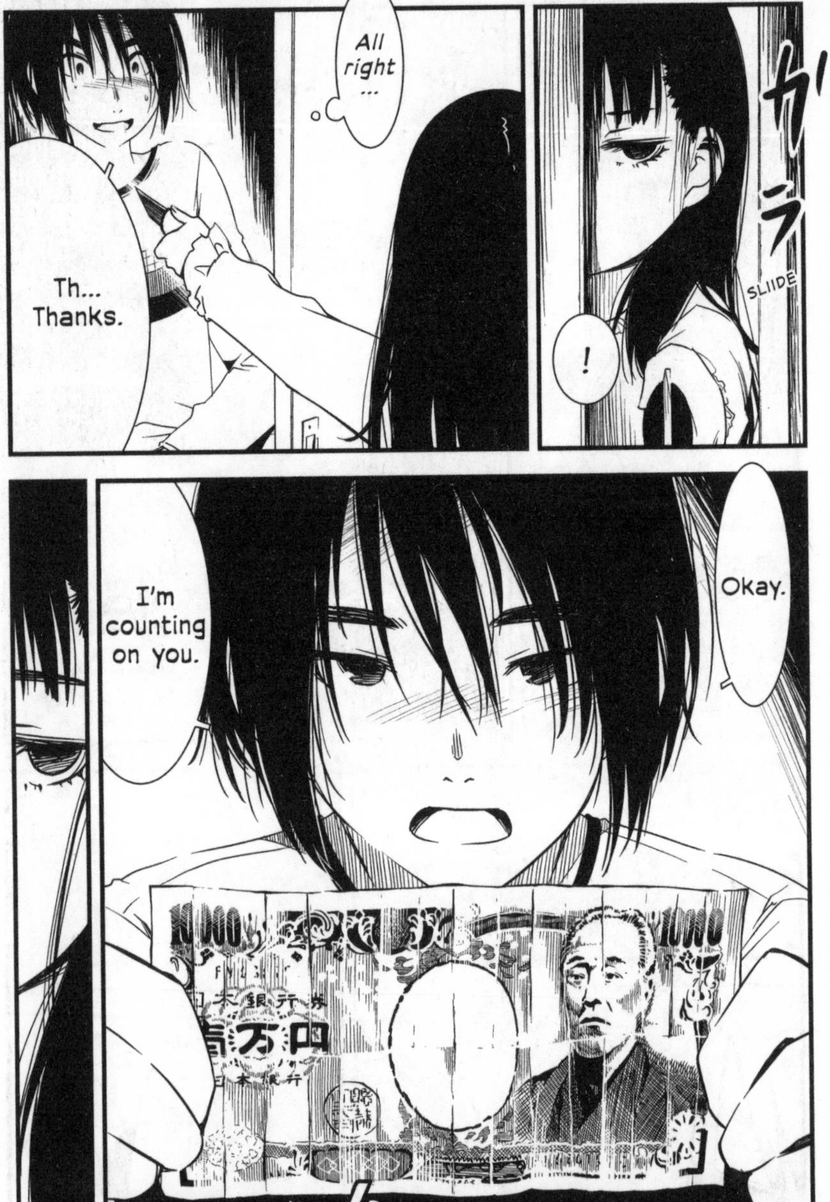
ガラ
SLIIDE
!
All right ...
Th... Thanks.
Okay.
I'm counting on you.
びっ
SNAP

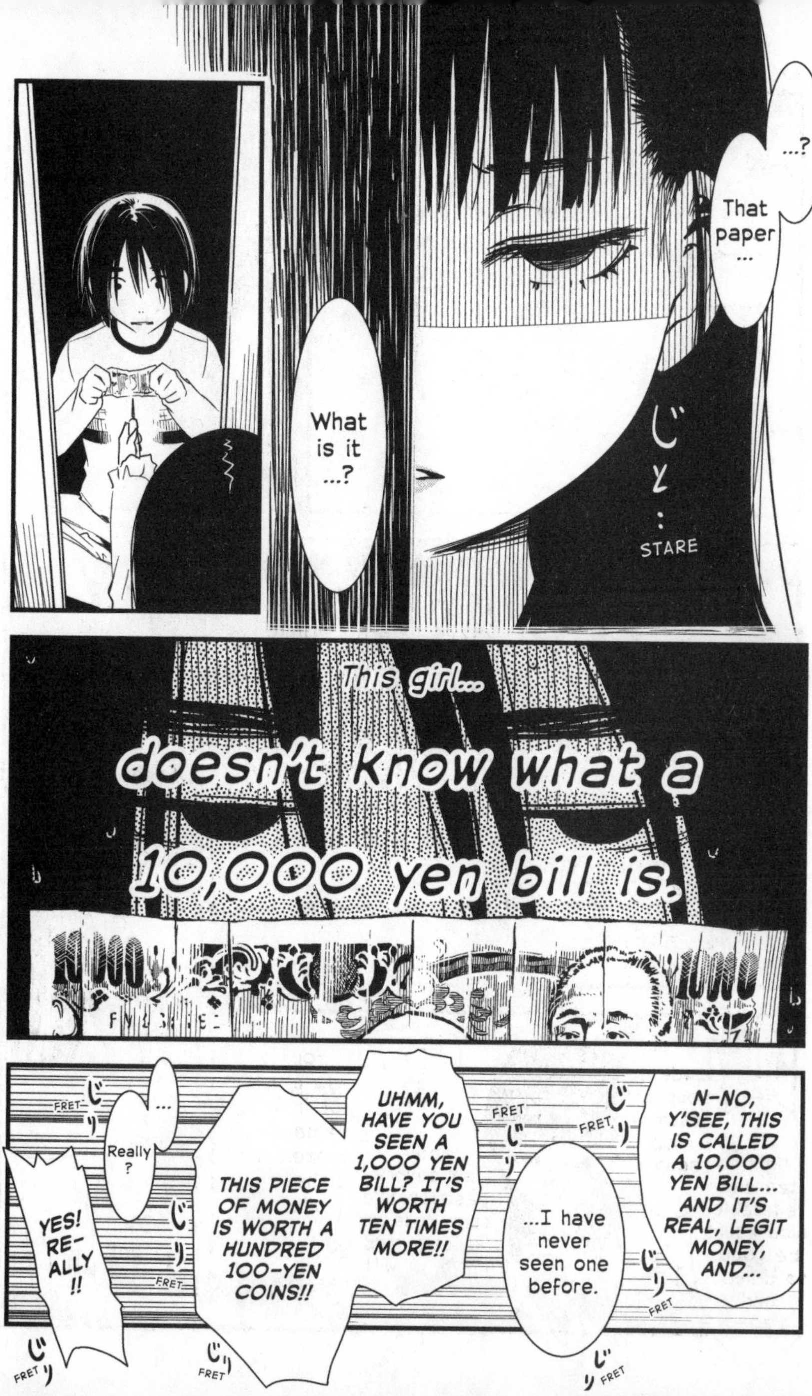
...?
That paper ...
What is it ...?
じっ
STARE
This girl...
doesn't know what a 10,000 yen bill is.
N-NO, Y'SEE, THIS IS CALLED A 10,000 YEN BILL... AND IT'S REAL, LEGIT MONEY, AND...
じり
FRET
...I have never seen one before.
UHMM, HAVE YOU SEEN A 1,000 YEN BILL? IT'S WORTH TEN TIMES MORE!!
THIS PIECE OF MONEY IS WORTH A HUNDRED 100-YEN COINS!!
...
Really ?
YES! RE-ALLY !!
じり
FRET

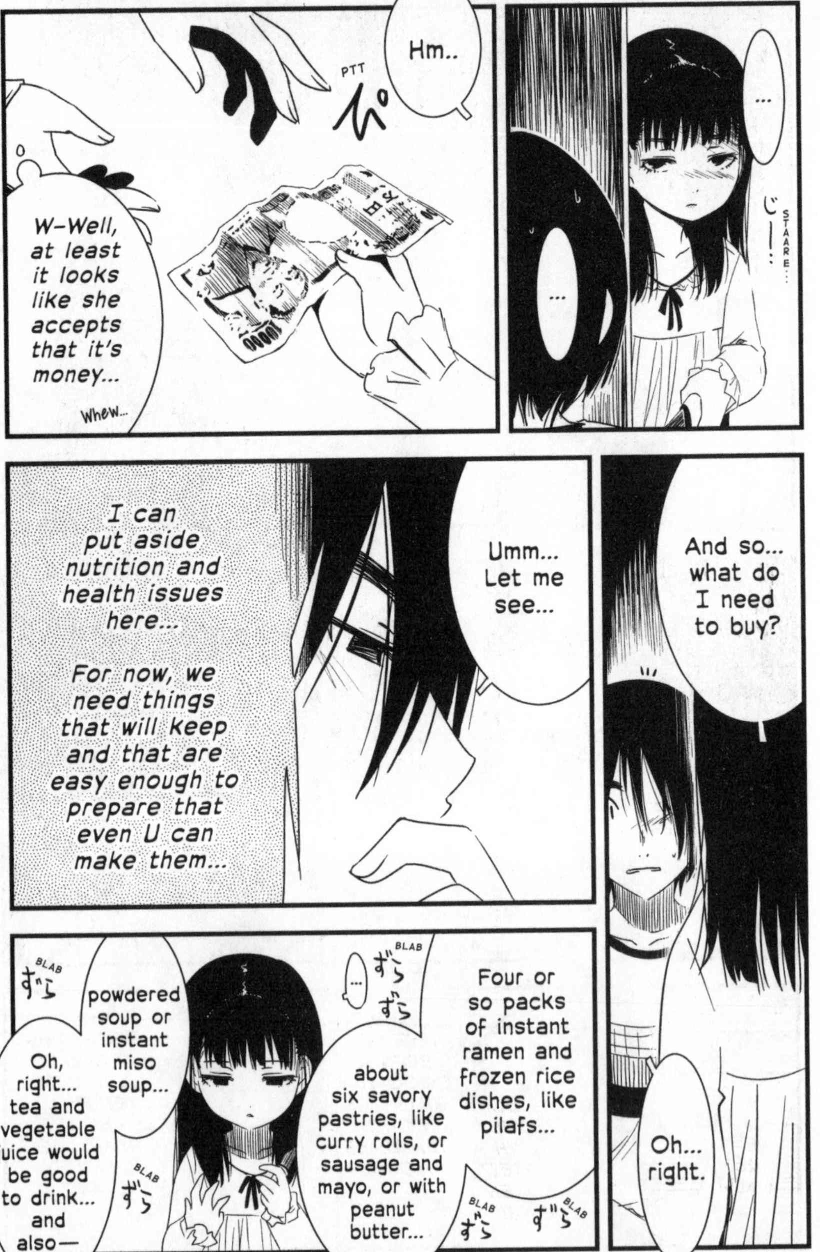
...
じー…
STARE...
...
Hm..
PTT
ぴ
W-Well, at least it looks like she accepts that it's money...
Whew...
And so... what do I need to buy?
Oh... right.
Umm... Let me see...
I can put aside nutrition and health issues here...
For now, we need things that will keep and that are easy enough to prepare that even U can make them...
Four or so packs of instant ramen and frozen rice dishes, like pilafs...
BLAB ずら
BLAB ずら
about six savory pastries, like curry rolls, or sausage and mayo, or with peanut butter...
BLAB ずら
ずら
...
powdered soup or instant miso soup...
BLAB ずら
BLAB ずら
Oh, right... tea and vegetable juice would be good to drink... and also—

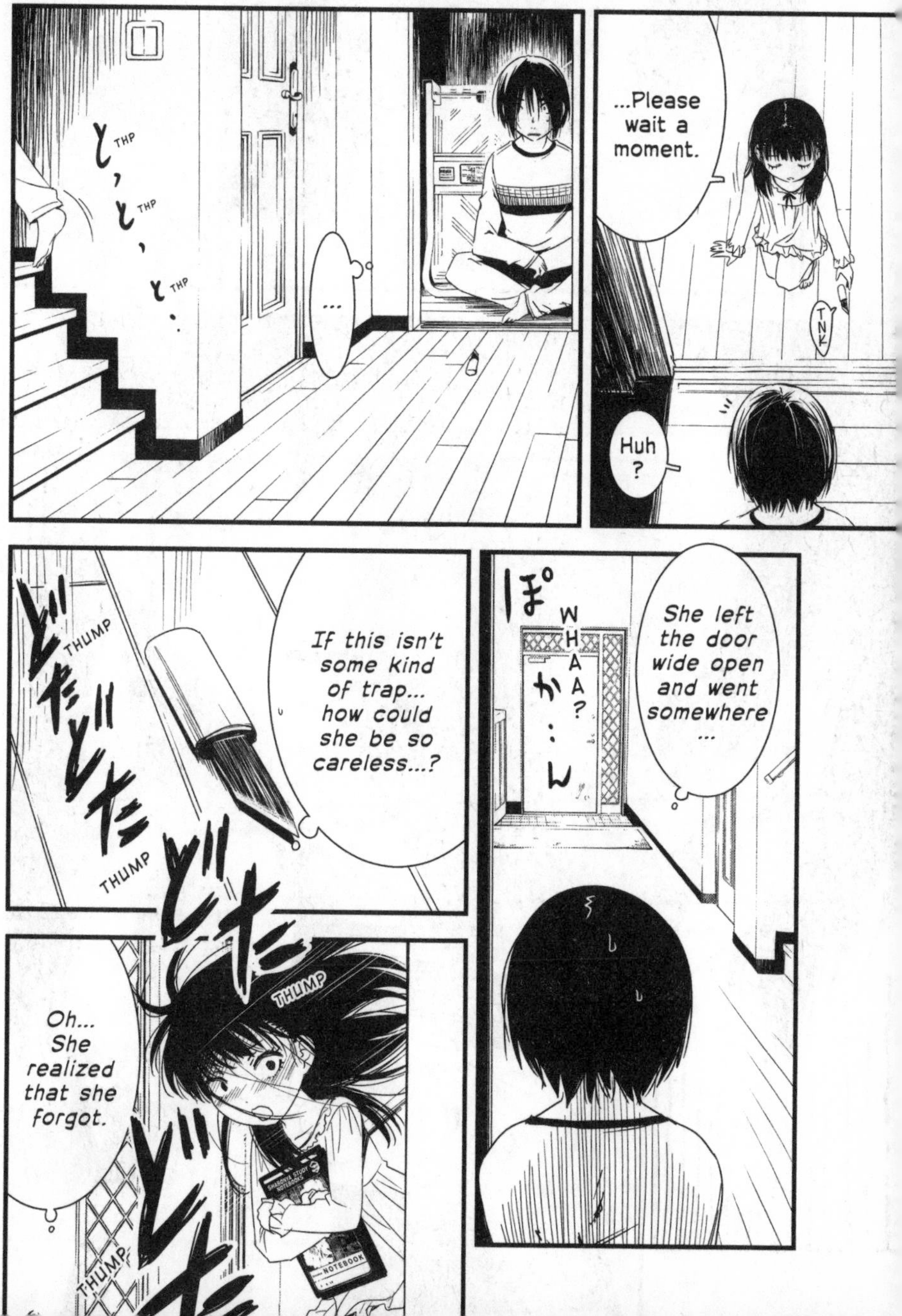
...Please wait a moment.
TNK
Huh?
THP
THP
THP
...
WHAA?
She left the door wide open and went somewhere ...
If this isn't some kind of trap... how could she be so careless...?
THUMP
THUMP
THUMP
Oh... She realized that she forgot.
NOTEBOOK
THUMP

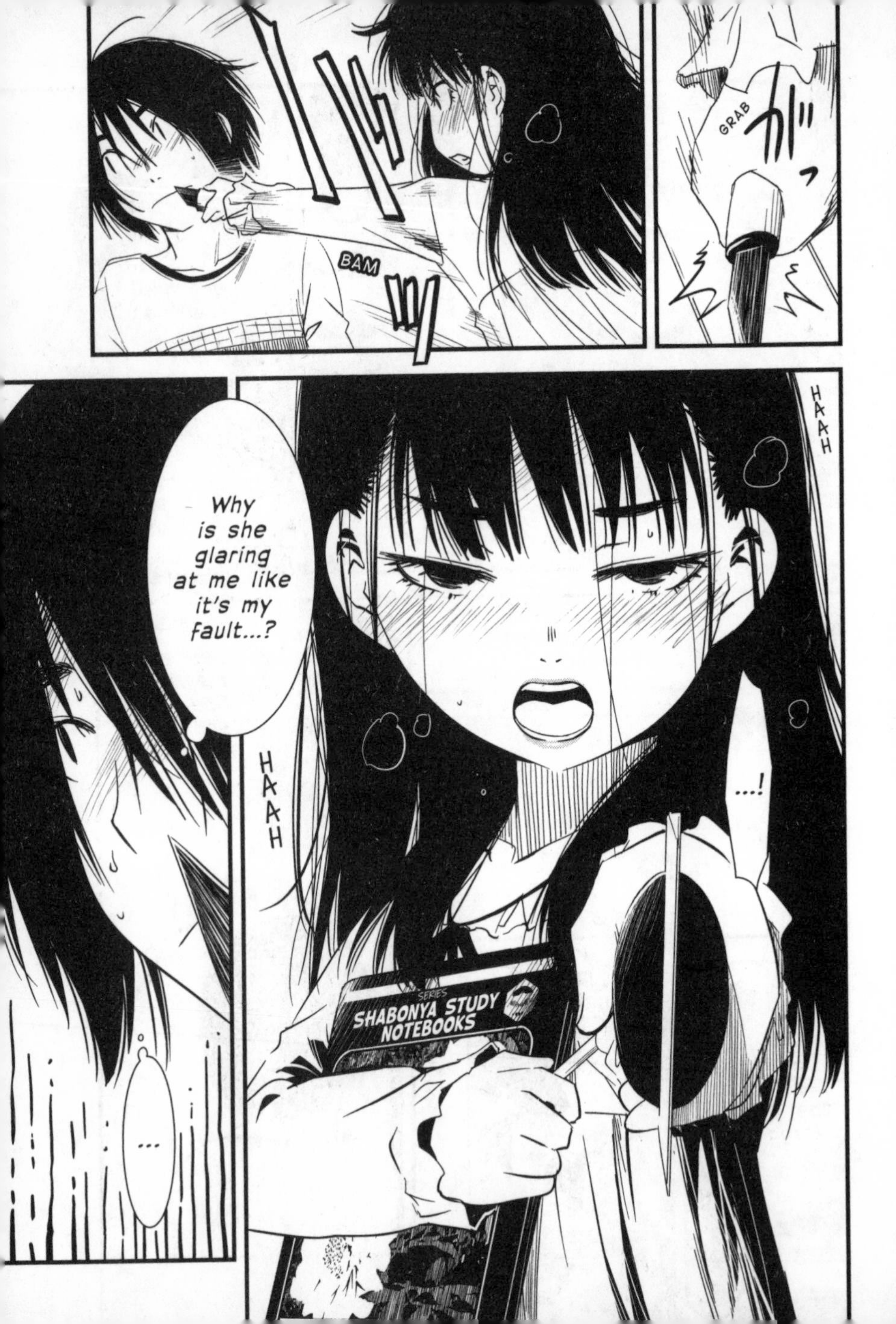
GRAB
BAM
HAAAH
...!
HAAAH
SERIES
SHABONYA STUDY NOTEBOOKS
Why is she glaring at me like it's my fault...?
...

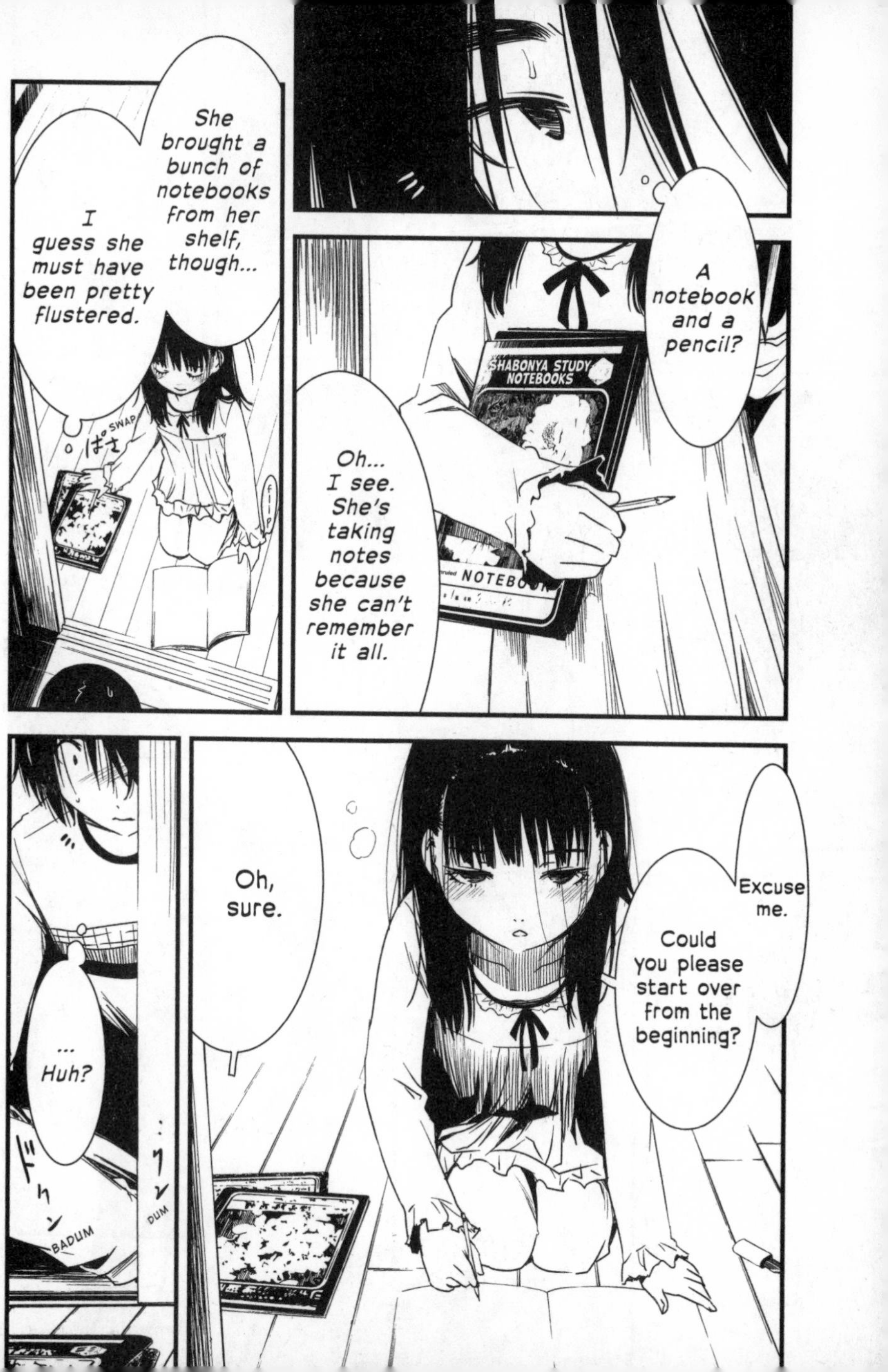
A notebook and a pencil?
SHABONYA STUDY NOTEBOOKS
NOTEBOOK
Oh... I see. She's taking notes because she can't remember it all.
She brought a bunch of notebooks from her shelf, though...
I guess she must have been pretty flustered.
SWAP
ぱさ
FLIP
Excuse me. Could you please start over from the beginning?
Oh, sure.
... Huh?
DUM
BADUM

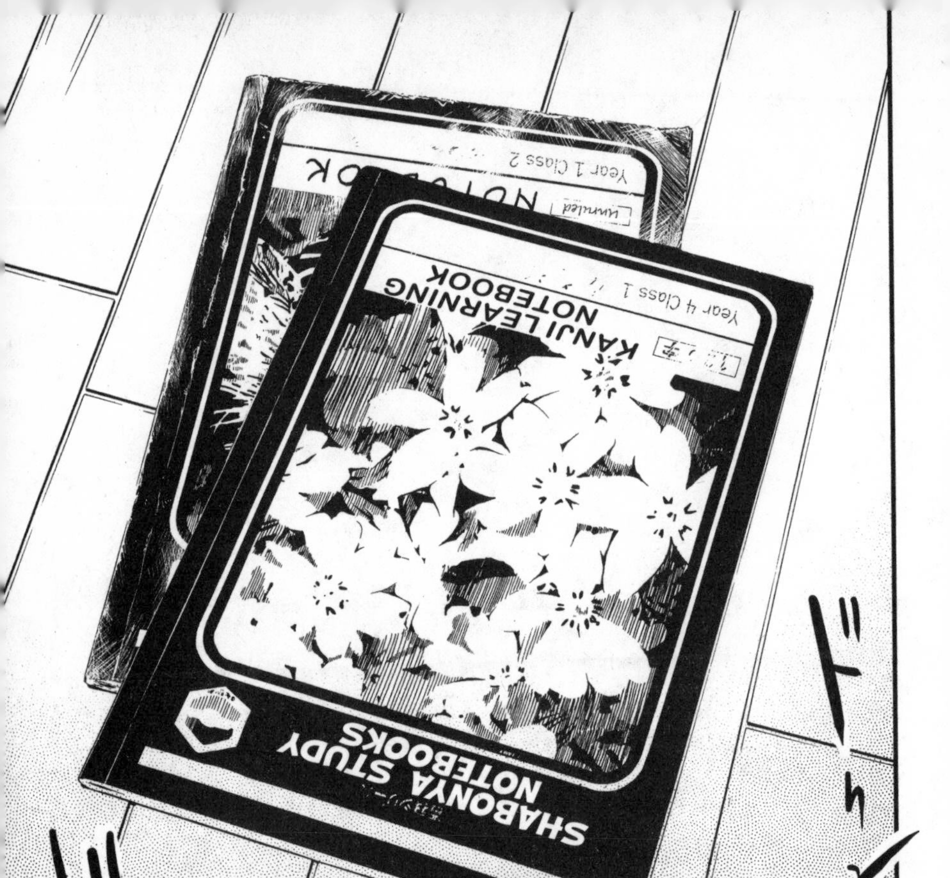
Year 1 Class 2
KANJI LEARNING NOTEBOOK
Year 4 Class 1
SHABONYA STUDY NOTEBOOKS
BADUM
BADUM
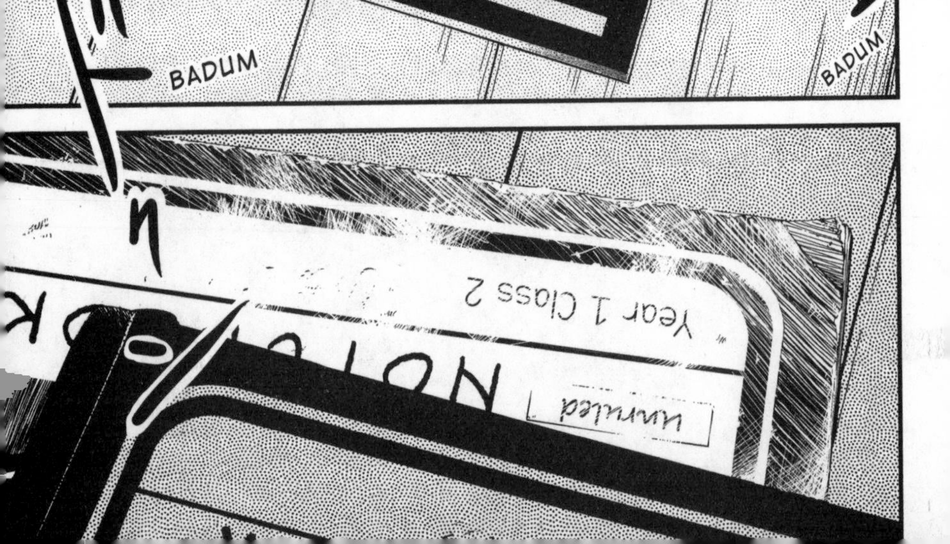
Year 1 Class 2

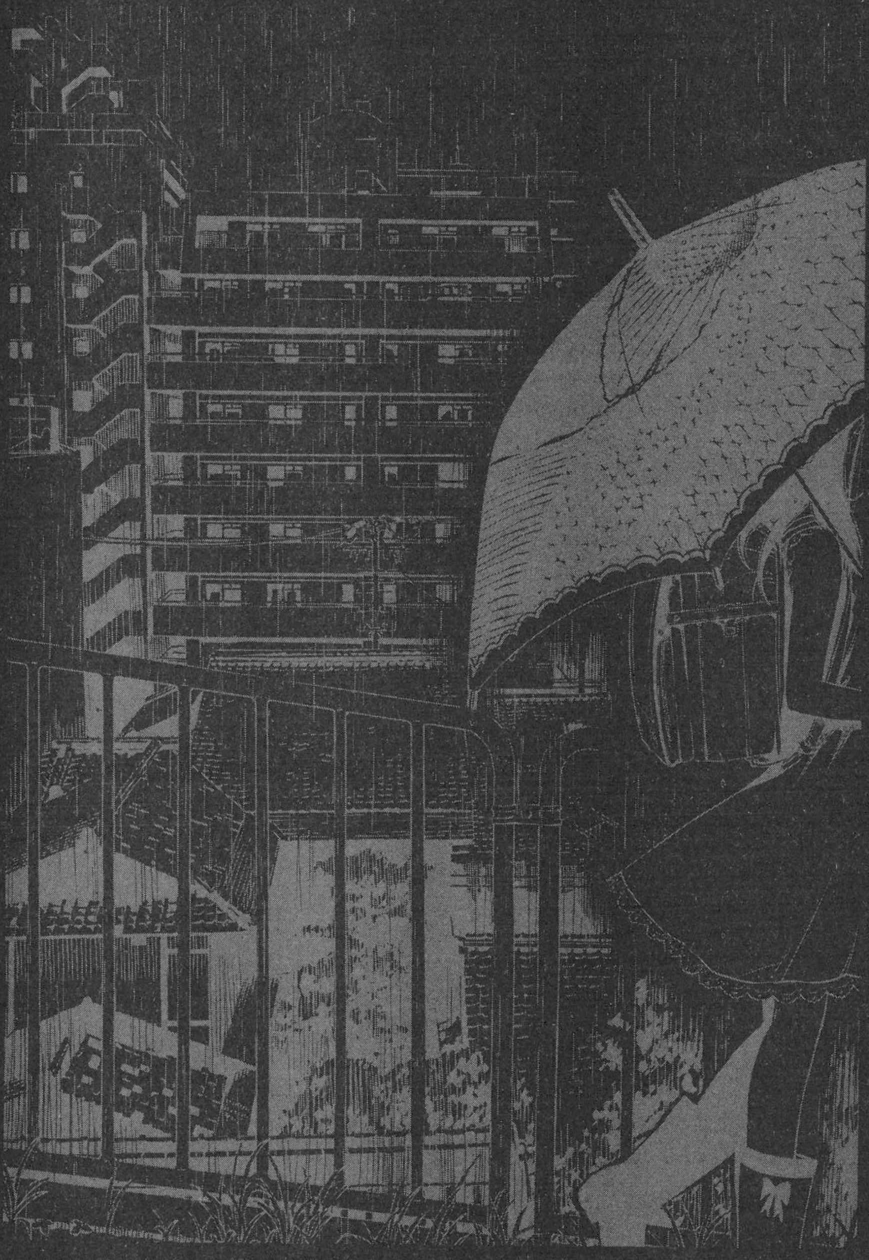

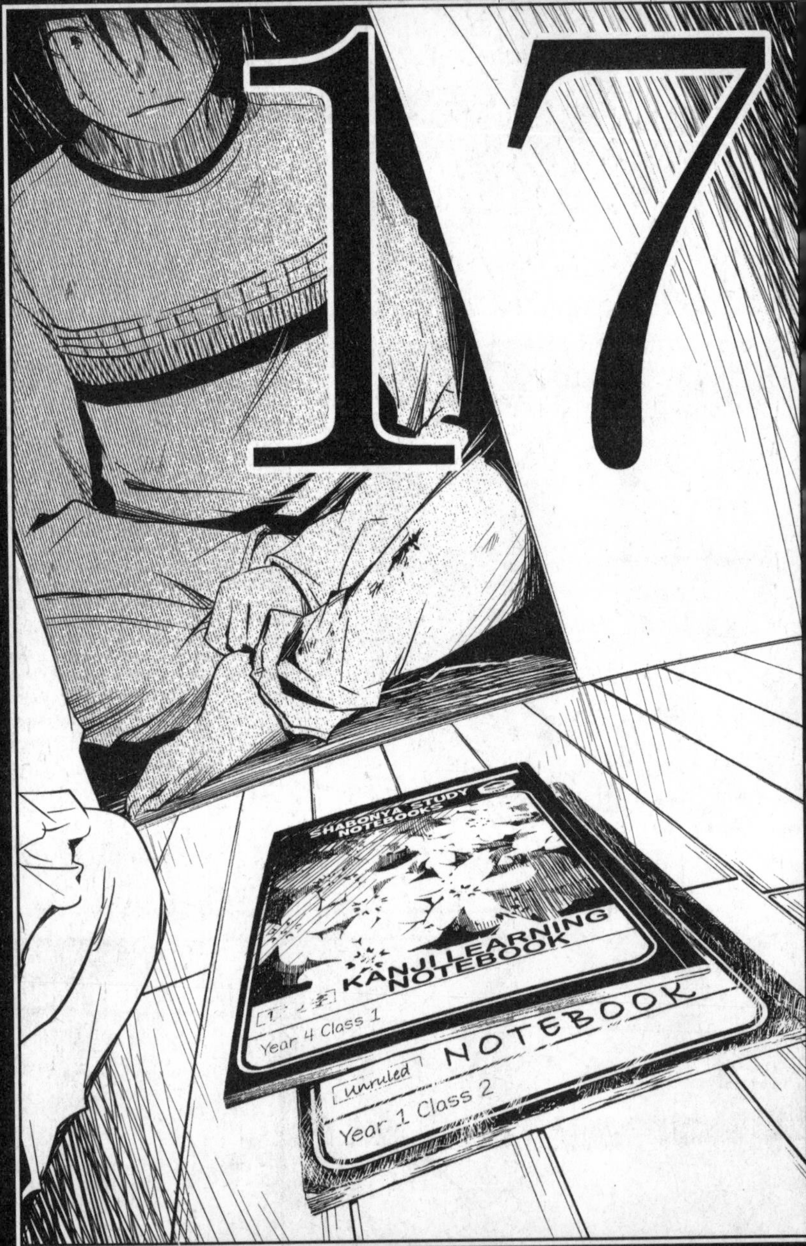
17
SHABONIYA STUDY NOTEBOOKS
KANJI LEARNING NOTEBOOK
Year 4 Class 1
Unruled
NOTEBOOK
Year 1 Class 2

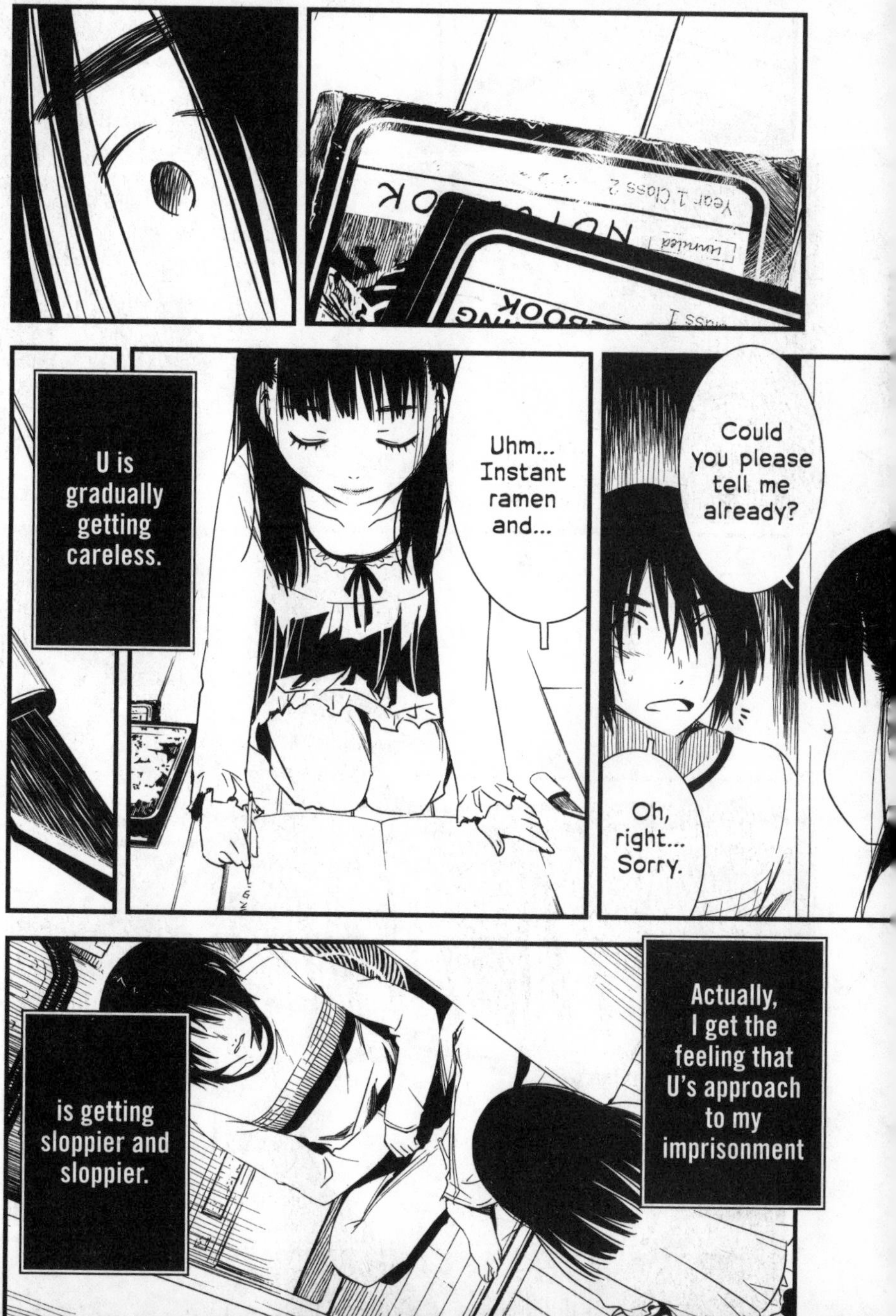
Year 1 Class 2
Could you please tell me already?
Oh, right... Sorry.
Uhm... Instant ramen and...
U is gradually getting careless.
Actually, I get the feeling that U's approach to my imprisonment
is getting sloppier and sloppier.

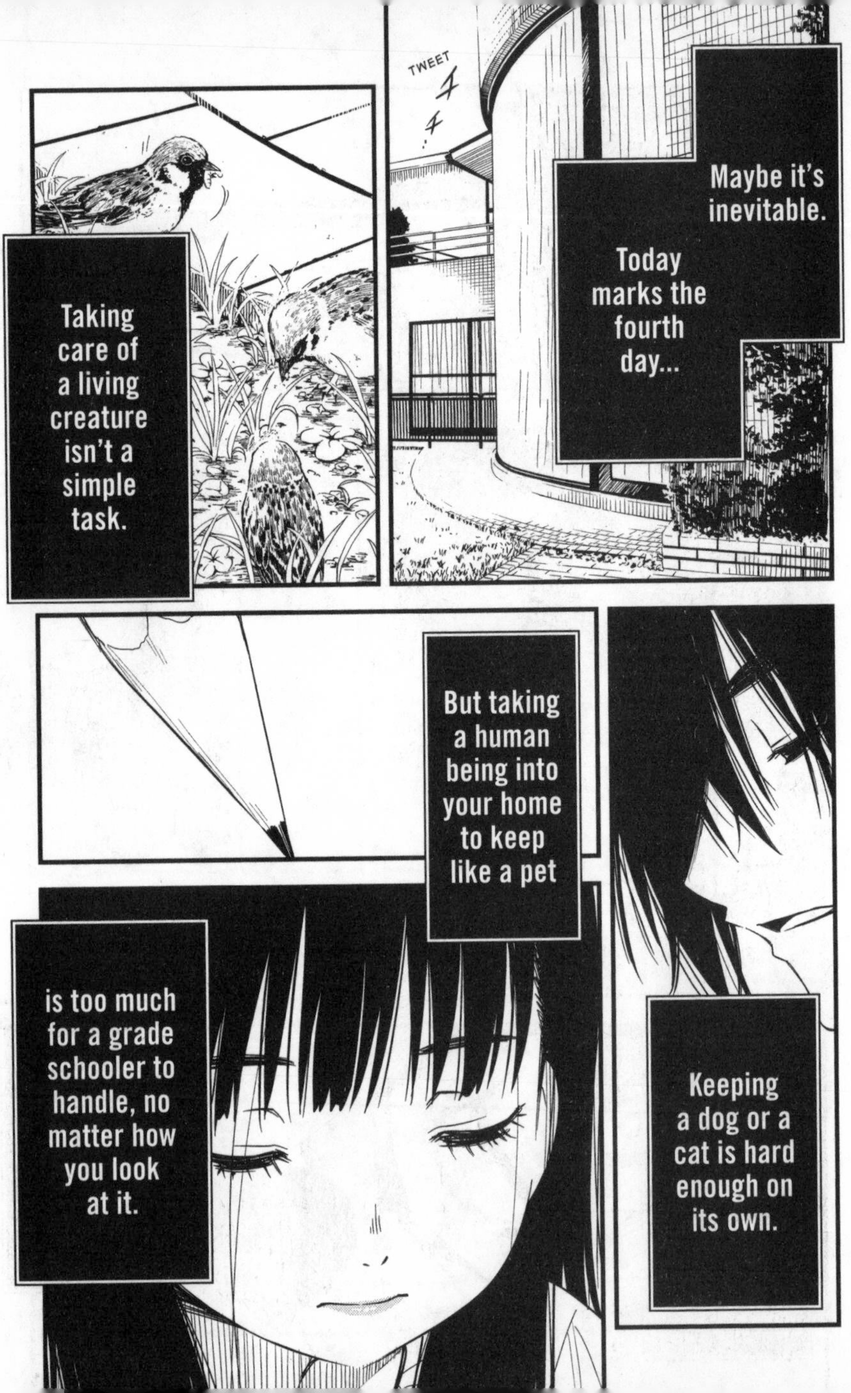
TWEET
Maybe it's inevitable.
Today marks the fourth day...
Taking care of a living creature isn't a simple task.
Keeping a dog or a cat is hard enough on its own.
But taking a human being into your home to keep like a pet
is too much for a grade schooler to handle, no matter how you look at it.

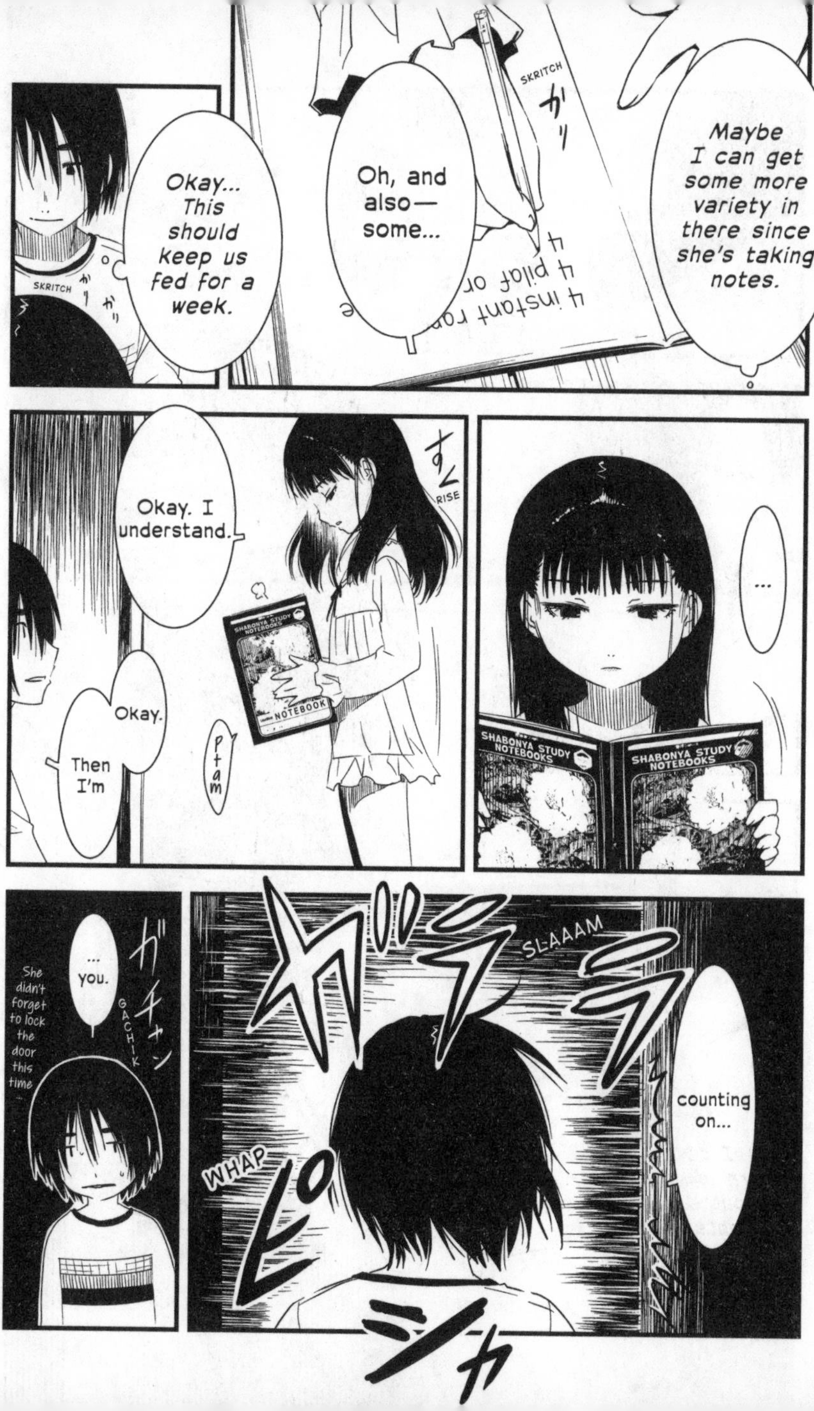

Maybe I can get some more variety in there since she's taking notes.
SKRITCH
ガリ
Oh, and also— some...
Okay... This should keep us fed for a week.
SKRITCH
がりがり
...
SHABONYA STUDY NOTEBOOKS
SHABONYA STUDY NOTEBOOKS
すく
RISE
Okay. I understand.
SHABONYA STUDY NOTEBOOKS
NOTEBOOK
Okay.
Then I'm
ptam
ガラ
SL-AAAM
counting on...
ピシ
WHAP
... you.
ガチャン
GACHIK
She didn't forget to lock the door this time...

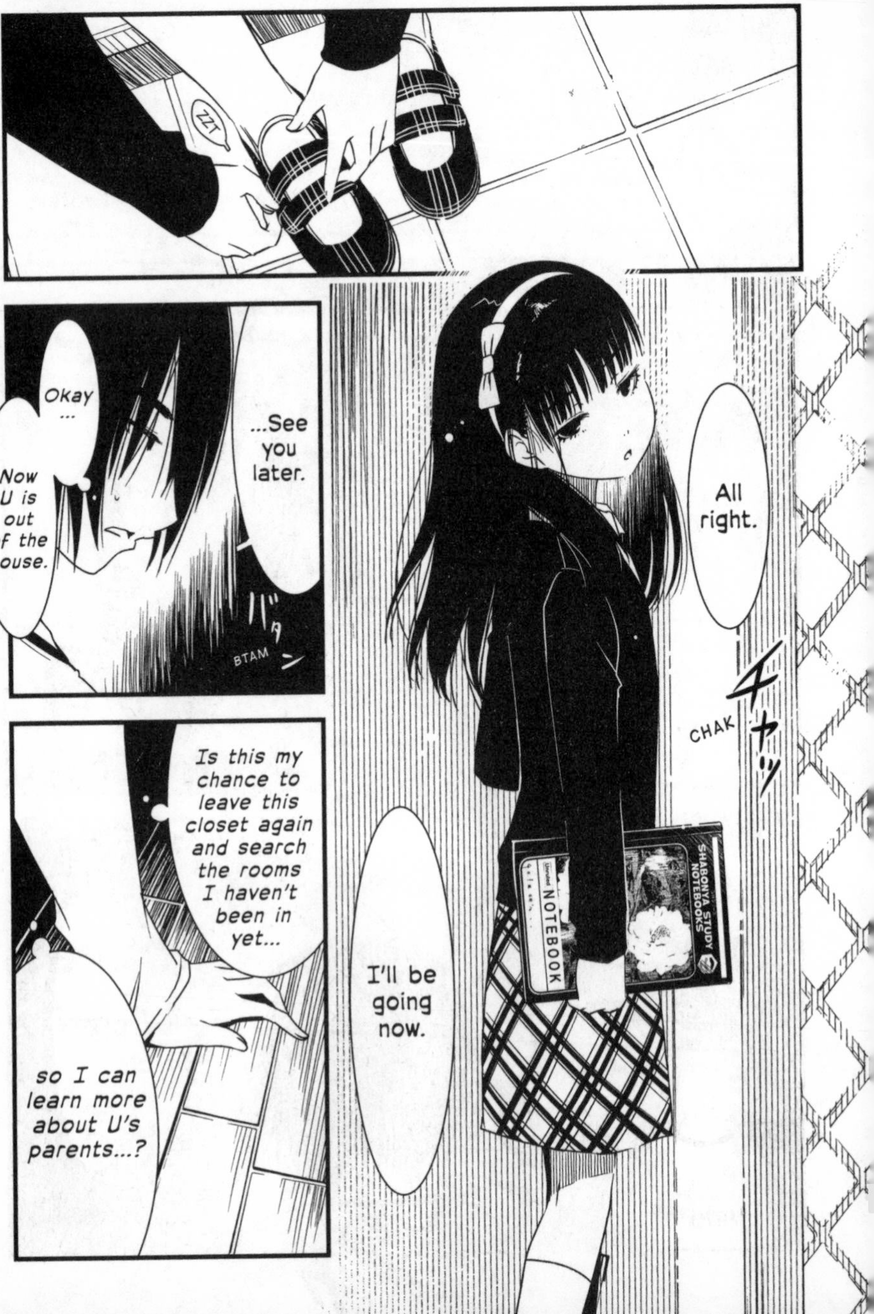
ZZT
All right.
CHAK
I'll be going now.
SHARONYA STUDY NOTEBOOKS
NOTEBOOK
...See you later.
BTAM
Okay ...
Now U is out of the house.
Is this my chance to leave this closet again and search the rooms I haven't been in yet...
so I can learn more about U's parents...?

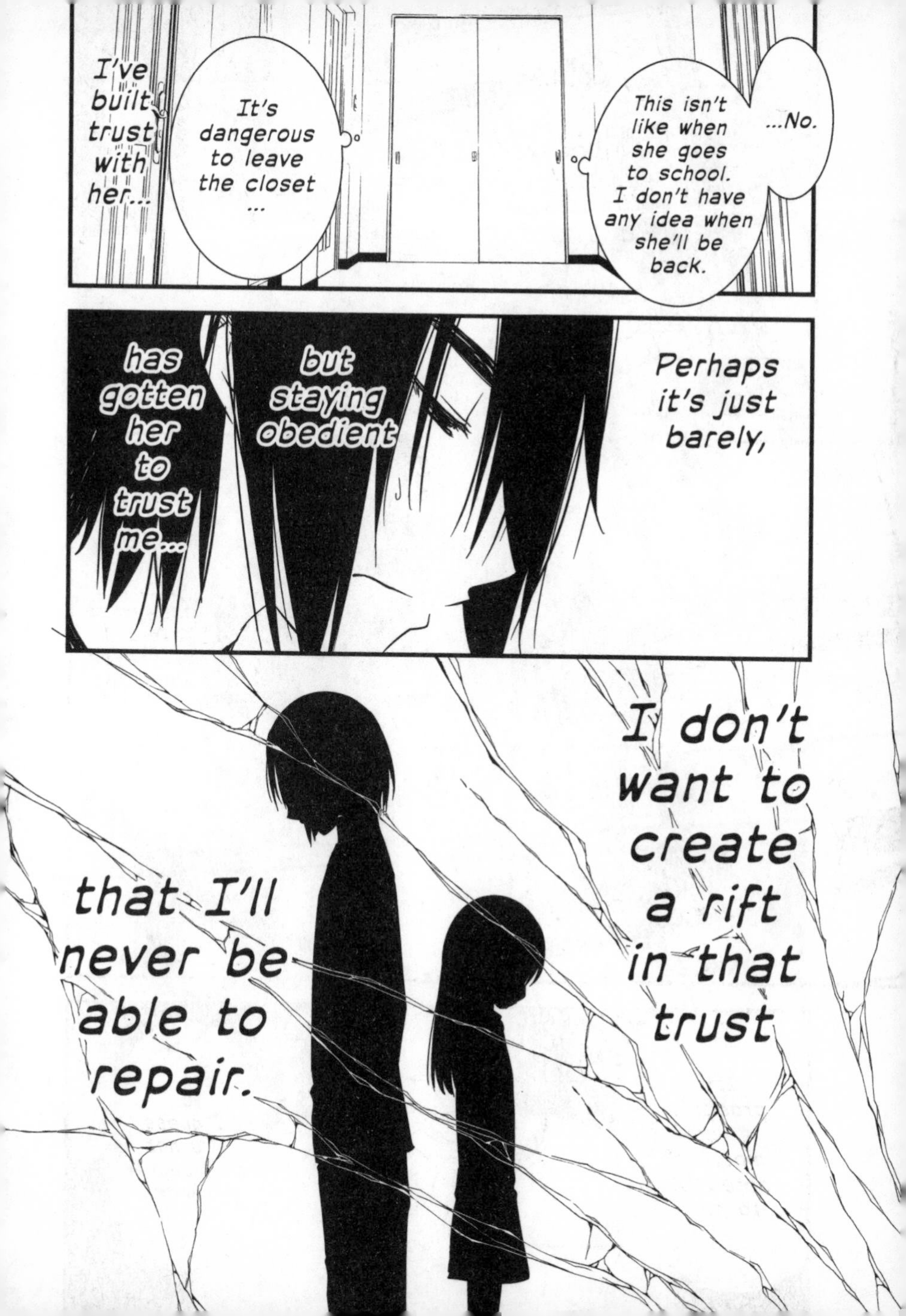
...No.
This isn't like when she goes to school. I don't have any idea when she'll be back.
It's dangerous to leave the closet ...
I've built trust with her...
Perhaps it's just barely,
but staying obedient
has gotten her to trust me...
I don't want to create a rift in that trust
that I'll never be able to repair.

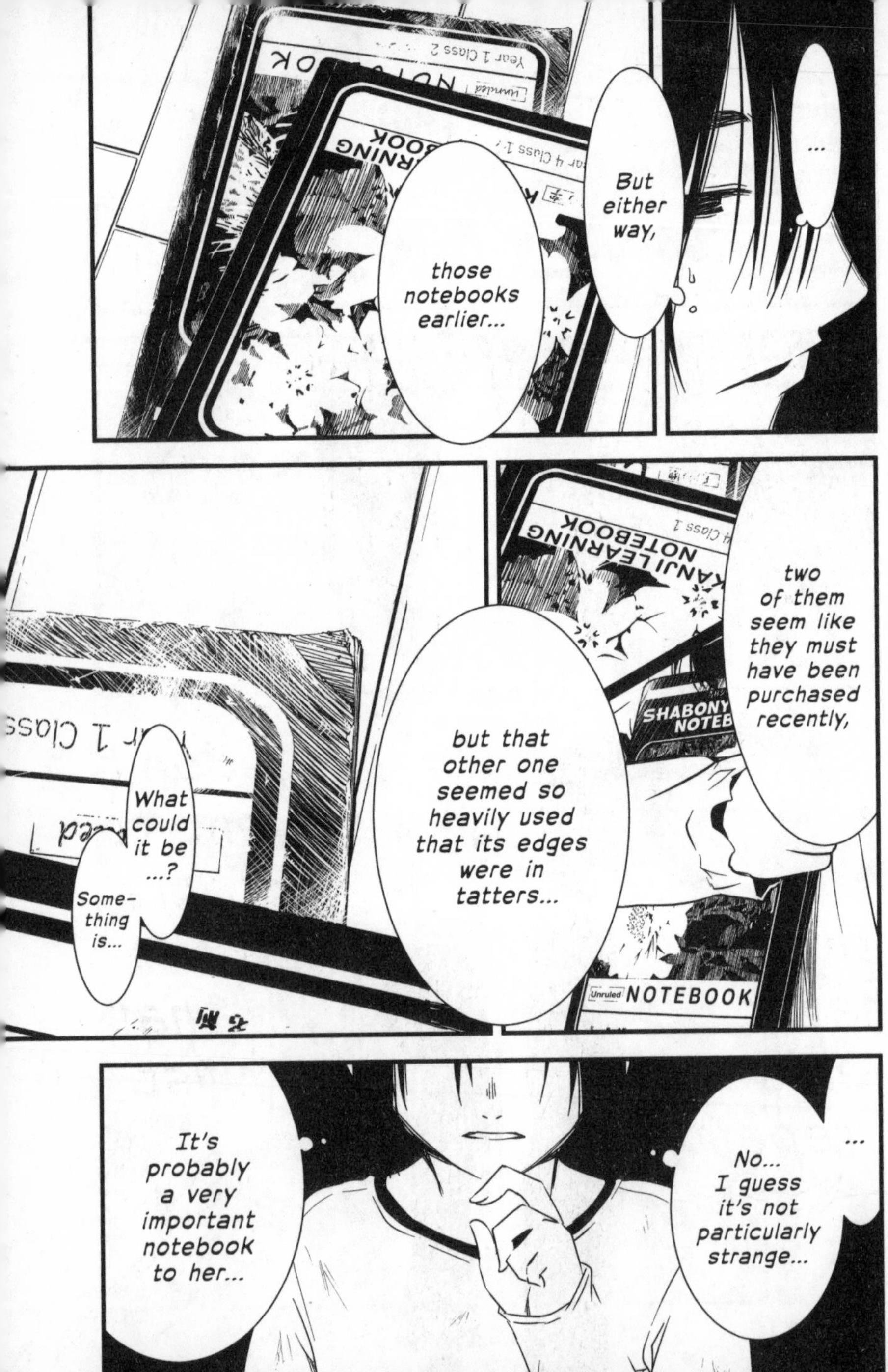
...
But either way,
those notebooks earlier...
two of them seem like they must have been purchased recently,
but that other one seemed so heavily used that its edges were in tatters...
What could it be ...?
Some-thing is...
...
No... I guess it's not particularly strange...
It's probably a very important notebook to her...

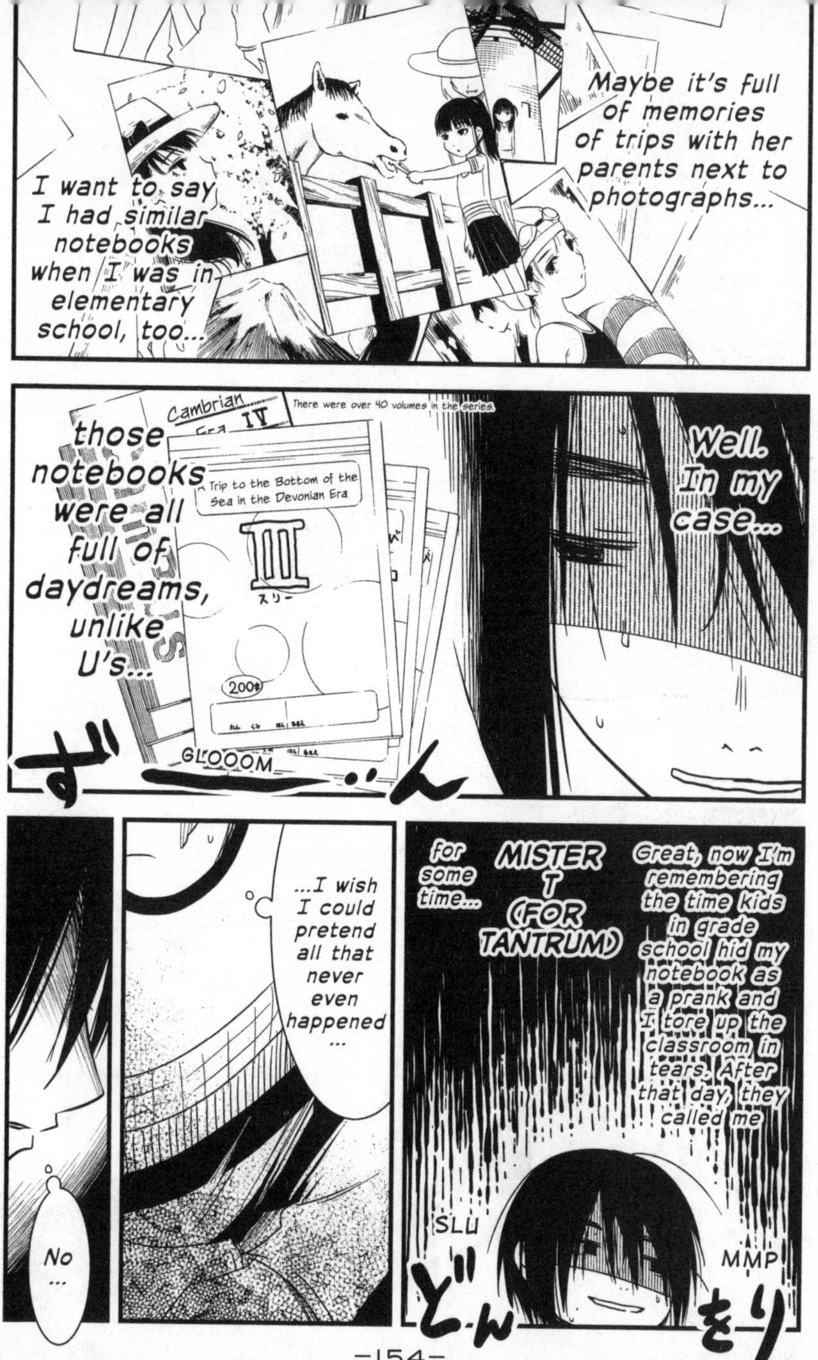
Maybe it's full of memories of trips with her parents next to photographs...
I want to say I had similar notebooks when I was in elementary school, too...
Well. In my case...
There were over 40 volumes in the series.
Cambrian Era IV
those notebooks were all full of daydreams, unlike U's...
Trip to the Bottom of the Sea in the Devonian Era
III
スリー
GLOOOM
ず————ん
Great, now I'm remembering the time kids in grade school hid my notebook as a prank and I tore up the classroom in tears. After that day, they called me
MISTER T (FOR TANTRUM)
for some time...
SLUMP
どんより
...I wish I could pretend all that never even happened...
No...

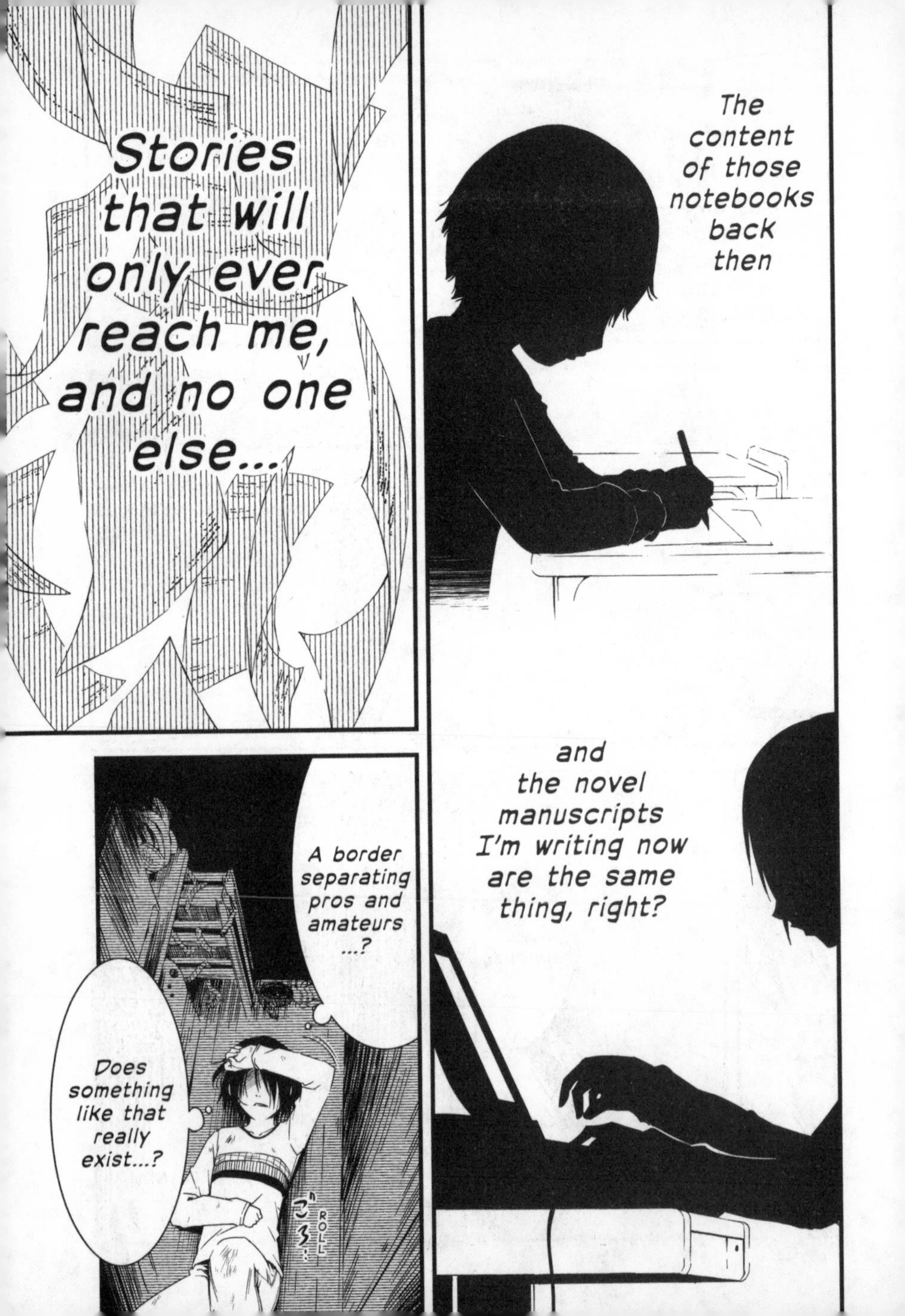
The content of those notebooks back then
Stories that will only ever reach me, and no one else...
and the novel manuscripts I'm writing now are the same thing, right?
A border separating pros and amateurs ...?
Does something like that really exist...?
ROLL

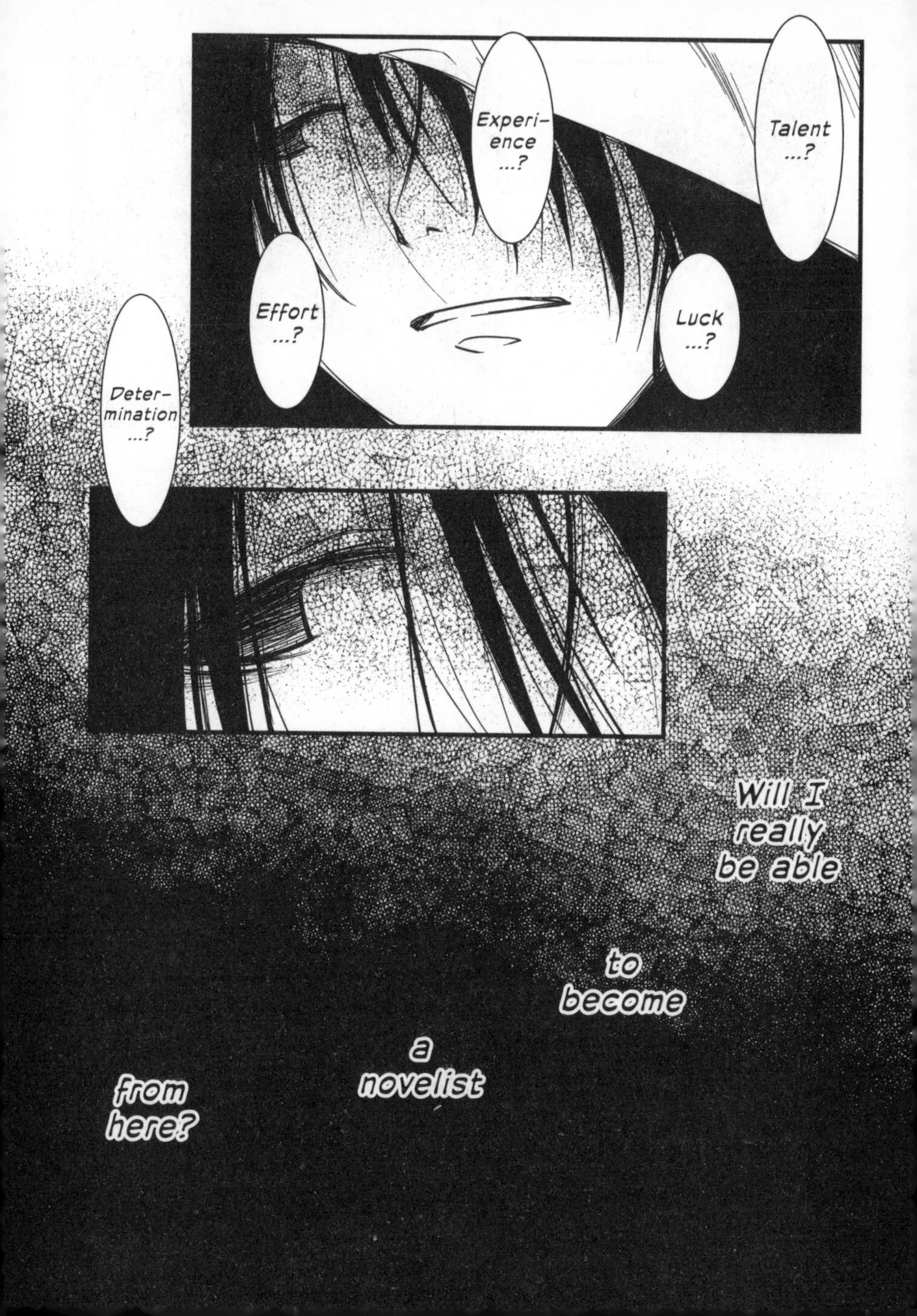
Talent ...?
Experi- ence ...?
Luck ...?
Effort ...?
Deter- mination ...?
Will I really be able
to become
a novelist
from here?

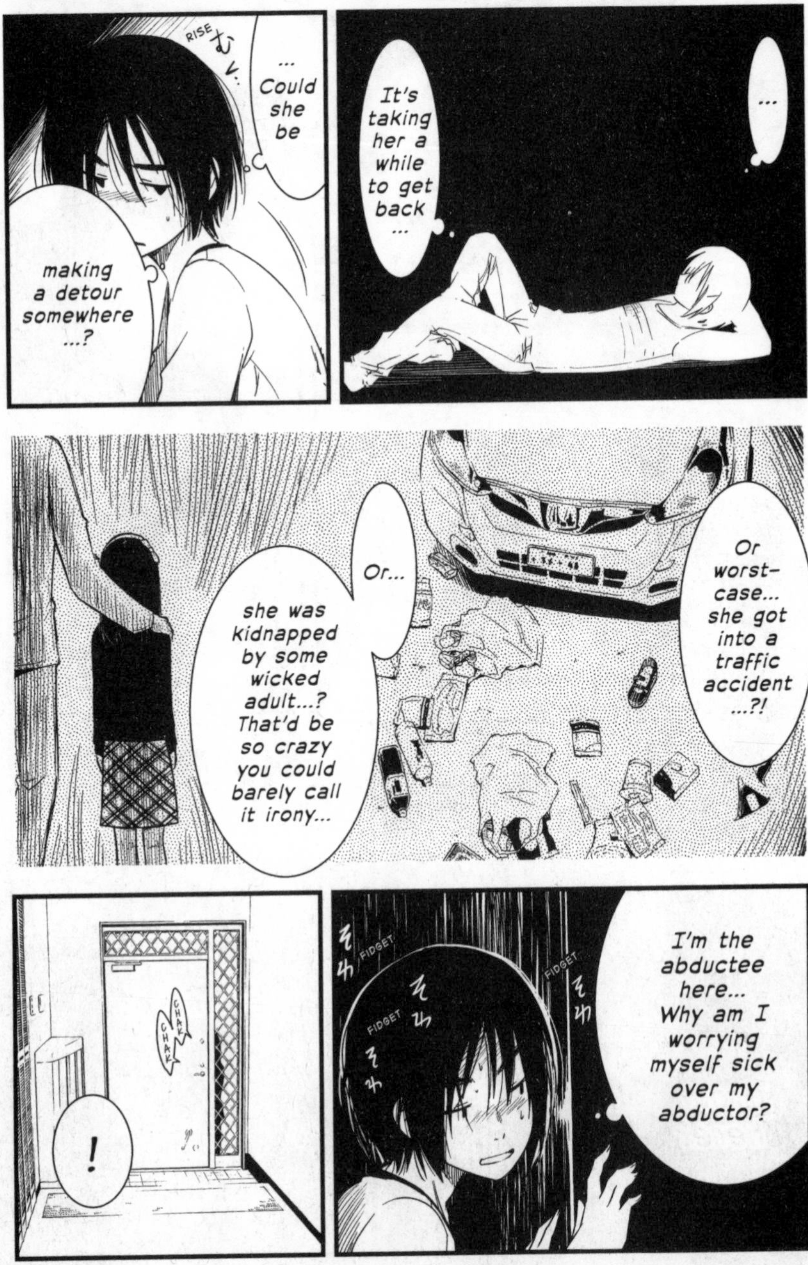
...
It's taking her a while to get back ...
RISE
... Could she be
making a detour somewhere ...?
Or worst-case... she got into a traffic accident ...?!
Or...
she was kidnapped by some wicked adult...? That'd be so crazy you could barely call it irony...
FIDGET
FIDGET
I'm the abductee here... Why am I worrying myself sick over my abductor?
CHAK CHAK
!

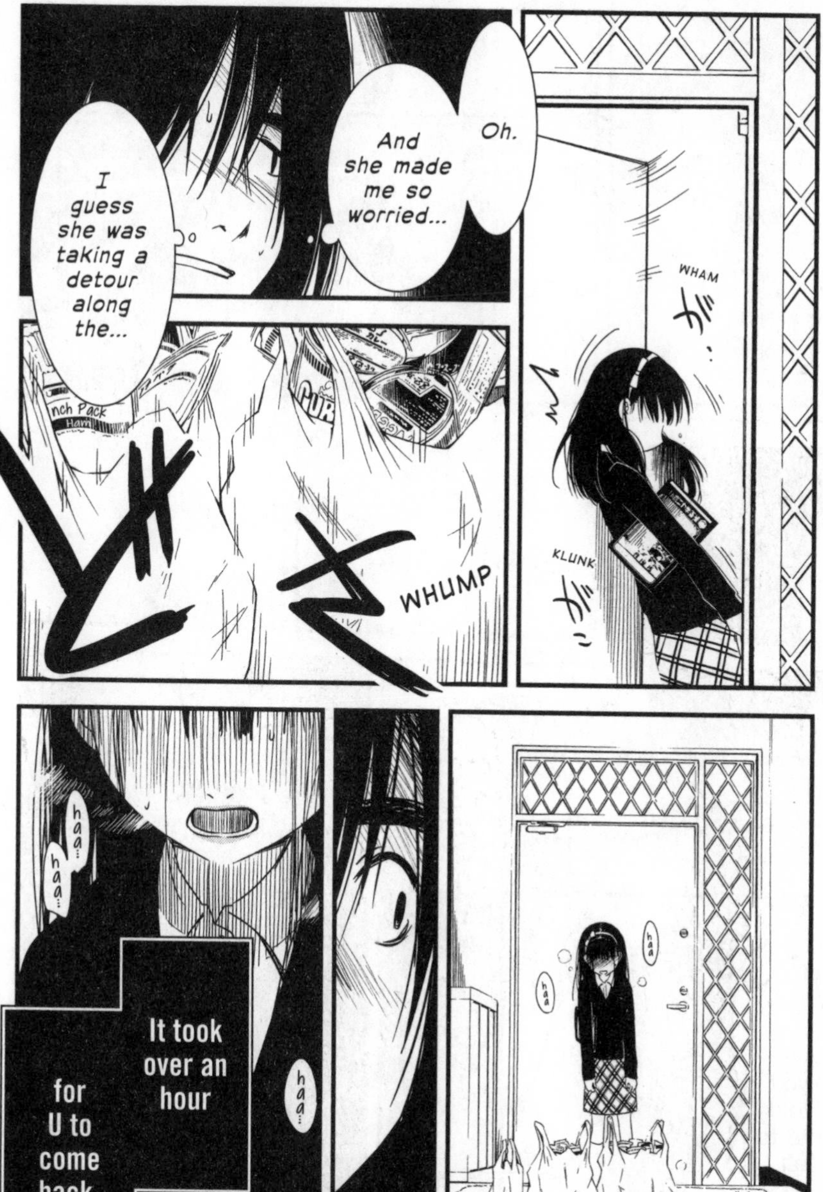

WHAM
KLUNK
Oh.
And she made me so worried...
I guess she was taking a detour along the...
nch Pack Ham
WHUMP
haa haa haa
haa...
haa... haa...
It took over an hour for U to come back.

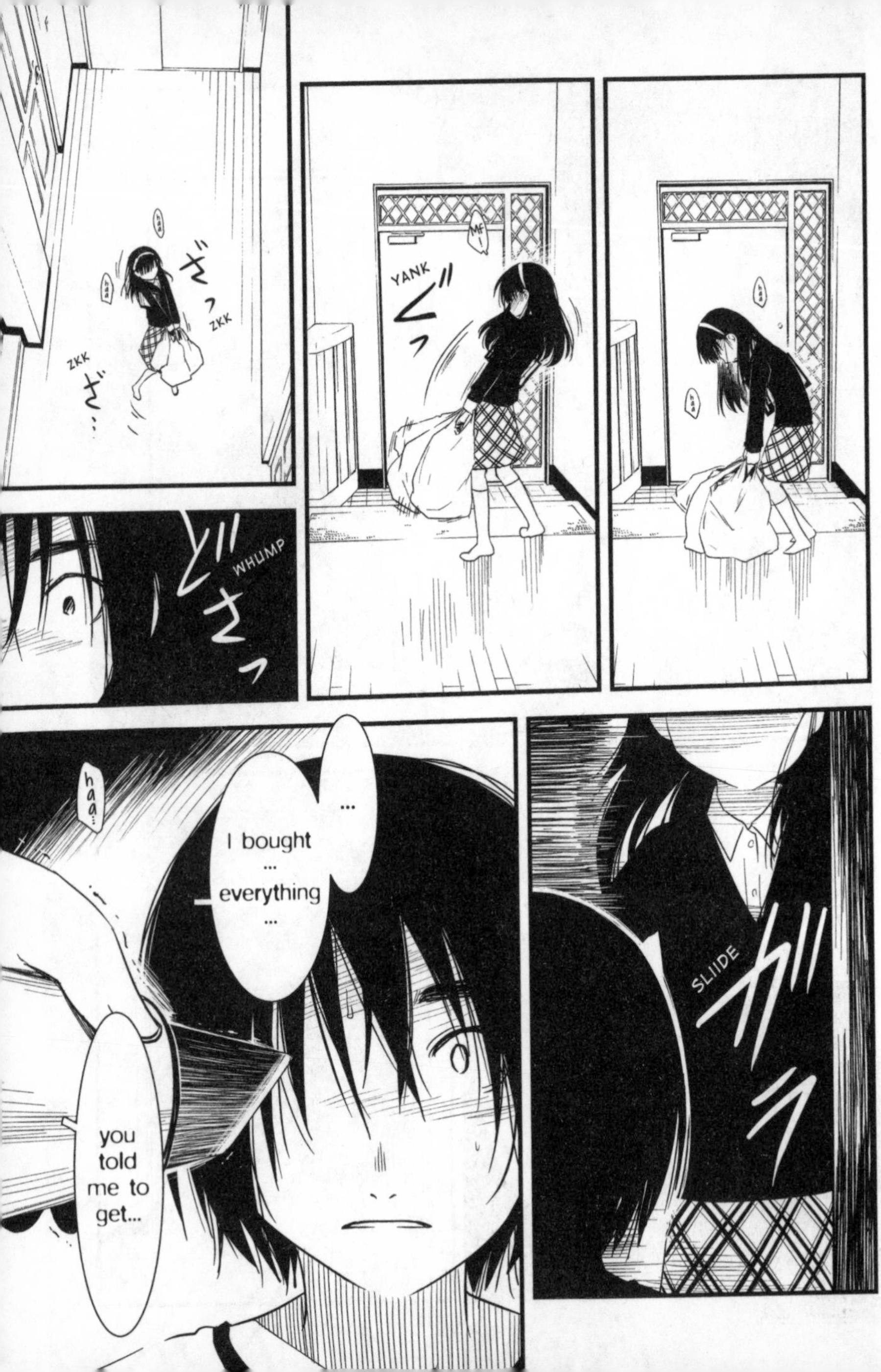
haa
haa
MF!
YANK
haa
haa
ZKK
ZKK
WHUMP
SLIIDE
haa...
... I bought ... everything ...
you told me to get...

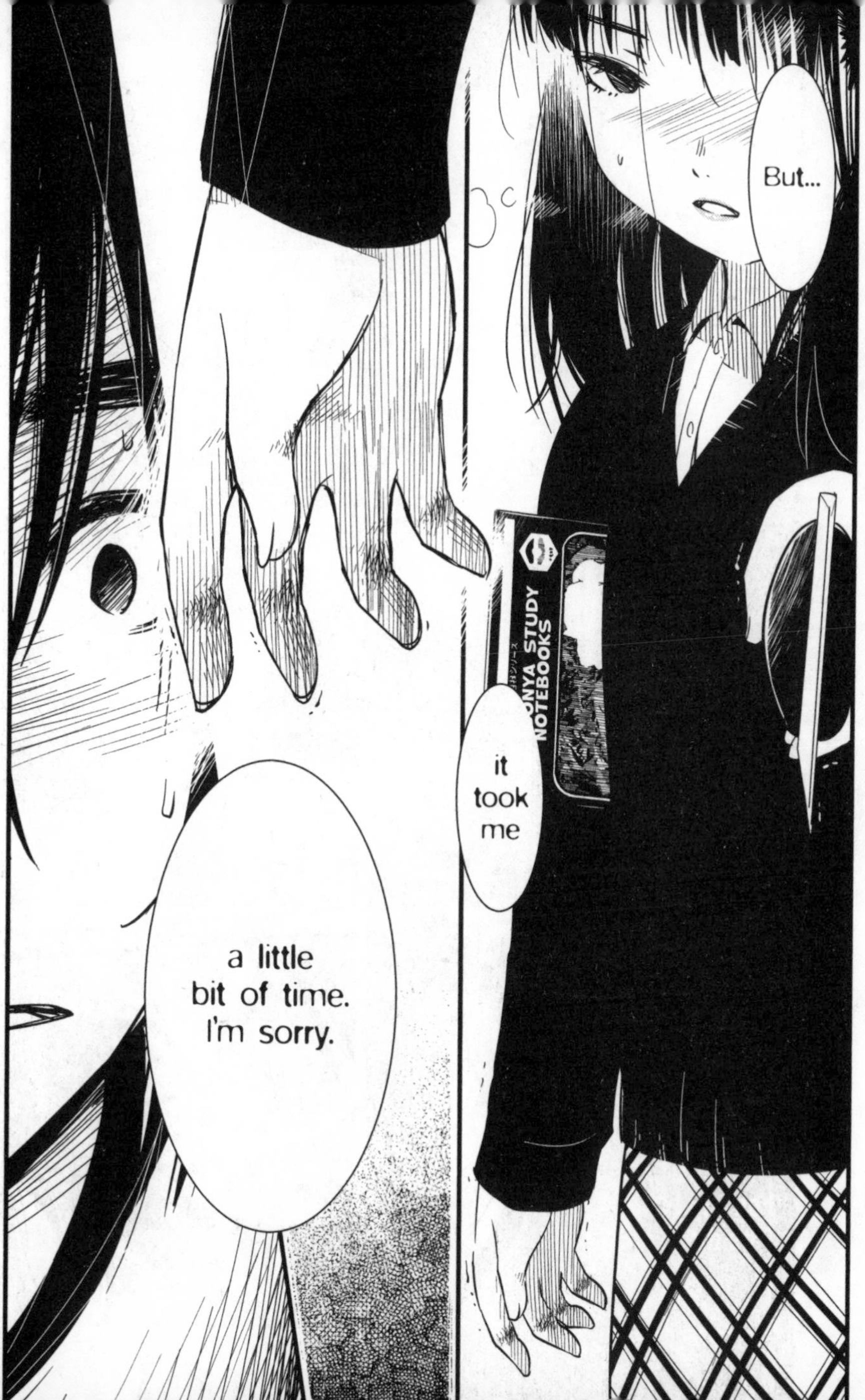
But...
ONYA STUDY NOTEBOOKS
it took me
a little bit of time. I'm sorry.

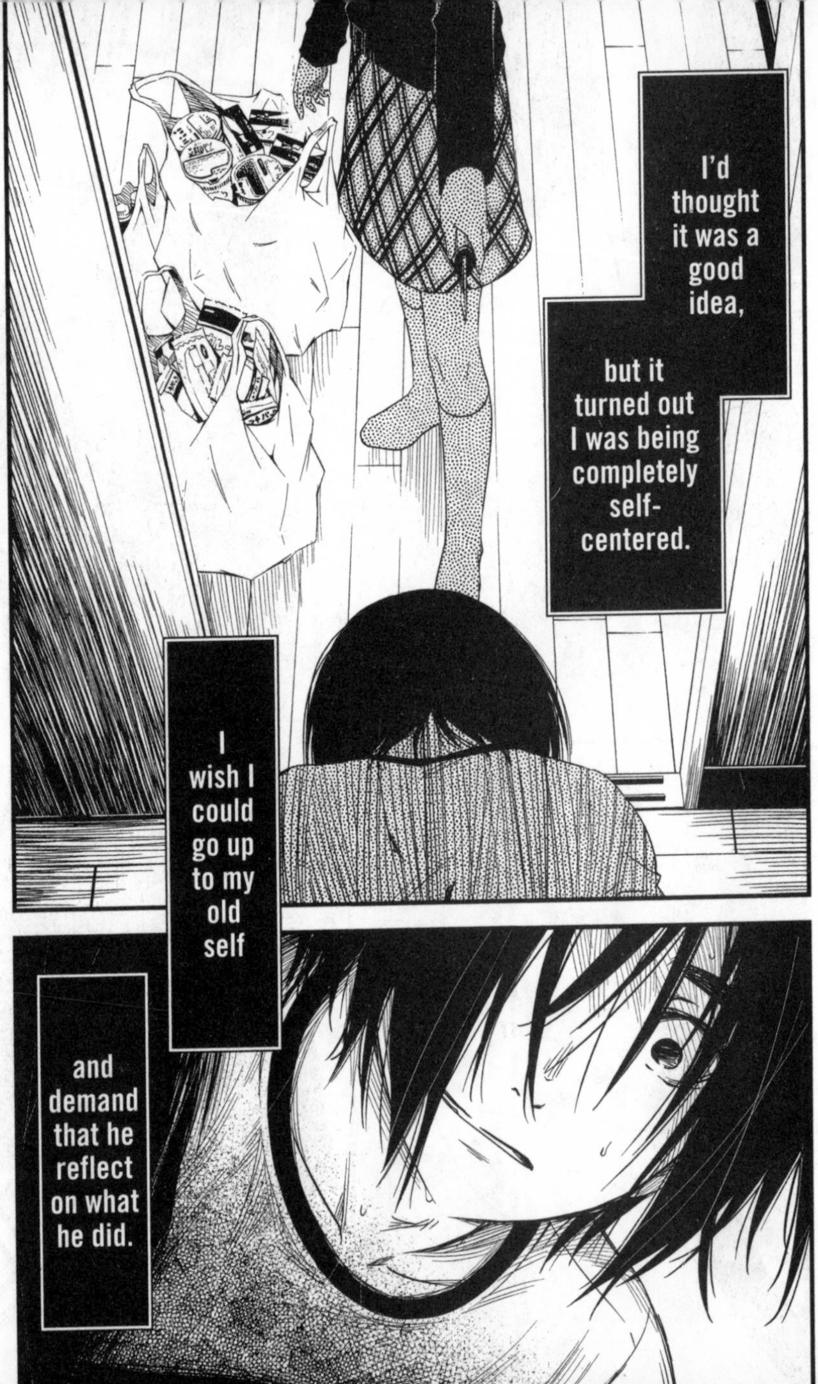
I'd thought it was a good idea,
but it turned out I was being completely self-centered.
I wish I could go up to my old self
and demand that he reflect on what he did.

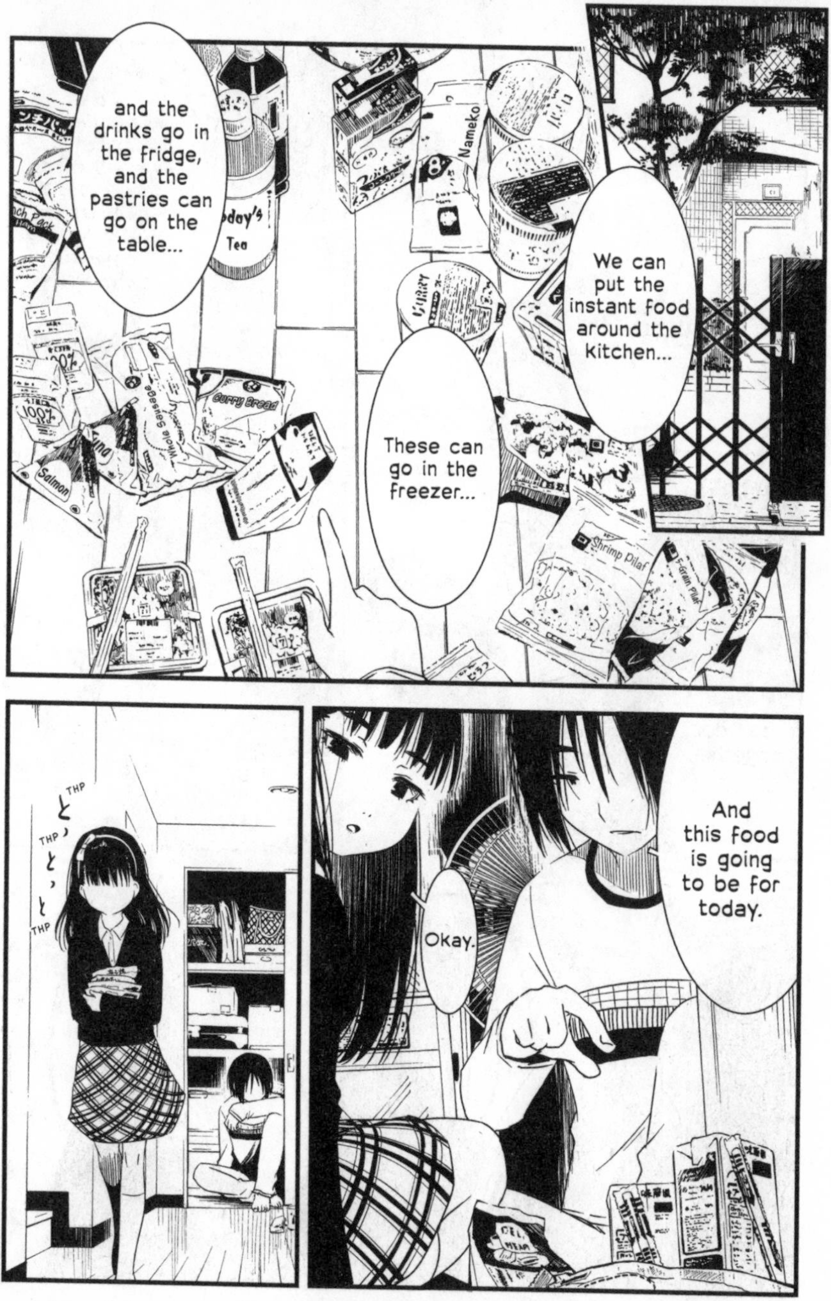
We can put the instant food around the kitchen...
These can go in the freezer...
and the drinks go in the fridge, and the pastries can go on the table...
Nameko
Tea
Curry Bread
Whole Sausage
Salmon
Shrimp Pilaf
5-Grain Pilaf
And this food is going to be for today.
Okay.
と、THP
と、THP
と THP

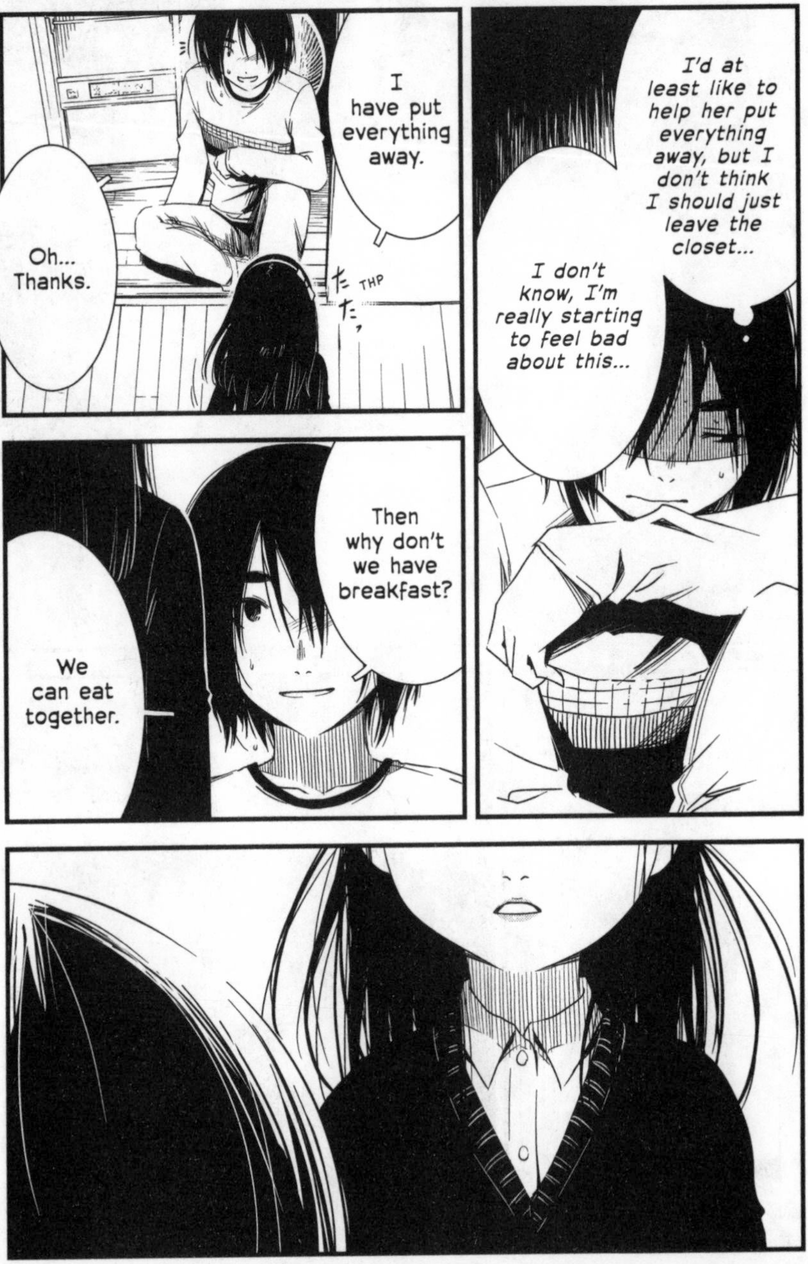
I'd at least like to help her put everything away, but I don't think I should just leave the closet...
I don't know, I'm really starting to feel bad about this...
I have put everything away.
Oh... Thanks.
たた, THP
Then why don't we have breakfast?
We can eat together.

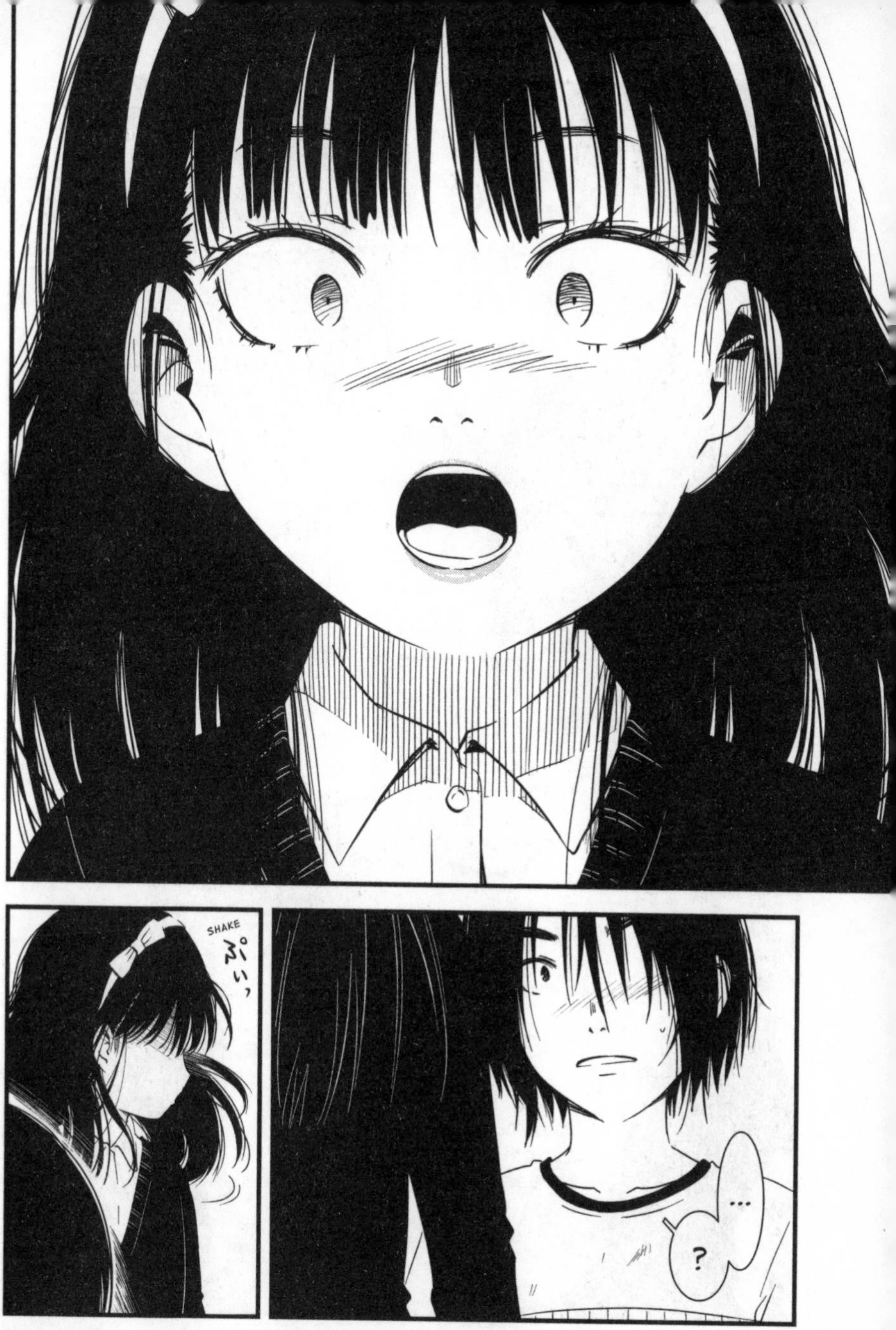
...
?
SHAKE
ぷい，

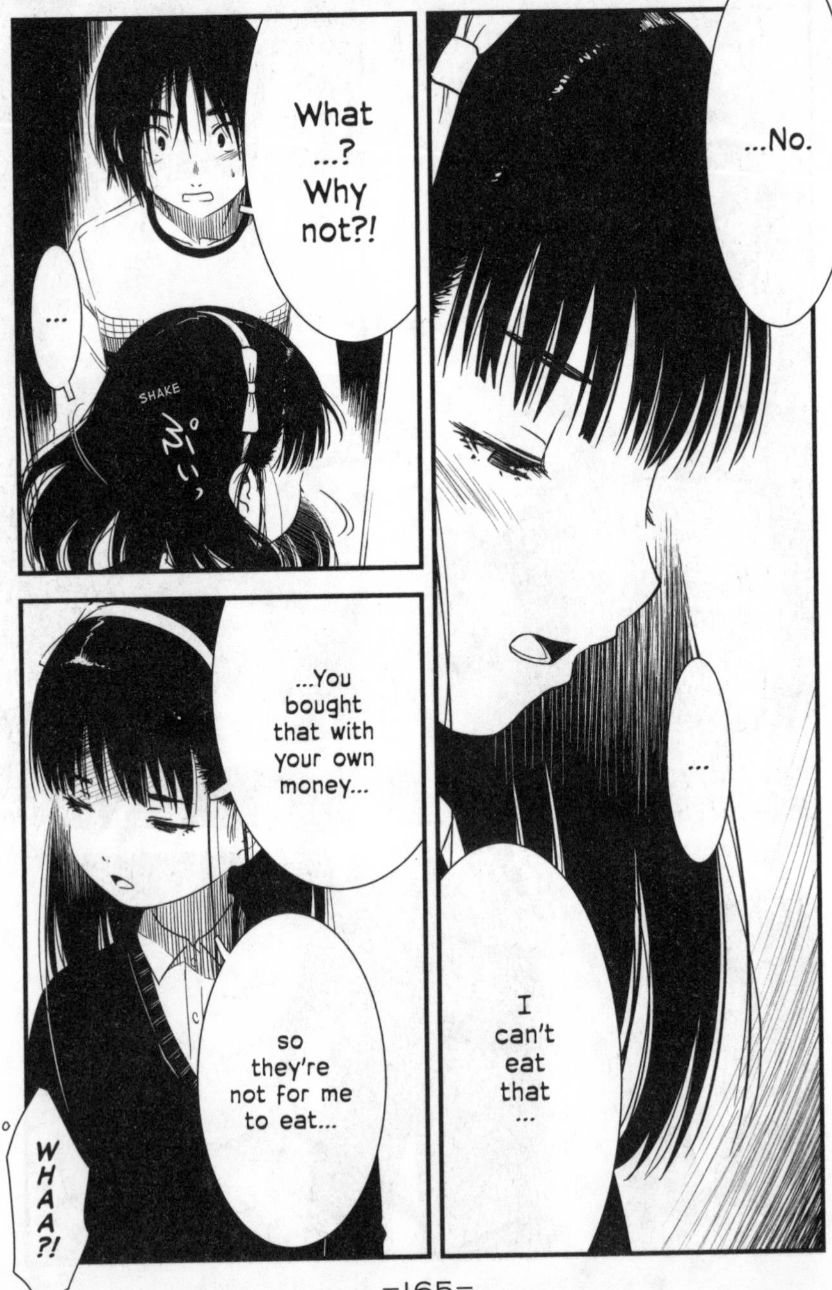
...No.
...
I can't eat that ...
What ...? Why not?!
...
SHAKE
...You bought that with your own money...
so they're not for me to eat...
WHAAA?!

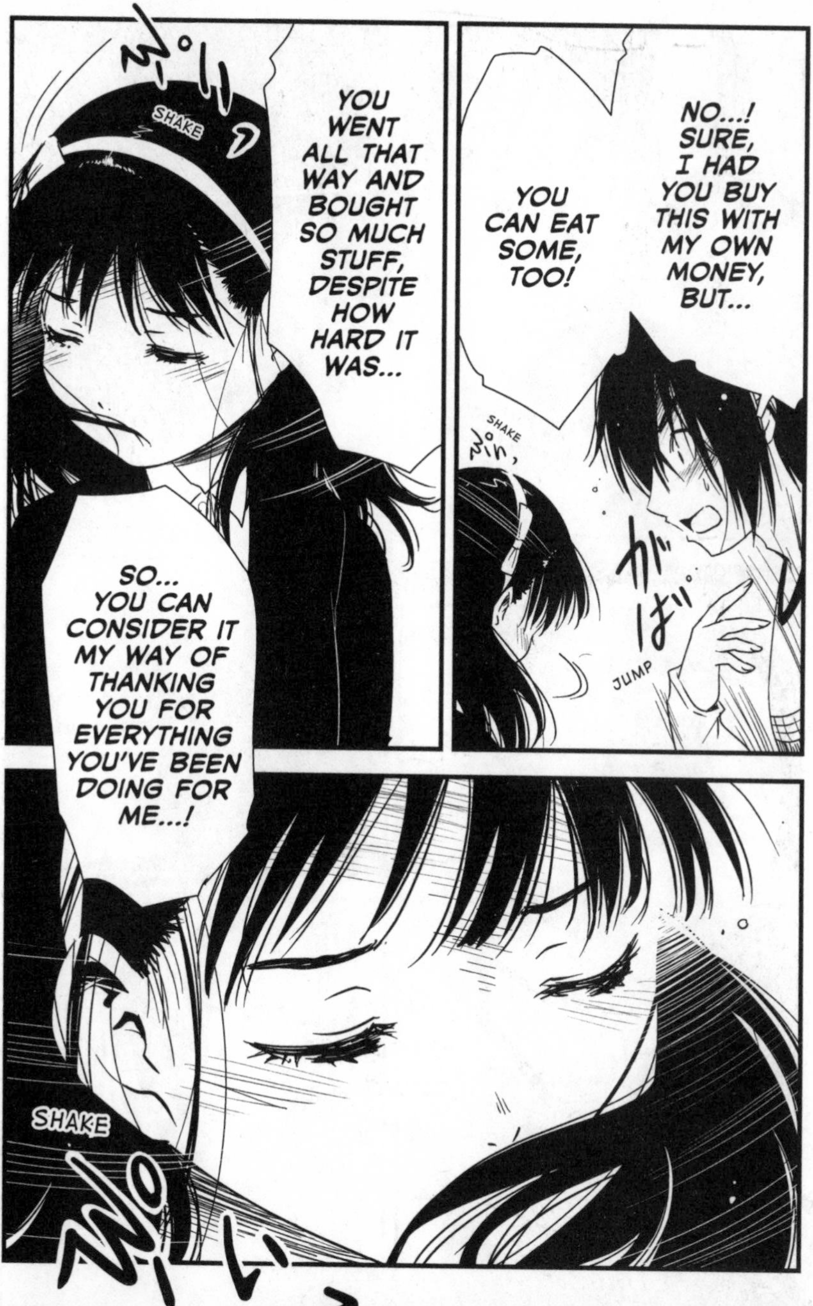
NO...! SURE, I HAD YOU BUY THIS WITH MY OWN MONEY, BUT...
YOU CAN EAT SOME, TOO!
SHAKE
JUMP
YOU WENT ALL THAT WAY AND BOUGHT SO MUCH STUFF, DESPITE HOW HARD IT WAS...
SHAKE
SO... YOU CAN CONSIDER IT MY WAY OF THANKING YOU FOR EVERYTHING YOU'VE BEEN DOING FOR ME...!
SHAKE

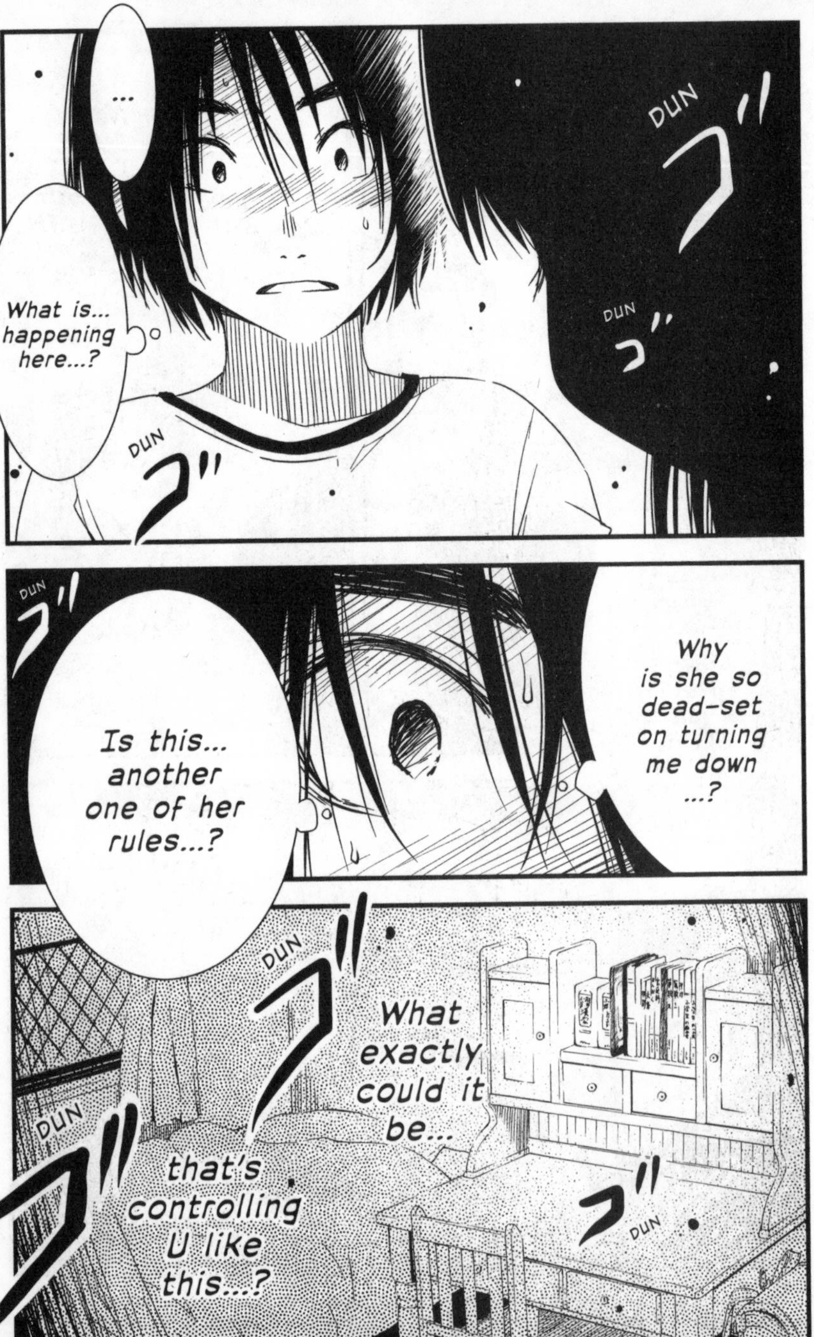
DUN ゴ
DUN ゴ
...
What is... happening here...?
DUN ゴ
Why is she so dead-set on turning me down ...?
DUN ゴ
Is this... another one of her rules...?
DUN ゴ
What exactly could it be...
DUN ゴ
that's controlling U like this...?
DUN ゴ

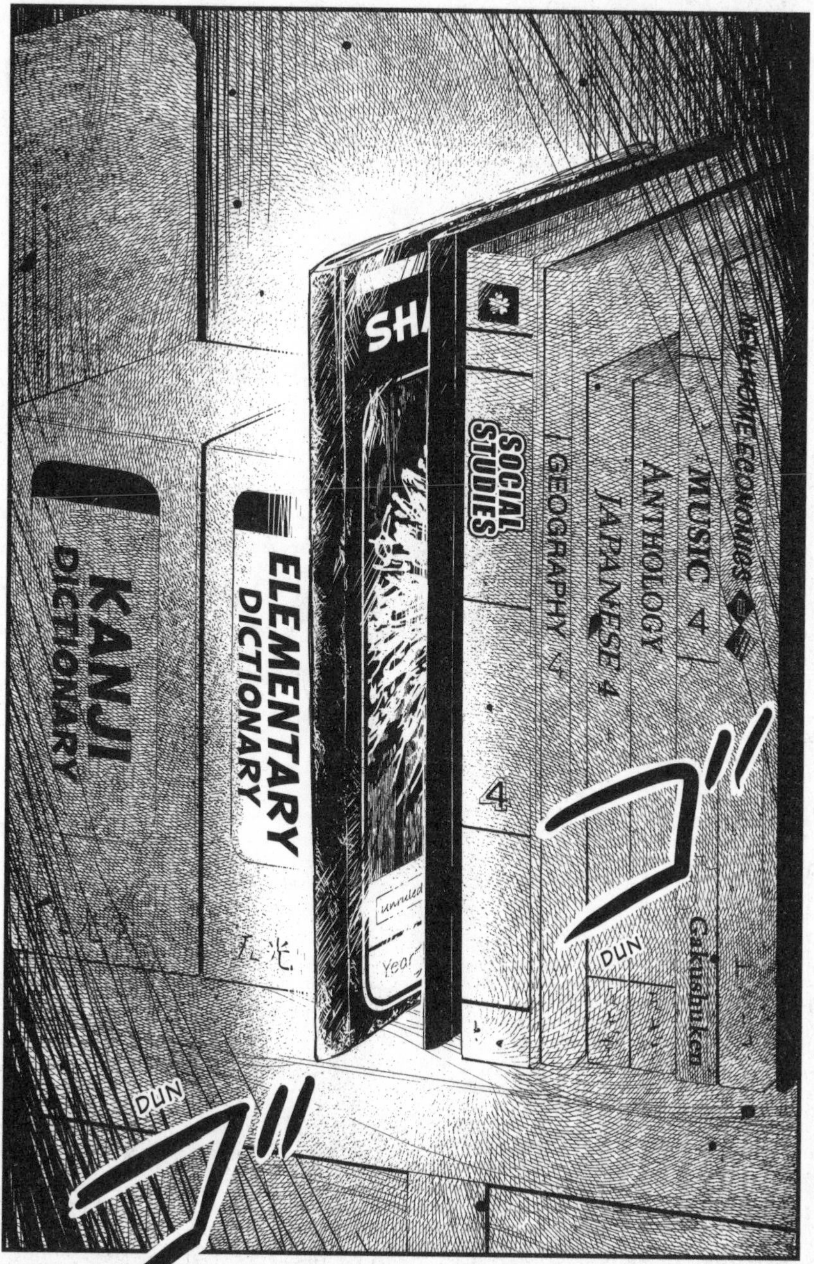
HOME ECONOMICS
MUSIC 4
ANTHOLOGY
JAPANESE 4
GEOGRAPHY 4
SOCIAL STUDIES
4
Gakushuken
DUN
SHA
unruled
Year
ELEMENTARY DICTIONARY
KANJI DICTIONARY
DUN

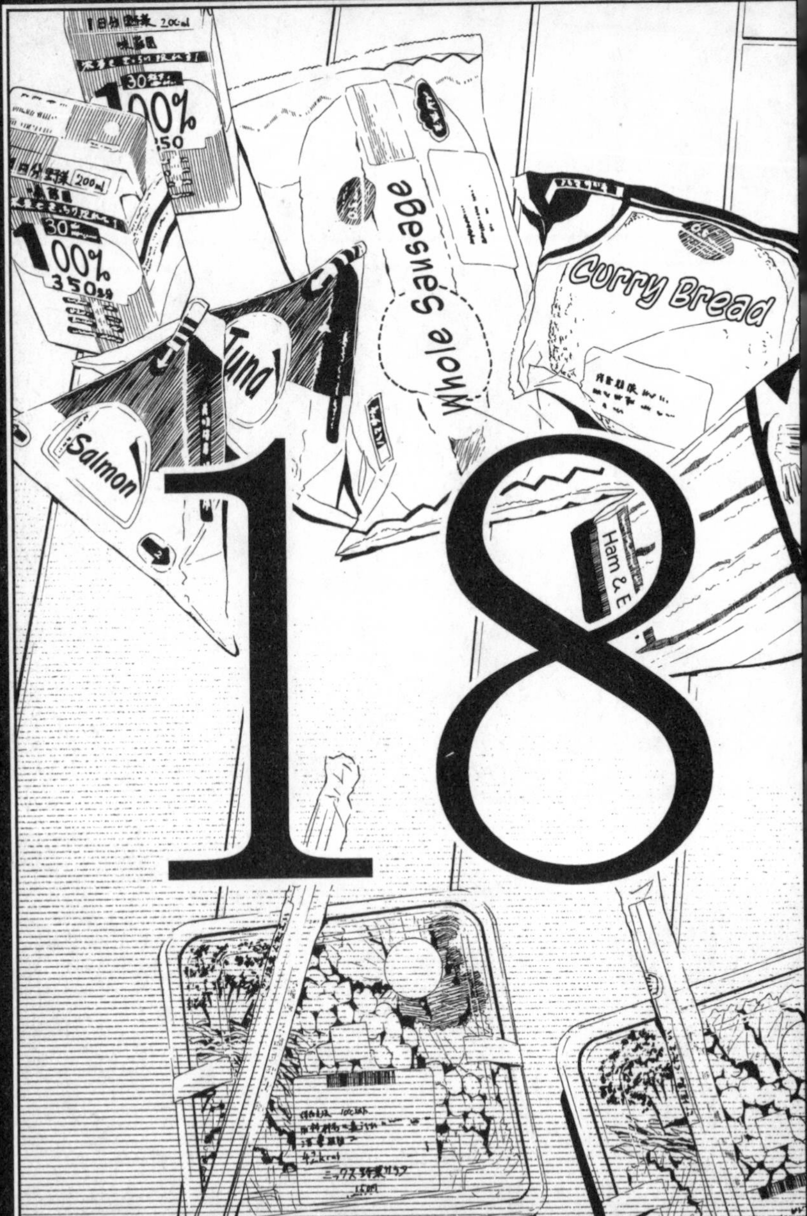
18
Curry Bread
Whole Sausage
Tuna
Salmon
Ham & E
100%
100%
350g

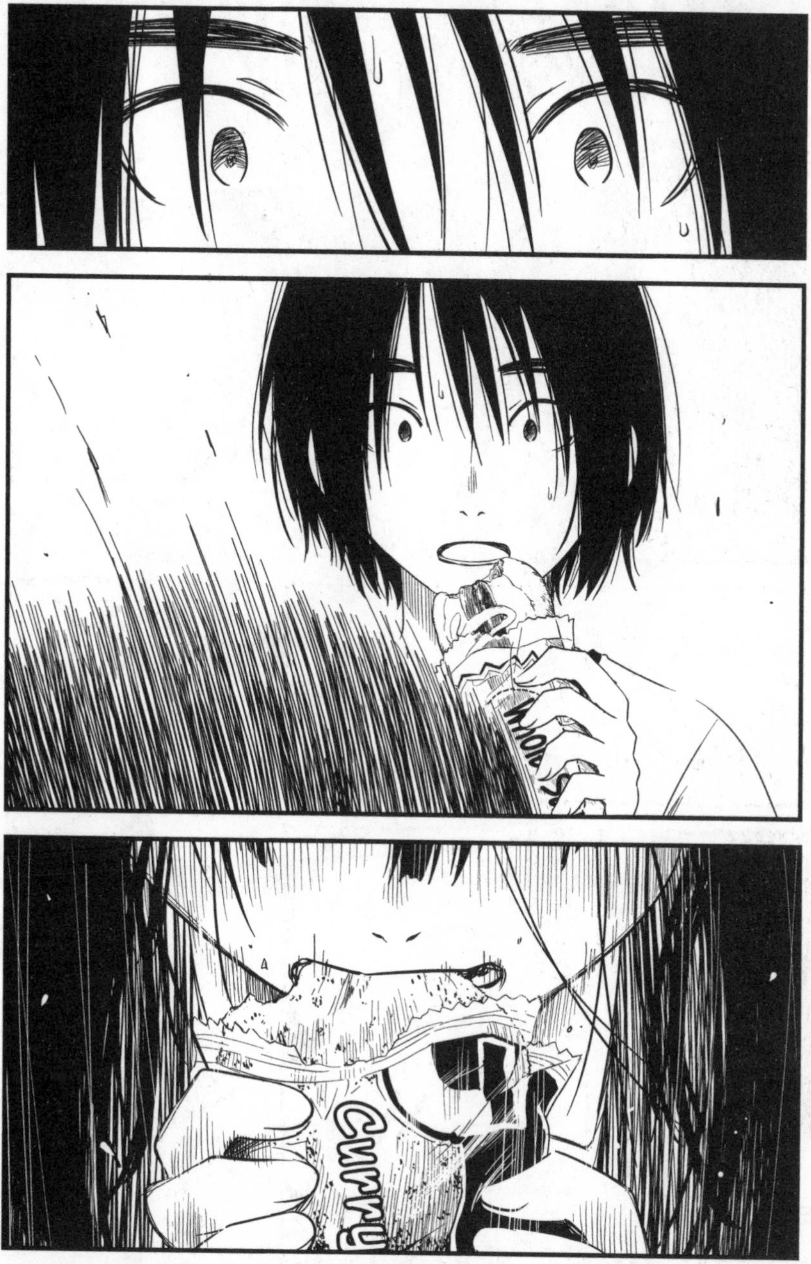
Curry

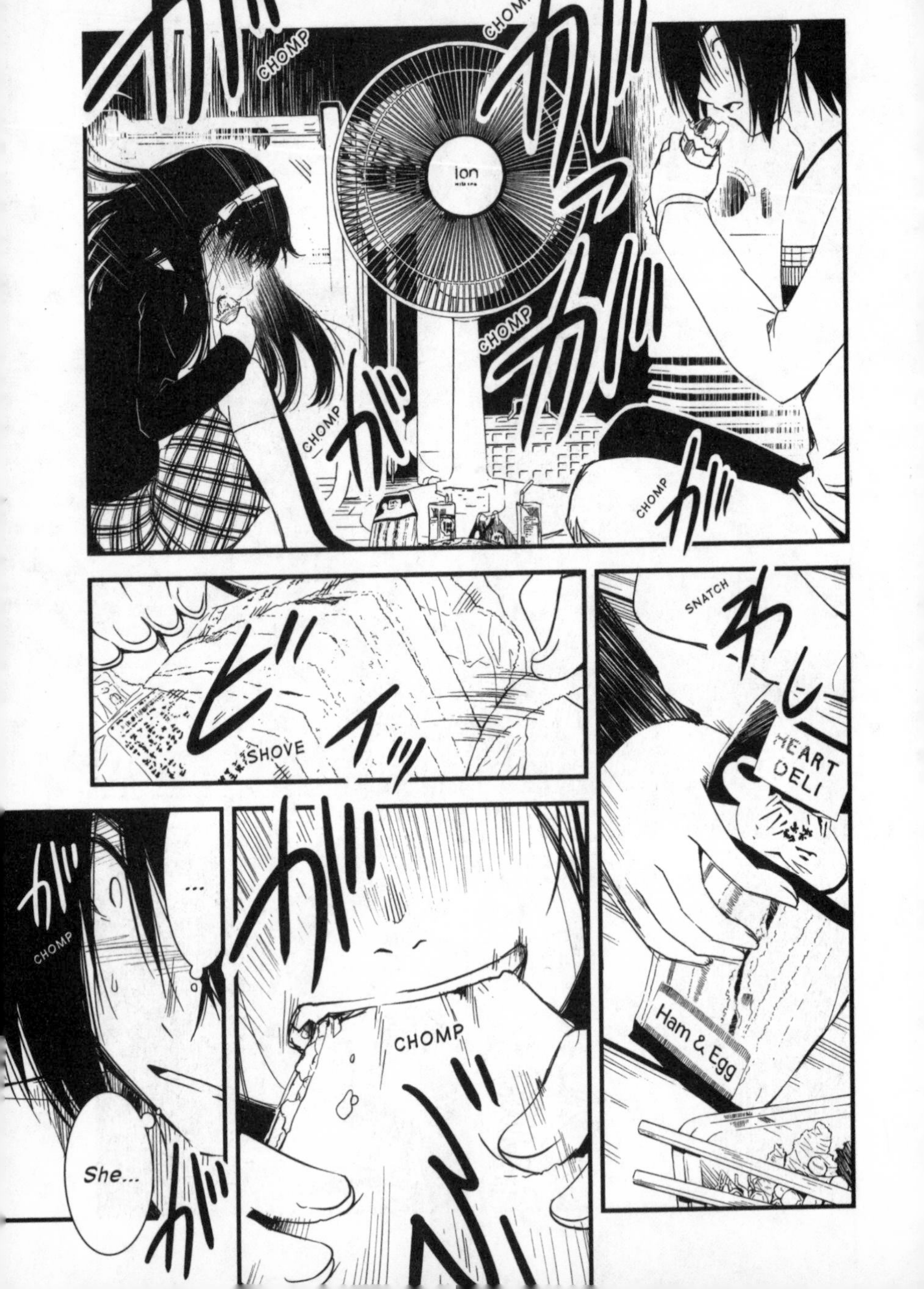
CHOMP
CHOMP
CHOMP
CHOMP
CHOMP
SNATCH
HEART DELI
Ham & Egg
SHOVE
CHOMP
...
CHOMP
She...

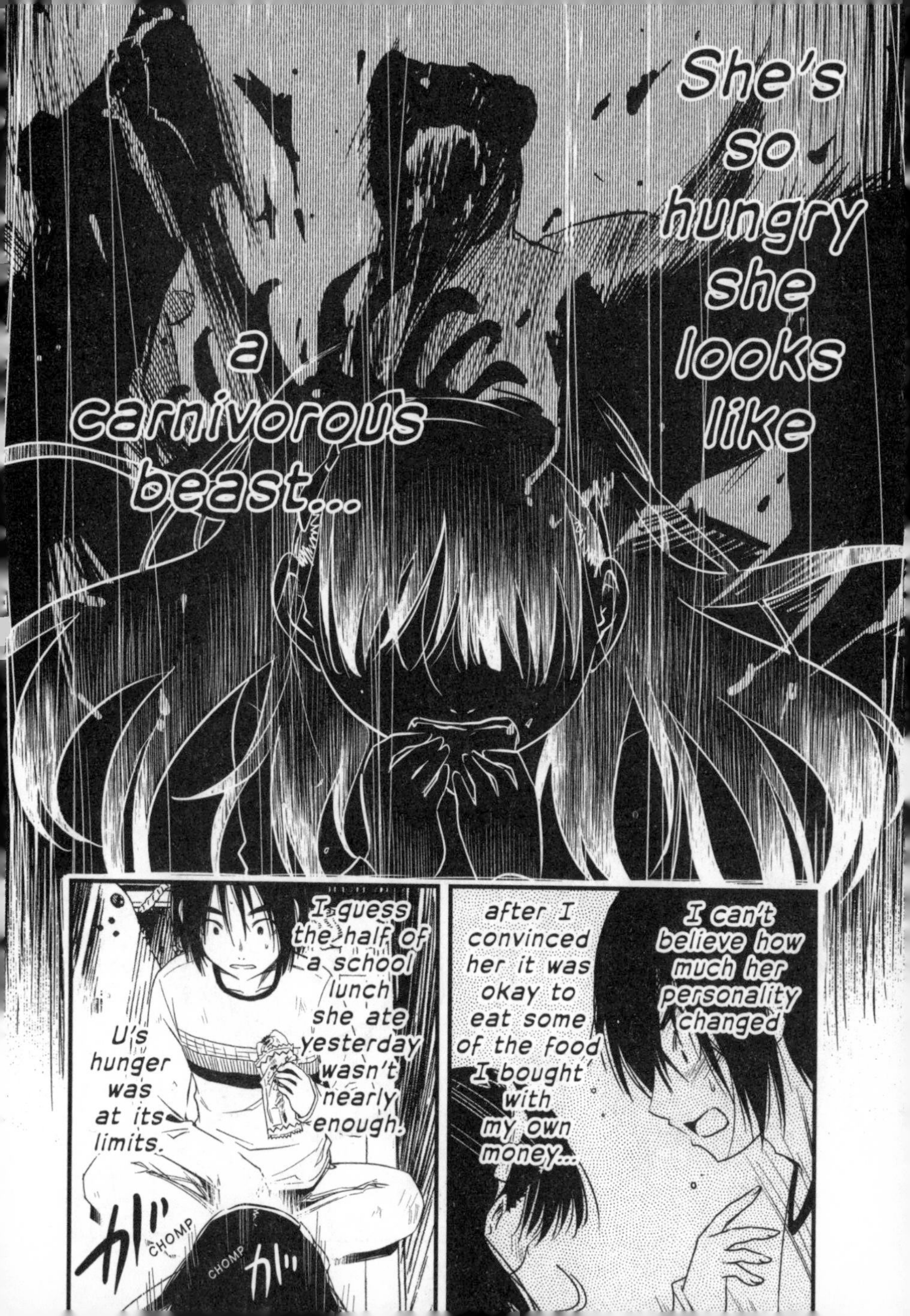
She's so hungry she looks like
a carnivorous beast...
I can't believe how much her personality changed
after I convinced her it was okay to eat some of the food I bought with my own money...
I guess the half of a school lunch she ate yesterday wasn't nearly enough.
U's hunger was at its limits.
CHOMP
CHOMP

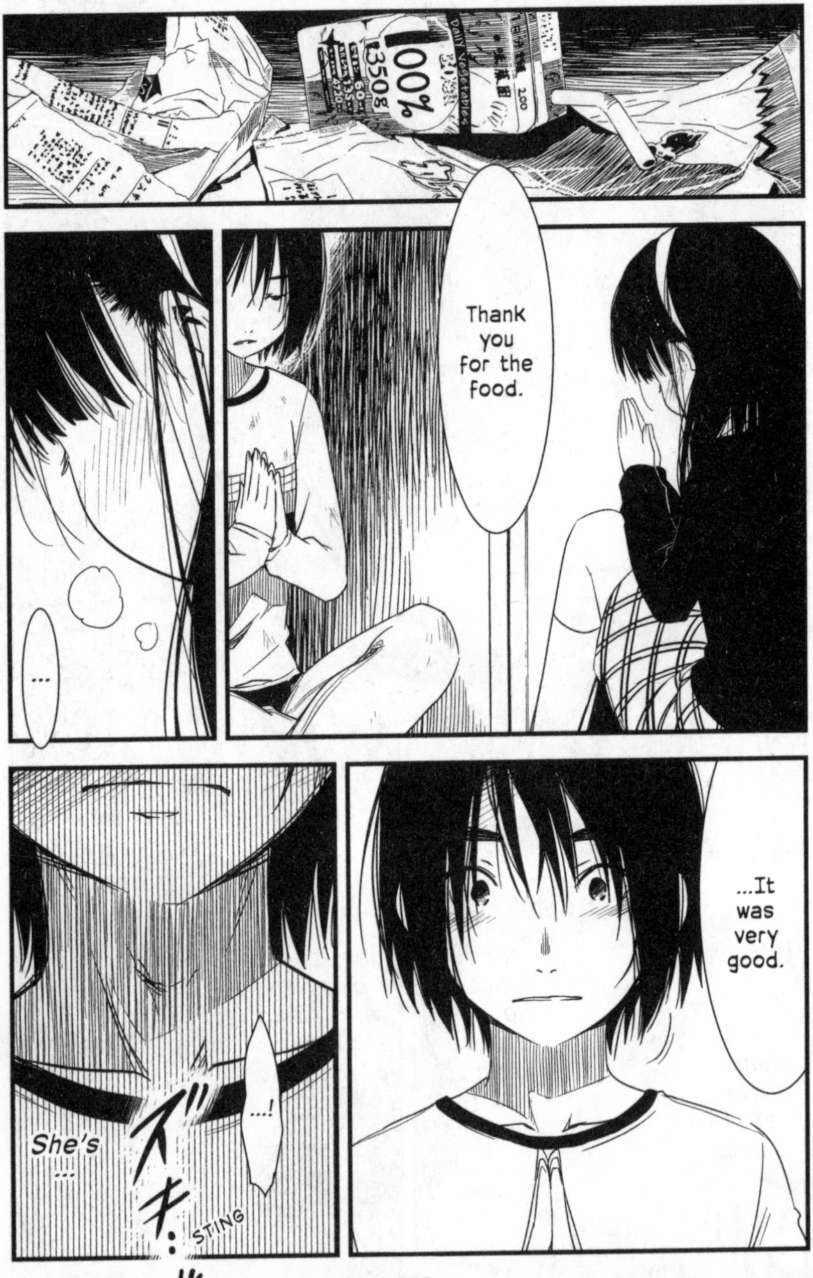
Daily Vegetables
100%
Thank you for the food.
...
...It was very good.
...!
She's ...
STING

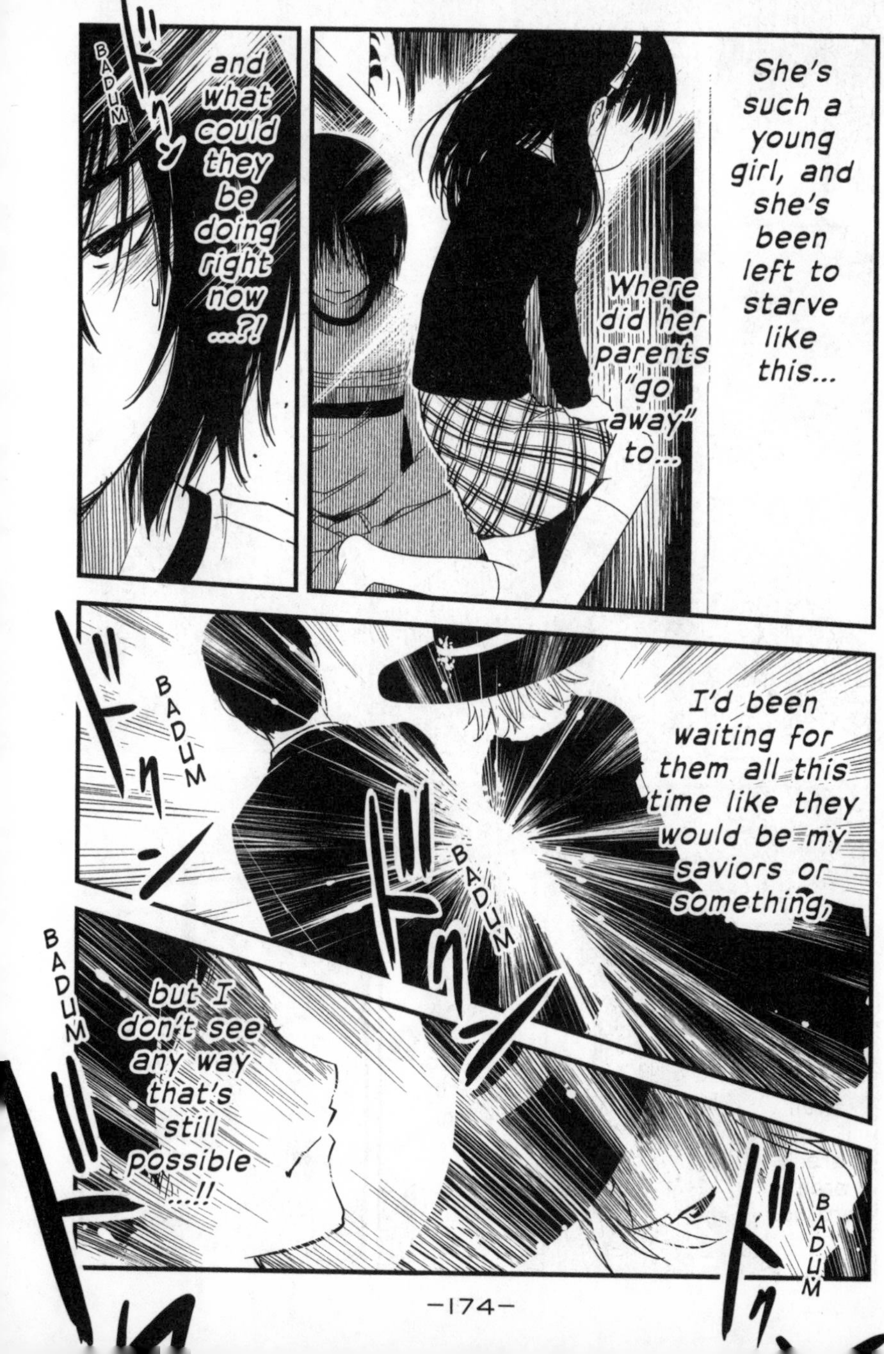
She's such a young girl, and she's been left to starve like this...
Where did her parents "go away" to...
BADUM
and what could they be doing right now ...?!
I'd been waiting for them all this time like they would be my saviors or something,
BADUM
BADUM
but I don't see any way that's still possible ...!!
BADUM
BADUM

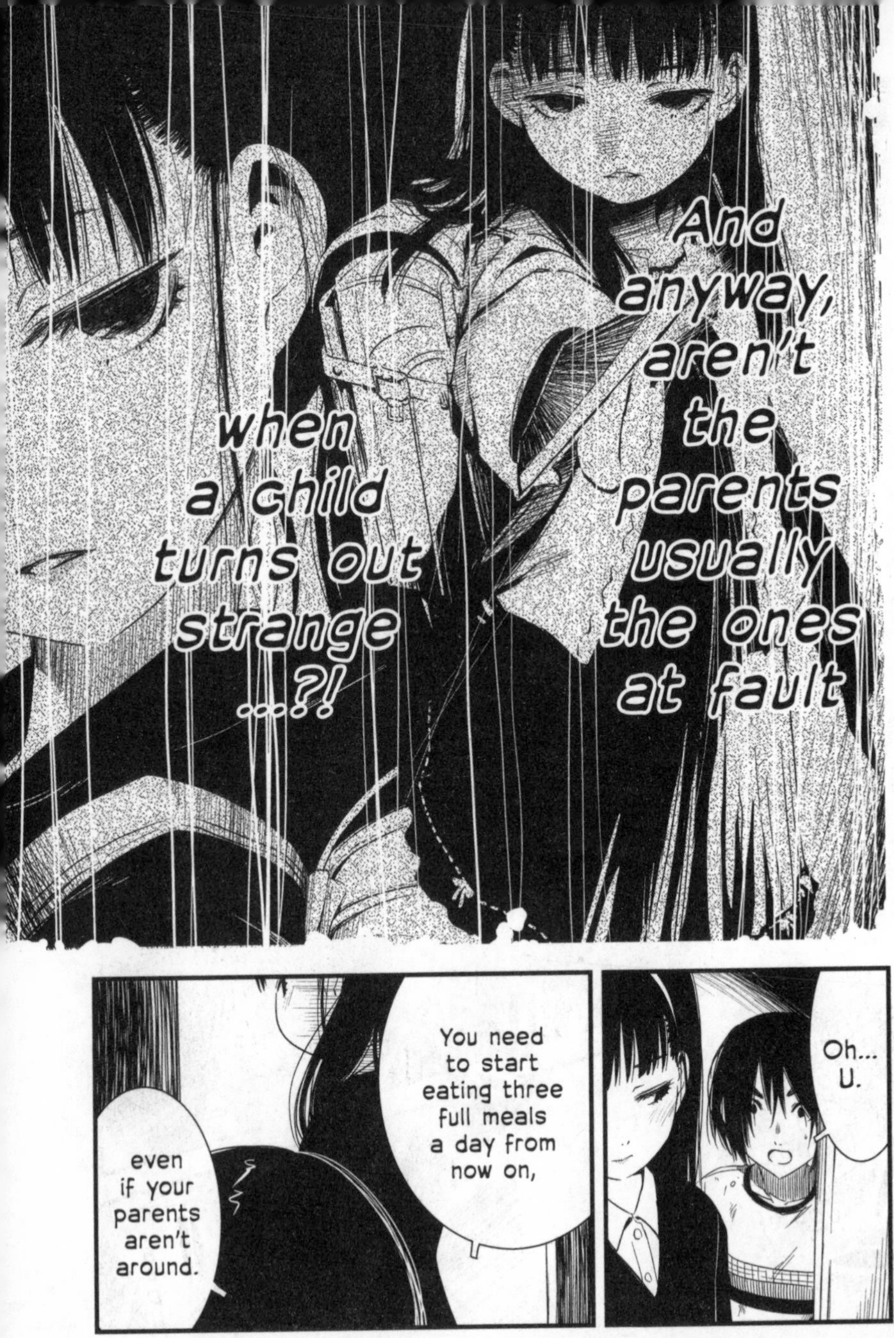
And anyway, aren't the parents usually the ones at fault
when a child turns out strange ...?!
Oh... U.
You need to start eating three full meals a day from now on,
even if your parents aren't around.

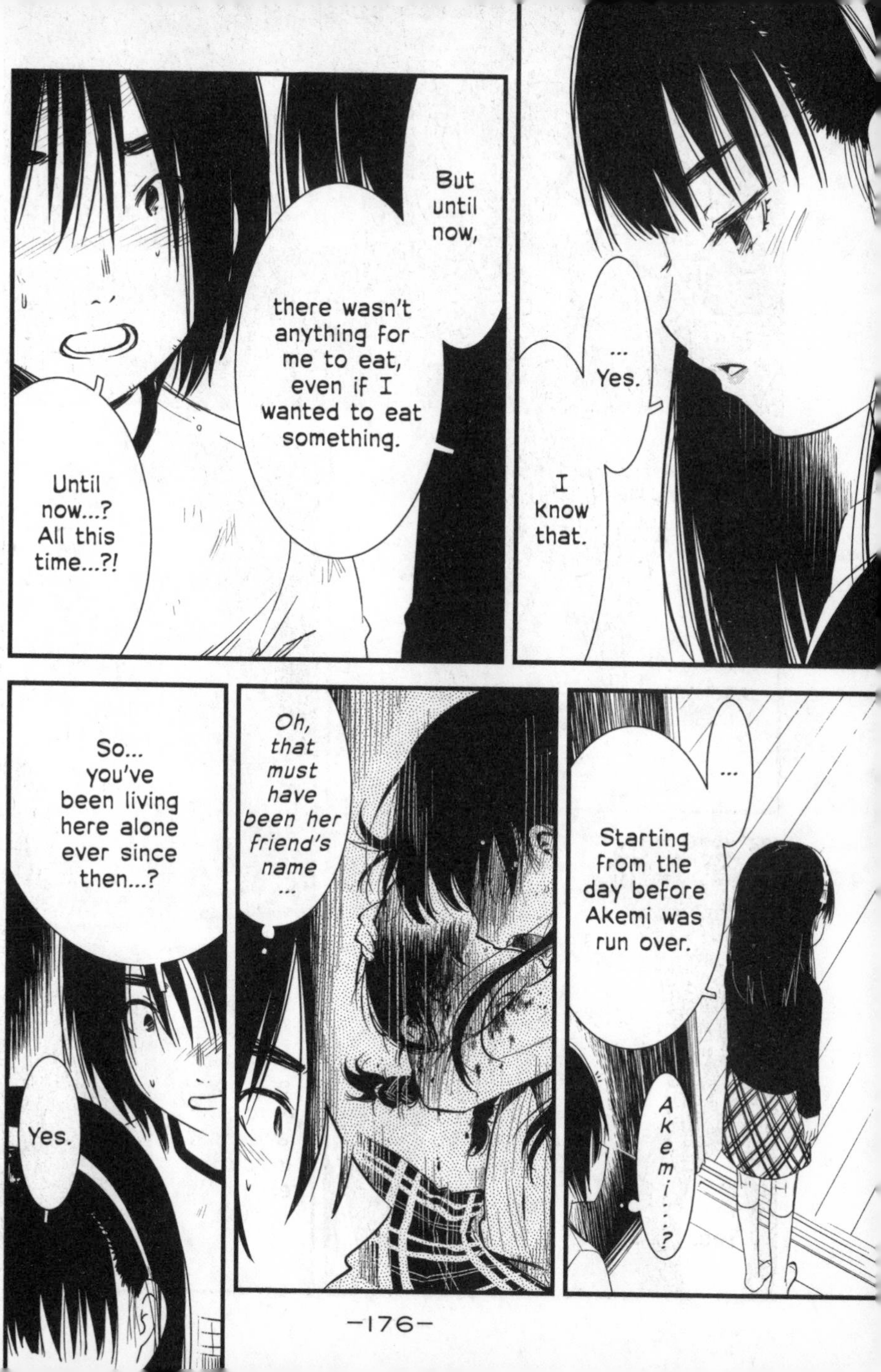

... Yes.
I know that.
But until now,
there wasn't anything for me to eat, even if I wanted to eat something.
Until now...? All this time...?!
...
Starting from the day before Akemi was run over.
Akemi...?
Oh, that must have been her friend's name ...
So... you've been living here alone ever since then...?
Yes.

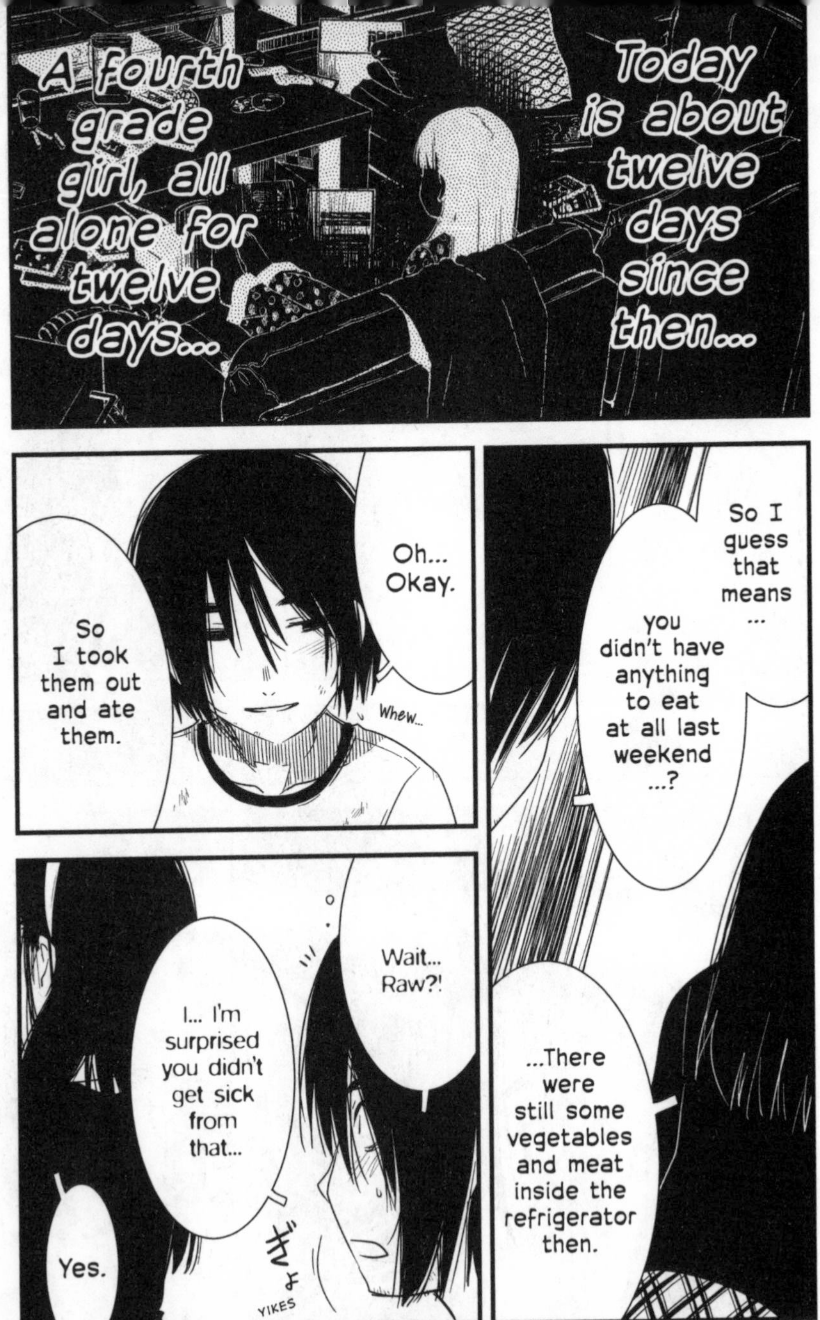
Today is about twelve days since then...
A fourth grade girl, all alone for twelve days...
So I guess that means...
you didn't have anything to eat at all last weekend...?
...There were still some vegetables and meat inside the refrigerator then.
Oh... Okay.
So I took them out and ate them.
Whew...
Wait... Raw?!
I... I'm surprised you didn't get sick from that...
YIKES
Yes.

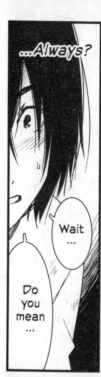

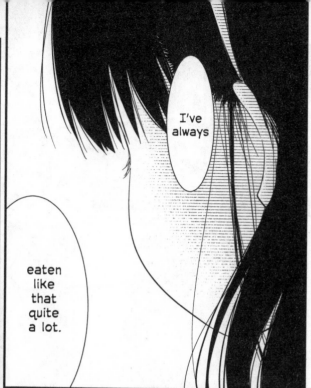

I've always
eaten like that quite a lot.
...Always?
Wait...
Do you mean...
I'm taking a nap.
Excuse me.
WHAPP
Ah...!
GACHIK
Heh...
Maybe she's sleepy from having a full stomach for the first time in a while...

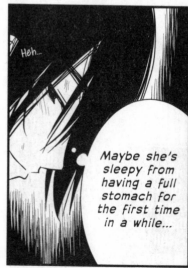

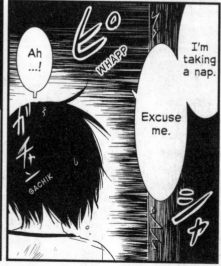

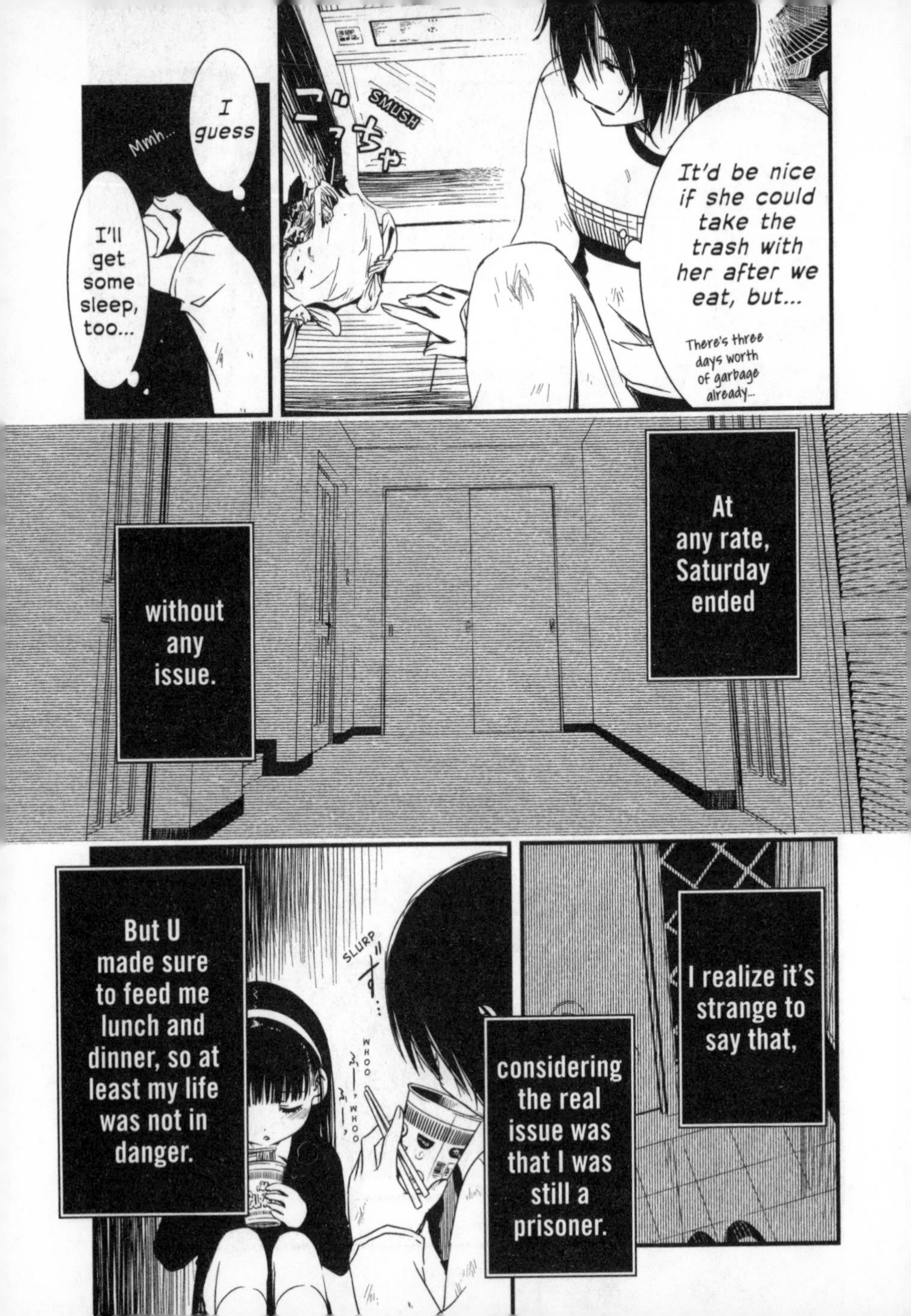
SMUSH
It'd be nice if she could take the trash with her after we eat, but...
There's three days worth of garbage already...
I guess
Mmh...
I'll get some sleep, too...
At any rate, Saturday ended
without any issue.
I realize it's strange to say that,
considering the real issue was that I was still a prisoner.
But U made sure to feed me lunch and dinner, so at least my life was not in danger.
SLURP
WHOO
WHOO

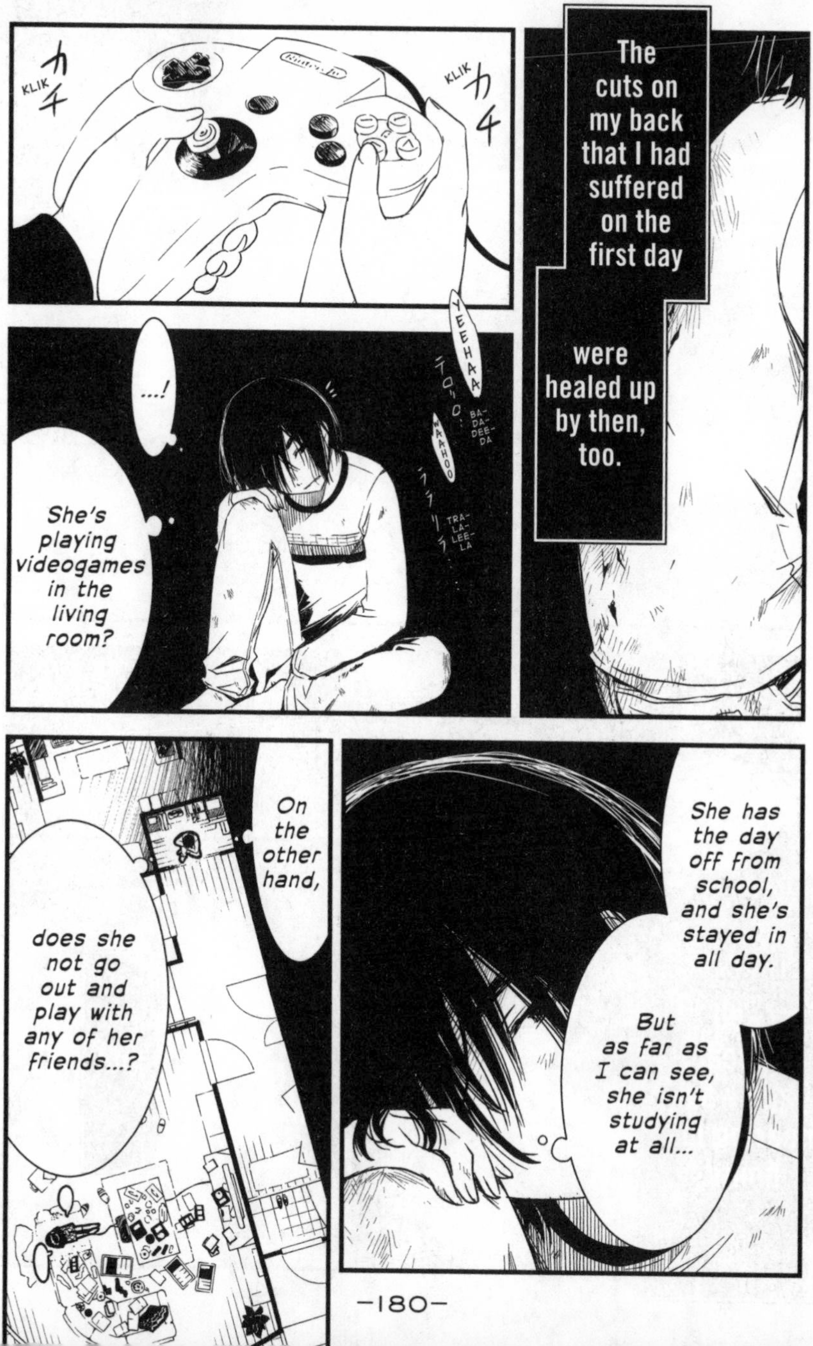

The cuts on my back that I had suffered on the first day
were healed up by then, too.
KLIK
カチ
KLIK
カチ
YEEHAA
BA-DA-DEE-DA
WAAHOO
TRA-LA-LEE-LA
...!
She's playing videogames in the living room?
She has the day off from school, and she's stayed in all day.
But as far as I can see, she isn't studying at all...
On the other hand,
does she not go out and play with any of her friends...?

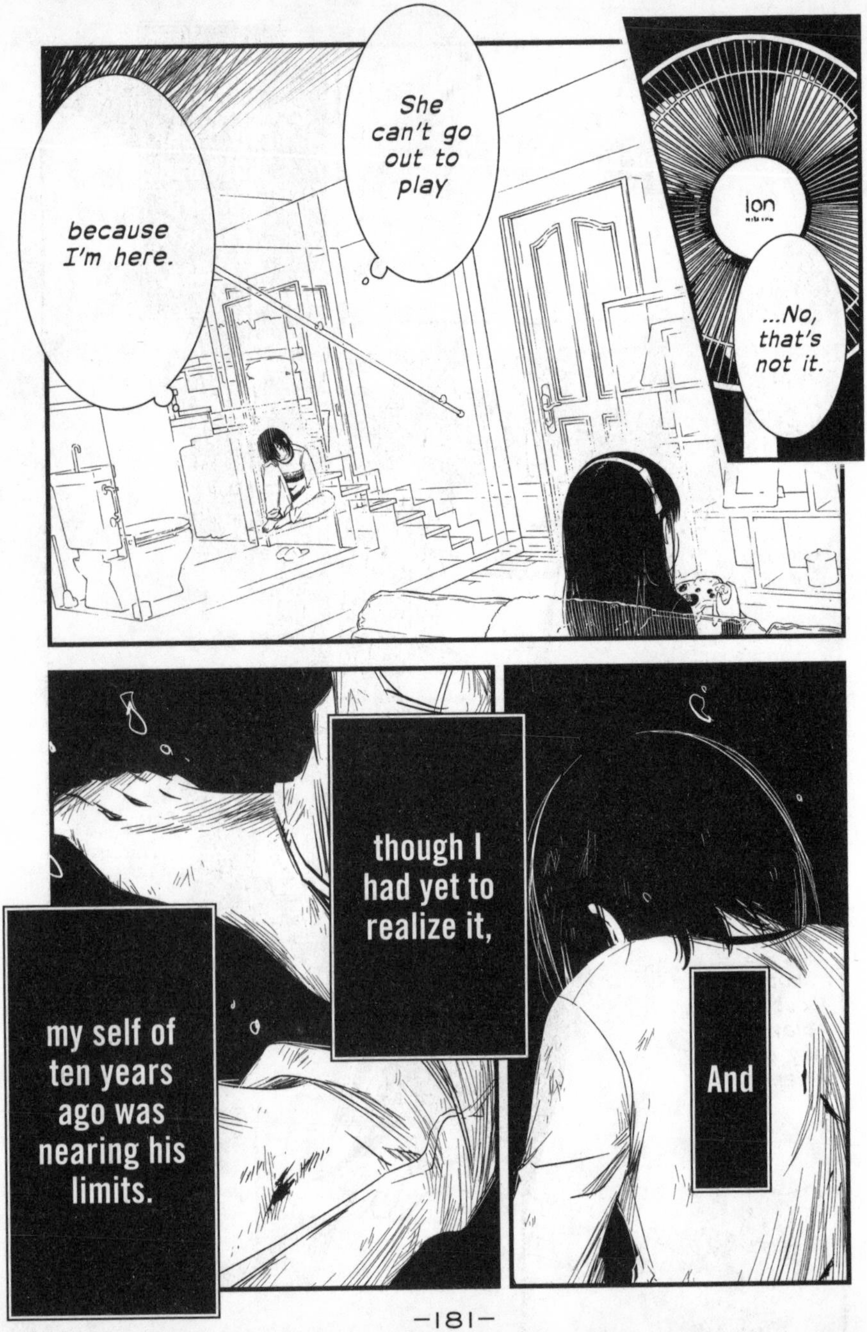
ion
...No, that's not it.
She can't go out to play
because I'm here.
And
though I had yet to realize it,
my self of ten years ago was nearing his limits.

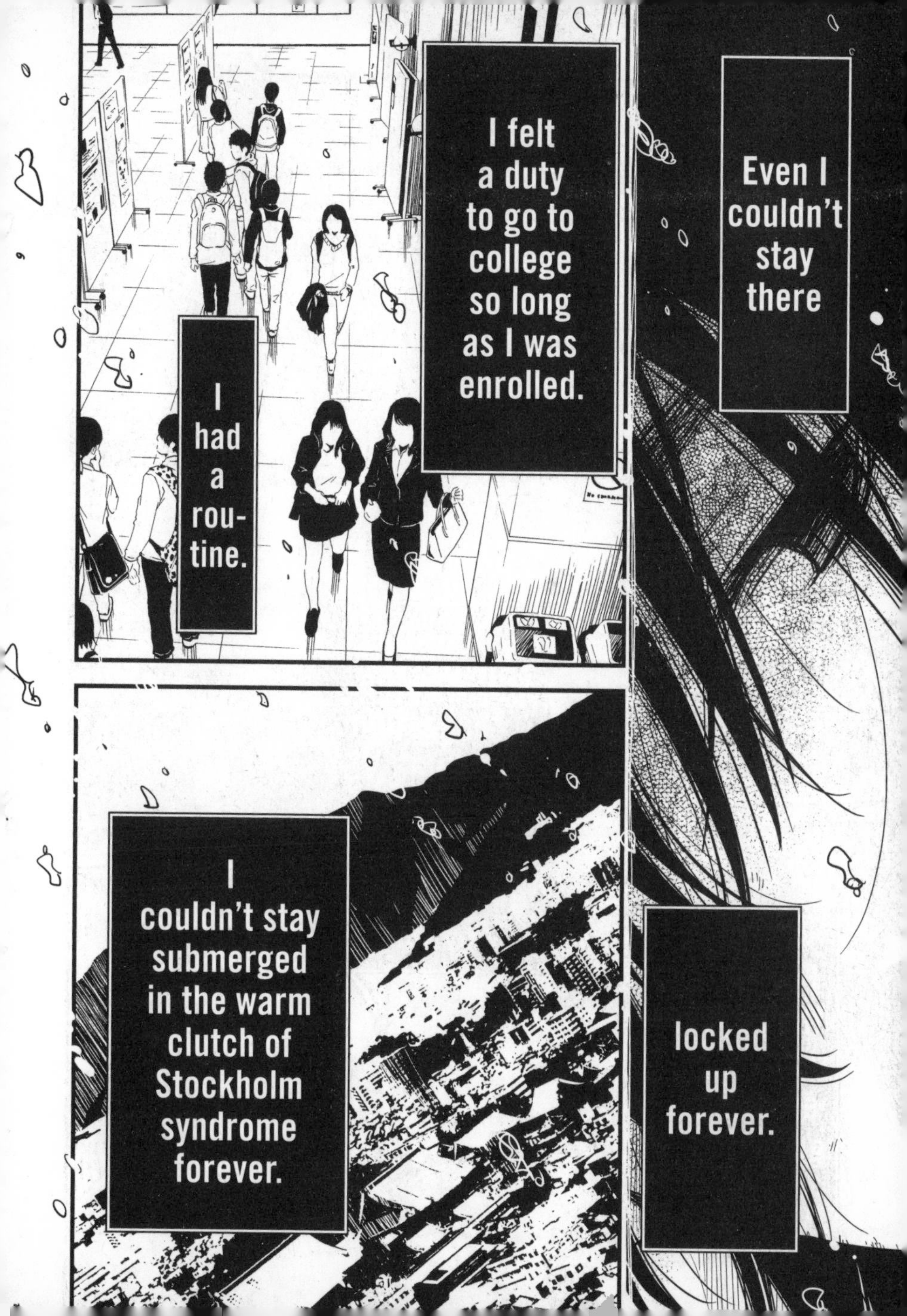
Even I couldn't stay there
locked up forever.
I felt a duty to go to college so long as I was enrolled.
I had a rou-tine.
I couldn't stay submerged in the warm clutch of Stockholm syndrome forever.

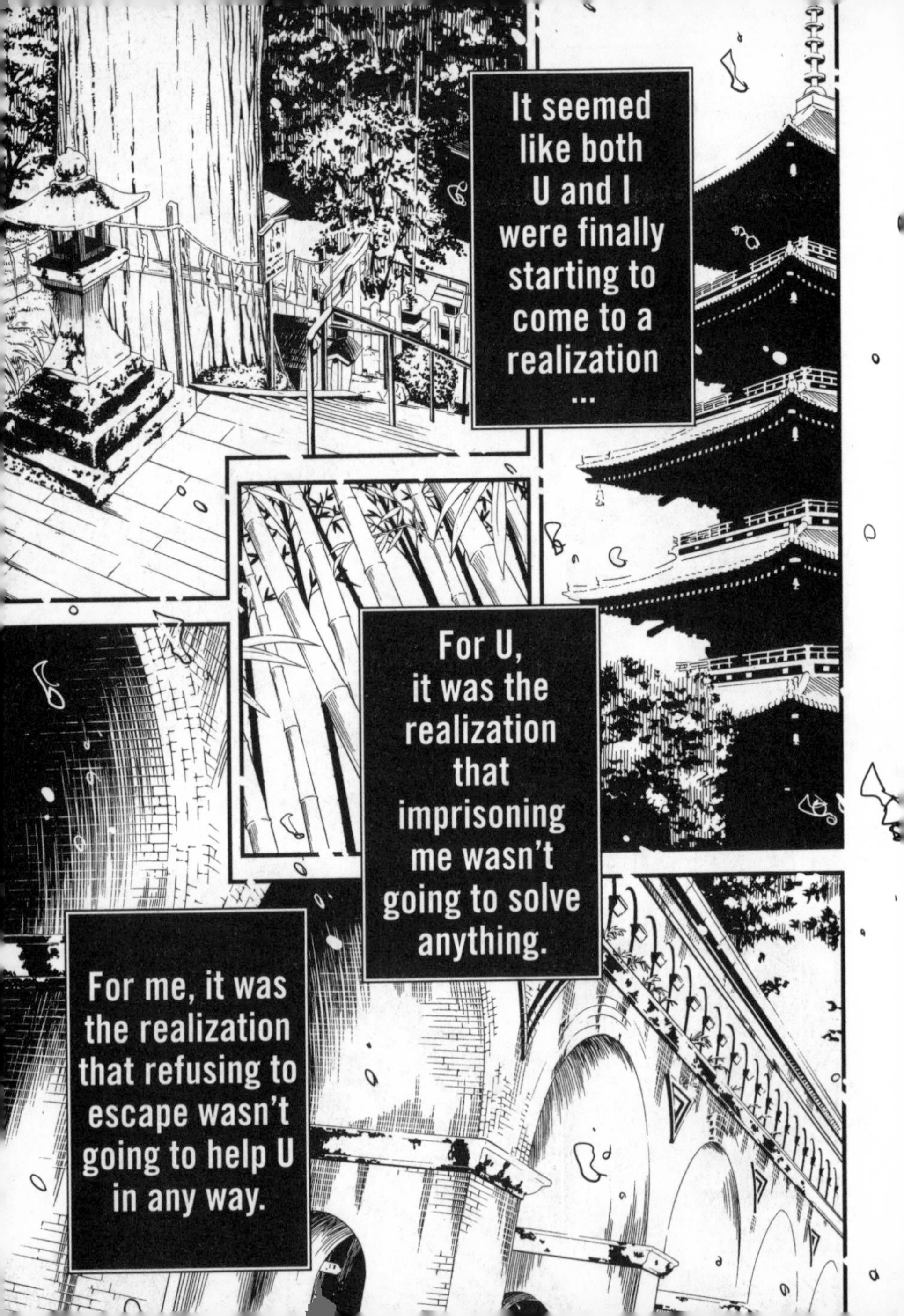
It seemed like both U and I were finally starting to come to a realization ...
For U, it was the realization that imprisoning me wasn't going to solve anything.
For me, it was the realization that refusing to escape wasn't going to help U in any way.

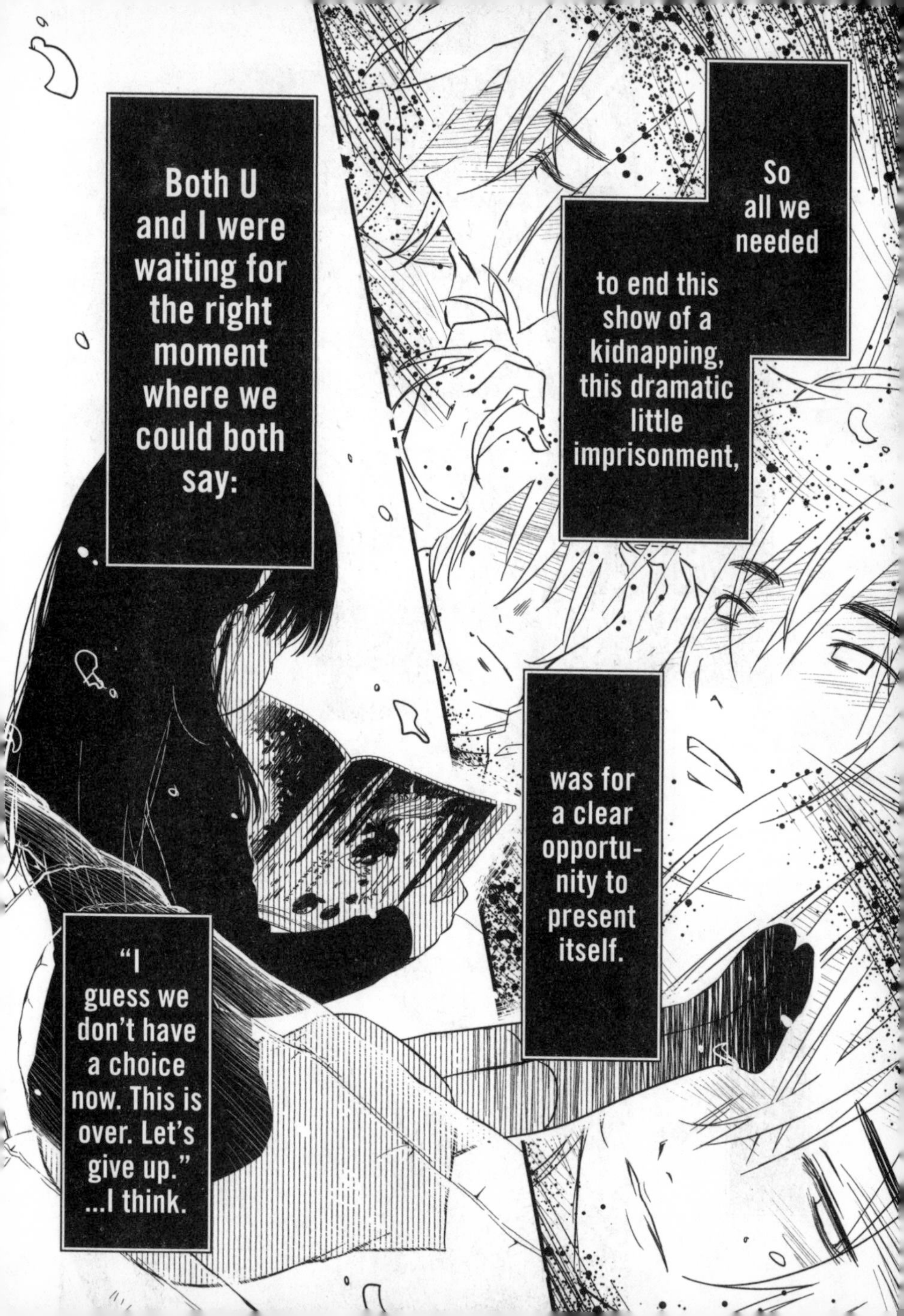
So all we needed to end this show of a kidnapping, this dramatic little imprisonment,
was for a clear opportunity to present itself.
Both U and I were waiting for the right moment where we could both say:
“I guess we don’t have a choice now. This is over. Let’s give up.” ...I think.

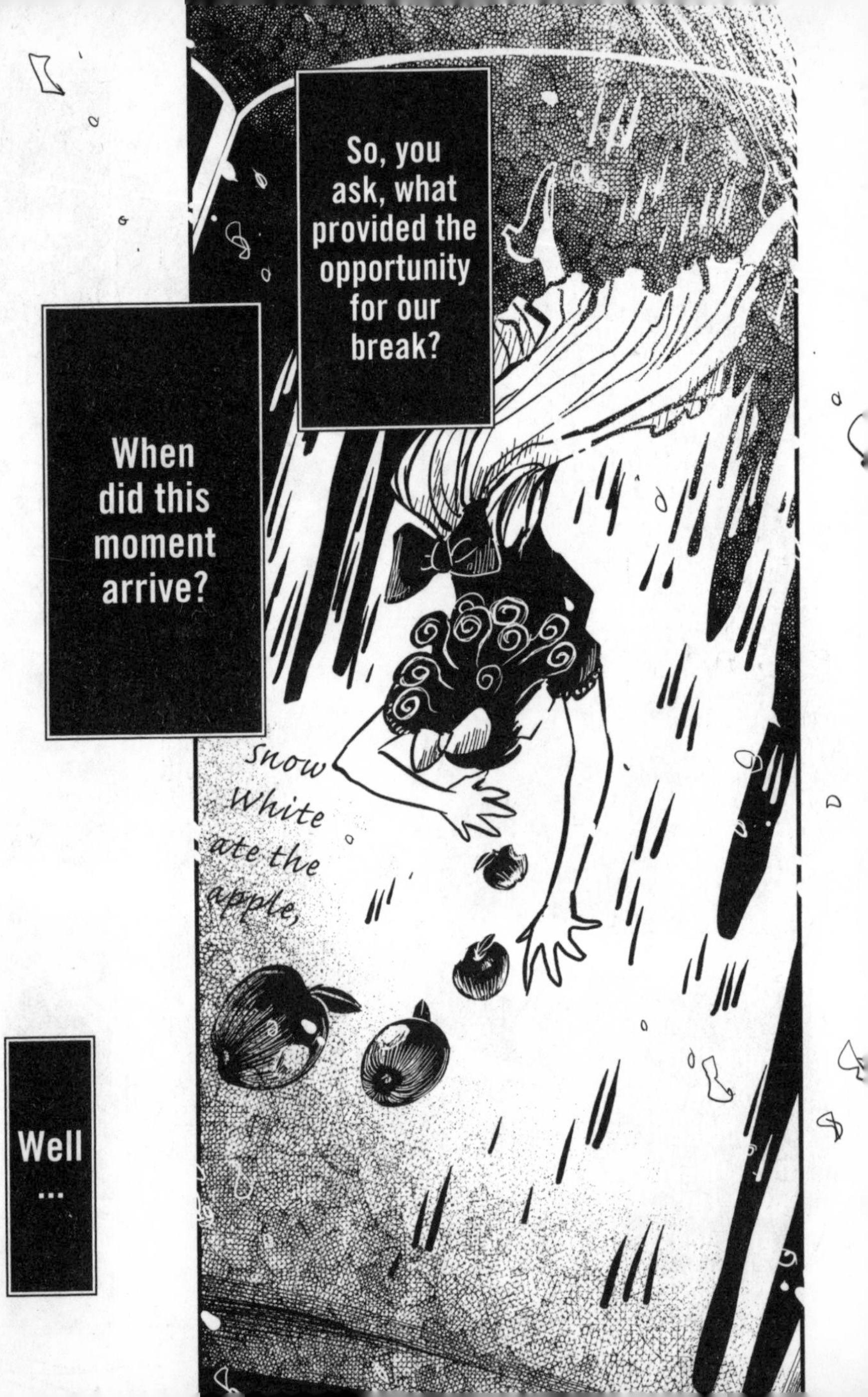
So, you ask, what provided the opportunity for our break?
When did this moment arrive?
Snow White ate the apple,
Well ...

Day 5 of Imprisonment

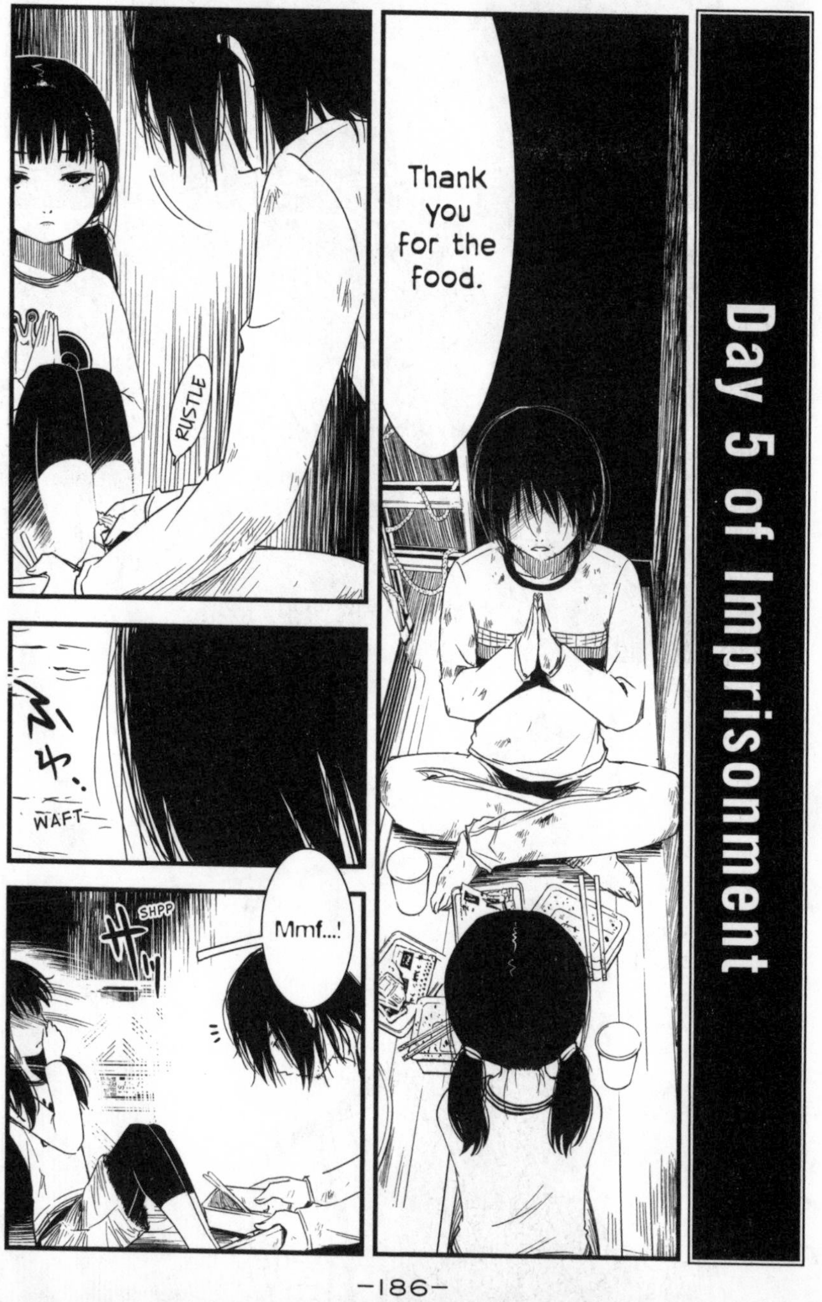
Thank you for the food.
RUSTLE
WAFT
SHPP
Mmf...!

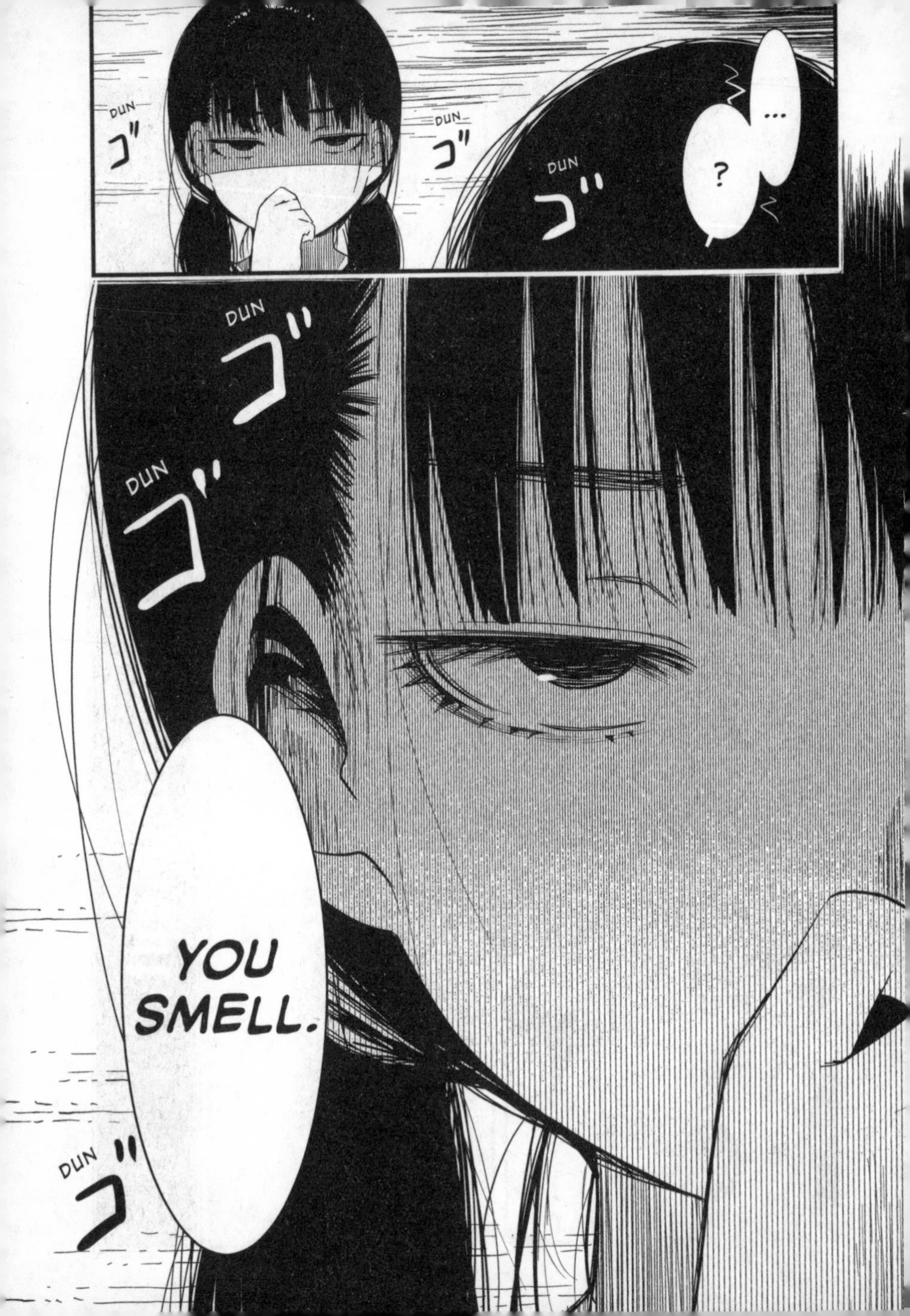
...
?
DUN ゴ"
DUN ゴ"
DUN ゴ"
DUN ゴ"
DUN ゴ"
YOU SMELL.
DUN ゴ"

Continued in Volume 3

Volume 3 Preview

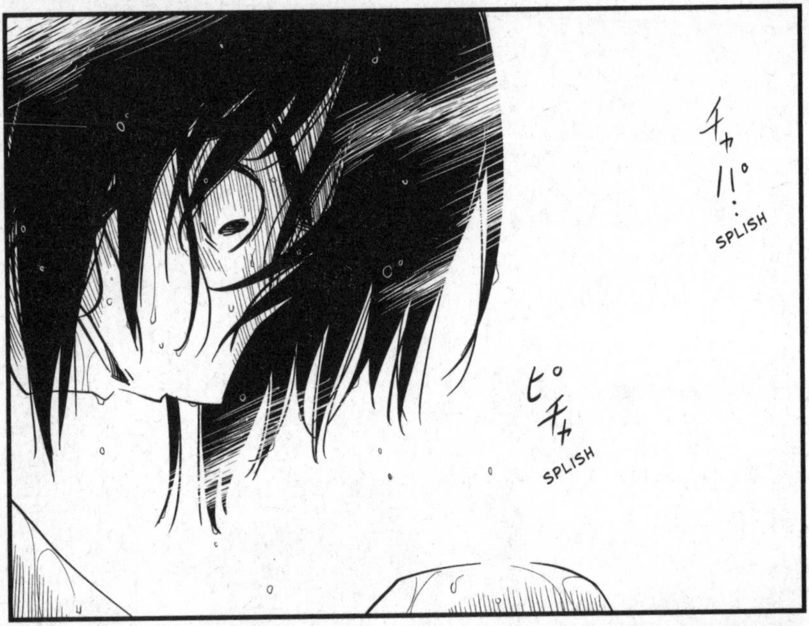
チャパ…
SPLISH
ピチャ
SPLISH

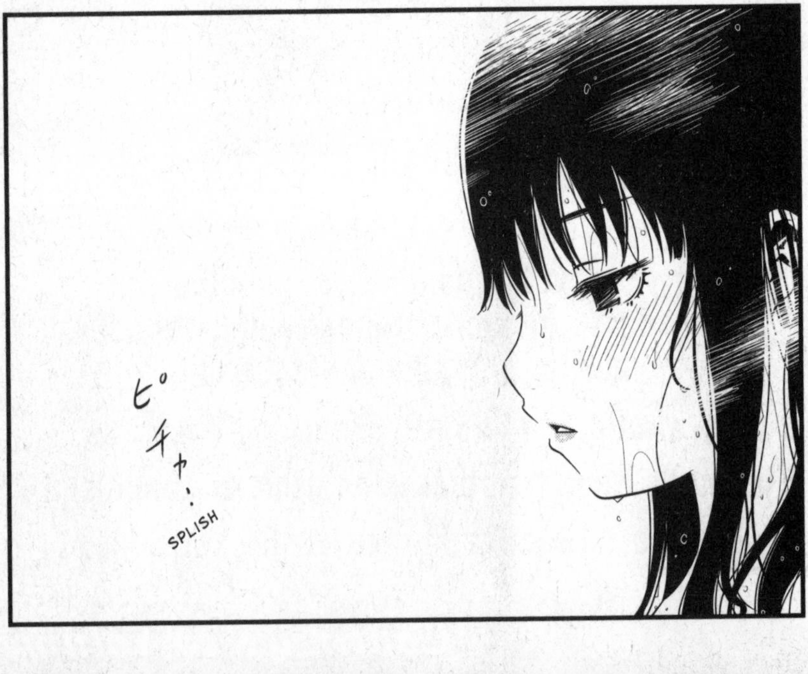
ピチャ…
SPLISH

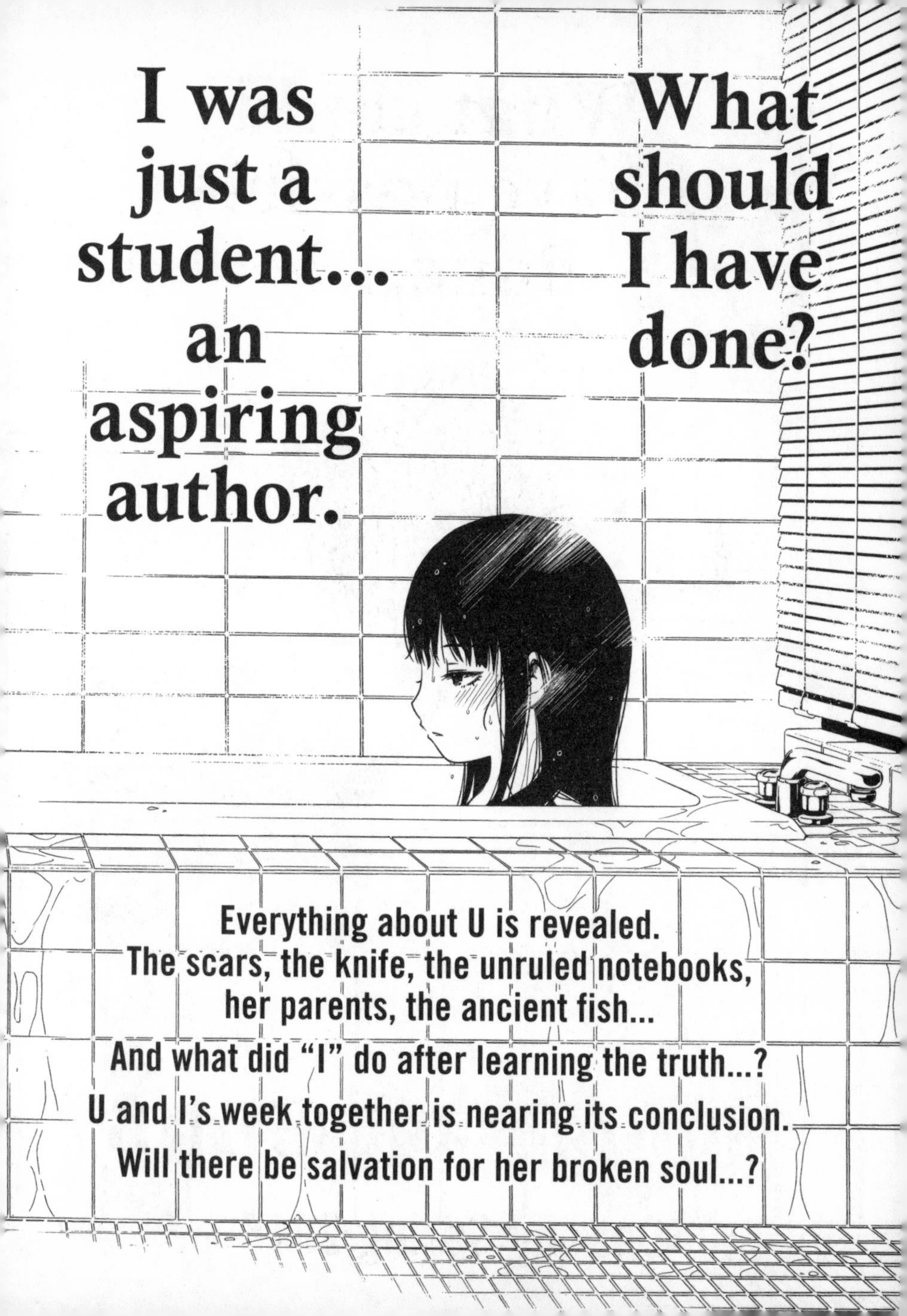
What should I have done?
I was just a student... an aspiring author.
Everything about U is revealed.
The scars, the knife, the unruled notebooks,
her parents, the ancient fish...
And what did "I" do after learning the truth...?
U and I's week together is nearing its conclusion.
Will there be salvation for her broken soul...?

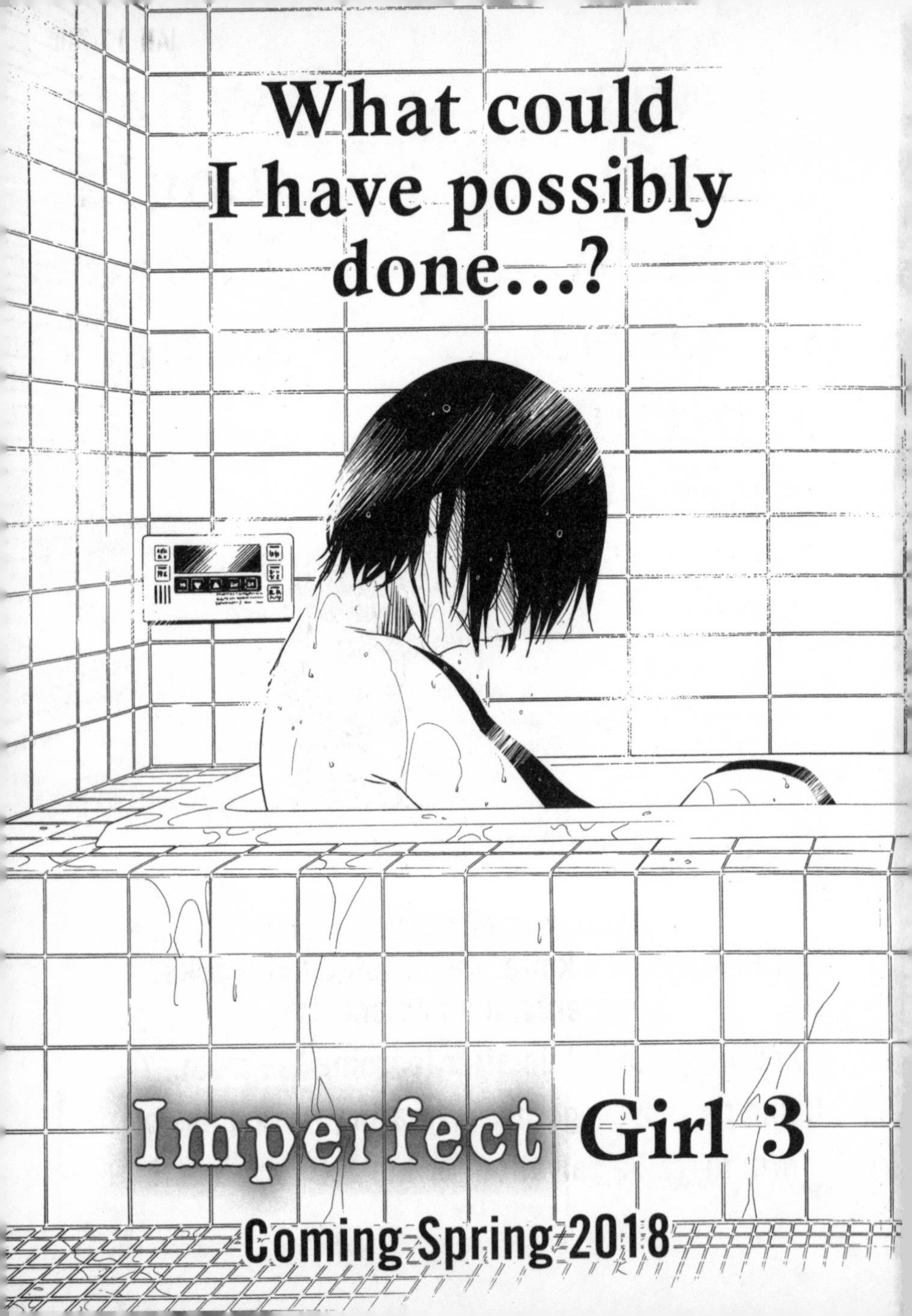
What could I have possibly done...?
Imperfect Girl 3
Coming Spring 2018

Imperfect Girl 2

A Vertical Comics Edition

Translation: Ko Ransom
Production: Grace Lu
Anthony Quintessenza

First published in Japan in 2016 by Kodansha, Ltd., Tokyo
Publication rights for this English edition arranged through Kodansha, Ltd., Tokyo
English language version produced by Vertical, Inc.

Translation provided by Vertical Comics, 2018
Published by Vertical Comics, an imprint of Vertical, Inc., New York

Originally published in Japanese as *Shoujo Fujuubun 2* by Kodansha, Ltd.
Shoujo Fujuubun first serialized in *Young Magazine*, Kodansha, Ltd., 2015-2016

ISBN: 978-1-945054-61-7

Manufactured in Canada

First Edition

Vertical, Inc.
451 Park Avenue South
7th Floor
New York, NY 10016
www.vertical-comics.com

Vertical books are distributed through Penguin-Random House Publisher Services.